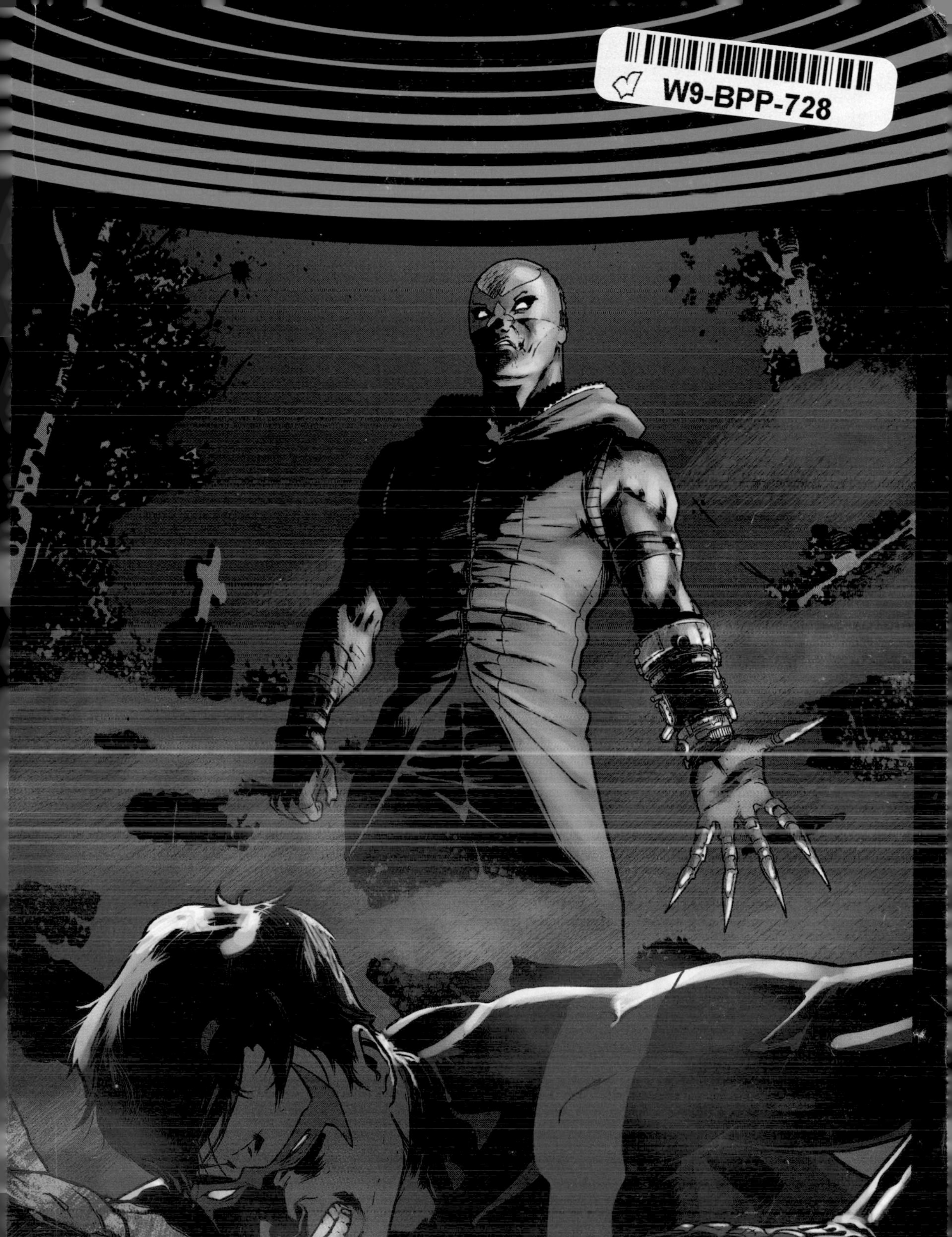

NIGHTWING

VOL.1 BETTER THAN BATMAN

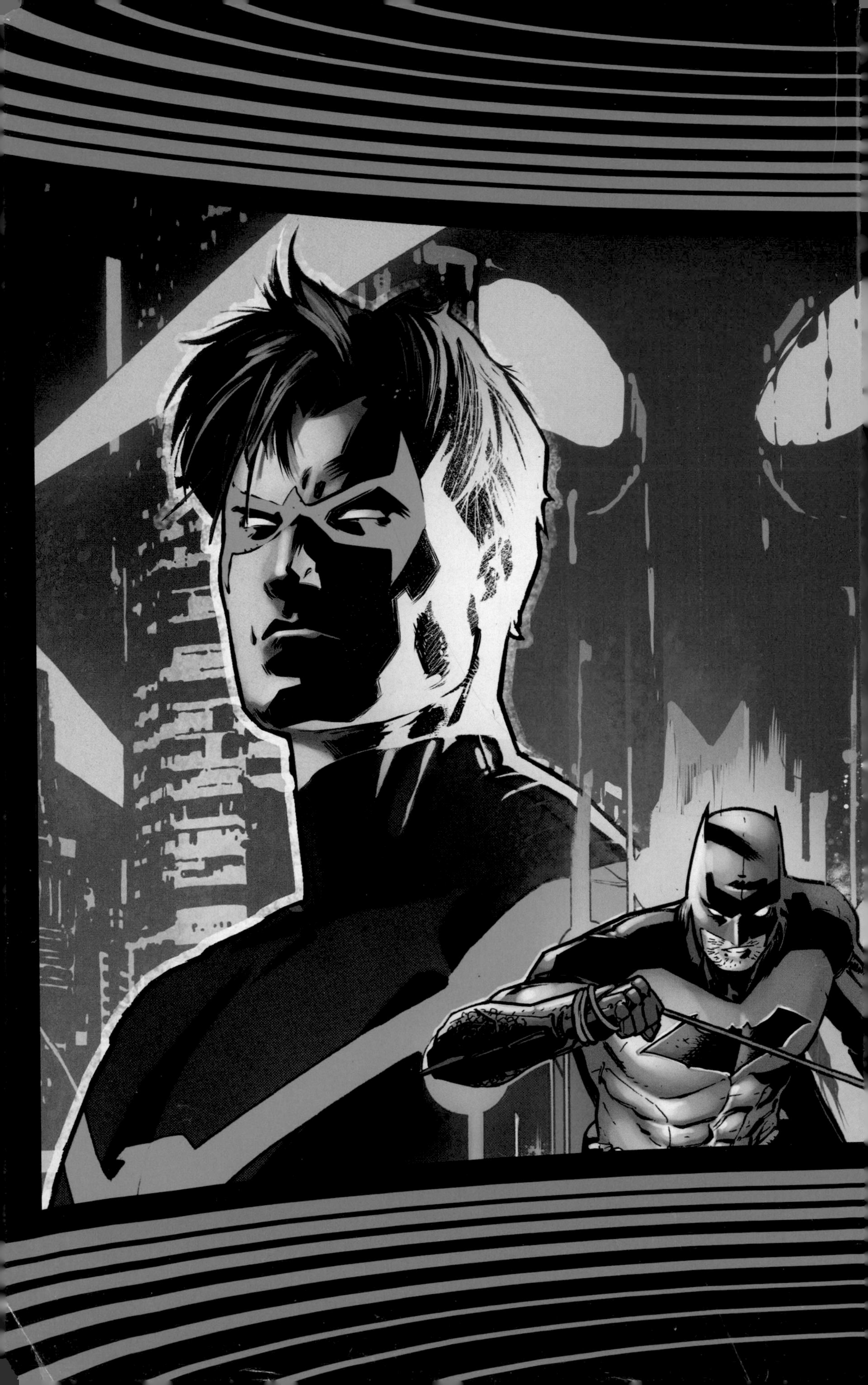

NIGHTWING

VOL.1 BETTER THAN BATMAN

TIM SEELEY
writer

JAVIER FERNÁNDEZ
YANICK PAQUETTE
artists

CHRIS SOTOMAYOR
NATHAN FAIRBAIRN
colorists

CARLOS M. MANGUAL
letterer

JAVIER FERNÁNDEZ and CHRIS SOTOMAYOR
collection cover artists

NIGHTWING created by MARV WOLFMAN and GEORGE PÉREZ

REBECCA TAYLOR Editor - Original Series • DAVE WIELGOSZ Assistant Editor - Original Series
JEB WOODARD Group Editor - Collected Editions • STEVE COOK Design Director - Books
CURTIS KING JR. Publication Design

BOB HARRAS Senior VP - Editor-in-Chief, DC Comics
PAT McCALLUM Executive Editor, DC Comics

DIANE NELSON President • DAN DiDIO Publisher • JIM LEE Publisher • GEOFF JOHNS President & Chief Creative Officer
AMIT DESAI Executive VP - Business & Marketing Strategy, Direct to Consumer & Global Franchise Management
SAM ADES Senior VP & General Manager, Digital Services • BOBBIE CHASE VP & Executive Editor, Young Reader & Talent Development
MARK CHIARELLO Senior VP - Art, Design & Collected Editions • JOHN CUNNINGHAM Senior VP - Sales & Trade Marketing
ANNE DePIES Senior VP - Business Strategy, Finance & Administration • DON FALLETTI VP - Manufacturing Operations
LAWRENCE GANEM VP - Editorial Administration & Talent Relations • ALISON GILL Senior VP - Manufacturing & Operations
HANK KANALZ Senior VP - Editorial Strategy & Administration • JAY KOGAN VP - Legal Affairs • JACK MAHAN VP - Business Affairs
NICK J. NAPOLITANO VP - Manufacturing Administration • EDDIE SCANNELL VP - Consumer Marketing
COURTNEY SIMMONS Senior VP - Publicity & Communications
JIM (SKI) SOKOLOWSKI VP - Comic Book Specialty Sales & Trade Marketing
NANCY SPEARS VP - Mass, Book, Digital Sales & Trade Marketing
MICHELE R. WELLS VP - Content Strategy

NIGHTWING VOLUME 1: BETTER THAN BATMAN

DC Comics 2900 West Alameda Ave. Burbank, CA 91505
Printed by LSC Communications, Kendallville, IN, USA. 9/15/17.
Second Printing.
ISBN: 978-1-4012-6803-9

Library of Congress Cataloging-in-Publication Data
Names: Seeley, Tim, author. | Fernández, Javier, artist. | Paquette, Yanick,
artist. | Sotomayor, Chris, colourist, artist. | Fairbairn, Nathan, colourist. | Mangual, Carlos M., letterer.
Title: Nightwing. Volume 1, Better than Batman / Tim Seeley, writer ;
Javier Fernández, Yanick Paquette, artists ; Chris Sotomayor,
colorists ; Carlos M. Mangual, letterer ; Javier Fernández and Chris Sotomayor, collection cover artists.
Other titles: Better than Batman
Description: Burbank, CA : DC Comics, [2017] | Series: Rebirth |
"Originally published in single magazine form in NIGHTWING: REBIRTH 1 and
NIGHTWING 1-4, 7-8." | "Nightwing created by Marv Wolfman and George Pérez"
Identifiers: LCCN 2016047061 | ISBN 9781401268039 (paperback)
Subjects: LCSH: Comic books, strips, etc. | BISAC: COMICS & GRAPHIC NOVELS / Superheroes.
Classification: LCC PN6728.N55 S44 2017 | DDC 741.5/973–dc23
LC record available at https://lccn.loc.gov/2016047061

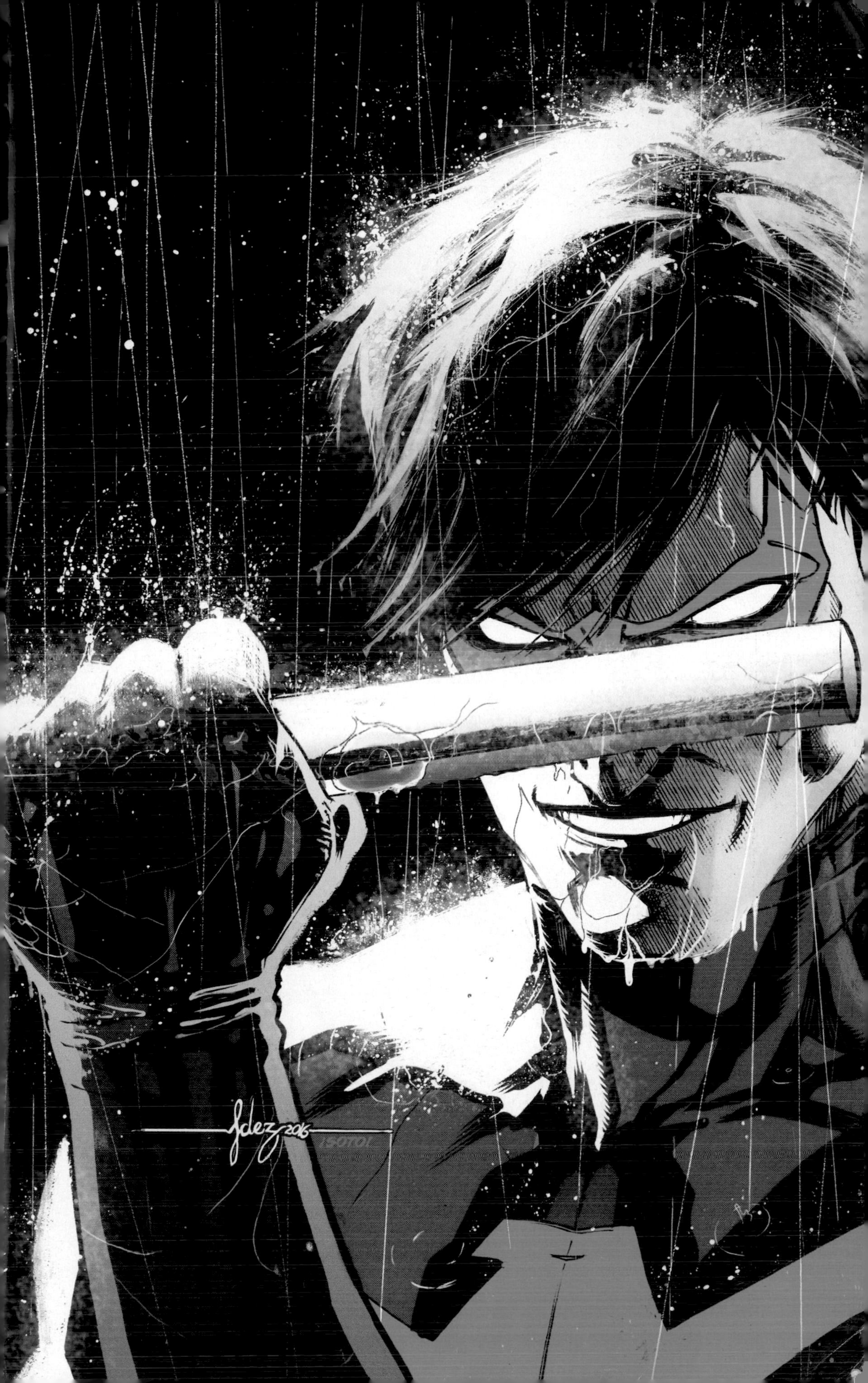

NIGHTWING: REBIRTH

TIM SEELEY writer * YANICK PAQUETTE artist * NATHAN FAIRBAIRN colorist
CARLOS M. MANGUAL letterer * JAVIER FERNÁNDEZ and CHRIS SOTOMAYOR cover artists

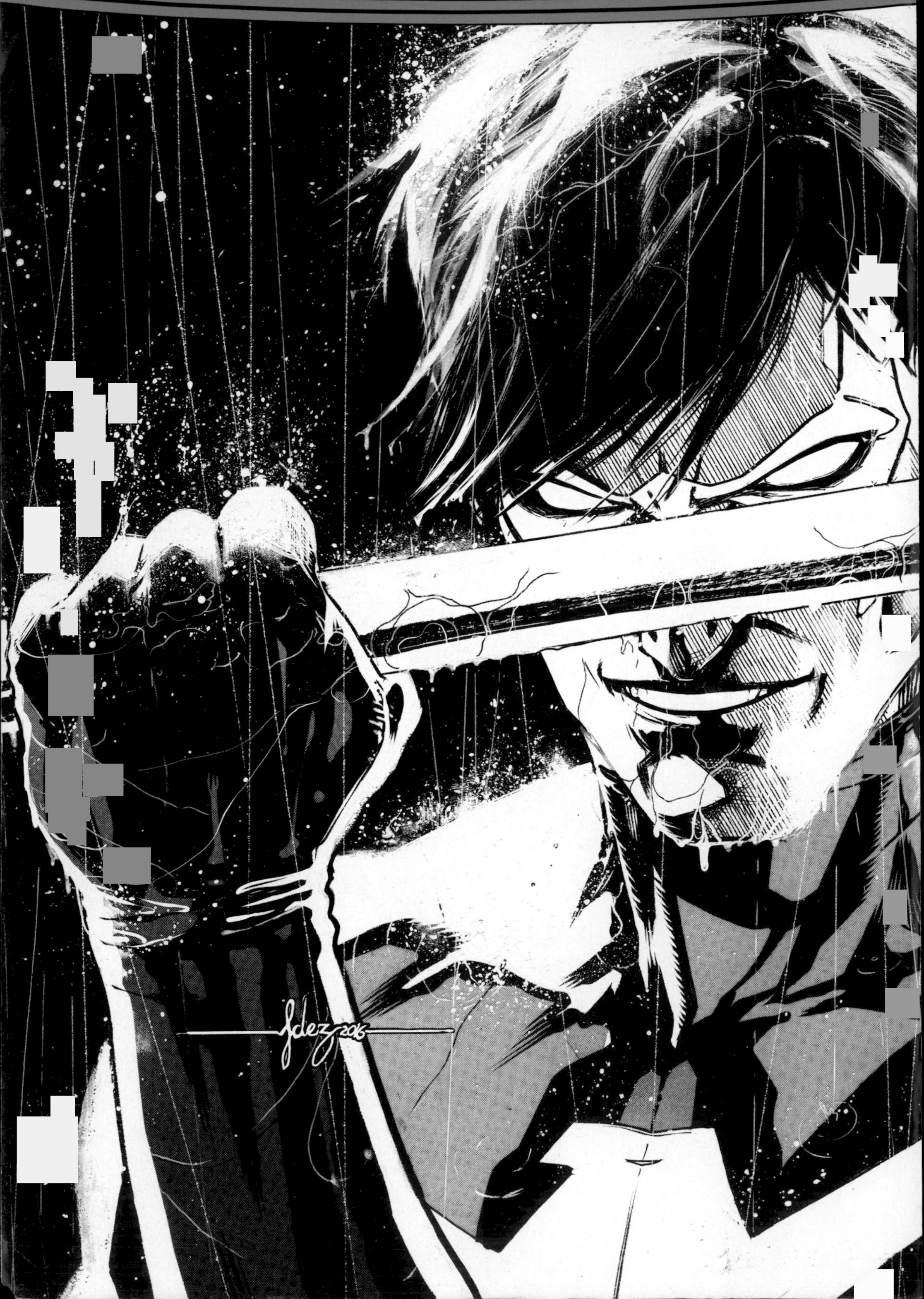

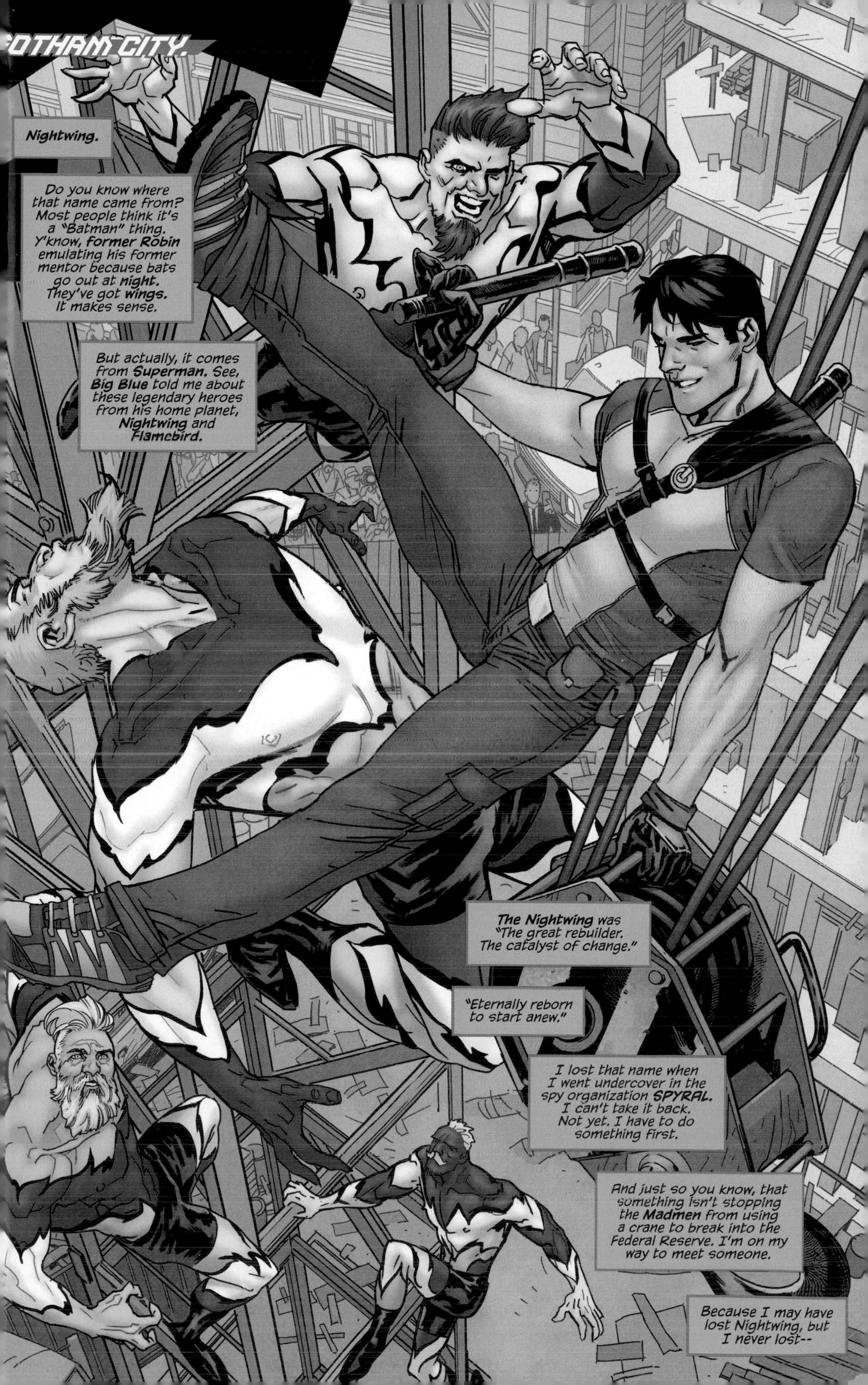

GOTHAM CITY.
Nightwing.
Do you know where that name came from? Most people think it's a "Batman" thing. Y'know, former Robin emulating his former mentor because bats go out at night. They've got wings. It makes sense.
But actually, it comes from Superman. See, Big Blue told me about these legendary heroes from his home planet, Nightwing and Flamebird.
The Nightwing was "The great rebuilder. The catalyst of change."
"Eternally reborn to start anew."
I lost that name when I went undercover in the spy organization SPYRAL. I can't take it back. Not yet. I have to do something first.
And just so you know, that something isn't stopping the Madmen from using a crane to break into the Federal Reserve. I'm on my way to meet someone.
Because I may have lost Nightwing, but I never lost--

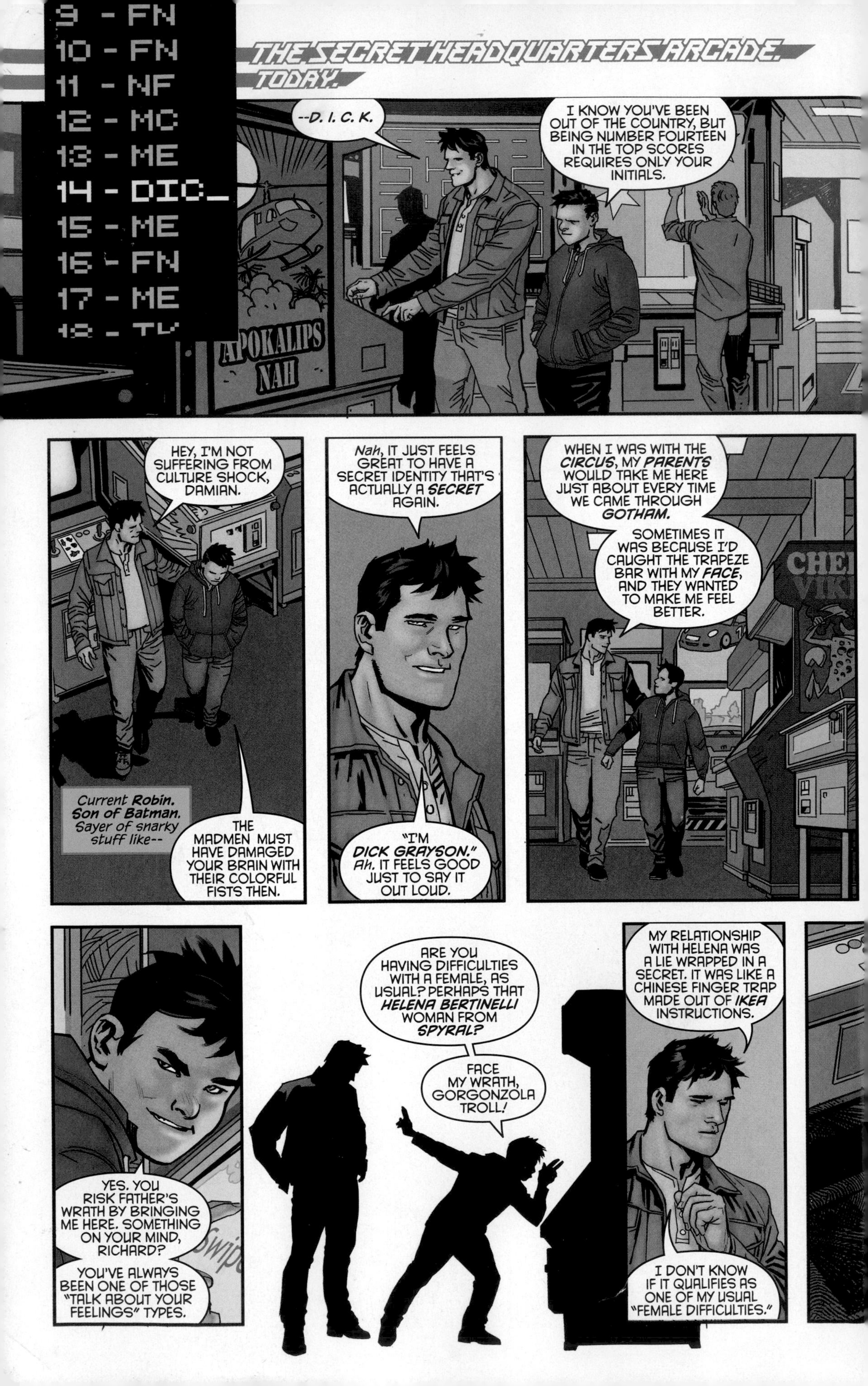
9 - FN
10 - FN
11 - NF
12 - MC
13 - ME
14 - DIC_
15 - ME
16 - FN
17 - ME
THE SECRET HEADQUARTERS ARCADE. TODAY.
--D. I. C. K.
I KNOW YOU'VE BEEN OUT OF THE COUNTRY, BUT BEING NUMBER FOURTEEN IN THE TOP SCORES REQUIRES ONLY YOUR INITIALS.
APOKALIPS NAH
HEY, I'M NOT SUFFERING FROM CULTURE SHOCK, DAMIAN.
Current Robin. Son of Batman. Sayer of snarky stuff like--
THE MADMEN MUST HAVE DAMAGED YOUR BRAIN WITH THEIR COLORFUL FISTS THEN.
Nah, IT JUST FEELS GREAT TO HAVE A SECRET IDENTITY THAT'S ACTUALLY A SECRET AGAIN.
"I'M DICK GRAYSON." Ah. IT FEELS GOOD JUST TO SAY IT OUT LOUD.
WHEN I WAS WITH THE CIRCUS, MY PARENTS WOULD TAKE ME HERE JUST ABOUT EVERY TIME WE CAME THROUGH GOTHAM.
SOMETIMES IT WAS BECAUSE I'D CAUGHT THE TRAPEZE BAR WITH MY FACE, AND THEY WANTED TO MAKE ME FEEL BETTER.
YES. YOU RISK FATHER'S WRATH BY BRINGING ME HERE. SOMETHING ON YOUR MIND, RICHARD?
YOU'VE ALWAYS BEEN ONE OF THOSE "TALK ABOUT YOUR FEELINGS" TYPES.
ARE YOU HAVING DIFFICULTIES WITH A FEMALE, AS USUAL? PERHAPS THAT HELENA BERTINELLI WOMAN FROM SPYRAL?
FACE MY WRATH, GORGONZOLA TROLL!
MY RELATIONSHIP WITH HELENA WAS A LIE WRAPPED IN A SECRET. IT WAS LIKE A CHINESE FINGER TRAP MADE OUT OF IKEA INSTRUCTIONS.
I DON'T KNOW IF IT QUALIFIES AS ONE OF MY USUAL "FEMALE DIFFICULTIES."

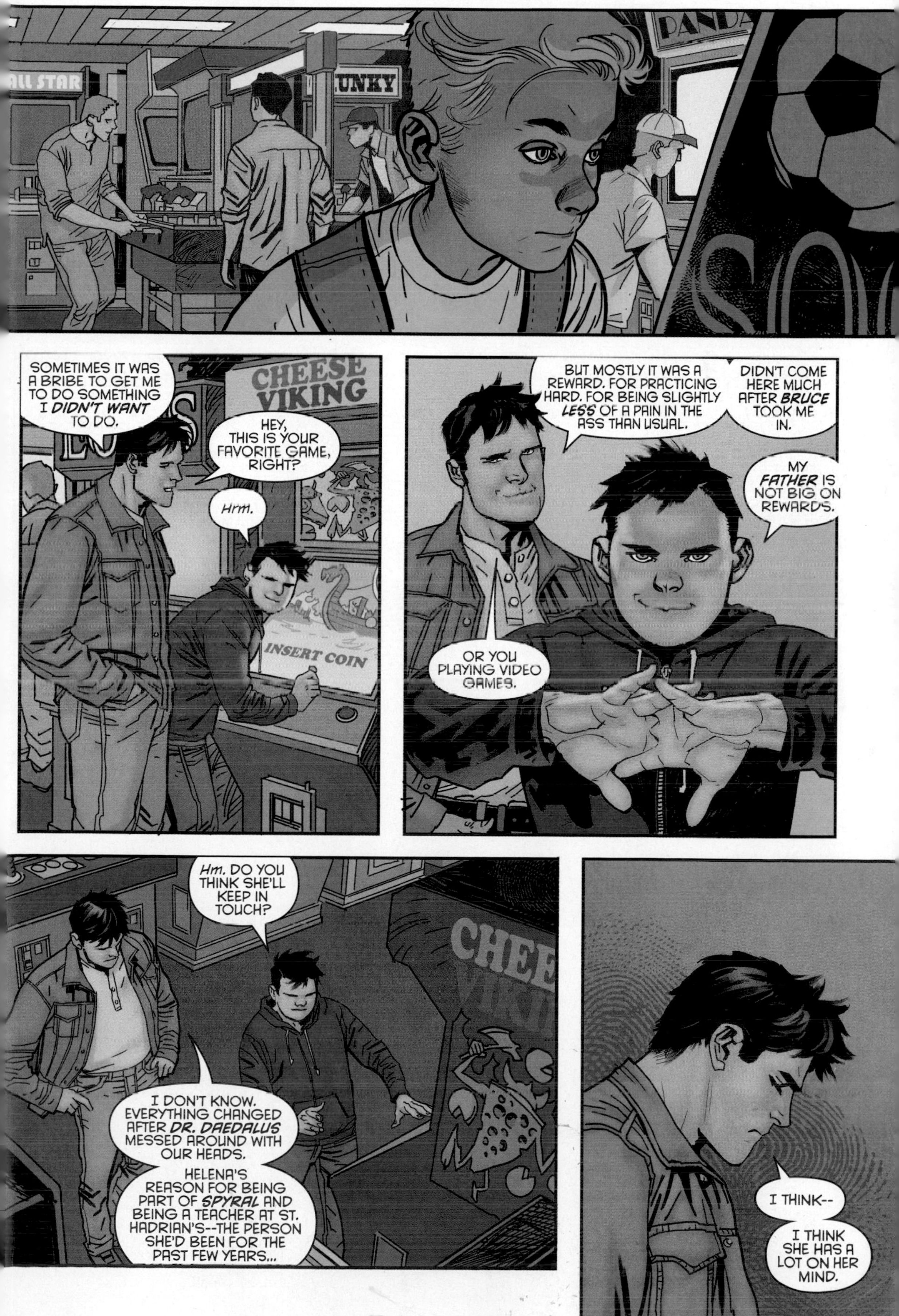
ALL STAR
UNKY
PANDA
SO
CHEESE VIKING
SOMETIMES IT WAS A BRIBE TO GET ME TO DO SOMETHING I *DIDN'T WANT* TO DO.
HEY, THIS IS YOUR FAVORITE GAME, RIGHT?
Hrm.
INSERT COIN
BUT MOSTLY IT WAS A REWARD. FOR PRACTICING HARD. FOR BEING SLIGHTLY *LESS* OF A PAIN IN THE ASS THAN USUAL.
DIDN'T COME HERE MUCH AFTER *BRUCE* TOOK ME IN.
MY *FATHER* IS NOT BIG ON REWARDS.
OR YOU PLAYING VIDEO GAMES.
Hm. DO YOU THINK SHE'LL KEEP IN TOUCH?
CHEE VIKI
I DON'T KNOW. EVERYTHING CHANGED AFTER *DR. DAEDALUS* MESSED AROUND WITH OUR HEADS.
HELENA'S REASON FOR BEING PART OF *SPYRAL* AND BEING A TEACHER AT ST. HADRIAN'S--THE PERSON SHE'D BEEN FOR THE PAST FEW YEARS...
I THINK--
I THINK SHE HAS A LOT ON HER MIND.

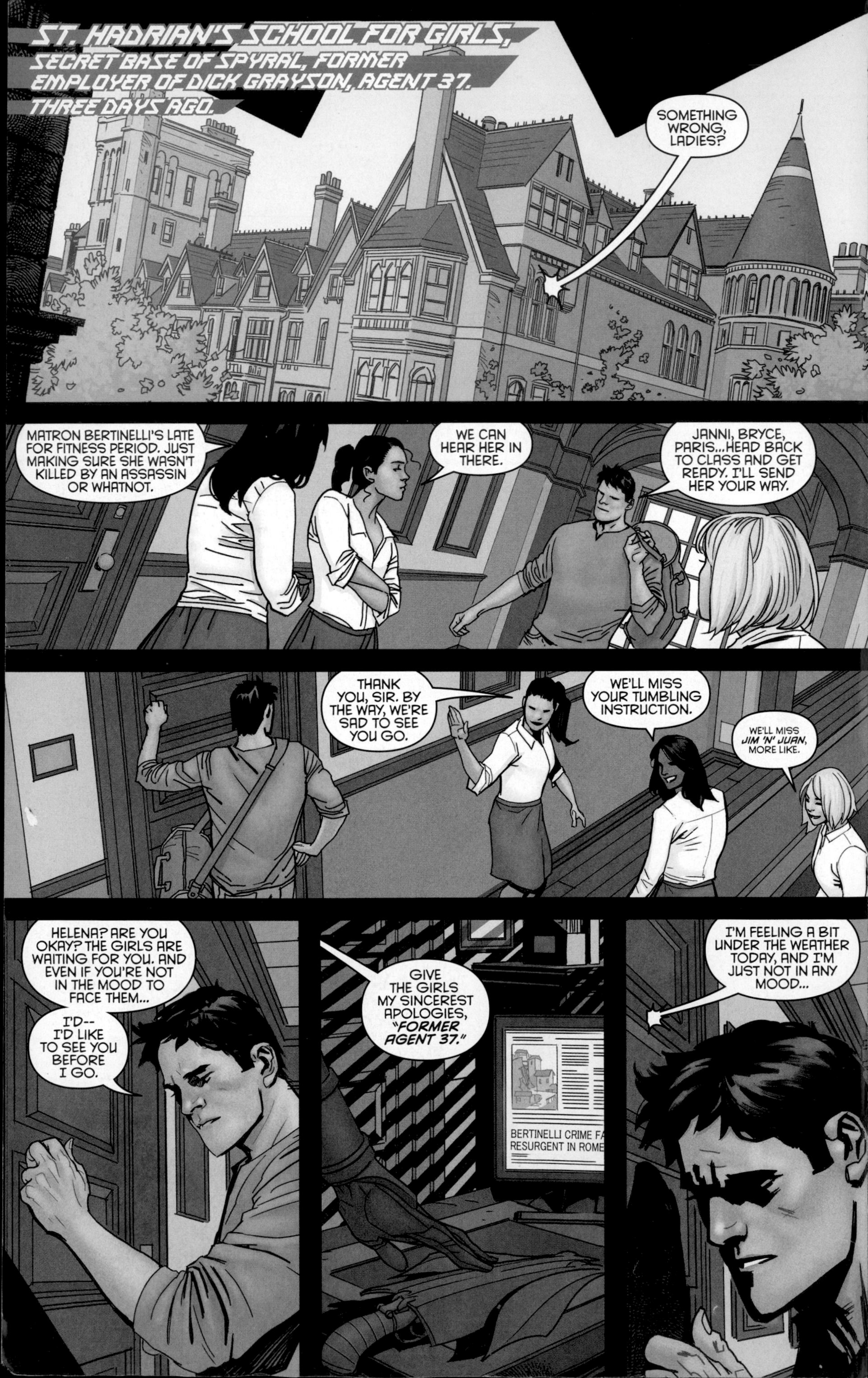
ST. HADRIAN'S SCHOOL FOR GIRLS,
SECRET BASE OF SPYRAL, FORMER EMPLOYER OF DICK GRAYSON, AGENT 37.
THREE DAYS AGO.
SOMETHING WRONG, LADIES?
MATRON BERTINELLI'S LATE FOR FITNESS PERIOD. JUST MAKING SURE SHE WASN'T KILLED BY AN ASSASSIN OR WHATNOT.
WE CAN HEAR HER IN THERE.
JANNI, BRYCE, PARIS...HEAD BACK TO CLASS AND GET READY. I'LL SEND HER YOUR WAY.
THANK YOU, SIR. BY THE WAY, WE'RE SAD TO SEE YOU GO.
WE'LL MISS YOUR TUMBLING INSTRUCTION.
WE'LL MISS JIM 'N' JUAN, MORE LIKE.
HELENA? ARE YOU OKAY? THE GIRLS ARE WAITING FOR YOU. AND EVEN IF YOU'RE NOT IN THE MOOD TO FACE THEM...
I'D-- I'D LIKE TO SEE YOU BEFORE I GO.
GIVE THE GIRLS MY SINCEREST APOLOGIES, "FORMER AGENT 37."
BERTINELLI CRIME FA
RESURGENT IN ROME
I'M FEELING A BIT UNDER THE WEATHER TODAY, AND I'M JUST NOT IN ANY MOOD...

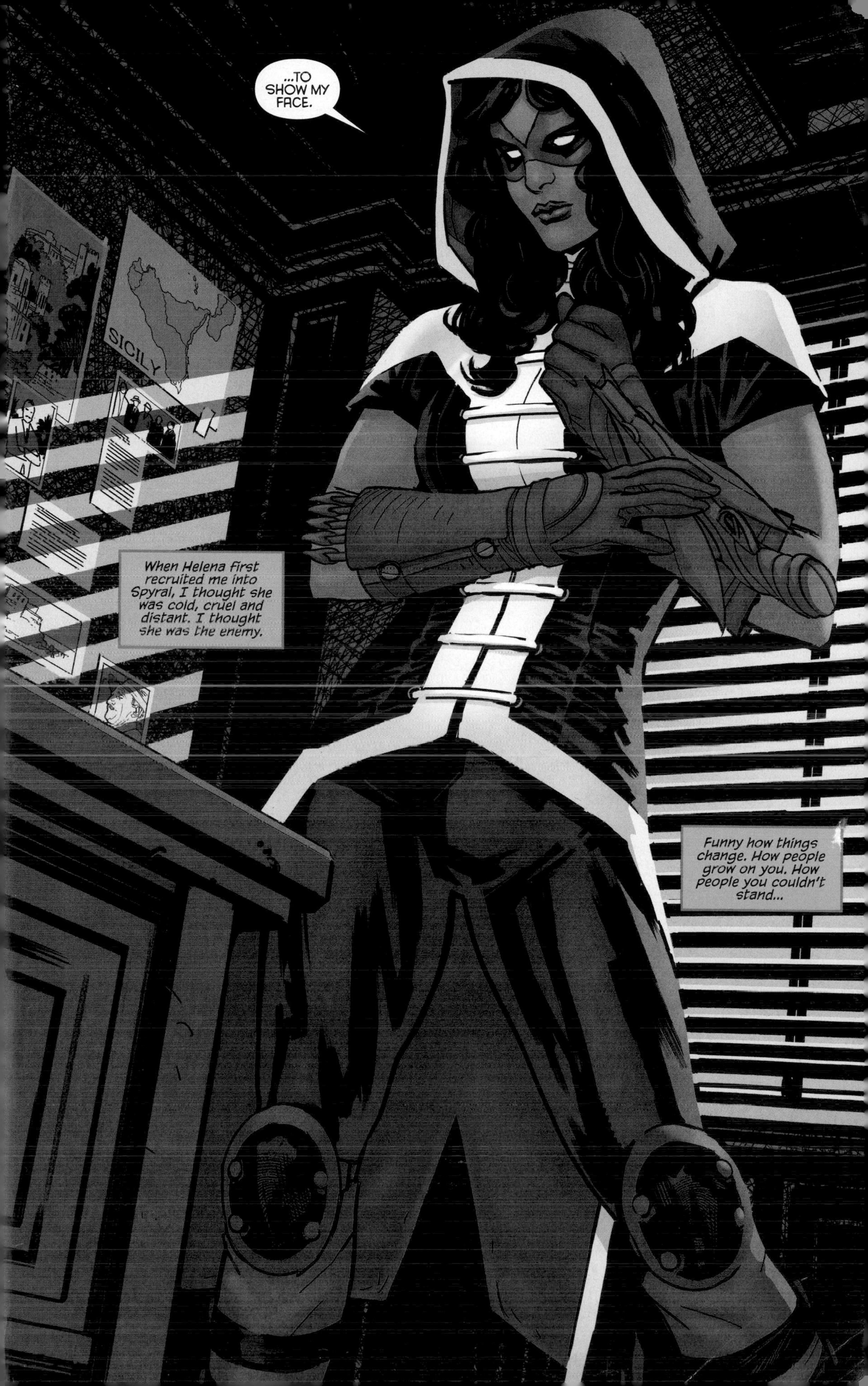
...TO SHOW MY FACE.
SICILY
When Helena first recruited me into Spyral, I thought she was cold, cruel and distant. I thought she was the enemy.
Funny how things change. How people grow on you. How people you couldn't stand...

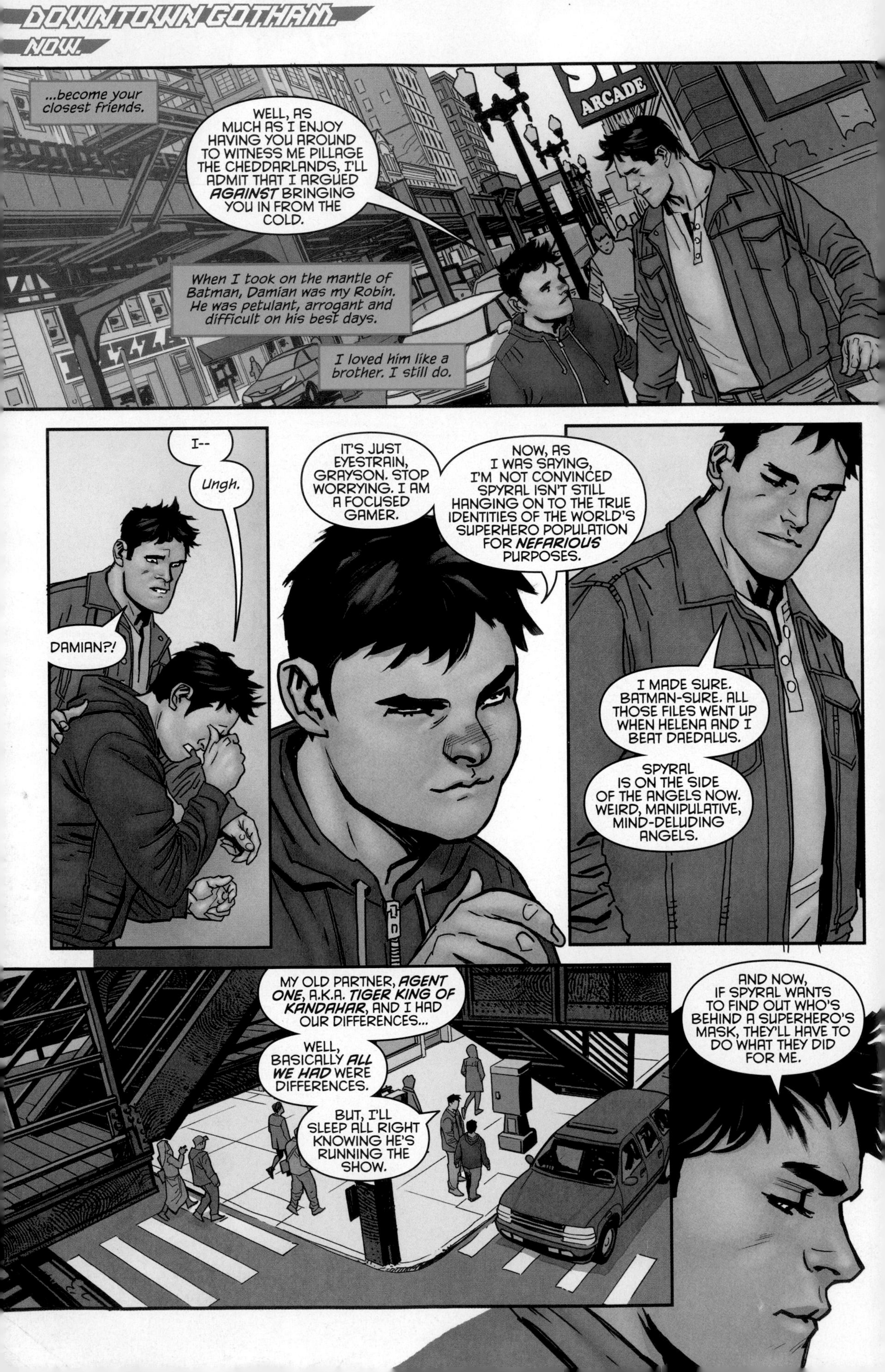
DOWNTOWN GOTHAM.
NOW.
...become your closest friends.
WELL, AS MUCH AS I ENJOY HAVING YOU AROUND TO WITNESS ME PILLAGE THE CHEDDARLANDS, I'LL ADMIT THAT I ARGUED AGAINST BRINGING YOU IN FROM THE COLD.
ARCADE
When I took on the mantle of Batman, Damian was my Robin. He was petulant, arrogant and difficult on his best days.
I loved him like a brother. I still do.
I--
Ungh.
DAMIAN?!
IT'S JUST EYESTRAIN, GRAYSON. STOP WORRYING. I AM A FOCUSED GAMER.
NOW, AS I WAS SAYING, I'M NOT CONVINCED SPYRAL ISN'T STILL HANGING ON TO THE TRUE IDENTITIES OF THE WORLD'S SUPERHERO POPULATION FOR NEFARIOUS PURPOSES.
I MADE SURE. BATMAN-SURE. ALL THOSE FILES WENT UP WHEN HELENA AND I BEAT DAEDALUS.
SPYRAL IS ON THE SIDE OF THE ANGELS NOW. WEIRD, MANIPULATIVE, MIND-DELUDING ANGELS.
MY OLD PARTNER, AGENT ONE, A.K.A. TIGER KING OF KANDAHAR, AND I HAD OUR DIFFERENCES...
WELL, BASICALLY ALL WE HAD WERE DIFFERENCES.
BUT, I'LL SLEEP ALL RIGHT KNOWING HE'S RUNNING THE SHOW.
AND NOW, IF SPYRAL WANTS TO FIND OUT WHO'S BEHIND A SUPERHERO'S MASK, THEY'LL HAVE TO DO WHAT THEY DID FOR ME.

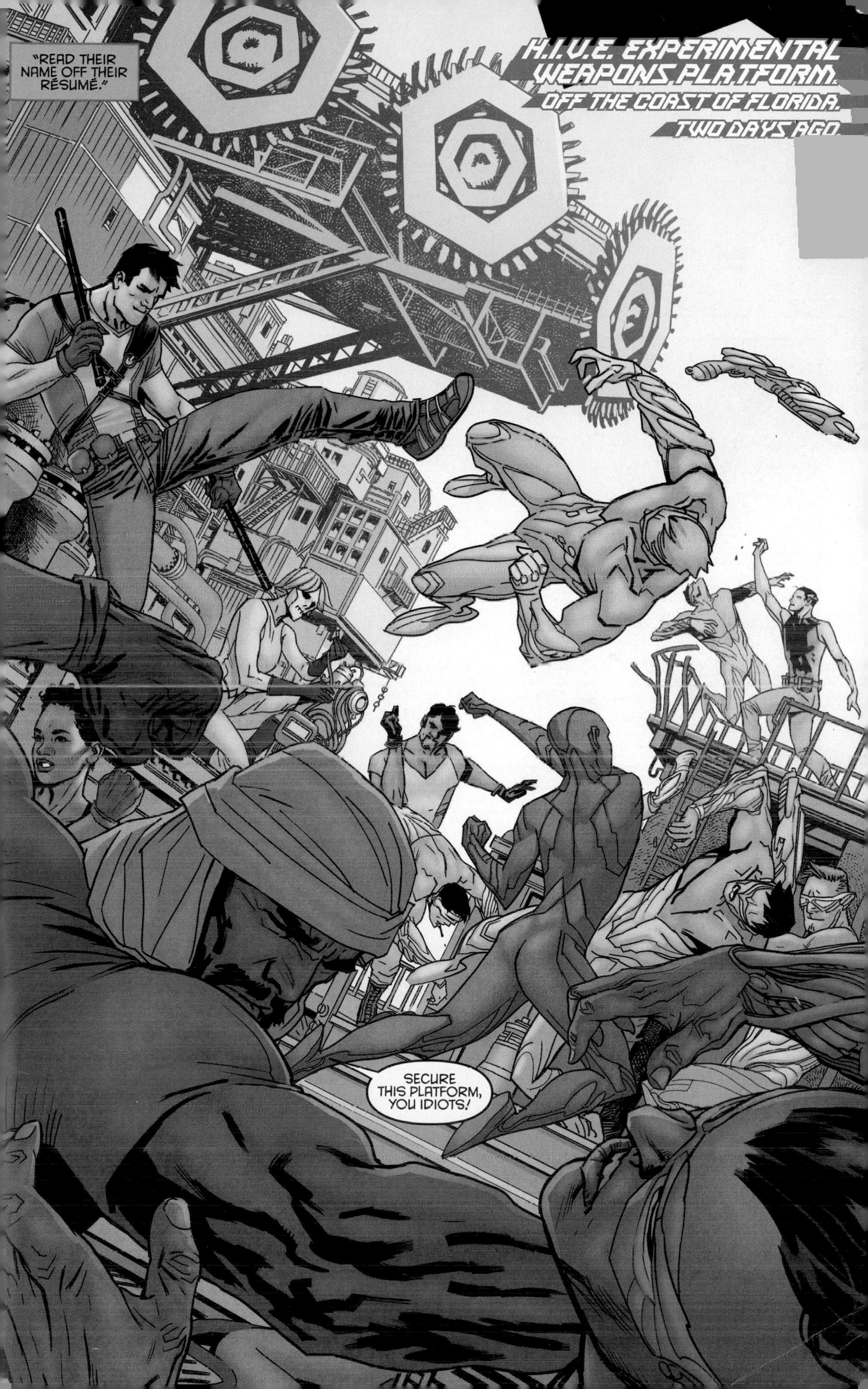
"READ THEIR NAME OFF THEIR RÉSUMÉ."
H.I.V.E. EXPERIMENTAL WEAPONS PLATFORM.
OFF THE COAST OF FLORIDA.
TWO DAYS AGO.
SECURE THIS PLATFORM, YOU IDIOTS!

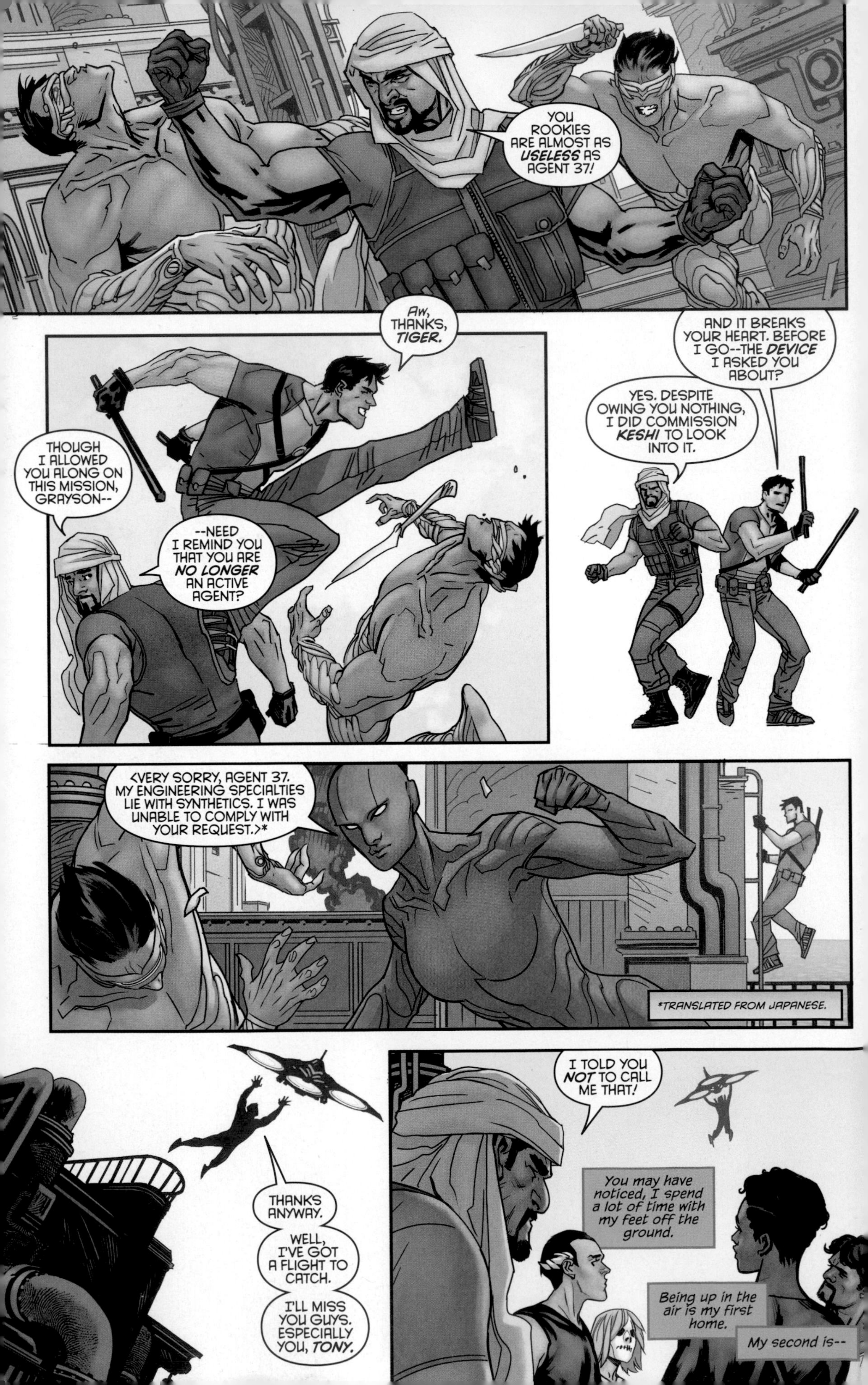
YOU ROOKIES ARE ALMOST AS USELESS AS AGENT 37!
AW, THANKS, TIGER.
THOUGH I ALLOWED YOU ALONG ON THIS MISSION, GRAYSON--
--NEED I REMIND YOU THAT YOU ARE NO LONGER AN ACTIVE AGENT?
AND IT BREAKS YOUR HEART. BEFORE I GO--THE DEVICE I ASKED YOU ABOUT?
YES. DESPITE OWING YOU NOTHING, I DID COMMISSION KESHI TO LOOK INTO IT.
<VERY SORRY, AGENT 37. MY ENGINEERING SPECIALTIES LIE WITH SYNTHETICS. I WAS UNABLE TO COMPLY WITH YOUR REQUEST.>*
*TRANSLATED FROM JAPANESE.
THANKS ANYWAY.
WELL, I'VE GOT A FLIGHT TO CATCH.
I'LL MISS YOU GUYS. ESPECIALLY YOU, TONY.
I TOLD YOU NOT TO CALL ME THAT!
You may have noticed, I spend a lot of time with my feet off the ground.
Being up in the air is my first home.
My second is--

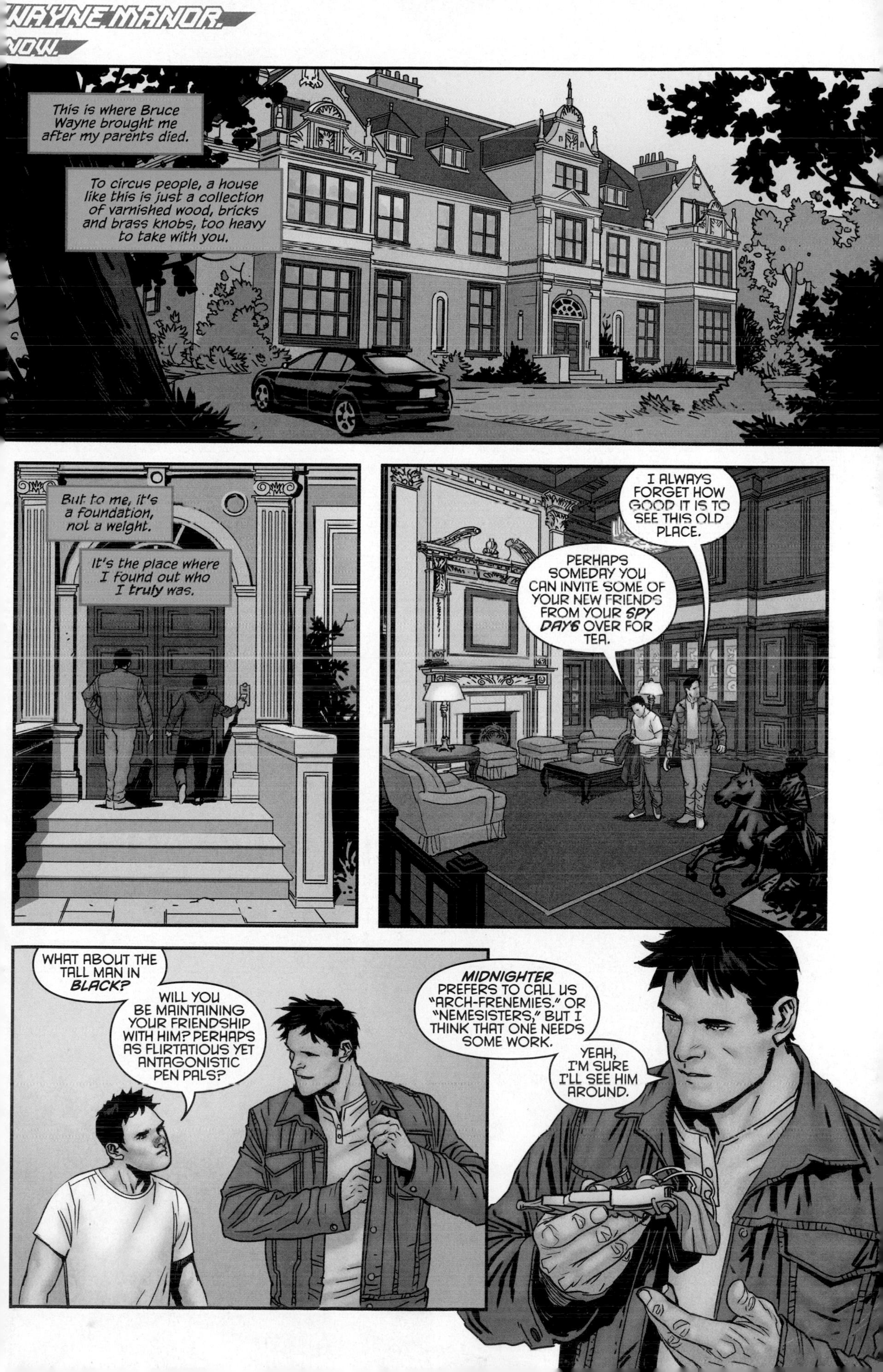
WAYNE MANOR.
NOW.
This is where Bruce Wayne brought me after my parents died.
To circus people, a house like this is just a collection of varnished wood, bricks and brass knobs, too heavy to take with you.
But to me, it's a foundation, not a weight.
It's the place where I found out who I truly was.
I ALWAYS FORGET HOW GOOD IT IS TO SEE THIS OLD PLACE.
PERHAPS SOMEDAY YOU CAN INVITE SOME OF YOUR NEW FRIENDS FROM YOUR SPY DAYS OVER FOR TEA.
WHAT ABOUT THE TALL MAN IN BLACK?
WILL YOU BE MAINTAINING YOUR FRIENDSHIP WITH HIM? PERHAPS AS FLIRTATIOUS YET ANTAGONISTIC PEN PALS?
MIDNIGHTER PREFERS TO CALL US "ARCH-FRENEMIES." OR "NEMESISTERS," BUT I THINK THAT ONE NEEDS SOME WORK.
YEAH, I'M SURE I'LL SEE HIM AROUND.

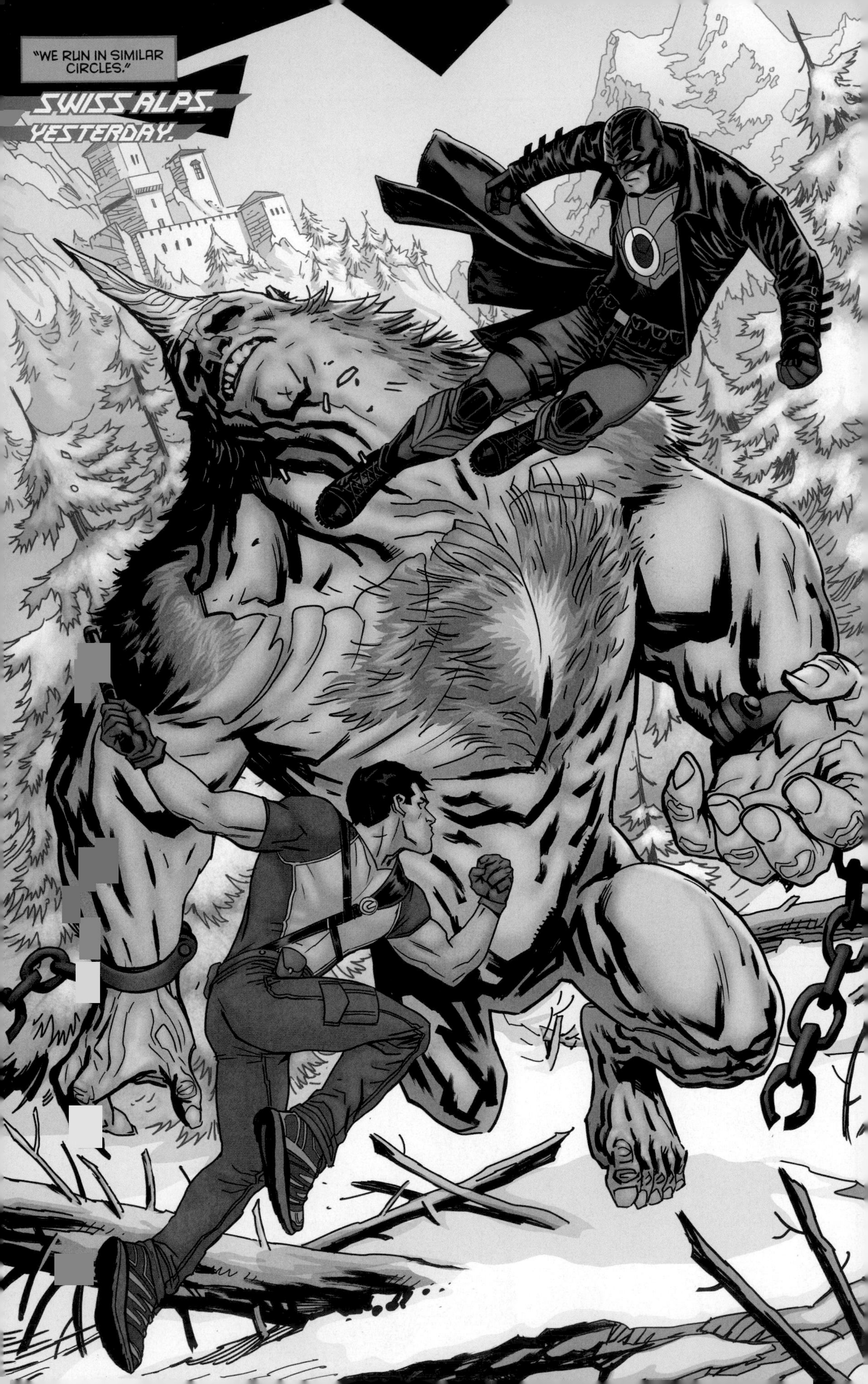
"WE RUN IN SIMILAR CIRCLES."
SWISS ALPS. YESTERDAY.

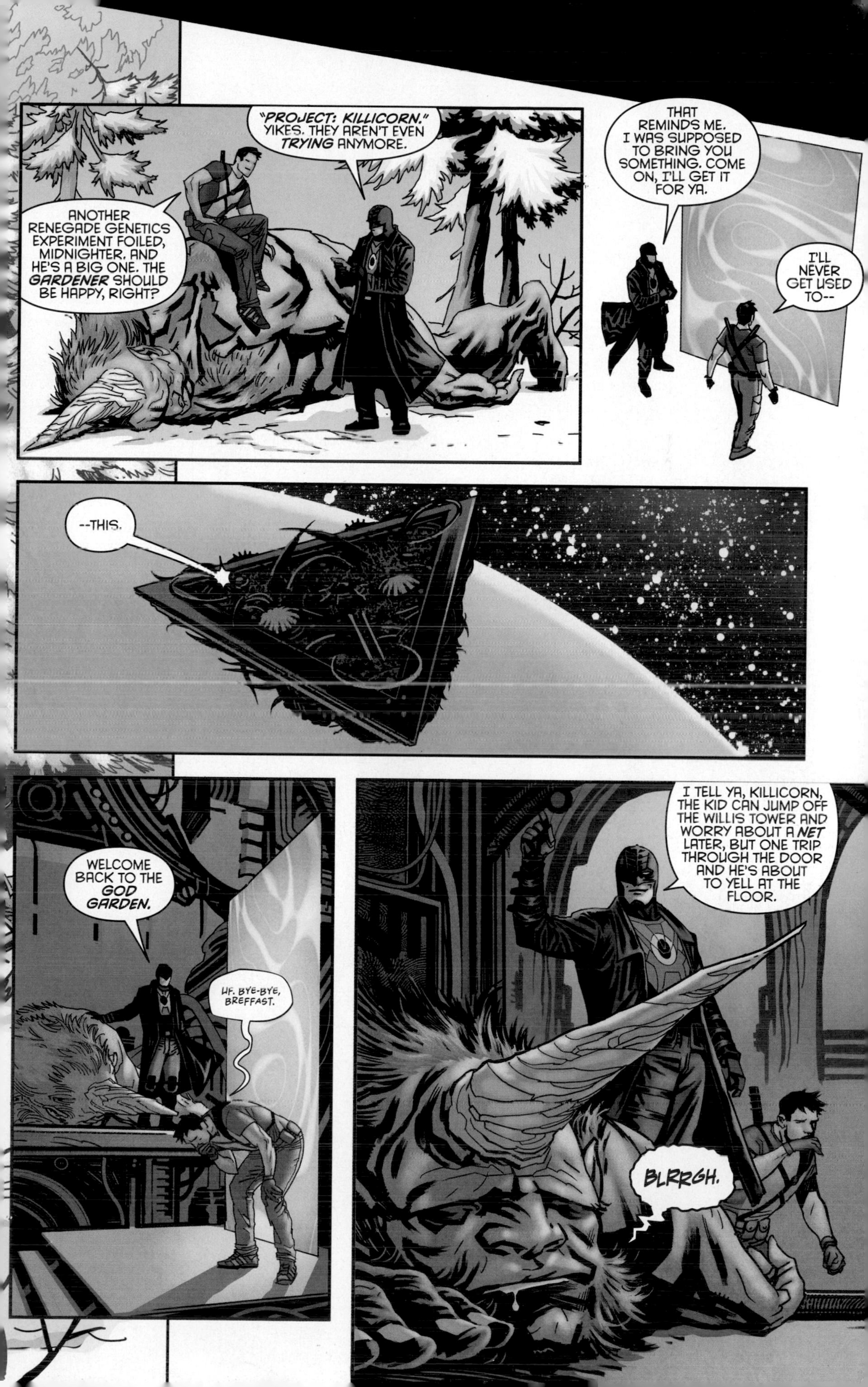

"PROJECT: KILLICORN." YIKES. THEY AREN'T EVEN TRYING ANYMORE.
ANOTHER RENEGADE GENETICS EXPERIMENT FOILED, MIDNIGHTER. AND HE'S A BIG ONE. THE GARDENER SHOULD BE HAPPY, RIGHT?
THAT REMINDS ME. I WAS SUPPOSED TO BRING YOU SOMETHING. COME ON, I'LL GET IT FOR YA.
I'LL NEVER GET USED TO--
--THIS.
WELCOME BACK TO THE GOD GARDEN.
UF. BYE-BYE, BREFFAST.
I TELL YA, KILLICORN, THE KID CAN JUMP OFF THE WILLIS TOWER AND WORRY ABOUT A NET LATER, BUT ONE TRIP THROUGH THE DOOR AND HE'S ABOUT TO YELL AT THE FLOOR.
BLRRGH.

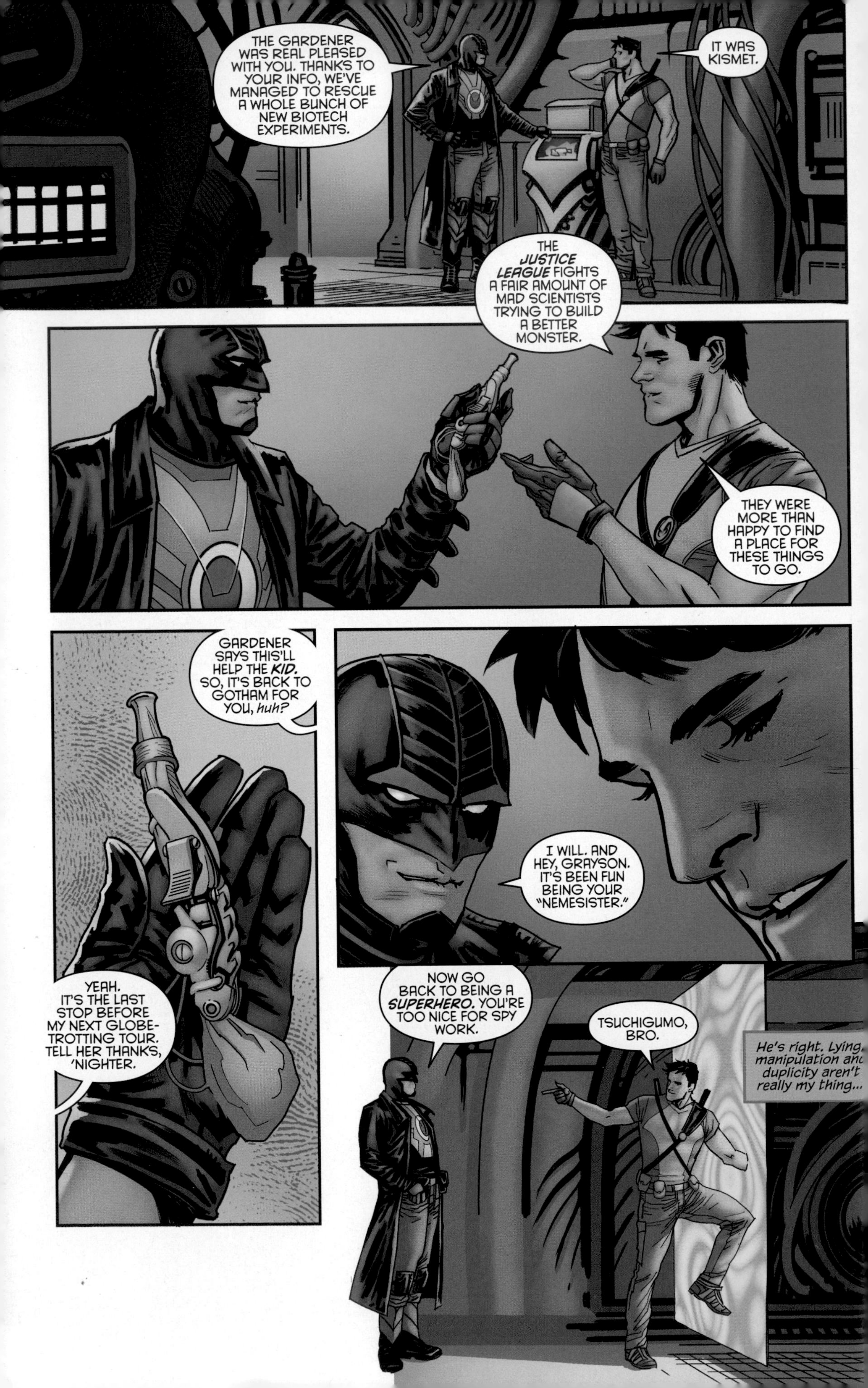
THE GARDENER WAS REAL PLEASED WITH YOU. THANKS TO YOUR INFO, WE'VE MANAGED TO RESCUE A WHOLE BUNCH OF NEW BIOTECH EXPERIMENTS.
IT WAS KISMET.
THE *JUSTICE LEAGUE* FIGHTS A FAIR AMOUNT OF MAD SCIENTISTS TRYING TO BUILD A BETTER MONSTER.
THEY WERE MORE THAN HAPPY TO FIND A PLACE FOR THESE THINGS TO GO.
GARDENER SAYS THIS'LL HELP THE *KID.* SO, IT'S BACK TO GOTHAM FOR YOU, *huh?*
YEAH. IT'S THE LAST STOP BEFORE MY NEXT GLOBE-TROTTING TOUR. TELL HER THANKS, 'NIGHTER.
I WILL. AND HEY, GRAYSON. IT'S BEEN FUN BEING YOUR "NEMESISTER."
NOW GO BACK TO BEING A *SUPERHERO.* YOU'RE TOO NICE FOR SPY WORK.
TSUCHIGUMO, BRO.
He's right. Lying, manipulation and duplicity aren't really my thing...

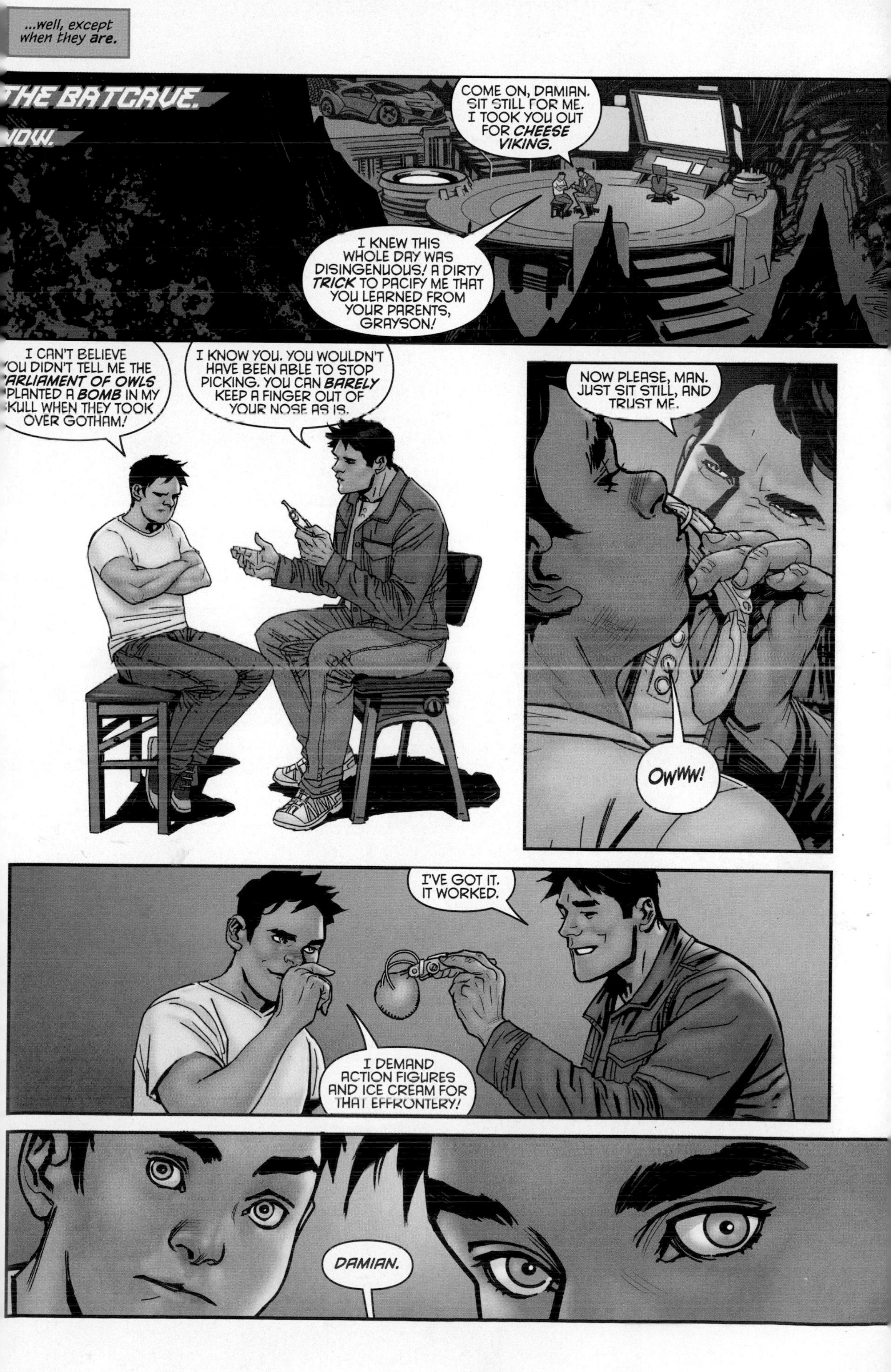
...well, except when they are.
THE BATCAVE.
NOW.
COME ON, DAMIAN. SIT STILL FOR ME. I TOOK YOU OUT FOR CHEESE VIKING.
I KNEW THIS WHOLE DAY WAS DISINGENUOUS! A DIRTY TRICK TO PACIFY ME THAT YOU LEARNED FROM YOUR PARENTS, GRAYSON!
I CAN'T BELIEVE YOU DIDN'T TELL ME THE PARLIAMENT OF OWLS PLANTED A BOMB IN MY SKULL WHEN THEY TOOK OVER GOTHAM!
I KNOW YOU. YOU WOULDN'T HAVE BEEN ABLE TO STOP PICKING. YOU CAN BARELY KEEP A FINGER OUT OF YOUR NOSE AS IS.
NOW PLEASE, MAN. JUST SIT STILL, AND TRUST ME.
OWWW!
I'VE GOT IT. IT WORKED.
I DEMAND ACTION FIGURES AND ICE CREAM FOR THAT EFFRONTERY!
DAMIAN.

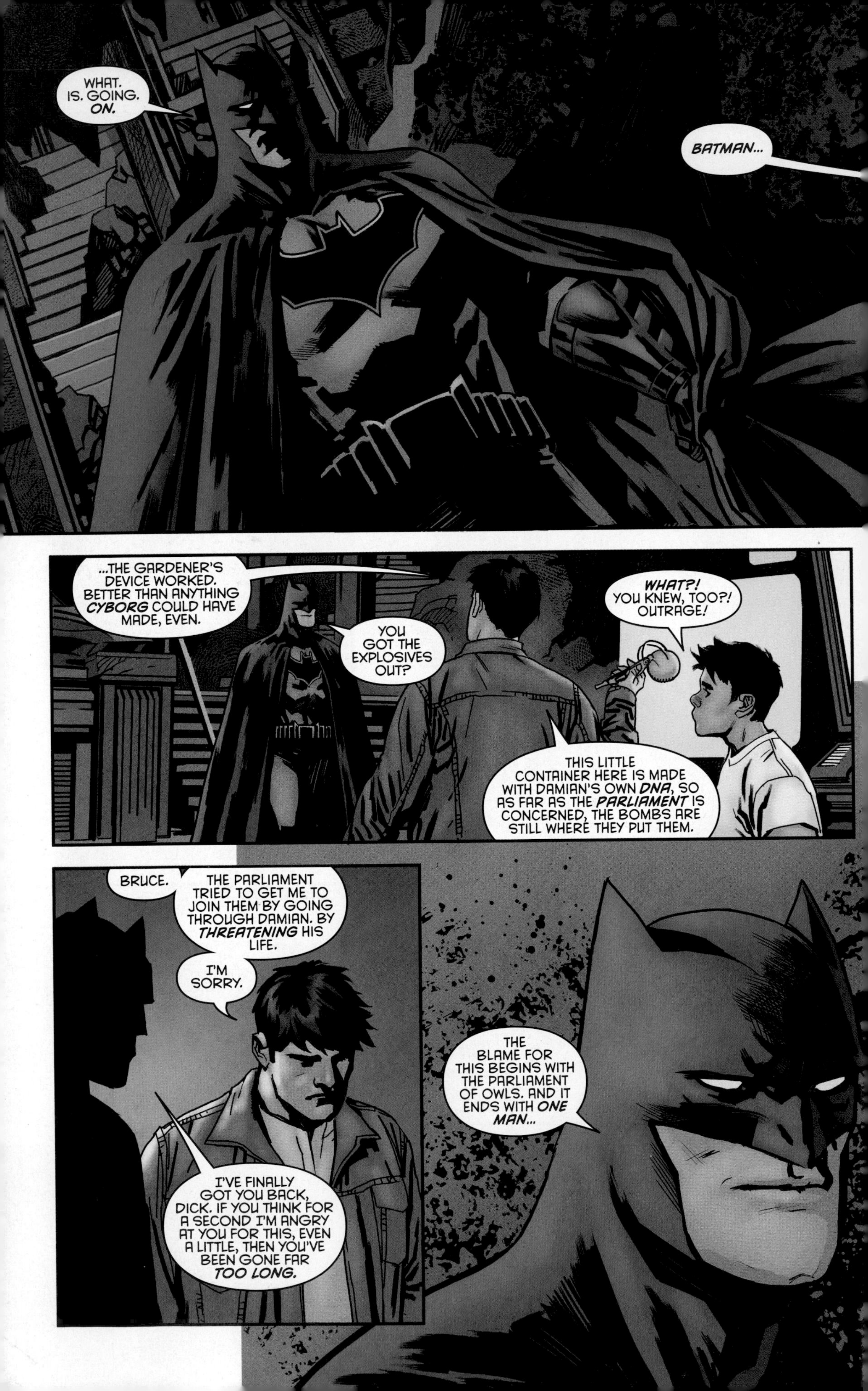
WHAT. IS. GOING. *ON.*
BATMAN...
...THE GARDENER'S DEVICE WORKED. BETTER THAN ANYTHING *CYBORG* COULD HAVE MADE, EVEN.
YOU GOT THE EXPLOSIVES OUT?
WHAT?! YOU KNEW, TOO?! OUTRAGE!
THIS LITTLE CONTAINER HERE IS MADE WITH DAMIAN'S OWN *DNA*, SO AS FAR AS THE *PARLIAMENT* IS CONCERNED, THE BOMBS ARE STILL WHERE THEY PUT THEM.
BRUCE.
THE PARLIAMENT TRIED TO GET ME TO JOIN THEM BY GOING THROUGH DAMIAN. BY *THREATENING* HIS LIFE.
I'M SORRY.
I'VE FINALLY GOT YOU BACK, DICK. IF YOU THINK FOR A SECOND I'M ANGRY AT YOU FOR THIS, EVEN A LITTLE, THEN YOU'VE BEEN GONE FAR *TOO LONG.*
THE BLAME FOR THIS BEGINS WITH THE PARLIAMENT OF OWLS. AND IT ENDS WITH *ONE MAN*...

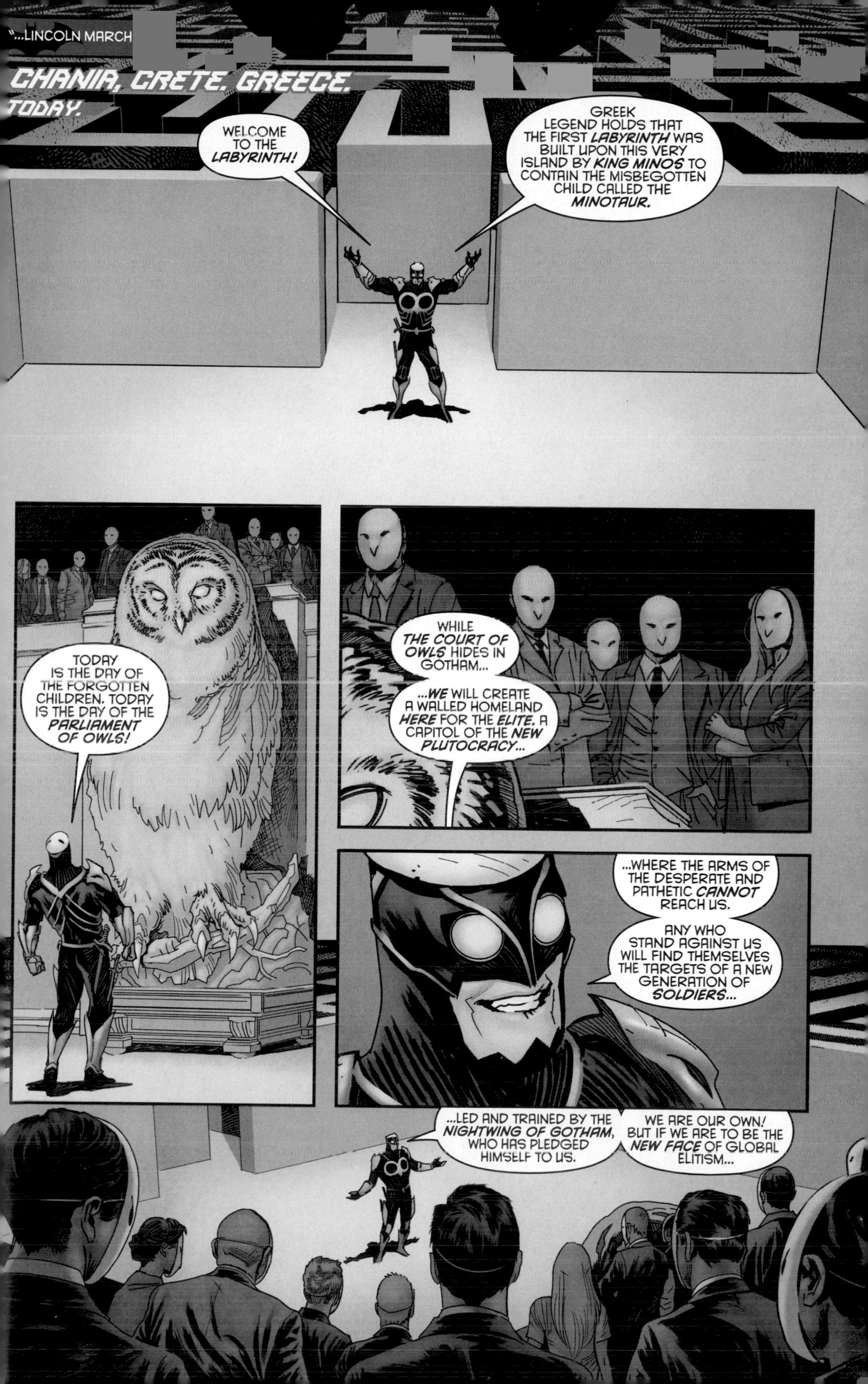
"...LINCOLN MARCH
CHANIA, CRETE. GREECE.
TODAY.
WELCOME TO THE LABYRINTH!
GREEK LEGEND HOLDS THAT THE FIRST LABYRINTH WAS BUILT UPON THIS VERY ISLAND BY KING MINOS TO CONTAIN THE MISBEGOTTEN CHILD CALLED THE MINOTAUR.
TODAY IS THE DAY OF THE FORGOTTEN CHILDREN. TODAY IS THE DAY OF THE PARLIAMENT OF OWLS!
WHILE THE COURT OF OWLS HIDES IN GOTHAM...
...WE WILL CREATE A WALLED HOMELAND HERE FOR THE ELITE. A CAPITOL OF THE NEW PLUTOCRACY...
...WHERE THE ARMS OF THE DESPERATE AND PATHETIC CANNOT REACH US.
ANY WHO STAND AGAINST US WILL FIND THEMSELVES THE TARGETS OF A NEW GENERATION OF SOLDIERS...
...LED AND TRAINED BY THE NIGHTWING OF GOTHAM, WHO HAS PLEDGED HIMSELF TO US.
WE ARE OUR OWN! BUT IF WE ARE TO BE THE NEW FACE OF GLOBAL ELITISM...

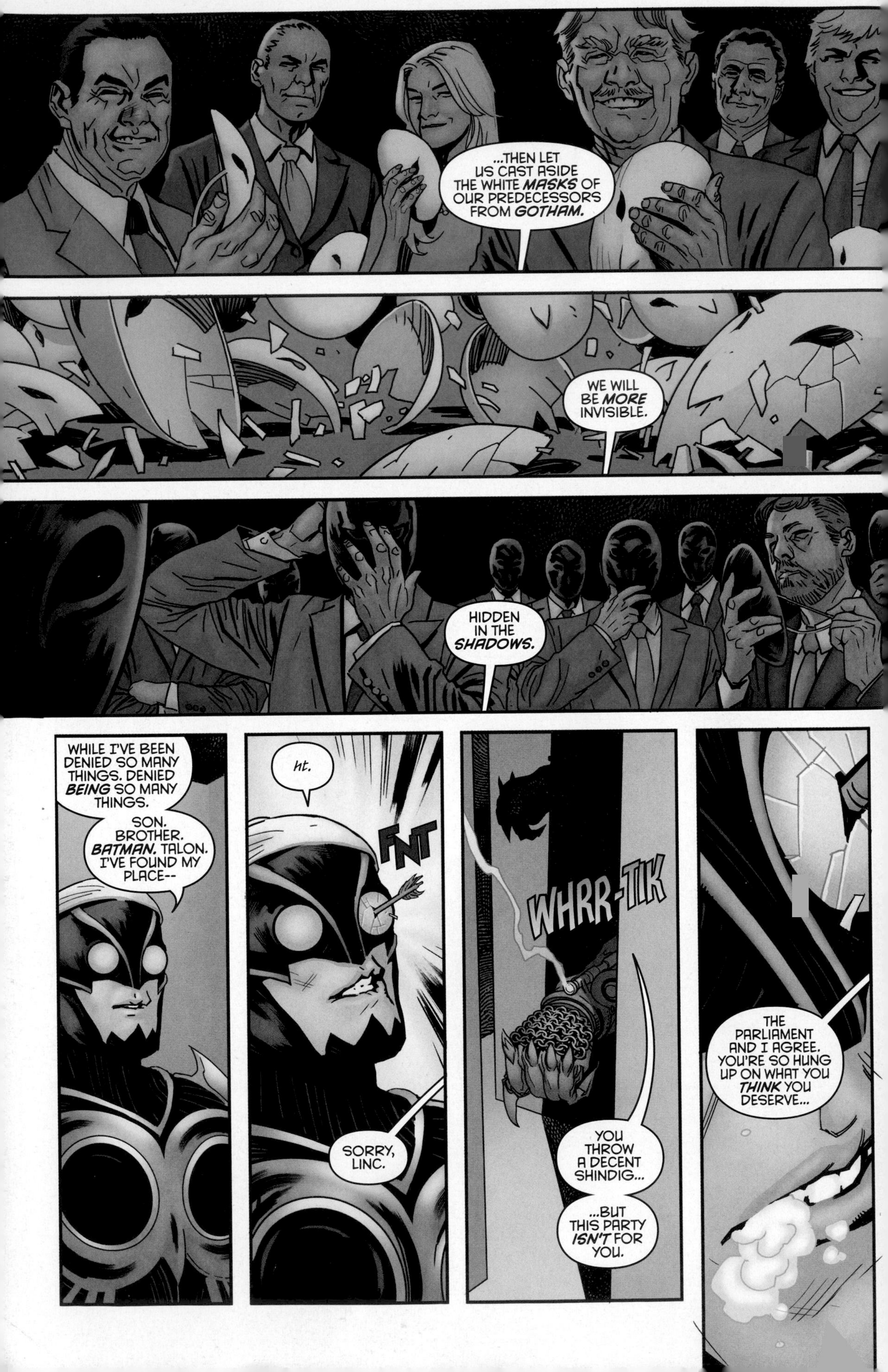
...THEN LET US CAST ASIDE THE WHITE MASKS OF OUR PREDECESSORS FROM GOTHAM.
WE WILL BE MORE INVISIBLE.
HIDDEN IN THE SHADOWS.
WHILE I'VE BEEN DENIED SO MANY THINGS. DENIED BEING SO MANY THINGS.
SON. BROTHER. BATMAN. TALON. I'VE FOUND MY PLACE--
ht.
FNT
SORRY, LINC.
WHRR-TIK
YOU THROW A DECENT SHINDIG...
...BUT THIS PARTY ISN'T FOR YOU.
THE PARLIAMENT AND I AGREE. YOU'RE SO HUNG UP ON WHAT YOU THINK YOU DESERVE...

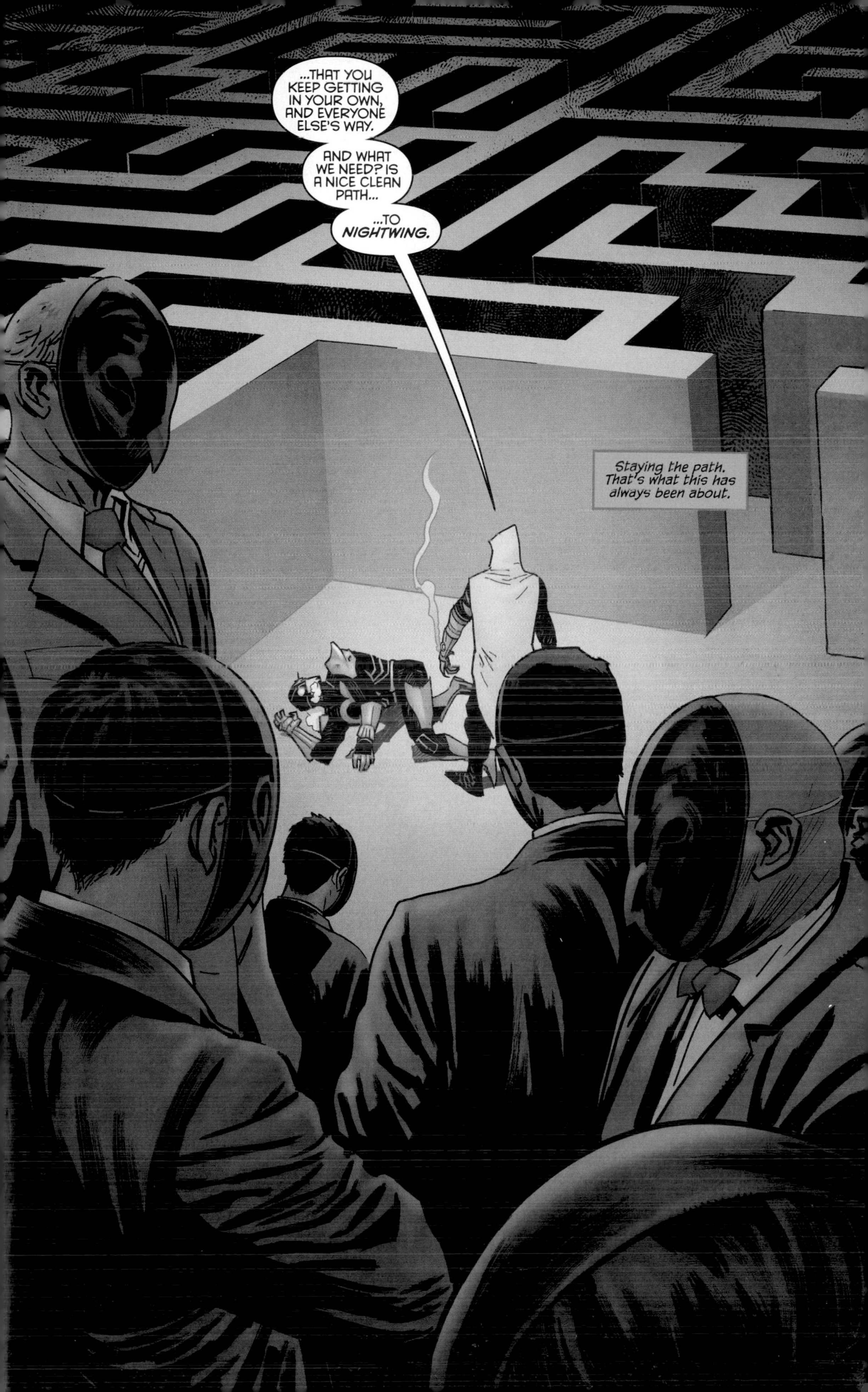
...THAT YOU KEEP GETTING IN YOUR OWN, AND EVERYONE ELSE'S WAY.
AND WHAT WE NEED? IS A NICE CLEAN PATH...
...TO NIGHTWING.
Staying the path. That's what this has always been about.

Balancing on a thin strip of *light*, surrounded by darkness.

For a second, I get to let my guard down. Breathe easy.

Before I step out again.

THE BATCAVE.

I'VE SENT DAMIAN ON A MISSION...TO THE ARCADE.

I WANTED TO TALK TO YOU, DICK. ALONE. I NEED TO KNOW...

...ARE YOU SURE THIS IS WHAT YOU WANT TO DO?

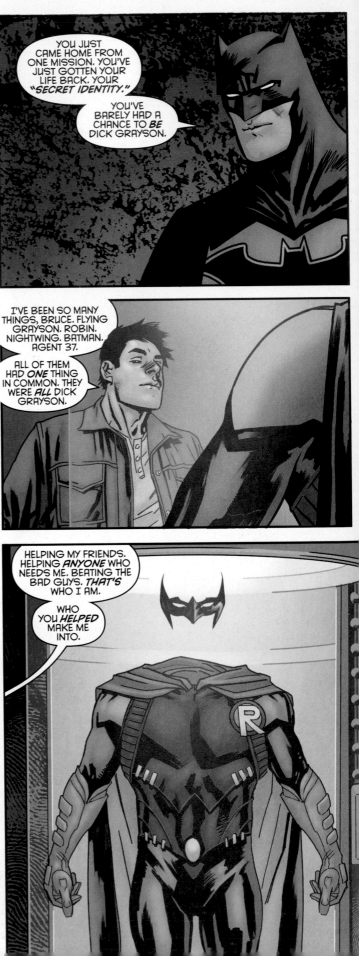

YOU JUST CAME HOME FROM ONE MISSION. YOU'VE JUST GOTTEN YOUR LIFE BACK. YOUR *"SECRET IDENTITY."*

YOU'VE BARELY HAD A CHANCE TO *BE* DICK GRAYSON.

I'VE BEEN SO MANY THINGS, BRUCE. FLYING GRAYSON. ROBIN. NIGHTWING. BATMAN. AGENT 37.

ALL OF THEM HAD *ONE* THING IN COMMON. THEY WERE *ALL* DICK GRAYSON.

HELPING MY FRIENDS. HELPING *ANYONE* WHO NEEDS ME. BEATING THE BAD GUYS. *THAT'S* WHO I AM.

WHO YOU *HELPED* MAKE ME INTO.

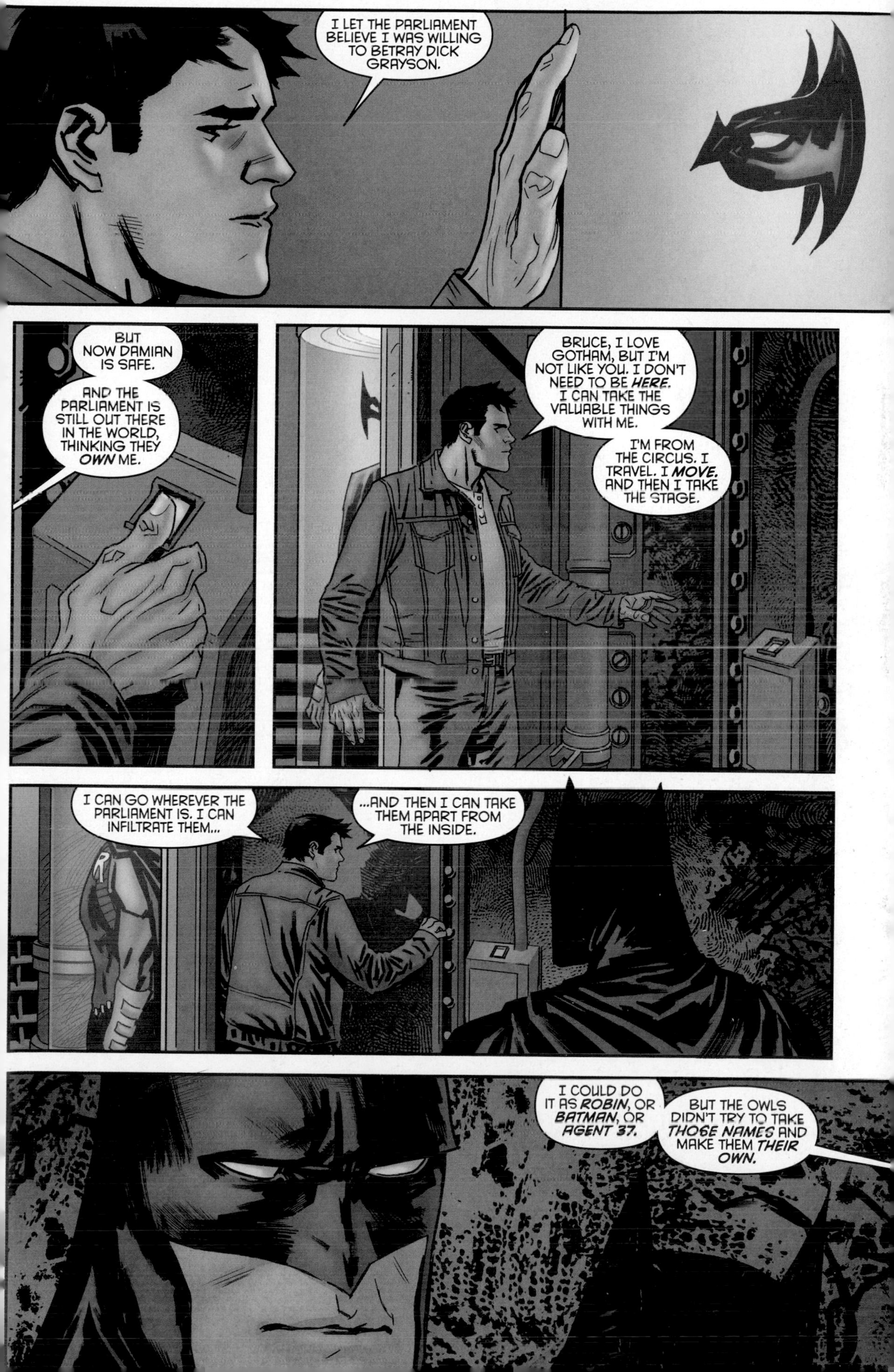
I LET THE PARLIAMENT BELIEVE I WAS WILLING TO BETRAY DICK GRAYSON.
BUT NOW DAMIAN IS SAFE.
AND THE PARLIAMENT IS STILL OUT THERE IN THE WORLD, THINKING THEY *OWN* ME.
BRUCE, I LOVE GOTHAM, BUT I'M NOT LIKE YOU. I DON'T NEED TO BE *HERE*. I CAN TAKE THE VALUABLE THINGS WITH ME.
I'M FROM THE CIRCUS. I TRAVEL. I *MOVE.* AND THEN I TAKE THE STAGE.
I CAN GO WHEREVER THE PARLIAMENT IS. I CAN INFILTRATE THEM...
...AND THEN I CAN TAKE THEM APART FROM THE INSIDE.
I COULD DO IT AS *ROBIN*, OR *BATMAN*, OR *AGENT 37.*
BUT THE OWLS DIDN'T TRY TO TAKE *THOSE NAMES* AND MAKE THEM *THEIR OWN.*

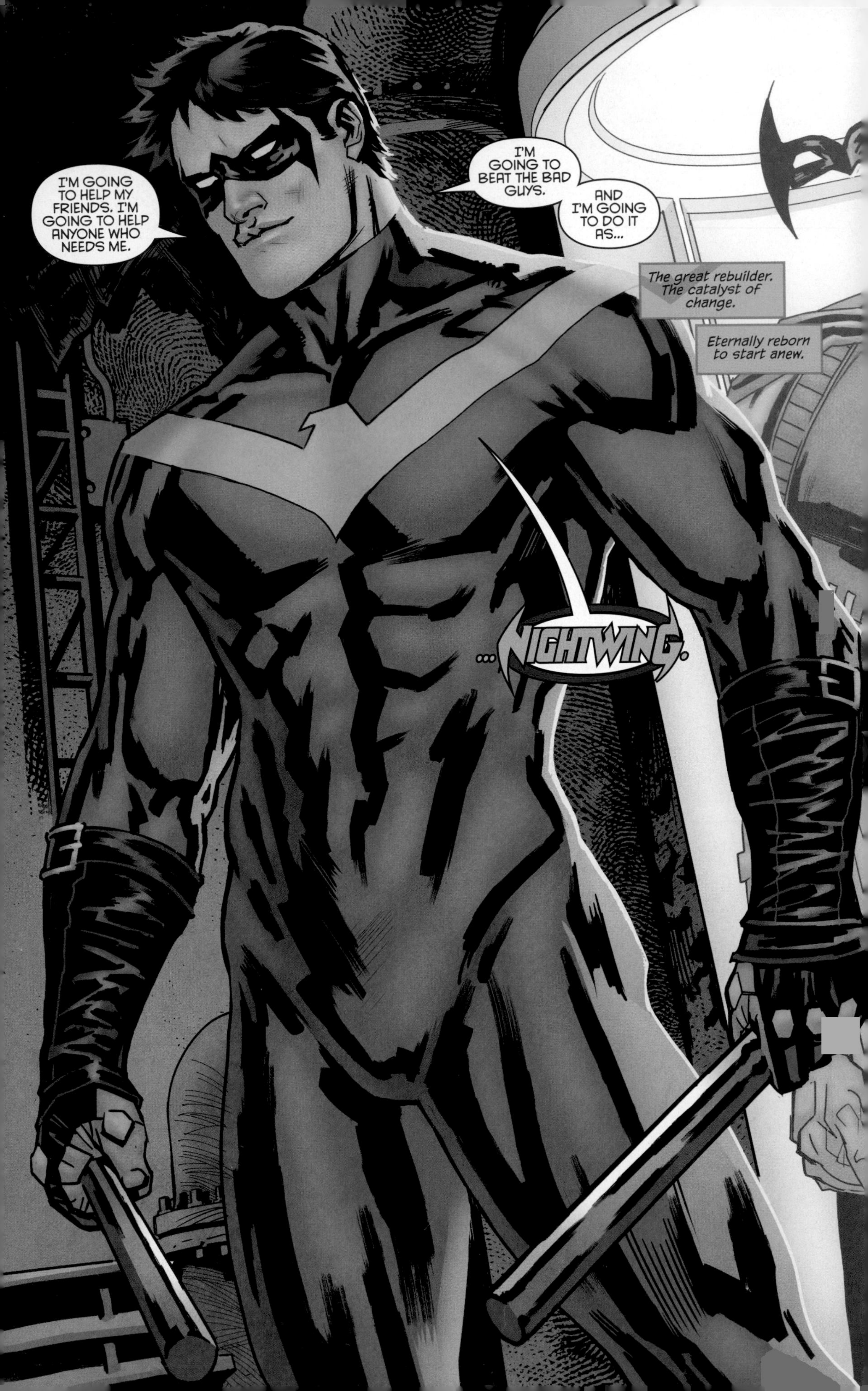

I'M GOING TO HELP MY FRIENDS. I'M GOING TO HELP ANYONE WHO NEEDS ME.
I'M GOING TO BEAT THE BAD GUYS.
AND I'M GOING TO DO IT AS...
The great rebuilder. The catalyst of change.
Eternally reborn to start anew.
...NIGHTWING.

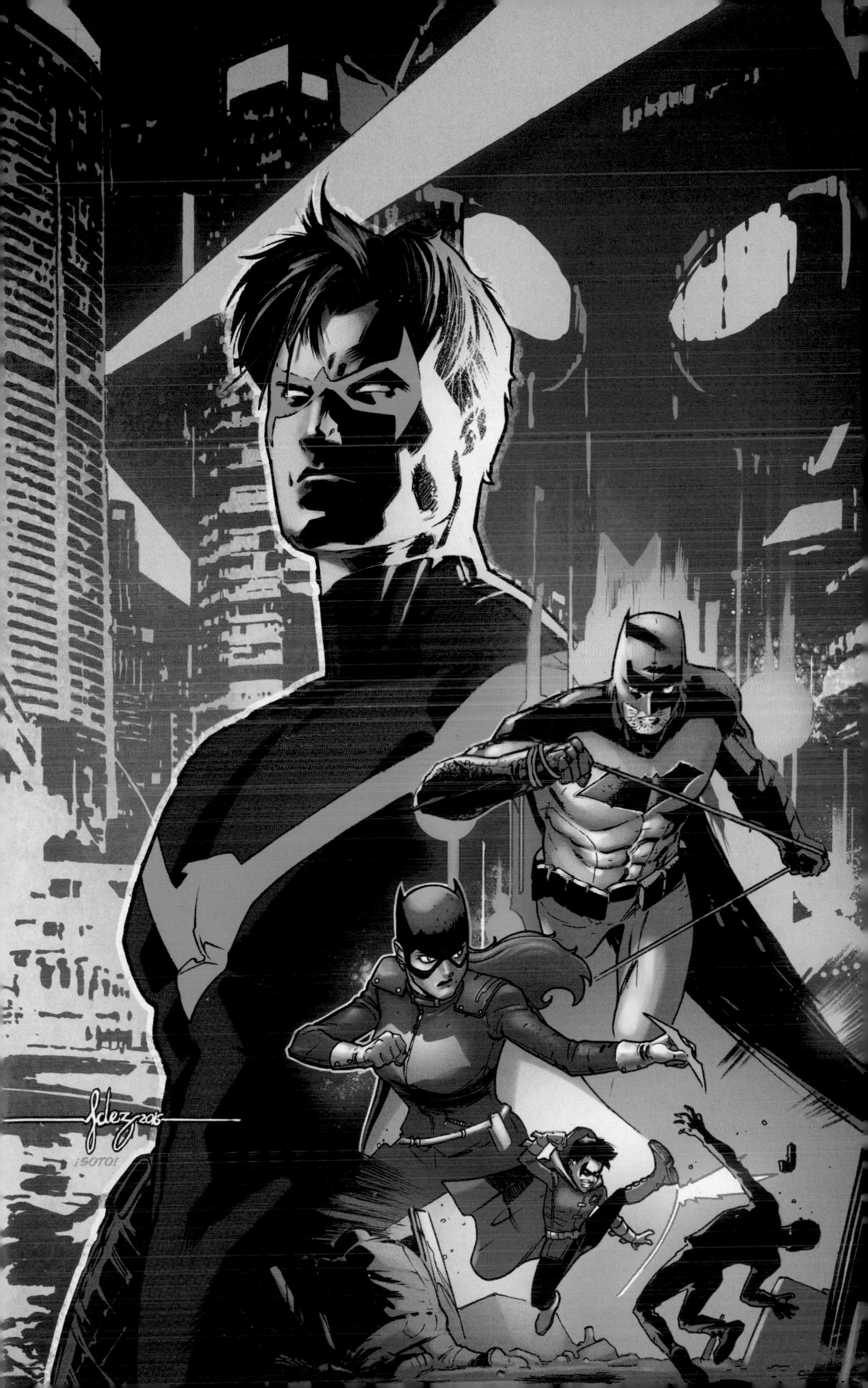
¡SOTO!

BETTER THAN BATMAN, PART 1

TIM SEELEY writer ∗ **JAVIER FERNÁNDEZ** artist ∗ **CHRIS SOTOMAYOR** colorist
CARLOS M. MANGUAL letterer ∗ **JAVIER FERNÁNDEZ** and **CHRIS SOTOMAYOR** cover artists

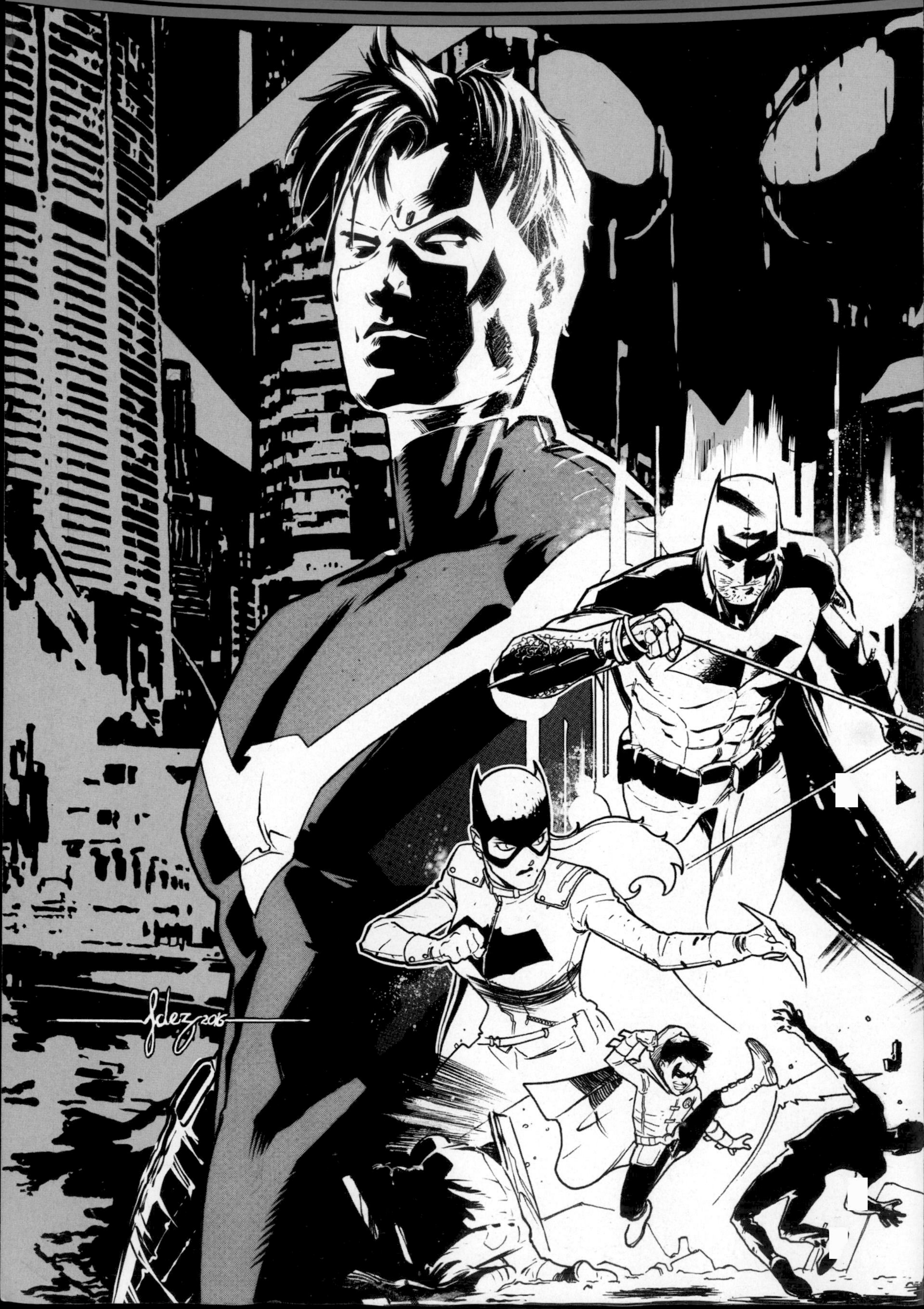

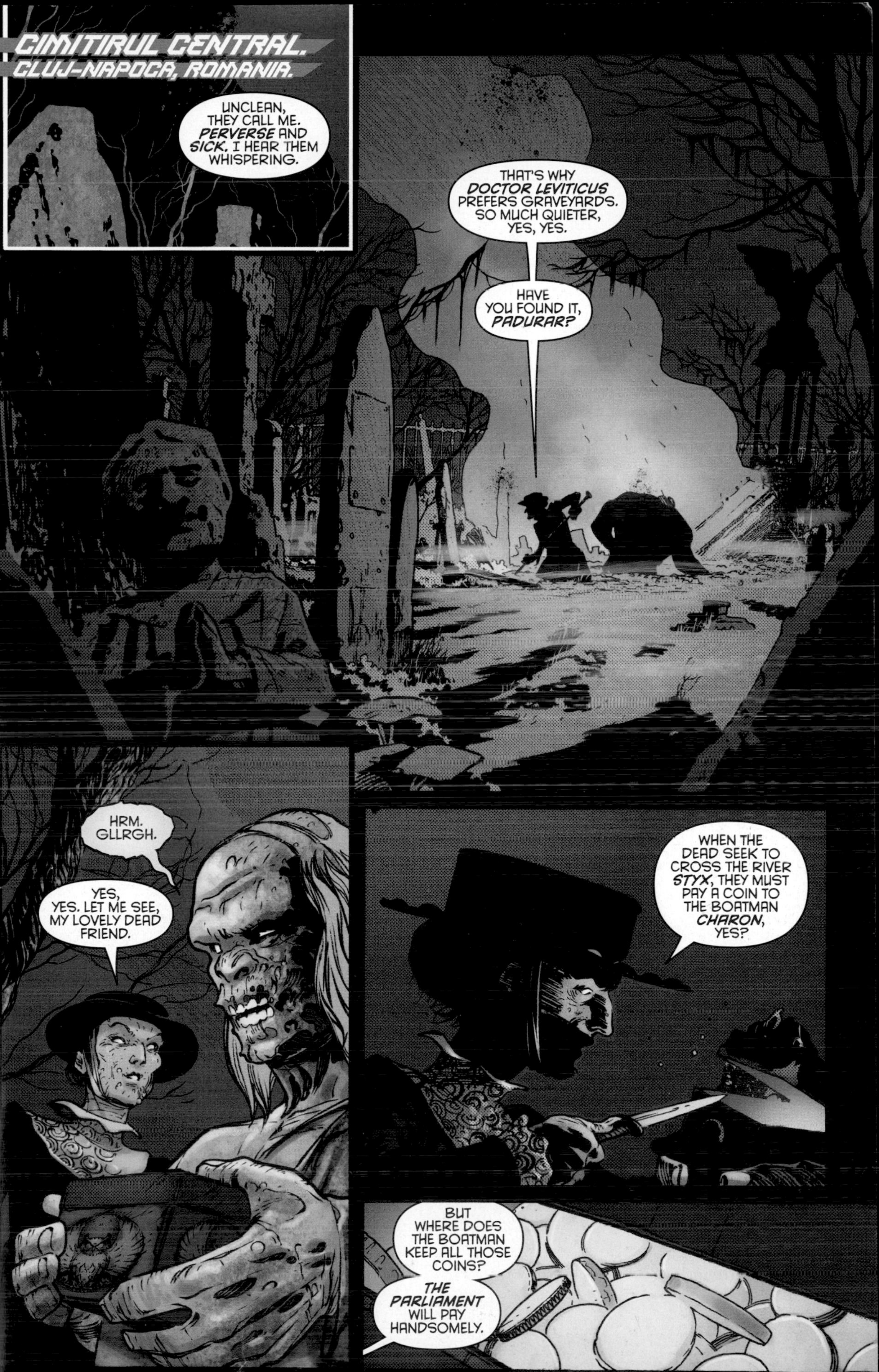
CIMITIRUL CENTRAL.
CLUJ-NAPOCA, ROMANIA.
UNCLEAN, THEY CALL ME. PERVERSE AND SICK. I HEAR THEM WHISPERING.
THAT'S WHY DOCTOR LEVITICUS PREFERS GRAVEYARDS. SO MUCH QUIETER, YES, YES.
HAVE YOU FOUND IT, PADURAR?
HRM. GLLRGH.
YES, YES. LET ME SEE, MY LOVELY DEAD FRIEND.
WHEN THE DEAD SEEK TO CROSS THE RIVER STYX, THEY MUST PAY A COIN TO THE BOATMAN CHARON, YES?
BUT WHERE DOES THE BOATMAN KEEP ALL THOSE COINS?
THE PARLIAMENT WILL PAY HANDSOMELY.

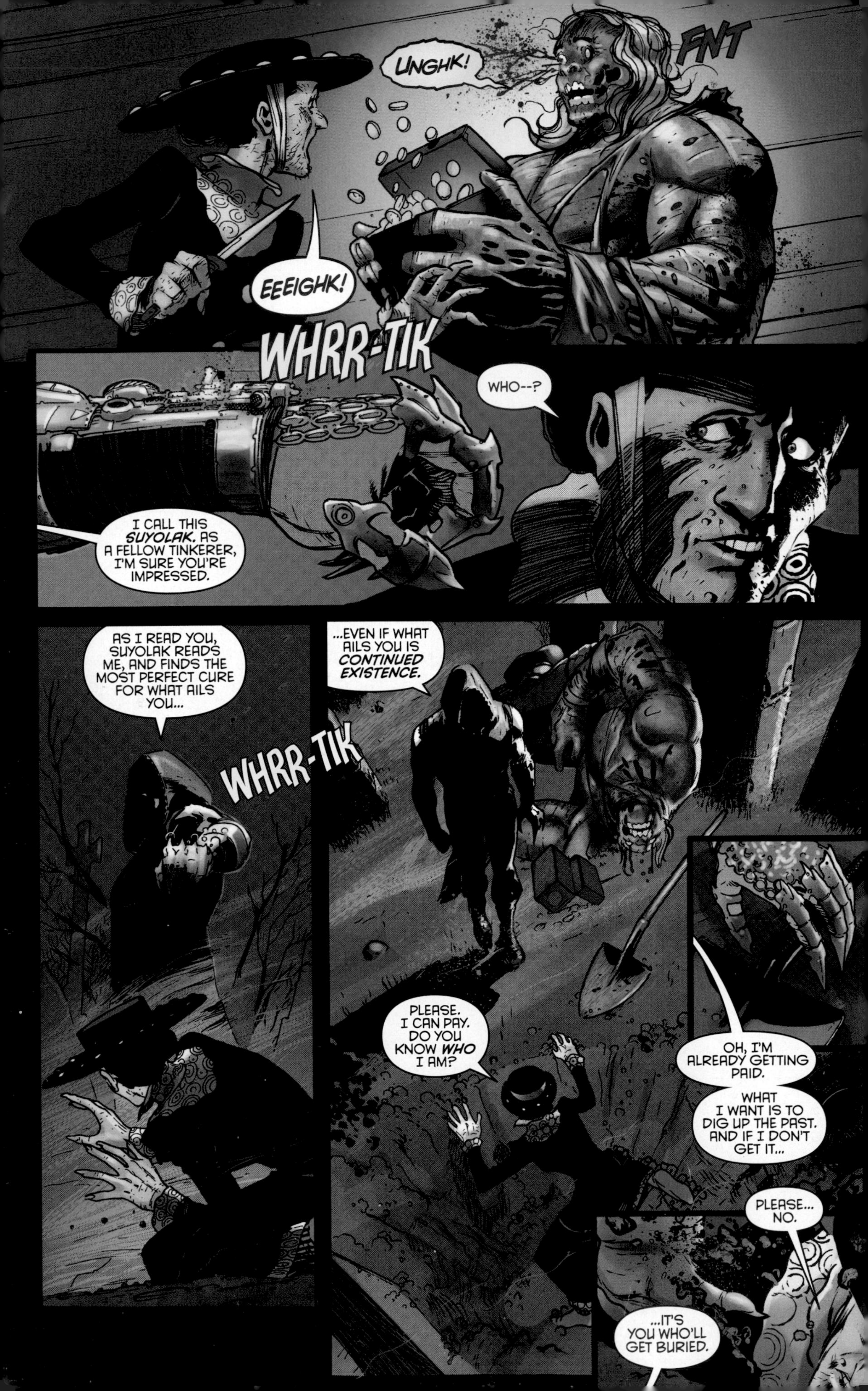
UNGHK!
FNT
EEEIGHK!
WHRR-TIK
WHO--?
I CALL THIS SUYOLAK. AS A FELLOW TINKERER, I'M SURE YOU'RE IMPRESSED.
AS I READ YOU, SUYOLAK READS ME, AND FINDS THE MOST PERFECT CURE FOR WHAT AILS YOU...
WHRR-TIK
...EVEN IF WHAT AILS YOU IS CONTINUED EXISTENCE.
PLEASE. I CAN PAY. DO YOU KNOW WHO I AM?
OH, I'M ALREADY GETTING PAID.
WHAT I WANT IS TO DIG UP THE PAST. AND IF I DON'T GET IT...
PLEASE... NO.
...IT'S YOU WHO'LL GET BURIED.

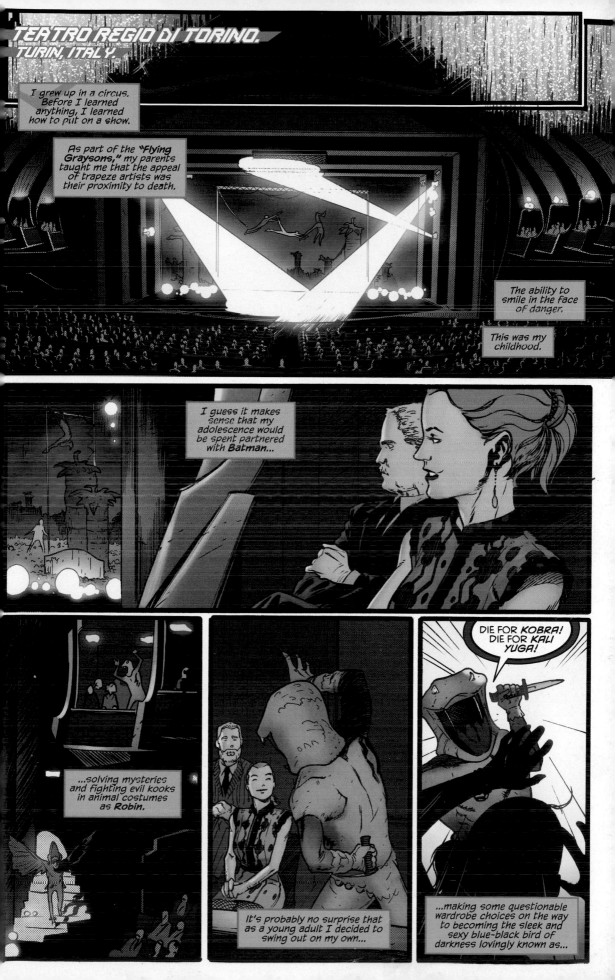

TEATRO REGIO DI TORINO.
TURIN, ITALY.

I grew up in a circus. Before I learned anything, I learned how to put on a show.

As part of the "Flying Graysons," my parents taught me that the appeal of trapeze artists was their proximity to death.

The ability to smile in the face of danger.

This was my childhood.

I guess it makes sense that my adolescence would be spent partnered with Batman...

...solving mysteries and fighting evil kooks in animal costumes as Robin.

It's probably no surprise that as a young adult I decided to swing out on my own...

DIE FOR KOBRA! DIE FOR KALI YUGA!

...making some questionable wardrobe choices on the way to becoming the sleek and sexy blue-black bird of darkness lovingly known as...

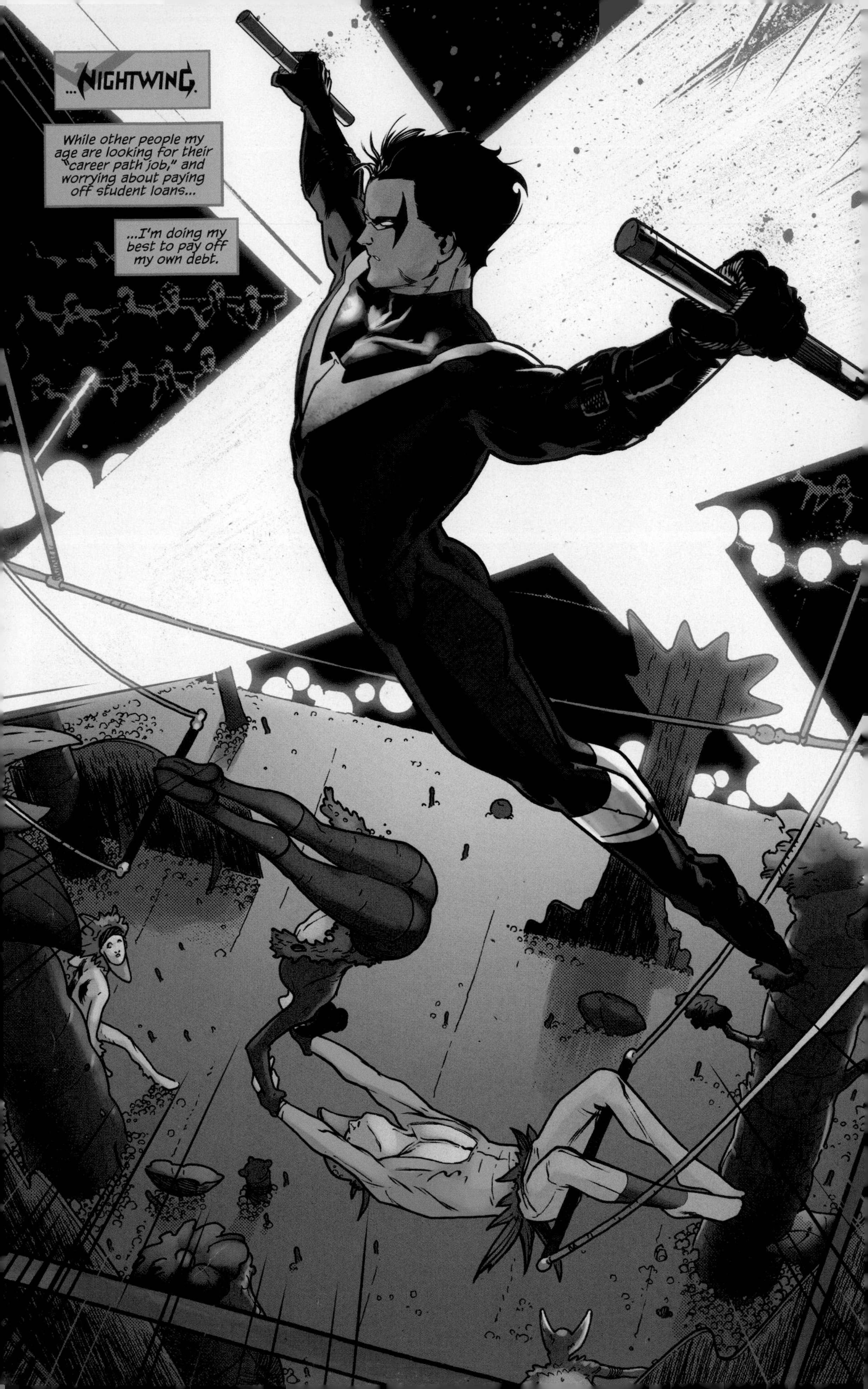
...NIGHTWING.
While other people my age are looking for their "career path job," and worrying about paying off student loans...
...I'm doing my best to pay off my own debt.

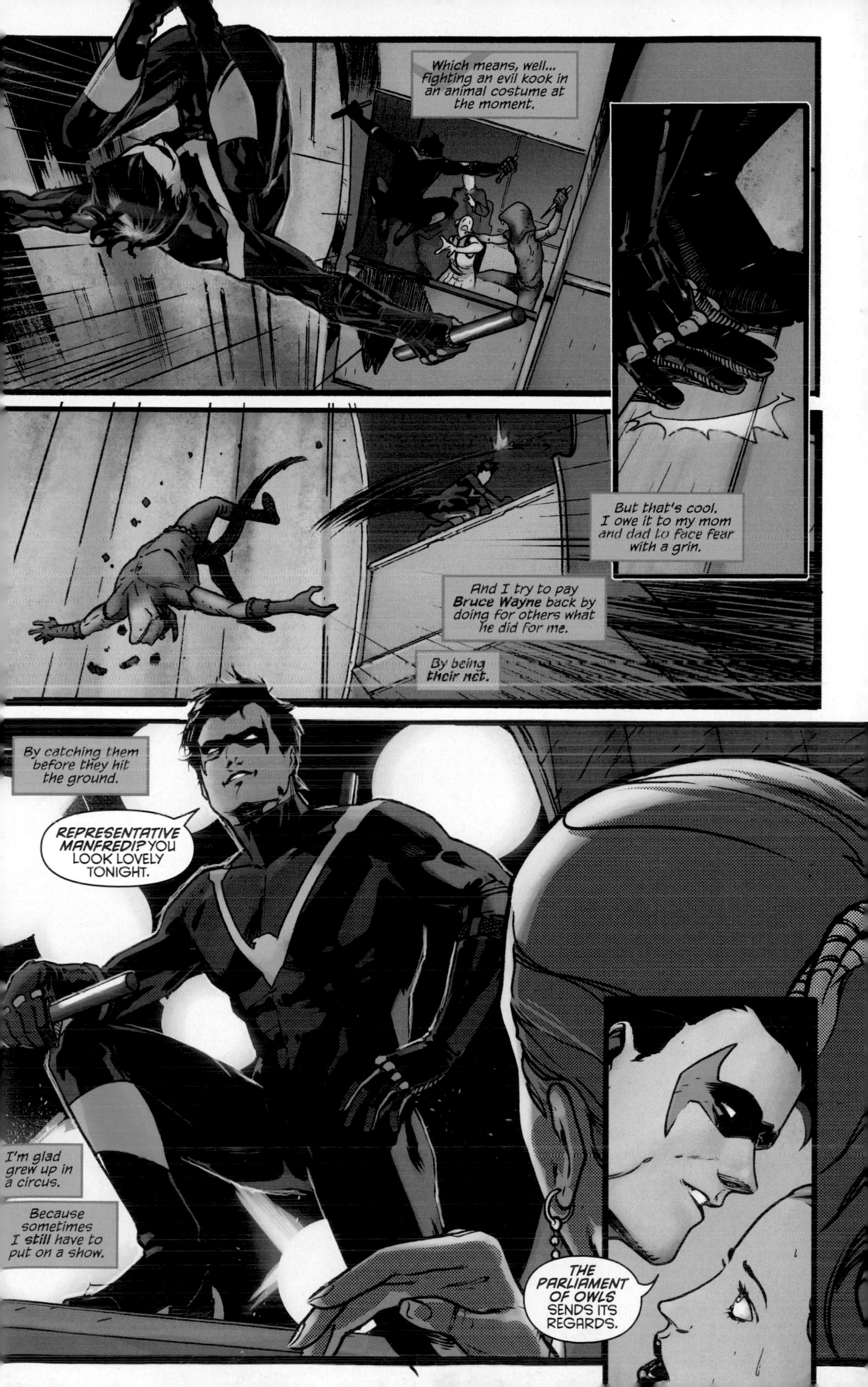
Which means, well... fighting an evil kook in an animal costume at the moment.
But that's cool. I owe it to my mom and dad to face fear with a grin.
And I try to pay Bruce Wayne back by doing for others what he did for me.
By being their net.
By catching them before they hit the ground.
REPRESENTATIVE MANFREDI? YOU LOOK LOVELY TONIGHT.
I'm glad grew up in a circus.
Because sometimes I still have to put on a show.
THE PARLIAMENT OF OWLS SENDS ITS REGARDS.

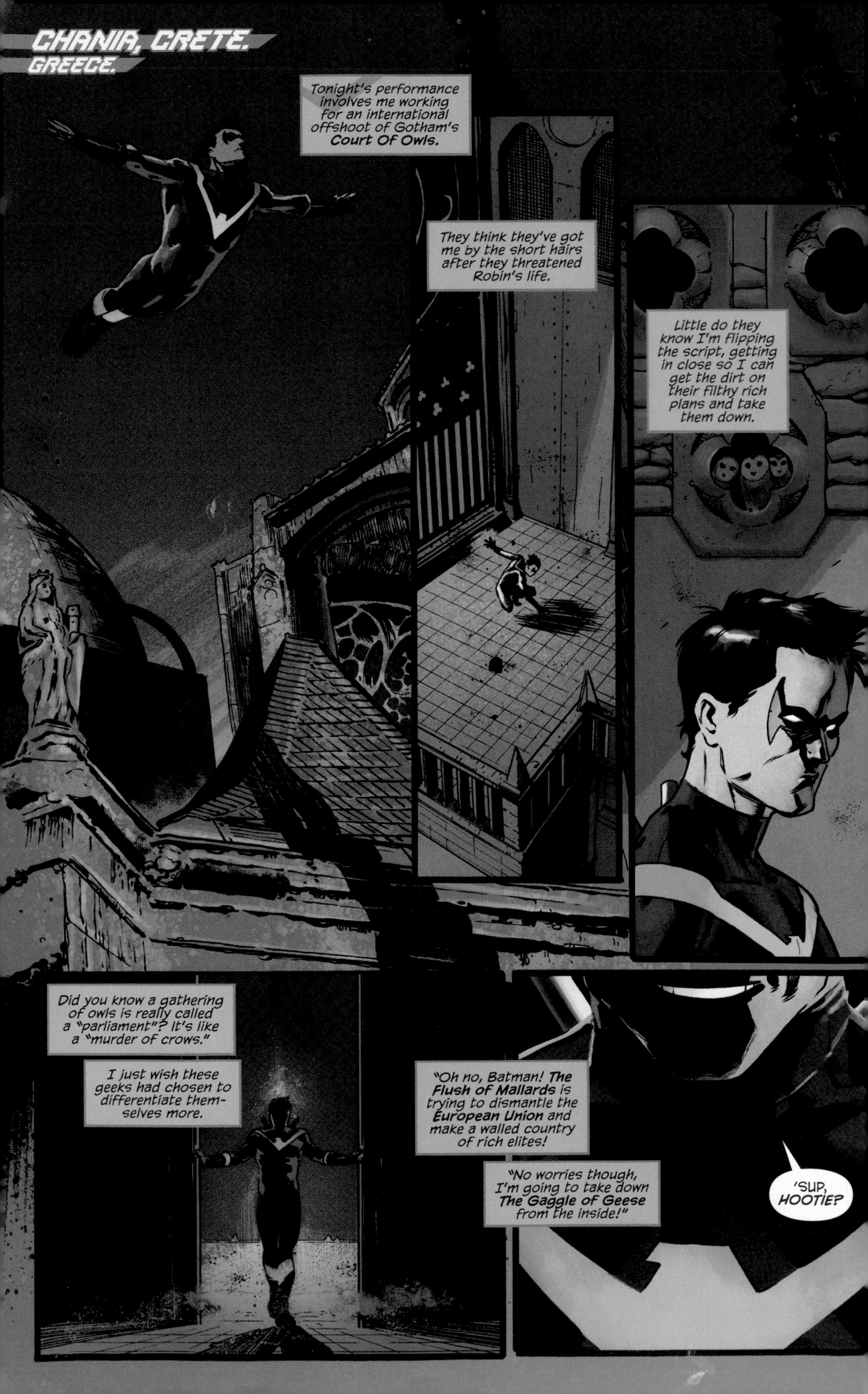
CHANIA, CRETE. GREECE.
Tonight's performance involves me working for an international offshoot of Gotham's Court Of Owls.
They think they've got me by the short hairs after they threatened Robin's life.
Little do they know I'm flipping the script, getting in close so I can get the dirt on their filthy rich plans and take them down.
Did you know a gathering of owls is really called a "parliament"? It's like a "murder of crows."
I just wish these geeks had chosen to differentiate them-selves more.
"Oh no, Batman! The Flush of Mallards is trying to dismantle the European Union and make a walled country of rich elites!
"No worries though, I'm going to take down The Gaggle of Geese from the inside!"
'SUP, HOOTIE?

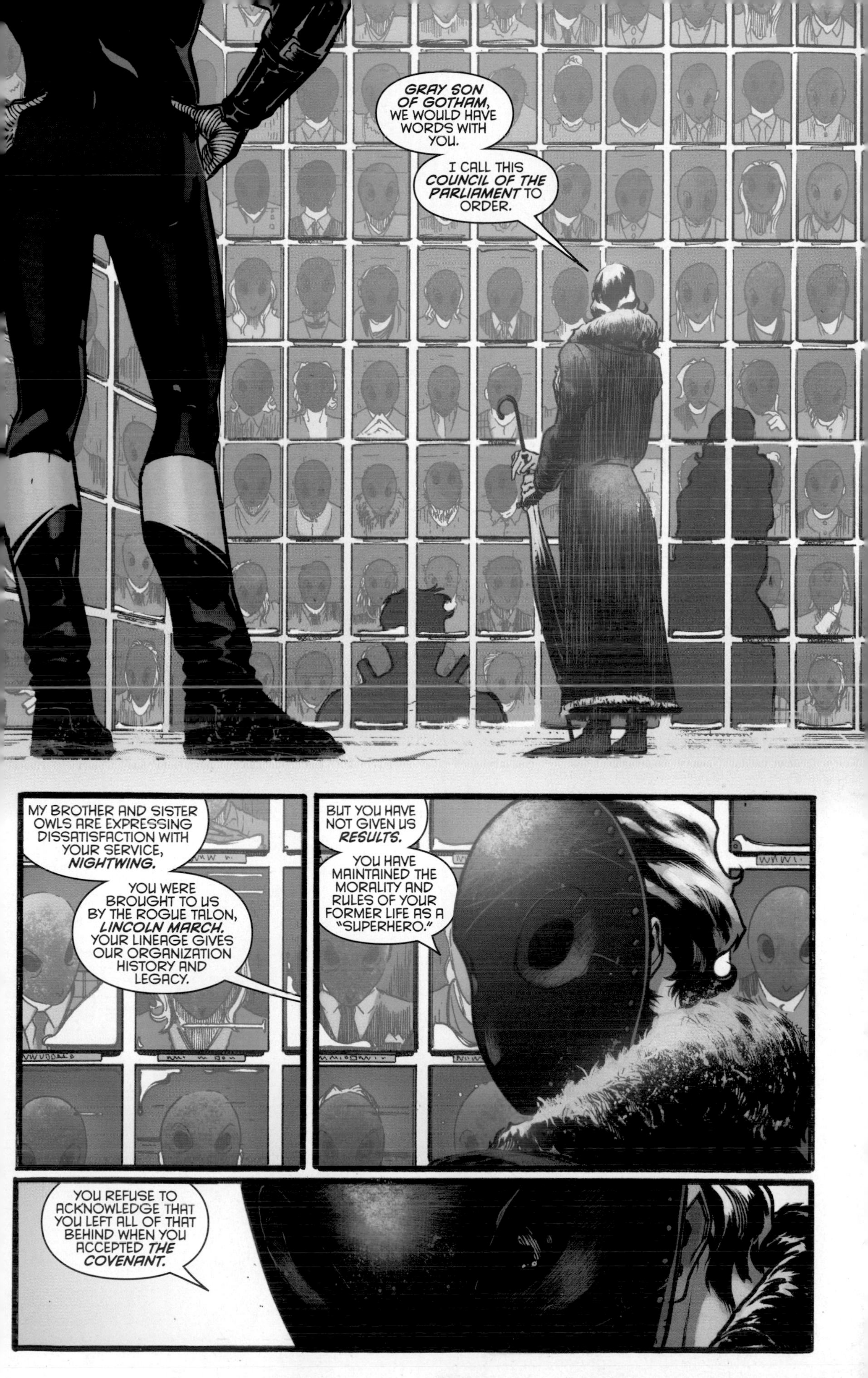
GRAY SON OF GOTHAM, WE WOULD HAVE WORDS WITH YOU.
I CALL THIS COUNCIL OF THE PARLIAMENT TO ORDER.
MY BROTHER AND SISTER OWLS ARE EXPRESSING DISSATISFACTION WITH YOUR SERVICE, NIGHTWING.
YOU WERE BROUGHT TO US BY THE ROGUE TALON, LINCOLN MARCH. YOUR LINEAGE GIVES OUR ORGANIZATION HISTORY AND LEGACY.
BUT YOU HAVE NOT GIVEN US RESULTS.
YOU HAVE MAINTAINED THE MORALITY AND RULES OF YOUR FORMER LIFE AS A "SUPERHERO."
YOU REFUSE TO ACKNOWLEDGE THAT YOU LEFT ALL OF THAT BEHIND WHEN YOU ACCEPTED THE COVENANT.

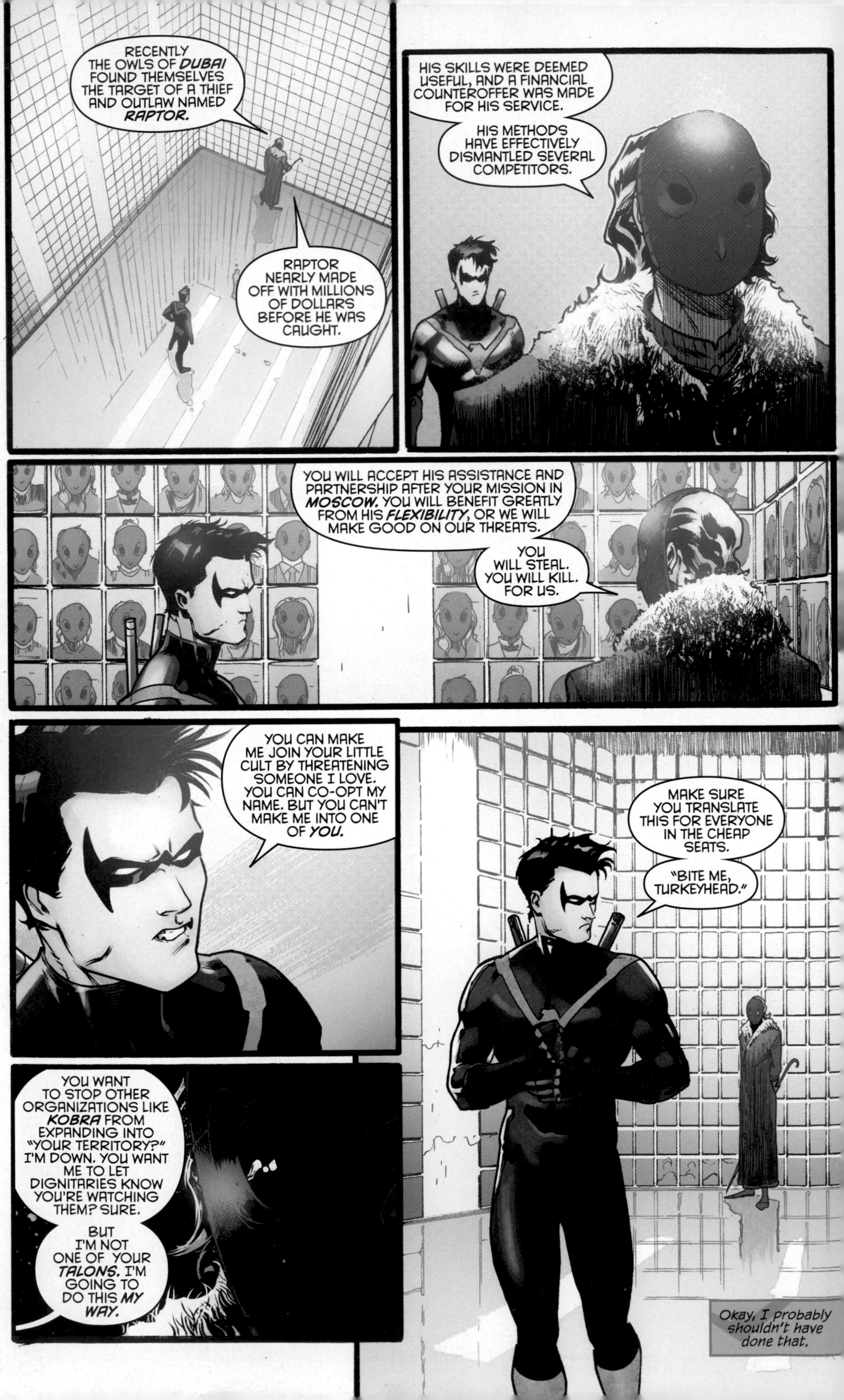
RECENTLY THE OWLS OF DUBAI FOUND THEMSELVES THE TARGET OF A THIEF AND OUTLAW NAMED RAPTOR.
RAPTOR NEARLY MADE OFF WITH MILLIONS OF DOLLARS BEFORE HE WAS CAUGHT.
HIS SKILLS WERE DEEMED USEFUL, AND A FINANCIAL COUNTEROFFER WAS MADE FOR HIS SERVICE.
HIS METHODS HAVE EFFECTIVELY DISMANTLED SEVERAL COMPETITORS.
YOU WILL ACCEPT HIS ASSISTANCE AND PARTNERSHIP AFTER YOUR MISSION IN MOSCOW. YOU WILL BENEFIT GREATLY FROM HIS FLEXIBILITY, OR WE WILL MAKE GOOD ON OUR THREATS.
YOU WILL STEAL. YOU WILL KILL. FOR US.
YOU CAN MAKE ME JOIN YOUR LITTLE CULT BY THREATENING SOMEONE I LOVE. YOU CAN CO-OPT MY NAME. BUT YOU CAN'T MAKE ME INTO ONE OF YOU.
YOU WANT TO STOP OTHER ORGANIZATIONS LIKE KOBRA FROM EXPANDING INTO "YOUR TERRITORY?" I'M DOWN. YOU WANT ME TO LET DIGNITARIES KNOW YOU'RE WATCHING THEM? SURE.
BUT I'M NOT ONE OF YOUR TALONS. I'M GOING TO DO THIS MY WAY.
MAKE SURE YOU TRANSLATE THIS FOR EVERYONE IN THE CHEAP SEATS.
"BITE ME, TURKEYHEAD."
Okay, I probably shouldn't have done that.

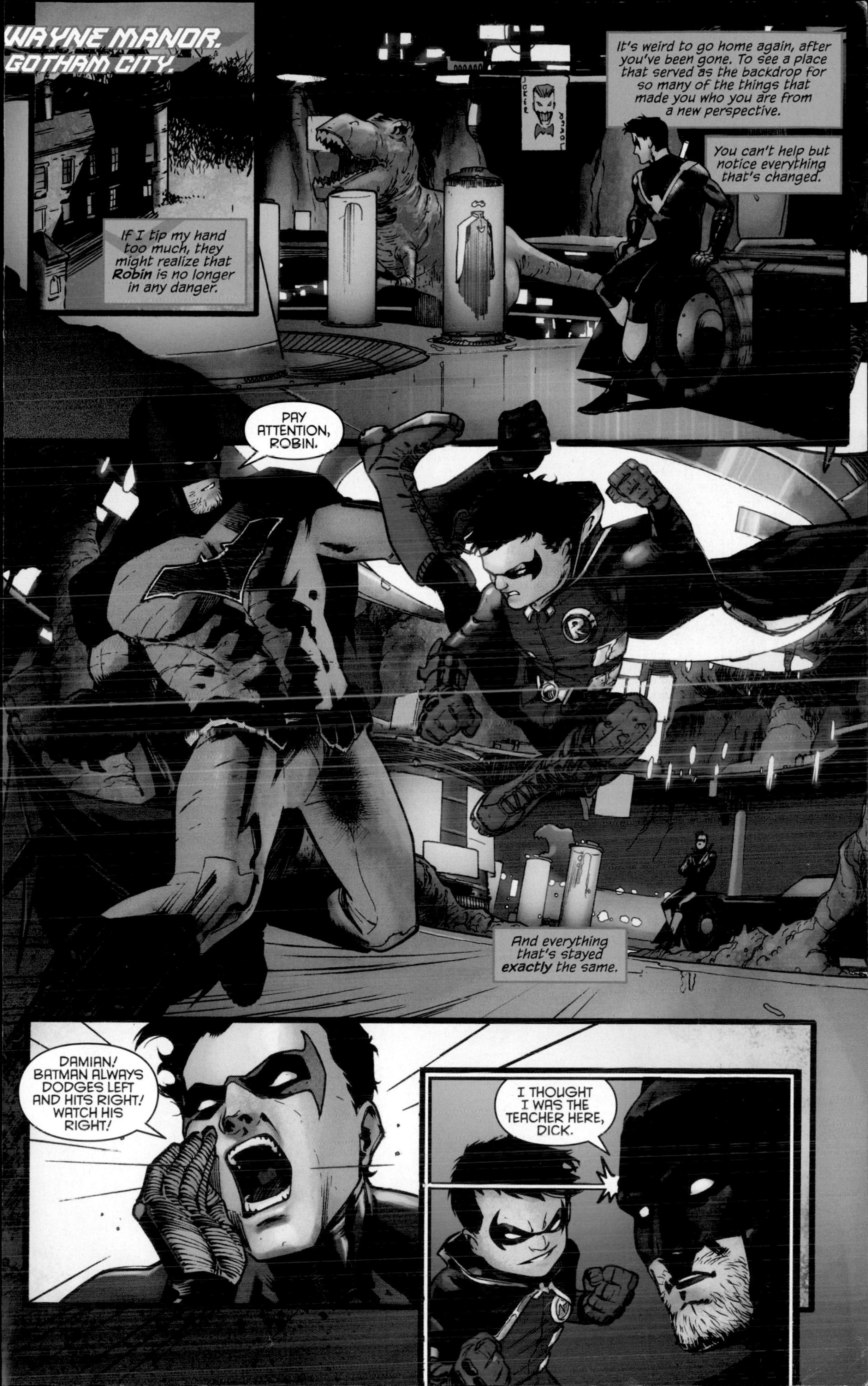
WAYNE MANOR. GOTHAM CITY.
It's weird to go home again, after you've been gone. To see a place that served as the backdrop for so many of the things that made you who you are from a new perspective.
You can't help but notice everything that's changed.
If I tip my hand too much, they might realize that Robin is no longer in any danger.
PAY ATTENTION, ROBIN.
And everything that's stayed exactly the same.
DAMIAN! BATMAN ALWAYS DODGES LEFT AND HITS RIGHT! WATCH HIS RIGHT!
I THOUGHT I WAS THE TEACHER HERE, DICK.

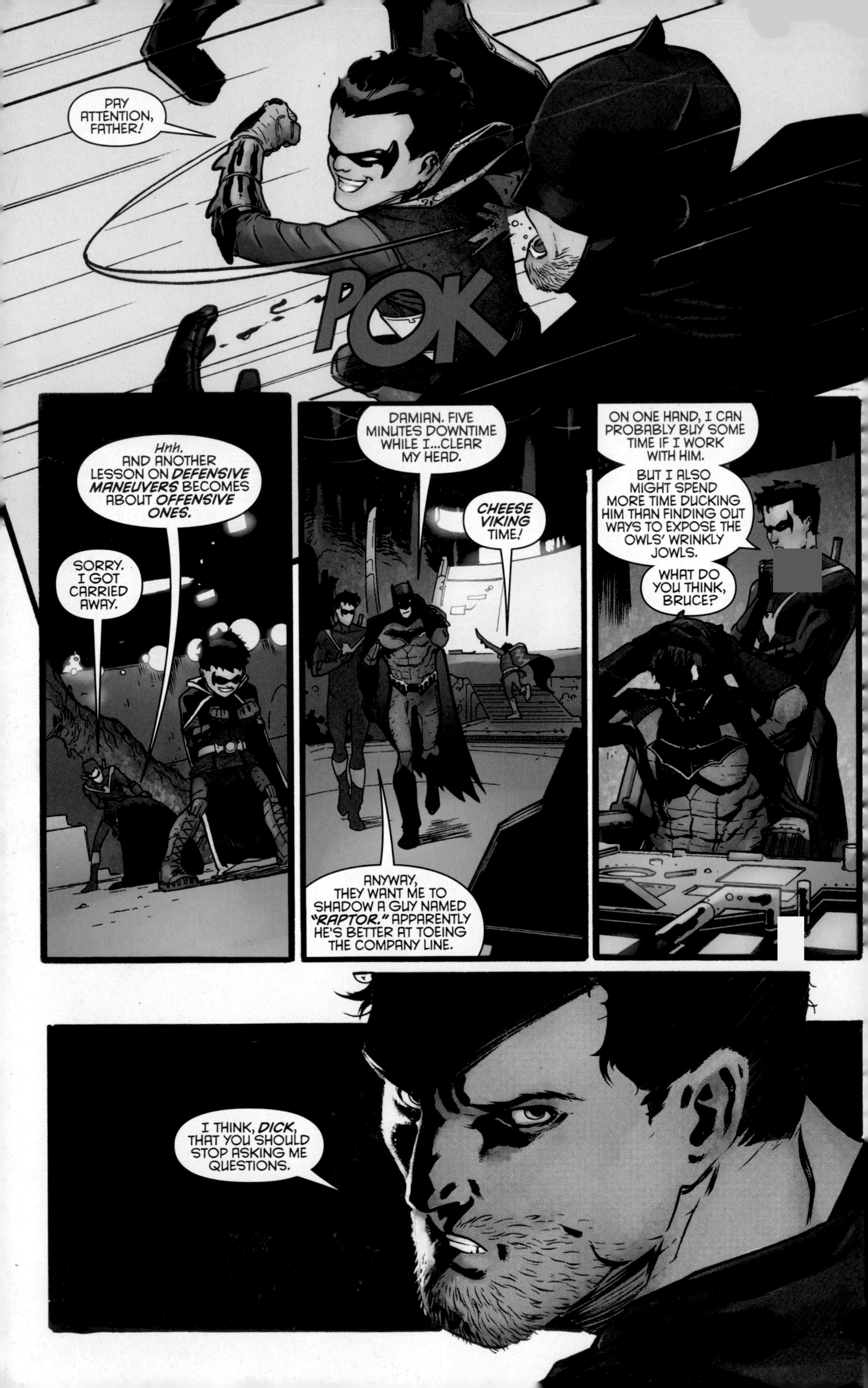
PAY ATTENTION, FATHER!
POK
Hnh. AND ANOTHER LESSON ON ***DEFENSIVE MANEUVERS*** BECOMES ABOUT ***OFFENSIVE ONES.***
SORRY. I GOT CARRIED AWAY.
DAMIAN. FIVE MINUTES DOWNTIME WHILE I...CLEAR MY HEAD.
CHEESE VIKING TIME!
ANYWAY, THEY WANT ME TO SHADOW A GUY NAMED ***"RAPTOR."*** APPARENTLY HE'S BETTER AT TOEING THE COMPANY LINE.
ON ONE HAND, I CAN PROBABLY BUY SOME TIME IF I WORK WITH HIM.
BUT I ALSO MIGHT SPEND MORE TIME DUCKING HIM THAN FINDING OUT WAYS TO EXPOSE THE OWLS' WRINKLY JOWLS.
WHAT DO YOU THINK, BRUCE?
I THINK, ***DICK***, THAT YOU SHOULD STOP ASKING ME QUESTIONS.

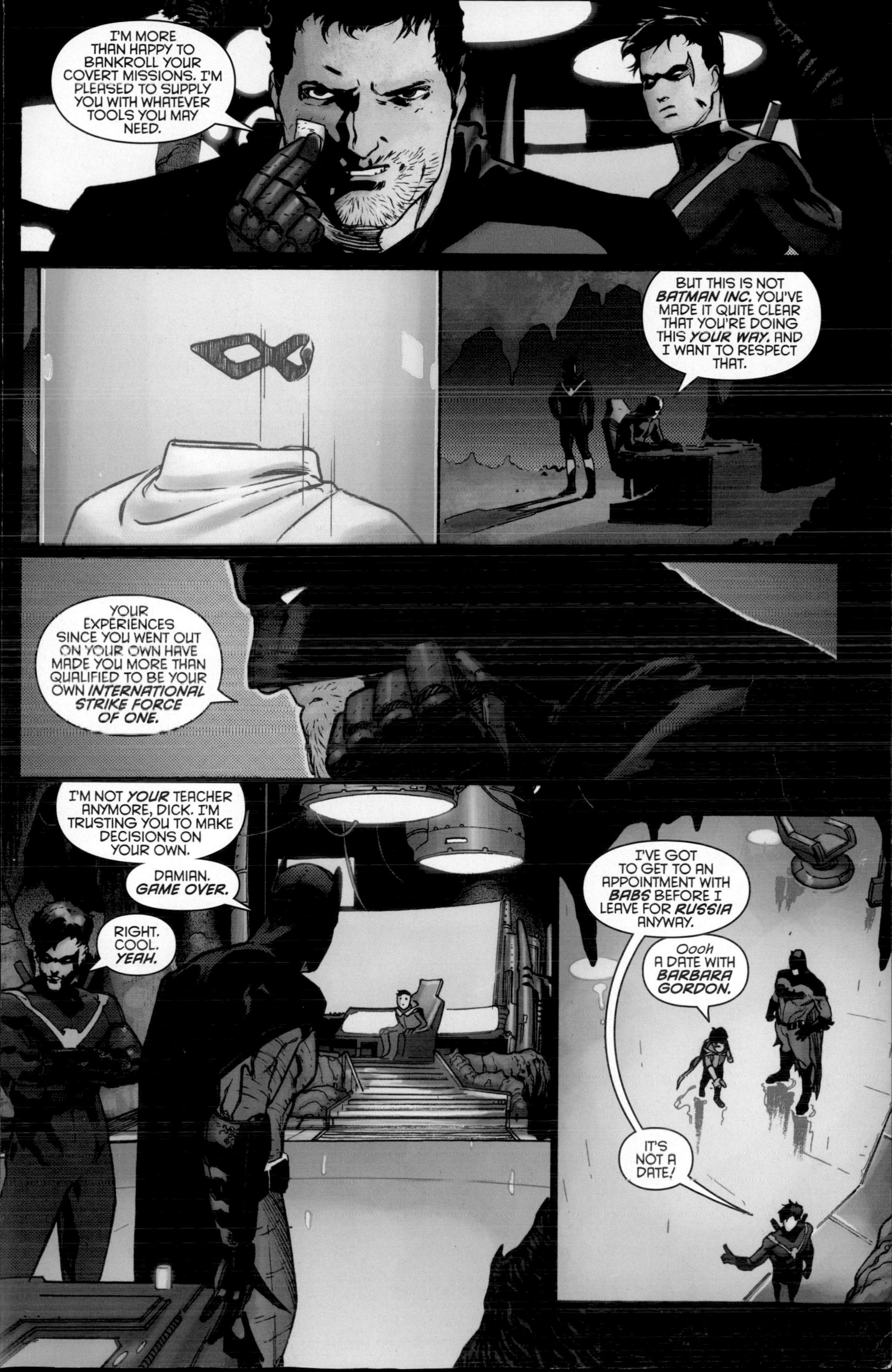
I'M MORE THAN HAPPY TO BANKROLL YOUR COVERT MISSIONS. I'M PLEASED TO SUPPLY YOU WITH WHATEVER TOOLS YOU MAY NEED.
BUT THIS IS NOT BATMAN INC. YOU'VE MADE IT QUITE CLEAR THAT YOU'RE DOING THIS YOUR WAY. AND I WANT TO RESPECT THAT.
YOUR EXPERIENCES SINCE YOU WENT OUT ON YOUR OWN HAVE MADE YOU MORE THAN QUALIFIED TO BE YOUR OWN INTERNATIONAL STRIKE FORCE OF ONE.
I'M NOT YOUR TEACHER ANYMORE, DICK. I'M TRUSTING YOU TO MAKE DECISIONS ON YOUR OWN.
DAMIAN. GAME OVER.
RIGHT. COOL. YEAH.
I'VE GOT TO GET TO AN APPOINTMENT WITH BABS BEFORE I LEAVE FOR RUSSIA ANYWAY.
Oooh A DATE WITH BARBARA GORDON.
IT'S NOT A DATE!

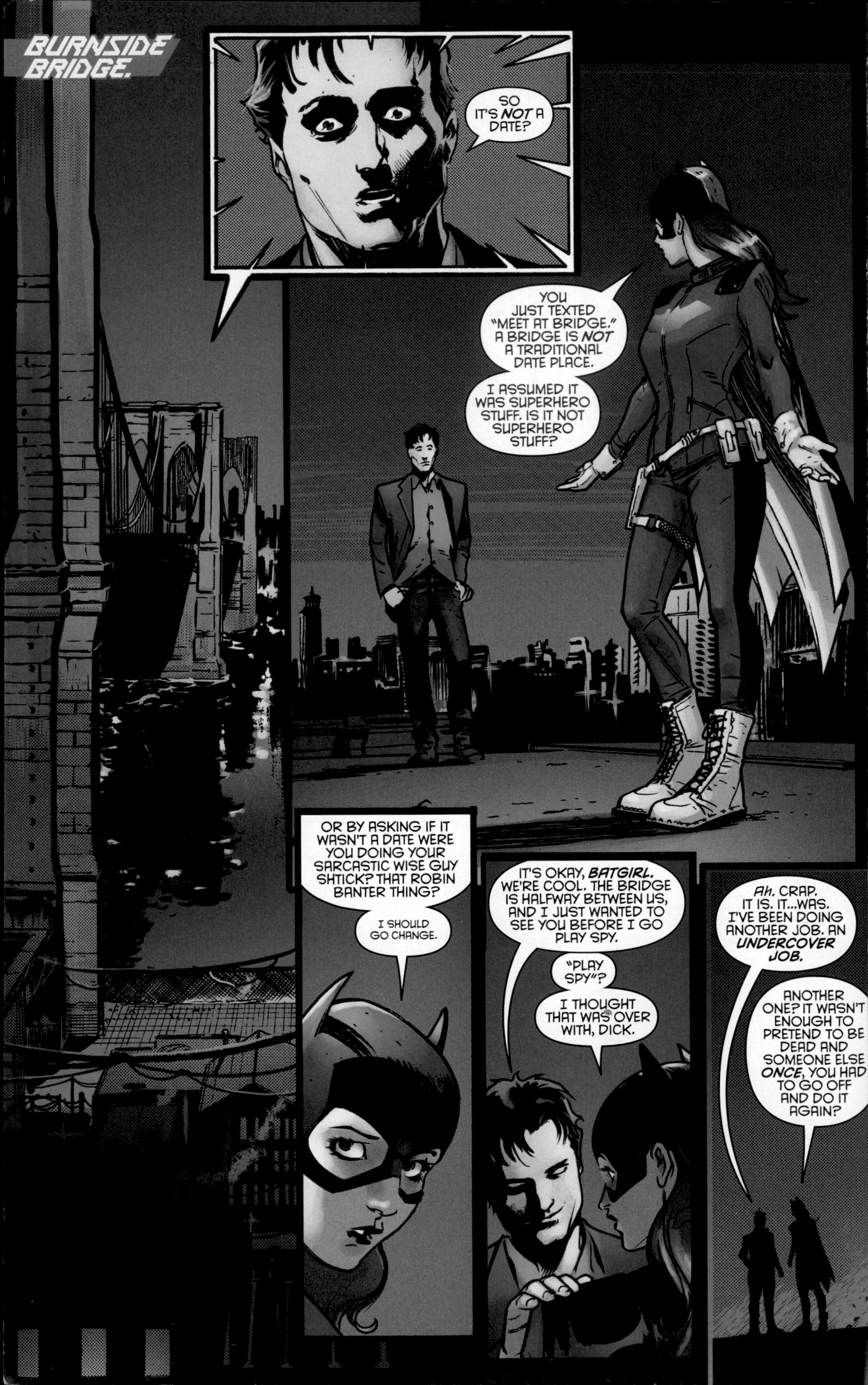
BURNSIDE BRIDGE.
SO IT'S NOT A DATE?
YOU JUST TEXTED "MEET AT BRIDGE." A BRIDGE IS NOT A TRADITIONAL DATE PLACE.
I ASSUMED IT WAS SUPERHERO STUFF. IS IT NOT SUPERHERO STUFF?
OR BY ASKING IF IT WASN'T A DATE WERE YOU DOING YOUR SARCASTIC WISE GUY SHTICK? THAT ROBIN BANTER THING?
I SHOULD GO CHANGE.
IT'S OKAY, BATGIRL. WE'RE COOL. THE BRIDGE IS HALFWAY BETWEEN US, AND I JUST WANTED TO SEE YOU BEFORE I GO PLAY SPY.
"PLAY SPY"?
I THOUGHT THAT WAS OVER WITH, DICK.
Ah. CRAP. IT IS. IT...WAS. I'VE BEEN DOING ANOTHER JOB. AN UNDERCOVER JOB.
ANOTHER ONE? IT WASN'T ENOUGH TO PRETEND TO BE DEAD AND SOMEONE ELSE ONCE, YOU HAD TO GO OFF AND DO IT AGAIN?

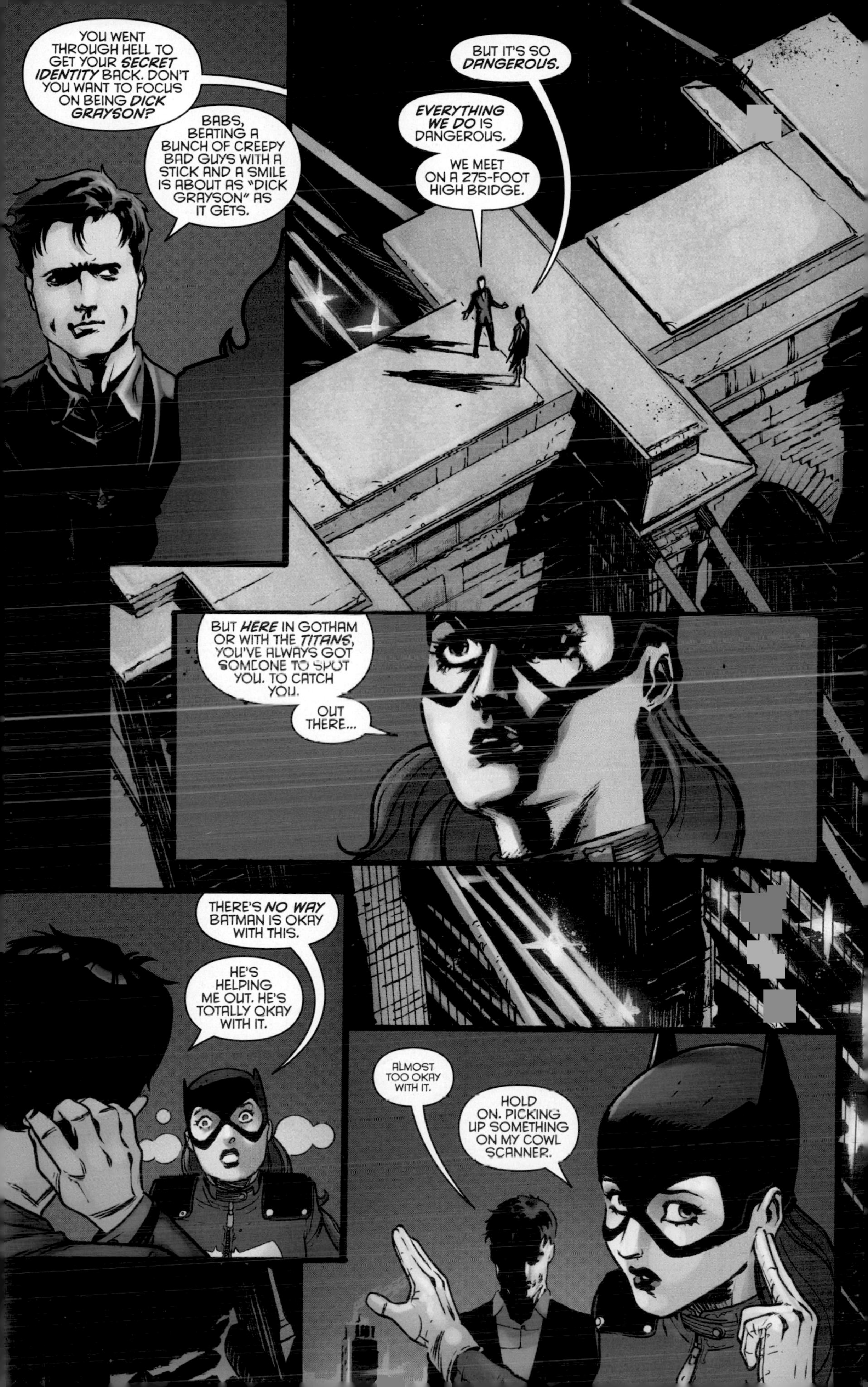
YOU WENT THROUGH HELL TO GET YOUR SECRET IDENTITY BACK. DON'T YOU WANT TO FOCUS ON BEING DICK GRAYSON?
BABS, BEATING A BUNCH OF CREEPY BAD GUYS WITH A STICK AND A SMILE IS ABOUT AS "DICK GRAYSON" AS IT GETS.
BUT IT'S SO DANGEROUS.
EVERYTHING WE DO IS DANGEROUS.
WE MEET ON A 275-FOOT HIGH BRIDGE.
BUT HERE IN GOTHAM OR WITH THE TITANS, YOU'VE ALWAYS GOT SOMEONE TO SPOT YOU. TO CATCH YOU.
OUT THERE...
THERE'S NO WAY BATMAN IS OKAY WITH THIS.
HE'S HELPING ME OUT. HE'S TOTALLY OKAY WITH IT.
ALMOST TOO OKAY WITH IT.
HOLD ON. PICKING UP SOMETHING ON MY COWL SCANNER.

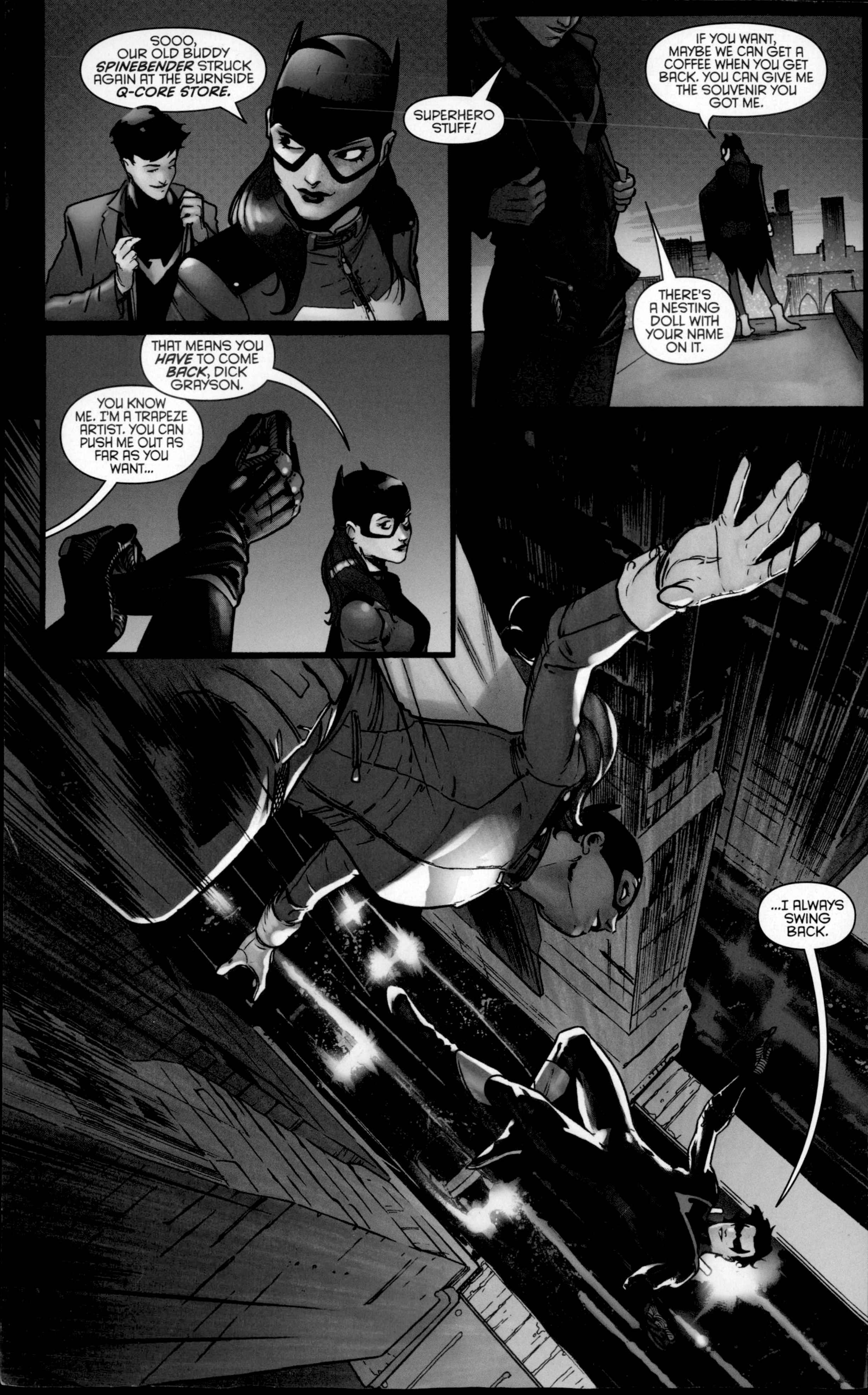
SOOO, OUR OLD BUDDY SPINEBENDER STRUCK AGAIN AT THE BURNSIDE Q-CORE STORE.
SUPERHERO STUFF!
IF YOU WANT, MAYBE WE CAN GET A COFFEE WHEN YOU GET BACK. YOU CAN GIVE ME THE SOUVENIR YOU GOT ME.
THERE'S A NESTING DOLL WITH YOUR NAME ON IT.
THAT MEANS YOU HAVE TO COME BACK, DICK GRAYSON.
YOU KNOW ME. I'M A TRAPEZE ARTIST. YOU CAN PUSH ME OUT AS FAR AS YOU WANT...
...I ALWAYS SWING BACK.

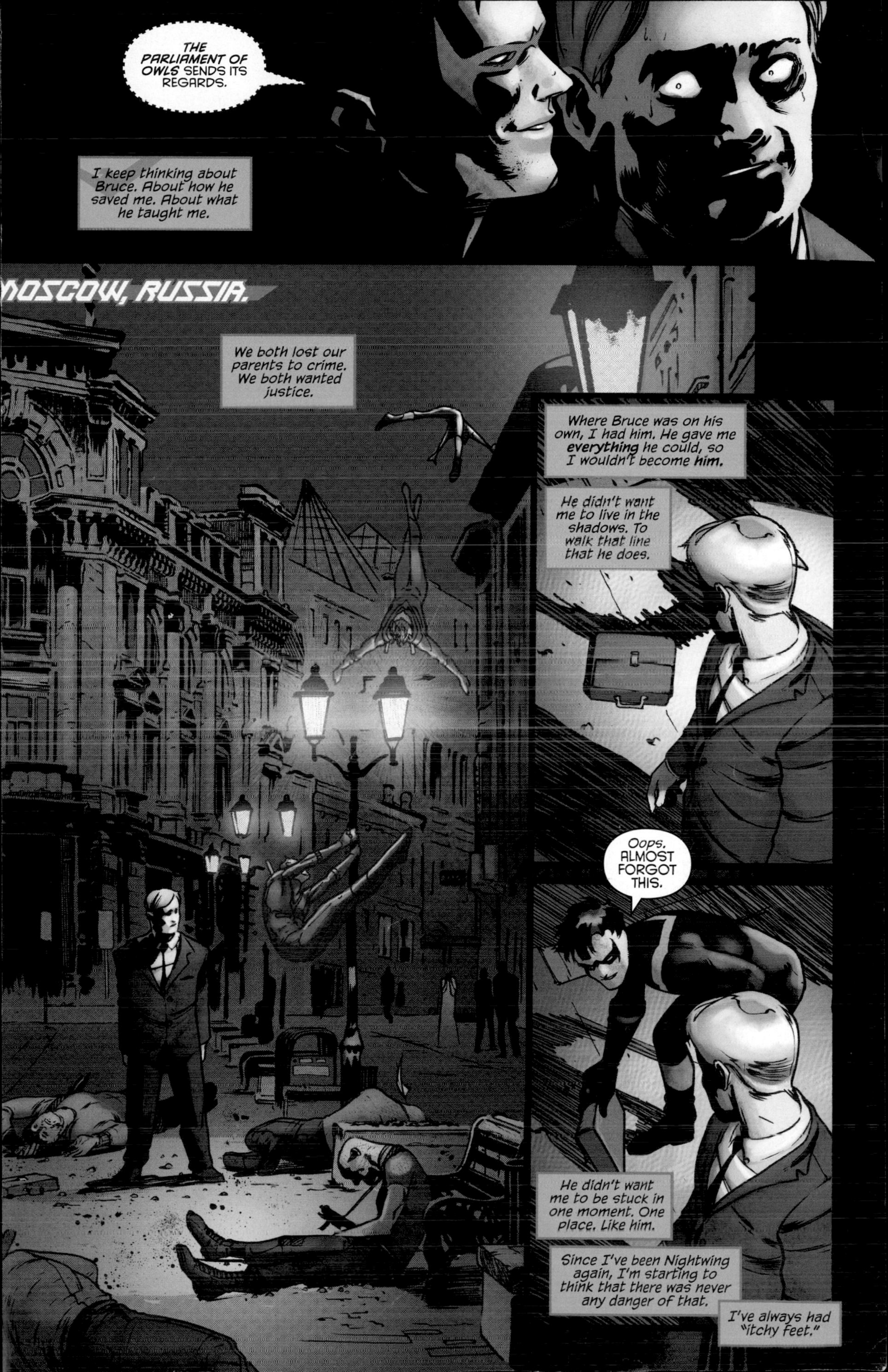

THE PARLIAMENT OF OWLS SENDS ITS REGARDS.
I keep thinking about Bruce. About how he saved me. About what he taught me.
MOSCOW, RUSSIA.
We both lost our parents to crime. We both wanted justice.
Where Bruce was on his own, I had him. He gave me everything he could, so I wouldn't become him.
He didn't want me to live in the shadows. To walk that line that he does.
Oops. ALMOST FORGOT THIS.
He didn't want me to be stuck in one moment. One place. Like him.
Since I've been Nightwing again, I'm starting to think that there was never any danger of that.
I've always had "itchy feet."

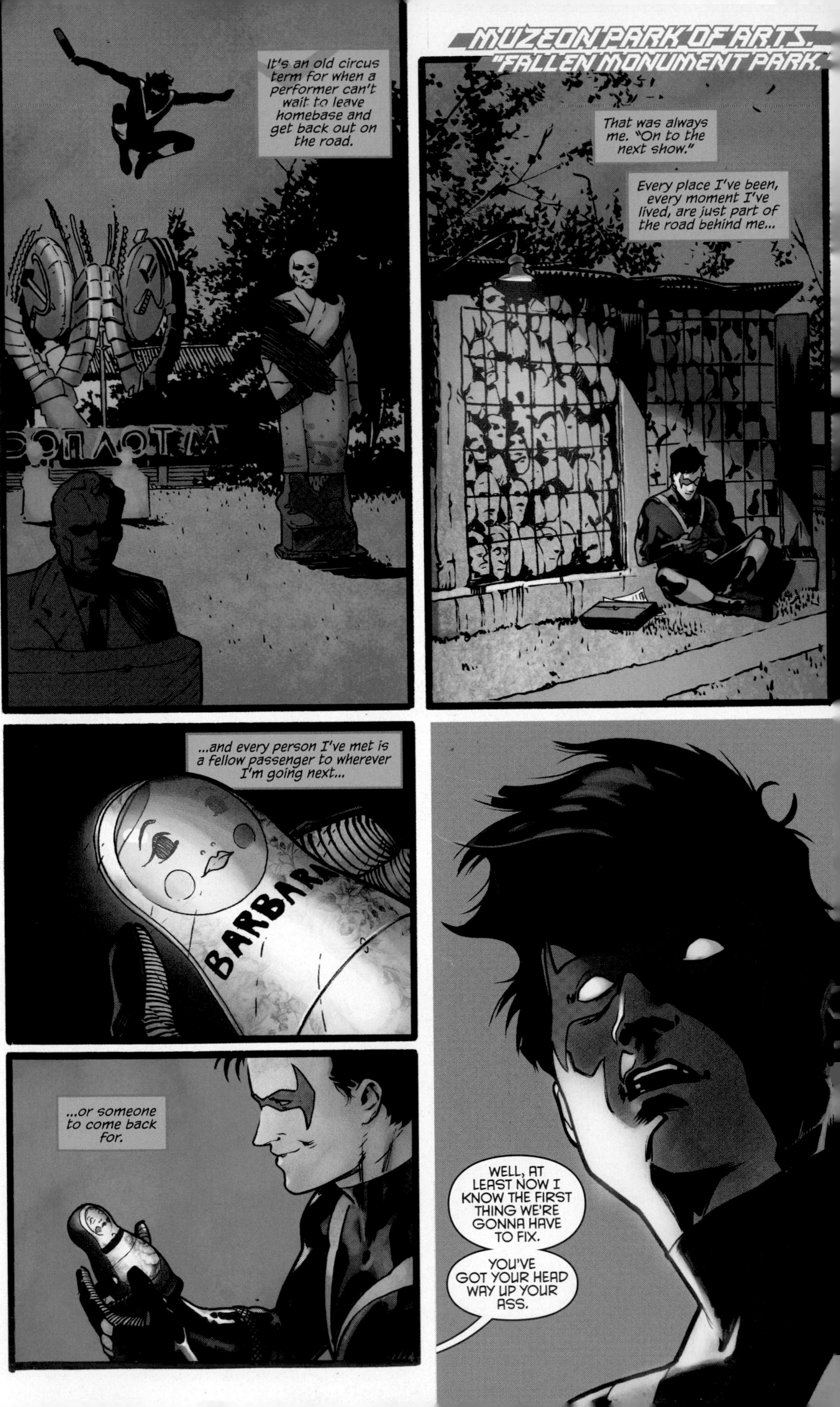

It's an old circus term for when a performer can't wait to leave homebase and get back out on the road.
MUZEON PARK OF ARTS. "FALLEN MONUMENT PARK."
That was always me. "On to the next show."
Every place I've been, every moment I've lived, are just part of the road behind me...
...and every person I've met is a fellow passenger to wherever I'm going next...
BARBAR
...or someone to come back for.
WELL, AT LEAST NOW I KNOW THE FIRST THING WE'RE GONNA HAVE TO FIX.
YOU'VE GOT YOUR HEAD WAY UP YOUR ASS.

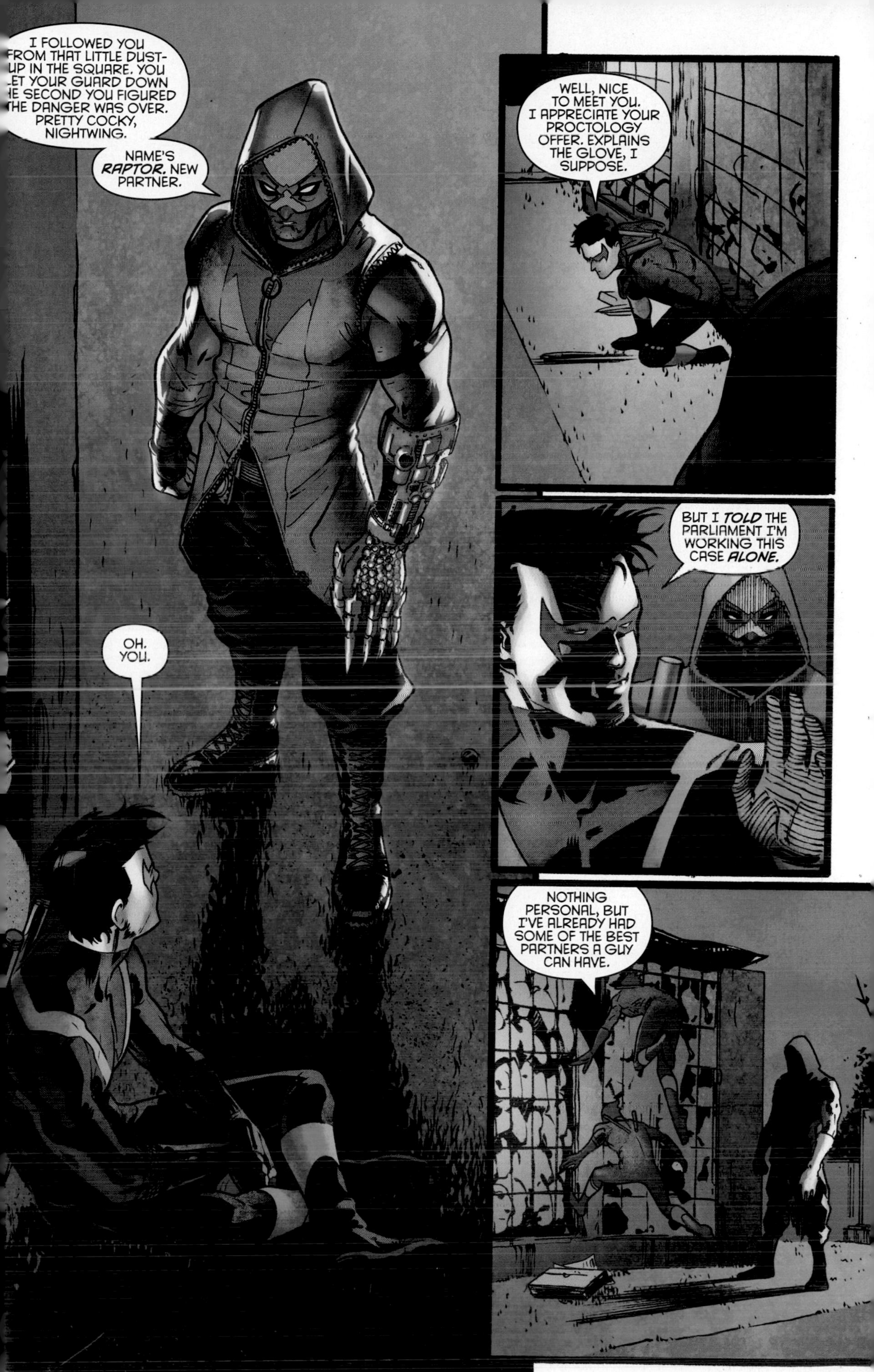
I FOLLOWED YOU FROM THAT LITTLE DUST-UP IN THE SQUARE. YOU LET YOUR GUARD DOWN THE SECOND YOU FIGURED THE DANGER WAS OVER. PRETTY COCKY, NIGHTWING.
NAME'S *RAPTOR.* NEW PARTNER.
OH. YOU.
WELL, NICE TO MEET YOU. I APPRECIATE YOUR PROCTOLOGY OFFER. EXPLAINS THE GLOVE, I SUPPOSE.
BUT I *TOLD* THE PARLIAMENT I'M WORKING THIS CASE *ALONE.*
NOTHING PERSONAL, BUT I'VE ALREADY HAD SOME OF THE BEST PARTNERS A GUY CAN HAVE.

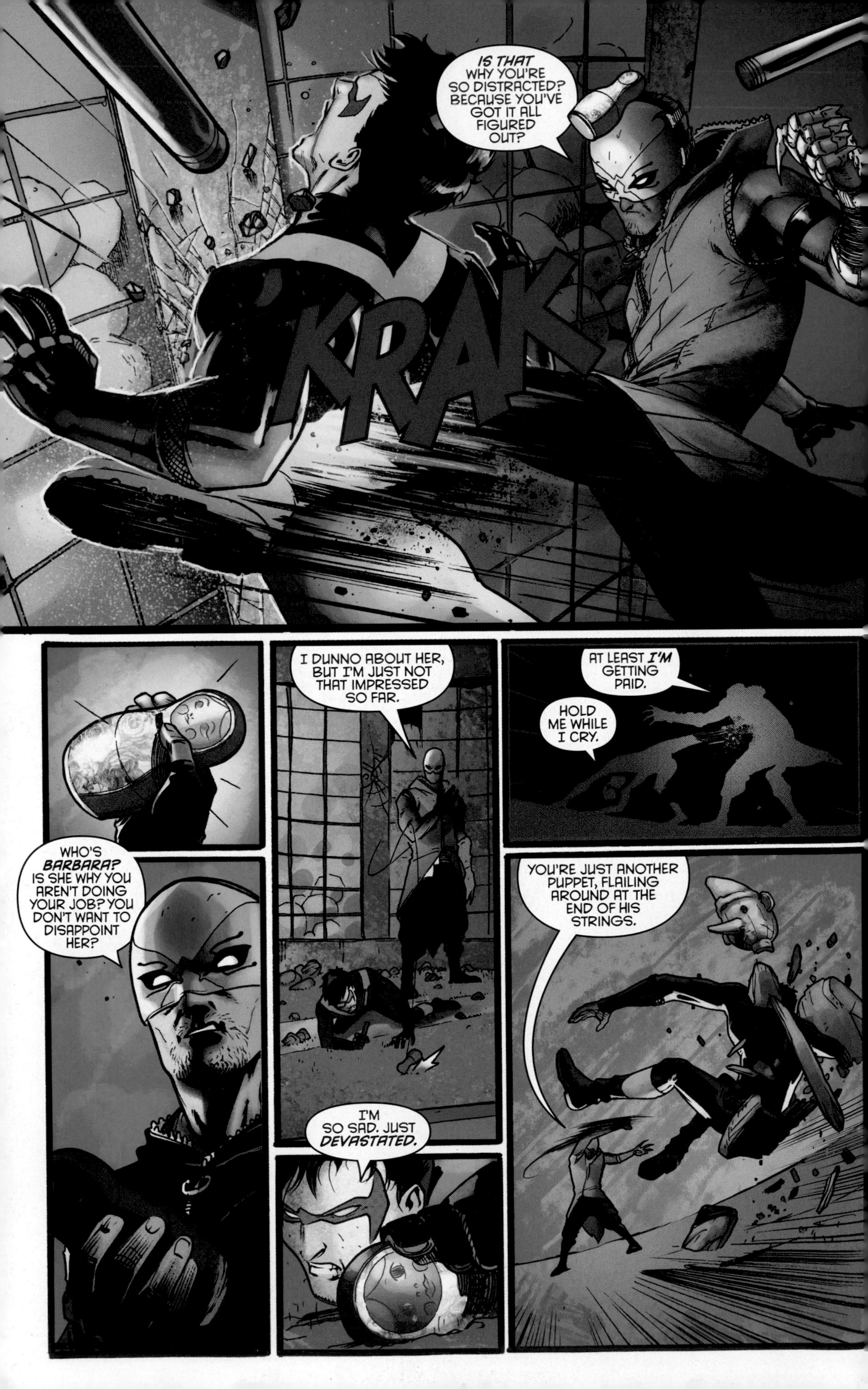
IS THAT WHY YOU'RE SO DISTRACTED? BECAUSE YOU'VE GOT IT ALL FIGURED OUT?
KRAK
I DUNNO ABOUT HER, BUT I'M JUST NOT THAT IMPRESSED SO FAR.
AT LEAST I'M GETTING PAID.
HOLD ME WHILE I CRY.
WHO'S BARBARA? IS SHE WHY YOU AREN'T DOING YOUR JOB? YOU DON'T WANT TO DISAPPOINT HER?
I'M SO SAD. JUST DEVASTATED.
YOU'RE JUST ANOTHER PUPPET, FLAILING AROUND AT THE END OF HIS STRINGS.

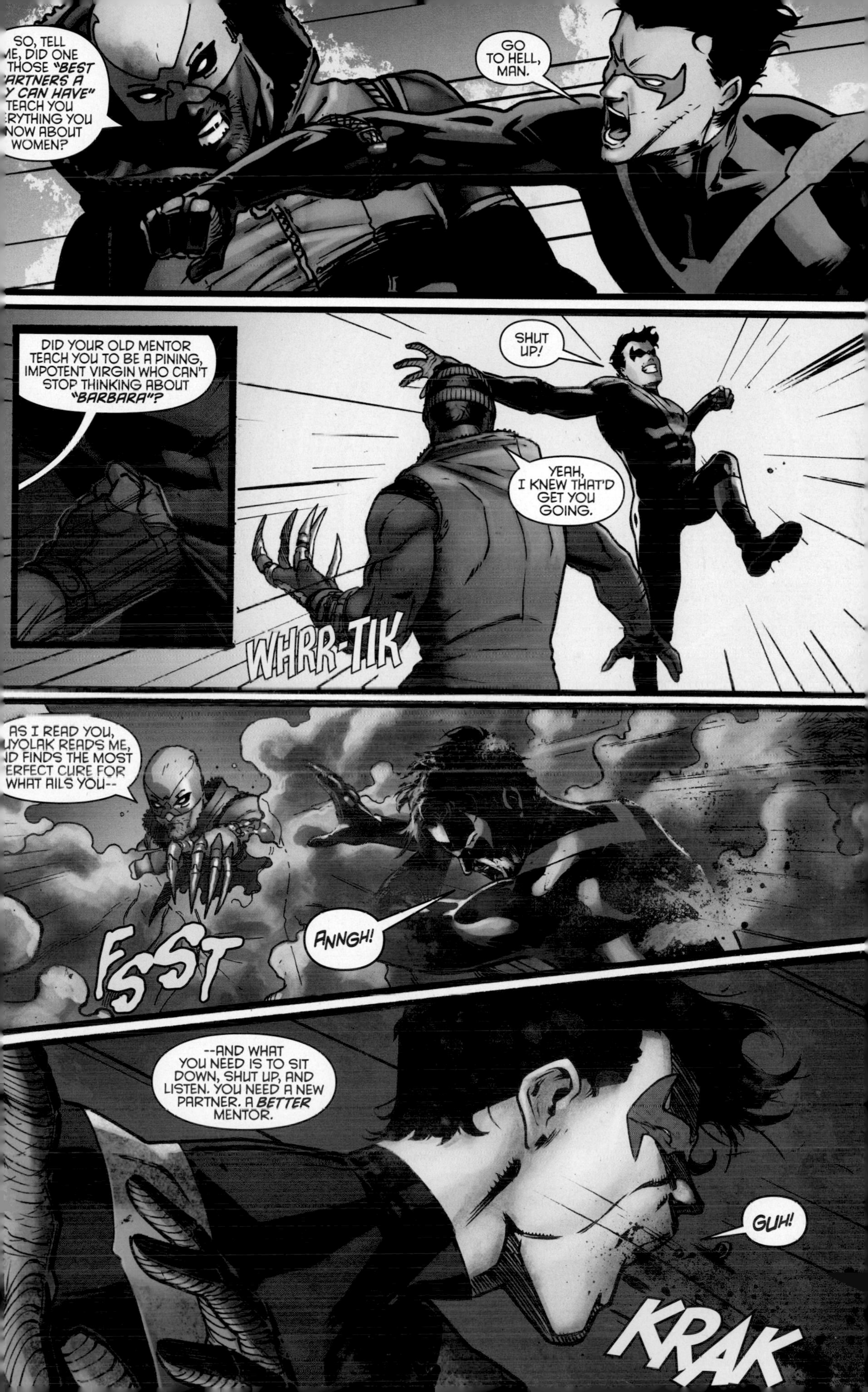
SO, TELL ME, DID ONE THOSE "BEST PARTNERS A Y CAN HAVE" TEACH YOU ERYTHING YOU NOW ABOUT WOMEN?
GO TO HELL, MAN.
DID YOUR OLD MENTOR TEACH YOU TO BE A PINING, IMPOTENT VIRGIN WHO CAN'T STOP THINKING ABOUT "BARBARA"?
SHUT UP!
YEAH, I KNEW THAT'D GET YOU GOING.
WHRR-TIK
AS I READ YOU, UYOLAK READS ME, ND FINDS THE MOST ERFECT CURE FOR WHAT AILS YOU--
FSST
ANNGH!
--AND WHAT YOU NEED IS TO SIT DOWN, SHUT UP, AND LISTEN. YOU NEED A NEW PARTNER. A BETTER MENTOR.
GUH!
KRAK

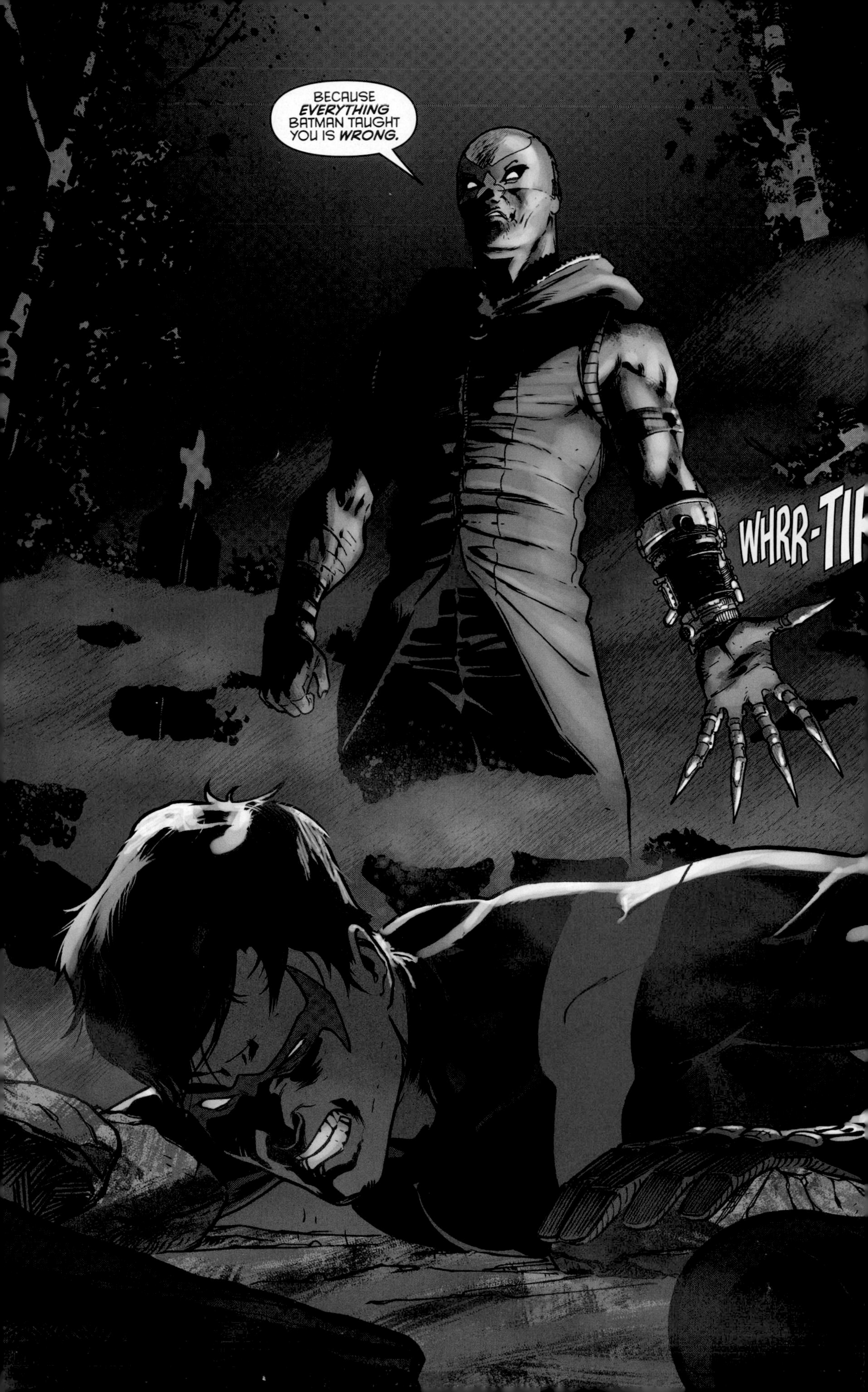
BECAUSE EVERYTHING BATMAN TAUGHT YOU IS WRONG.
WHRR-TIR

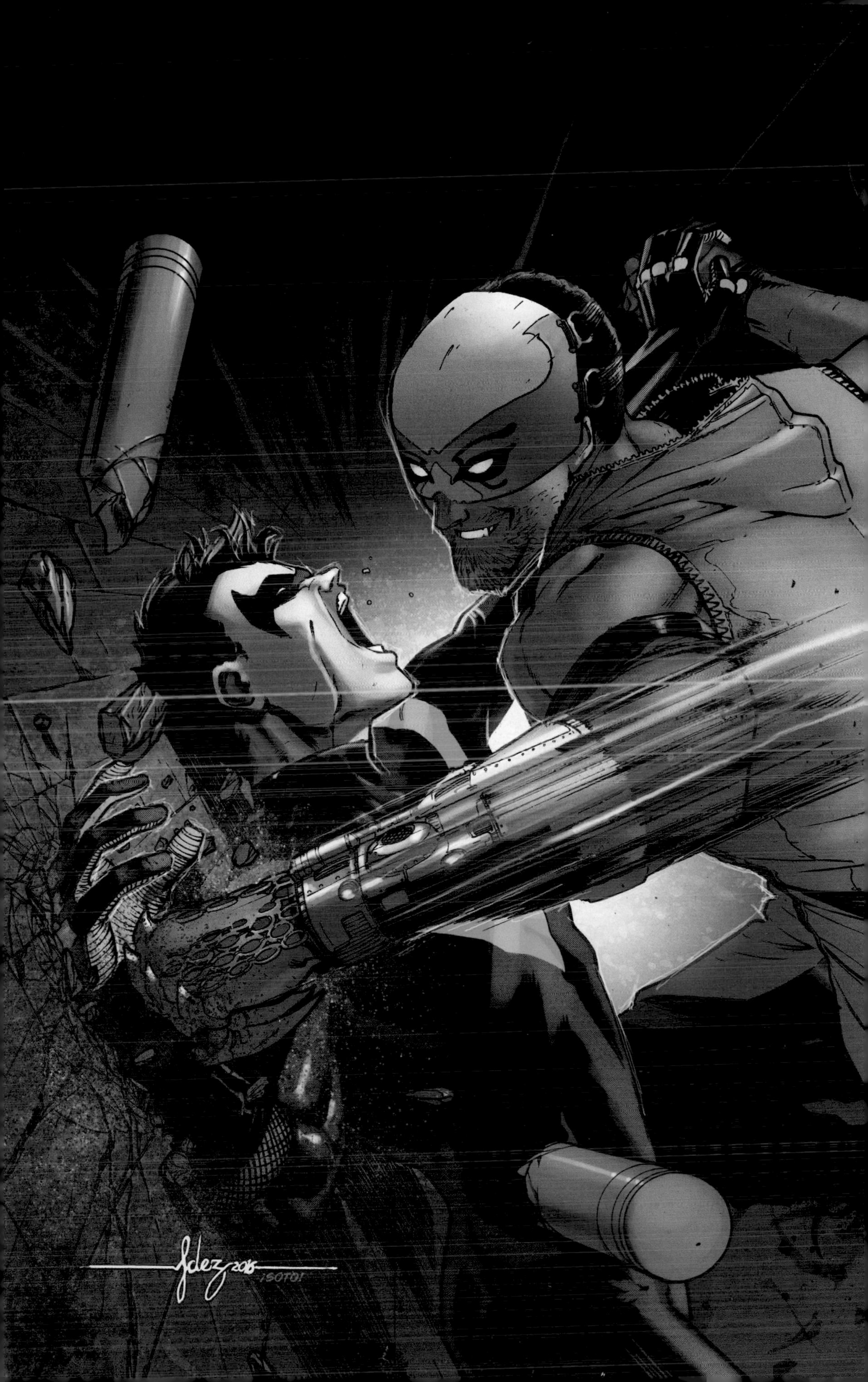
fdez 2016
¡SOTO!

BETTER THAN BATMAN, PART 2

TIM SEELEY writer * JAVIER FERNÁNDEZ artist * CHRIS SOTOMAYOR colorist
CARLOS M. MANGUAL letterer * JAVIER FERNÁNDEZ and CHRIS SOTOMAYOR cover artists

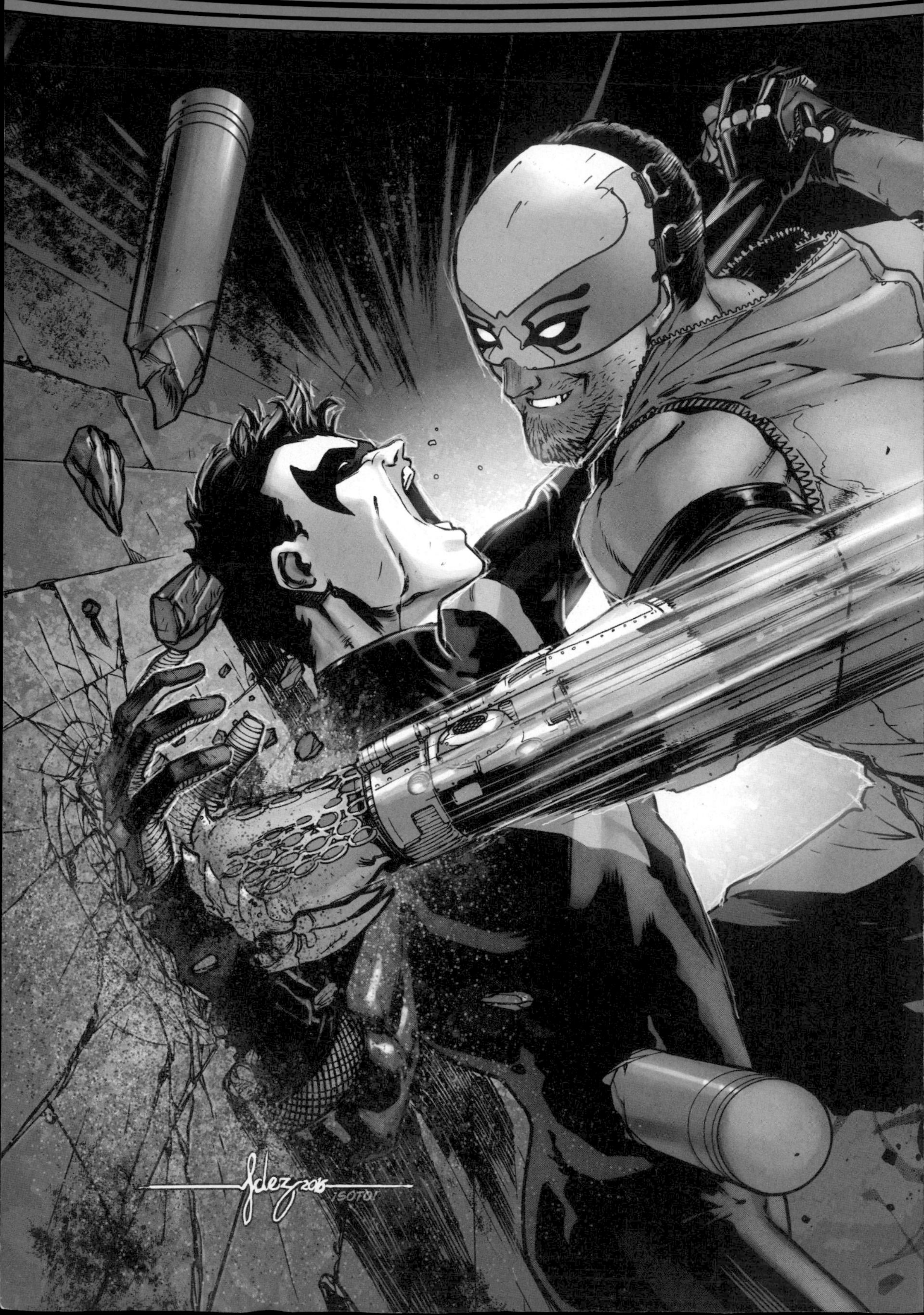

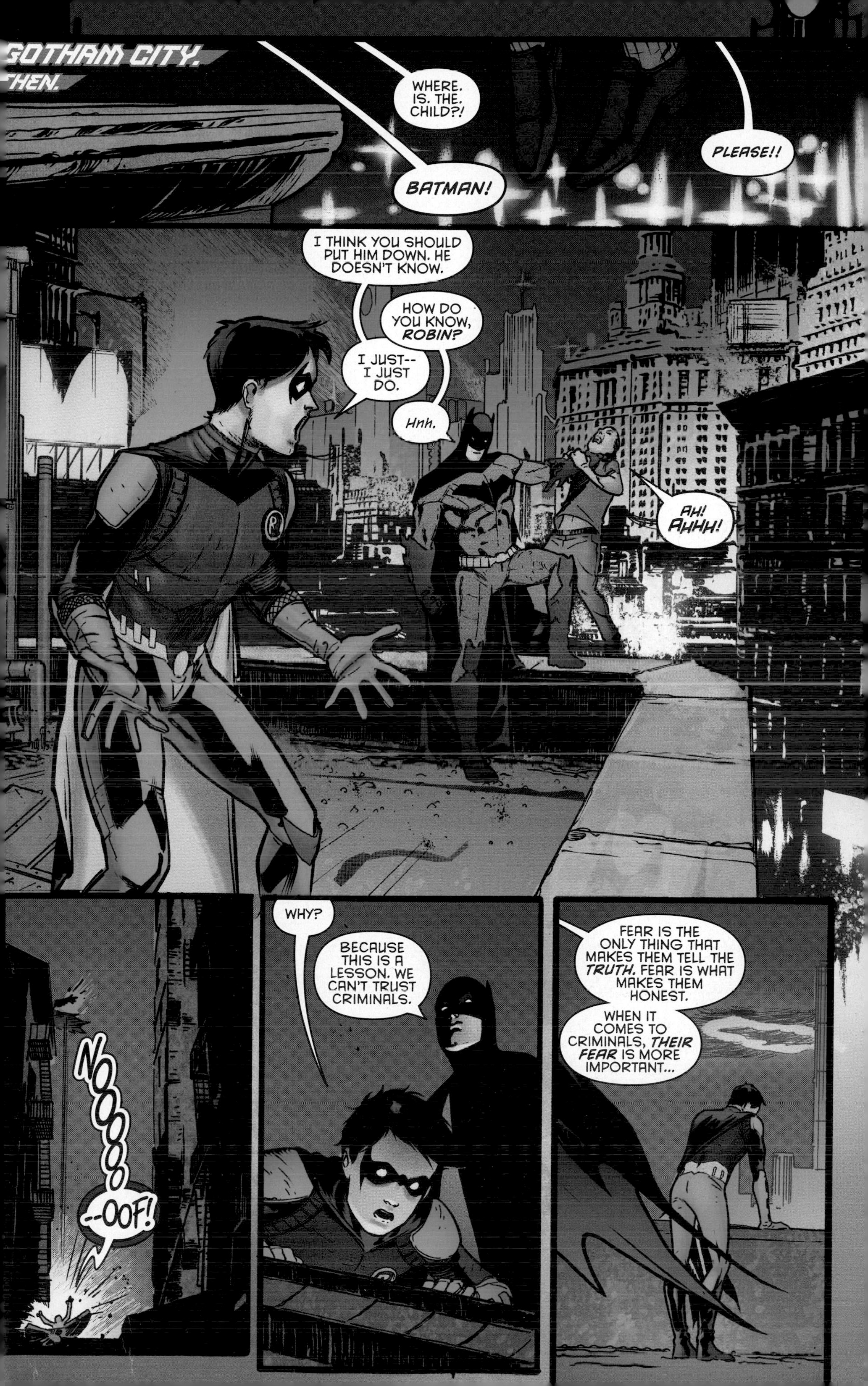
GOTHAM CITY.
THEN.
WHERE. IS. THE. CHILD?!
BATMAN!
PLEASE!!
I THINK YOU SHOULD PUT HIM DOWN. HE DOESN'T KNOW.
HOW DO YOU KNOW, ROBIN?
I JUST-- I JUST DO.
Hnh.
AH! AHHH!
NOOOOO
--OOF!
WHY?
BECAUSE THIS IS A LESSON. WE CAN'T TRUST CRIMINALS.
FEAR IS THE ONLY THING THAT MAKES THEM TELL THE TRUTH. FEAR IS WHAT MAKES THEM HONEST.
WHEN IT COMES TO CRIMINALS, THEIR FEAR IS MORE IMPORTANT...

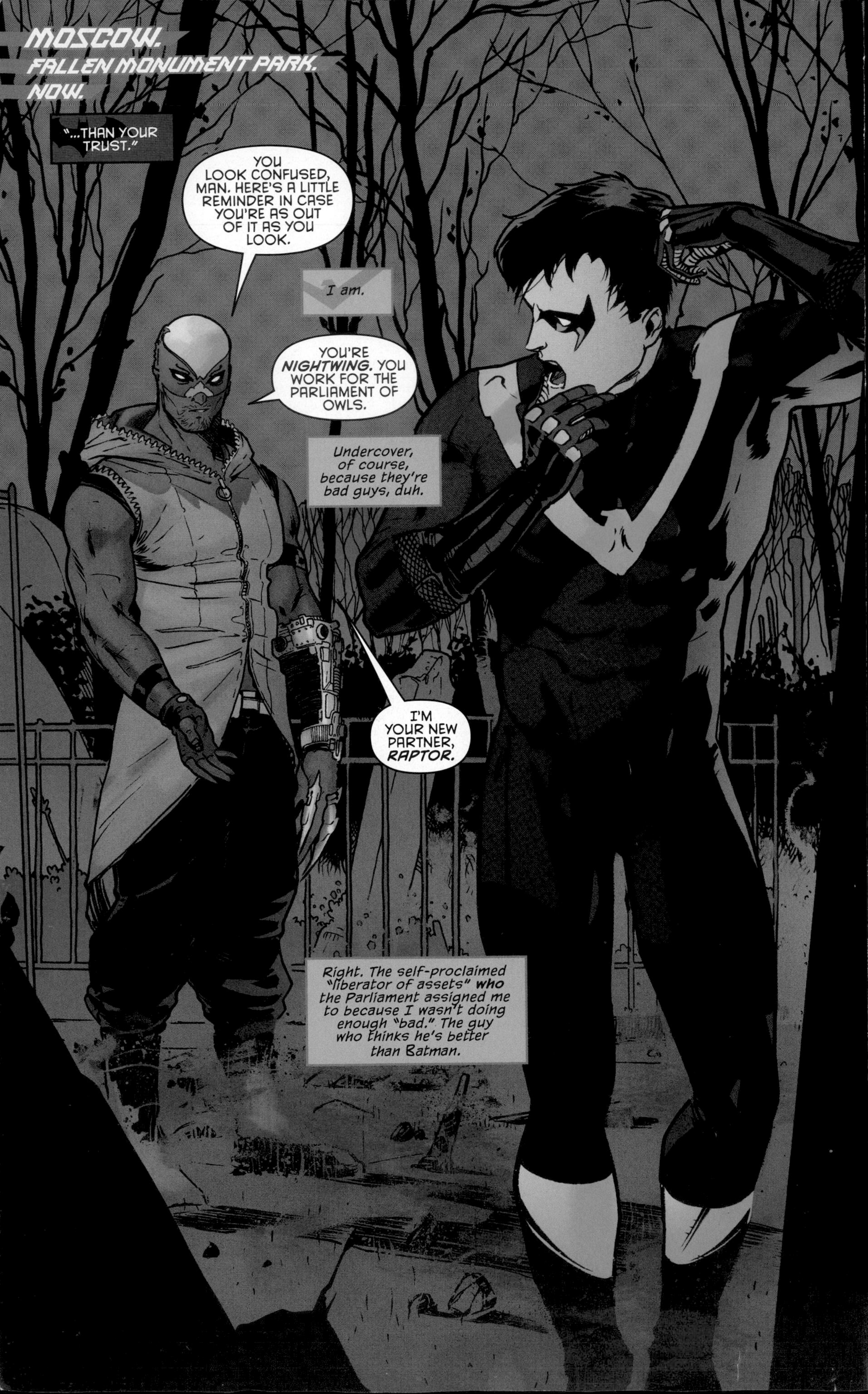
MOSCOW.
FALLEN MONUMENT PARK.
NOW.
"...THAN YOUR TRUST."
YOU LOOK CONFUSED, MAN. HERE'S A LITTLE REMINDER IN CASE YOU'RE AS OUT OF IT AS YOU LOOK.
I am.
YOU'RE NIGHTWING. YOU WORK FOR THE PARLIAMENT OF OWLS.
Undercover, of course, because they're bad guys, duh.
I'M YOUR NEW PARTNER, RAPTOR.
Right. The self-proclaimed "liberator of assets" who the Parliament assigned me to because I wasn't doing enough "bad." The guy who thinks he's better than Batman.

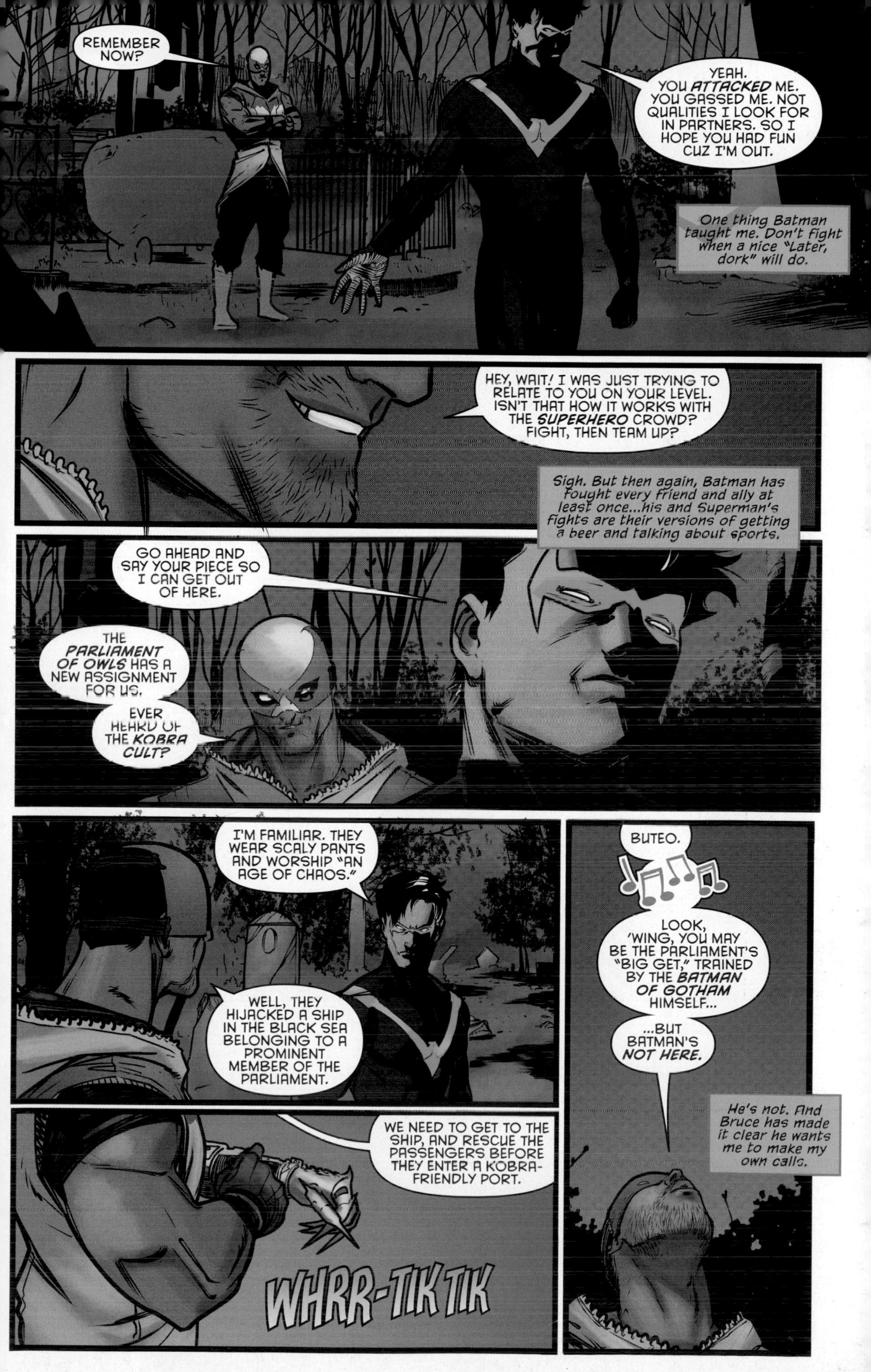
REMEMBER NOW?
YEAH. YOU ATTACKED ME. YOU GASSED ME. NOT QUALITIES I LOOK FOR IN PARTNERS. SO I HOPE YOU HAD FUN CUZ I'M OUT.
One thing Batman taught me. Don't fight when a nice "Later, dork" will do.
HEY, WAIT! I WAS JUST TRYING TO RELATE TO YOU ON YOUR LEVEL. ISN'T THAT HOW IT WORKS WITH THE SUPERHERO CROWD? FIGHT, THEN TEAM UP?
Sigh. But then again, Batman has fought every friend and ally at least once...his and Superman's fights are their versions of getting a beer and talking about sports.
GO AHEAD AND SAY YOUR PIECE SO I CAN GET OUT OF HERE.
THE PARLIAMENT OF OWLS HAS A NEW ASSIGNMENT FOR US.
EVER HEARD OF THE KOBRA CULT?
I'M FAMILIAR. THEY WEAR SCALY PANTS AND WORSHIP "AN AGE OF CHAOS."
WELL, THEY HIJACKED A SHIP IN THE BLACK SEA BELONGING TO A PROMINENT MEMBER OF THE PARLIAMENT.
WE NEED TO GET TO THE SHIP, AND RESCUE THE PASSENGERS BEFORE THEY ENTER A KOBRA-FRIENDLY PORT.
WHRR-TIK TIK
BUTEO.
LOOK, 'WING, YOU MAY BE THE PARLIAMENT'S "BIG GET," TRAINED BY THE BATMAN OF GOTHAM HIMSELF...
...BUT BATMAN'S NOT HERE.
He's not. And Bruce has made it clear he wants me to make my own calls.

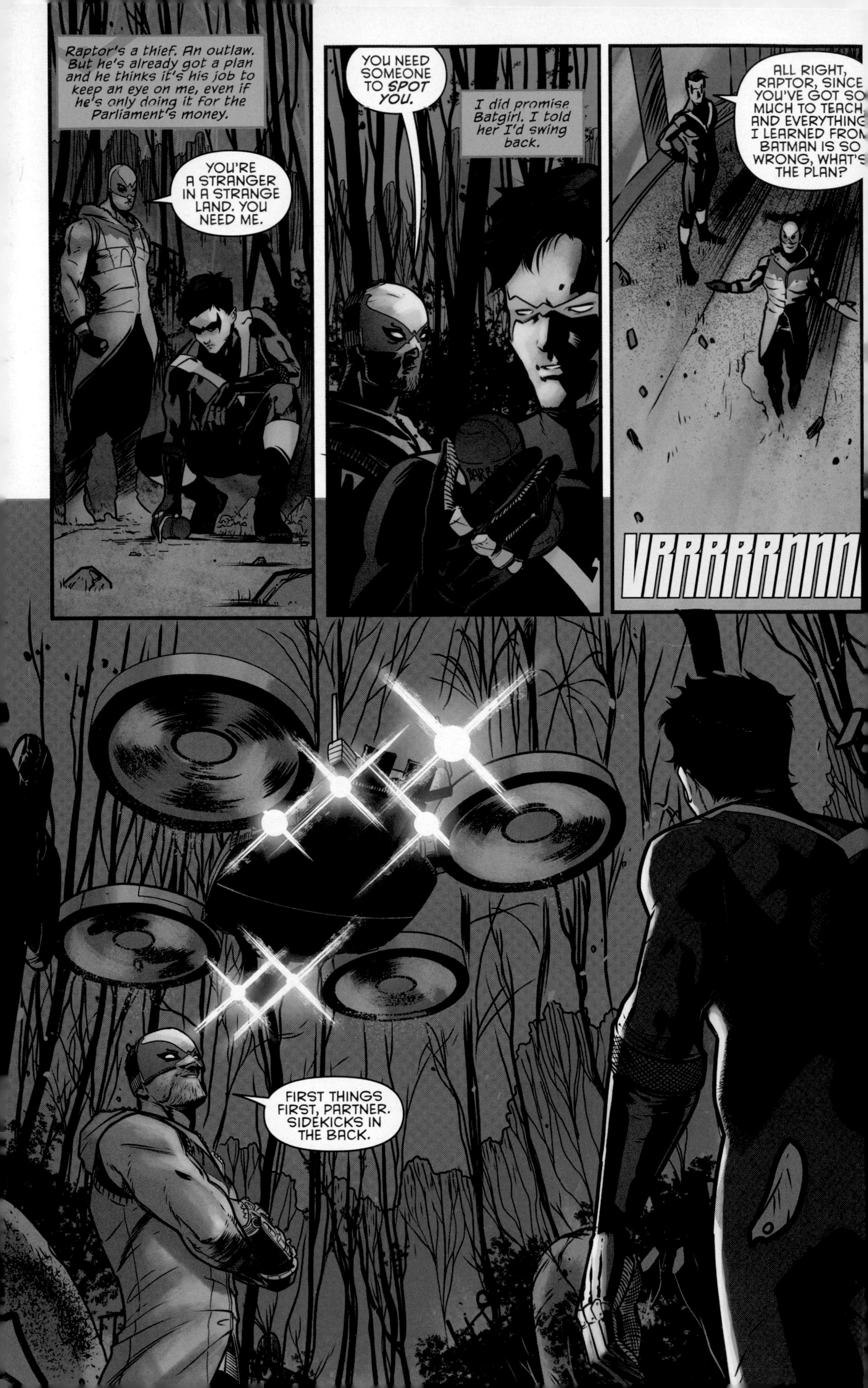
Raptor's a thief. An outlaw. But he's already got a plan and he thinks it's his job to keep an eye on me, even if he's only doing it for the Parliament's money.
YOU'RE A STRANGER IN A STRANGE LAND. YOU NEED ME.
YOU NEED SOMEONE TO SPOT YOU.
I did promise Batgirl. I told her I'd swing back.
ALL RIGHT, RAPTOR, SINCE YOU'VE GOT SO MUCH TO TEACH, AND EVERYTHING I LEARNED FROM BATMAN IS SO WRONG, WHAT'S THE PLAN?
VRRRRRNNN
FIRST THINGS FIRST, PARTNER. SIDEKICKS IN THE BACK.

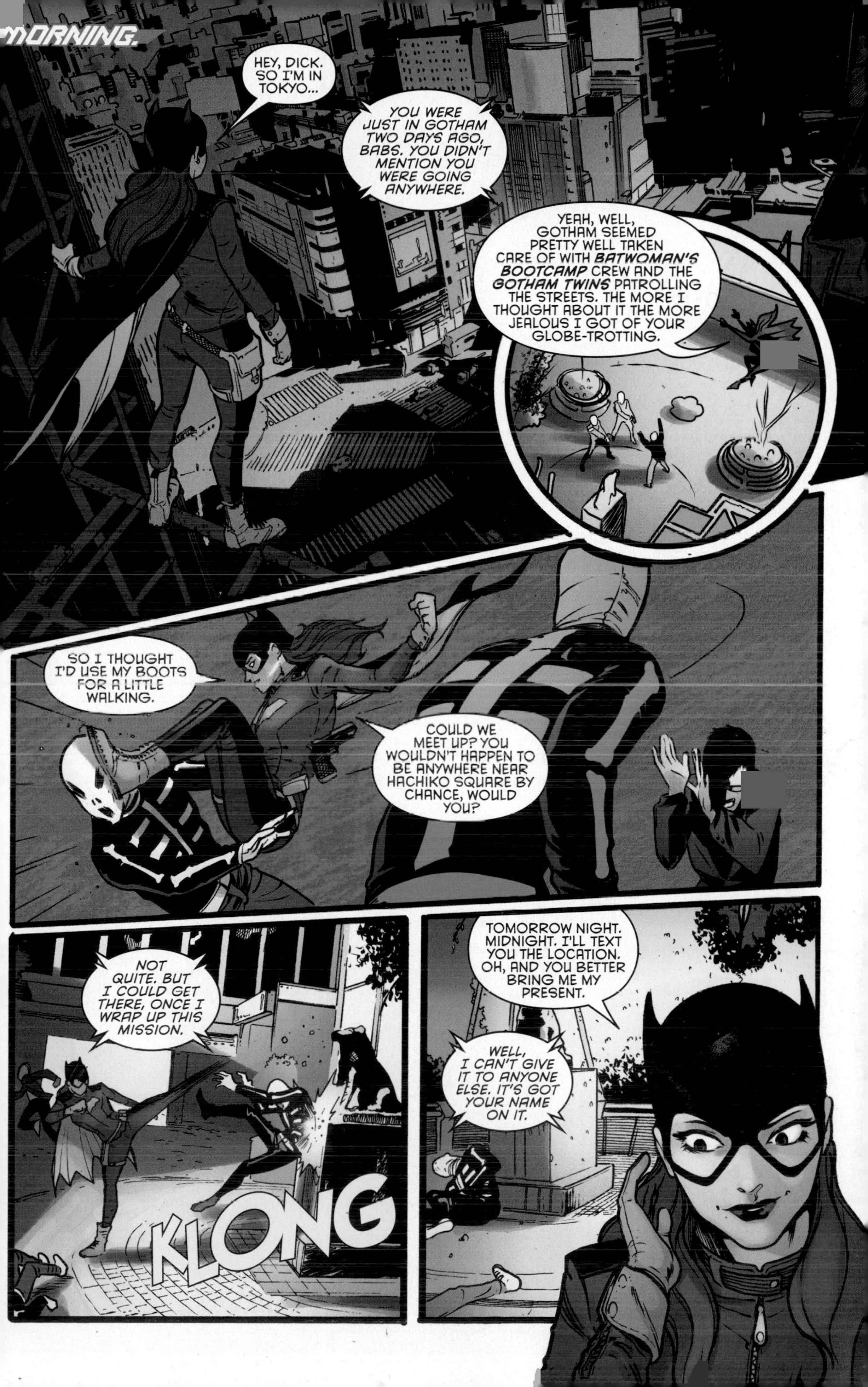
MORNING.
HEY, DICK. SO I'M IN TOKYO...
YOU WERE JUST IN GOTHAM TWO DAYS AGO, BABS. YOU DIDN'T MENTION YOU WERE GOING ANYWHERE.
YEAH, WELL, GOTHAM SEEMED PRETTY WELL TAKEN CARE OF WITH BATWOMAN'S BOOTCAMP CREW AND THE GOTHAM TWINS PATROLLING THE STREETS. THE MORE I THOUGHT ABOUT IT THE MORE JEALOUS I GOT OF YOUR GLOBE-TROTTING.
SO I THOUGHT I'D USE MY BOOTS FOR A LITTLE WALKING.
COULD WE MEET UP? YOU WOULDN'T HAPPEN TO BE ANYWHERE NEAR HACHIKO SQUARE BY CHANCE, WOULD YOU?
NOT QUITE. BUT I COULD GET THERE, ONCE I WRAP UP THIS MISSION.
KLONG
TOMORROW NIGHT. MIDNIGHT. I'LL TEXT YOU THE LOCATION. OH, AND YOU BETTER BRING ME MY PRESENT.
WELL, I CAN'T GIVE IT TO ANYONE ELSE. IT'S GOT YOUR NAME ON IT.

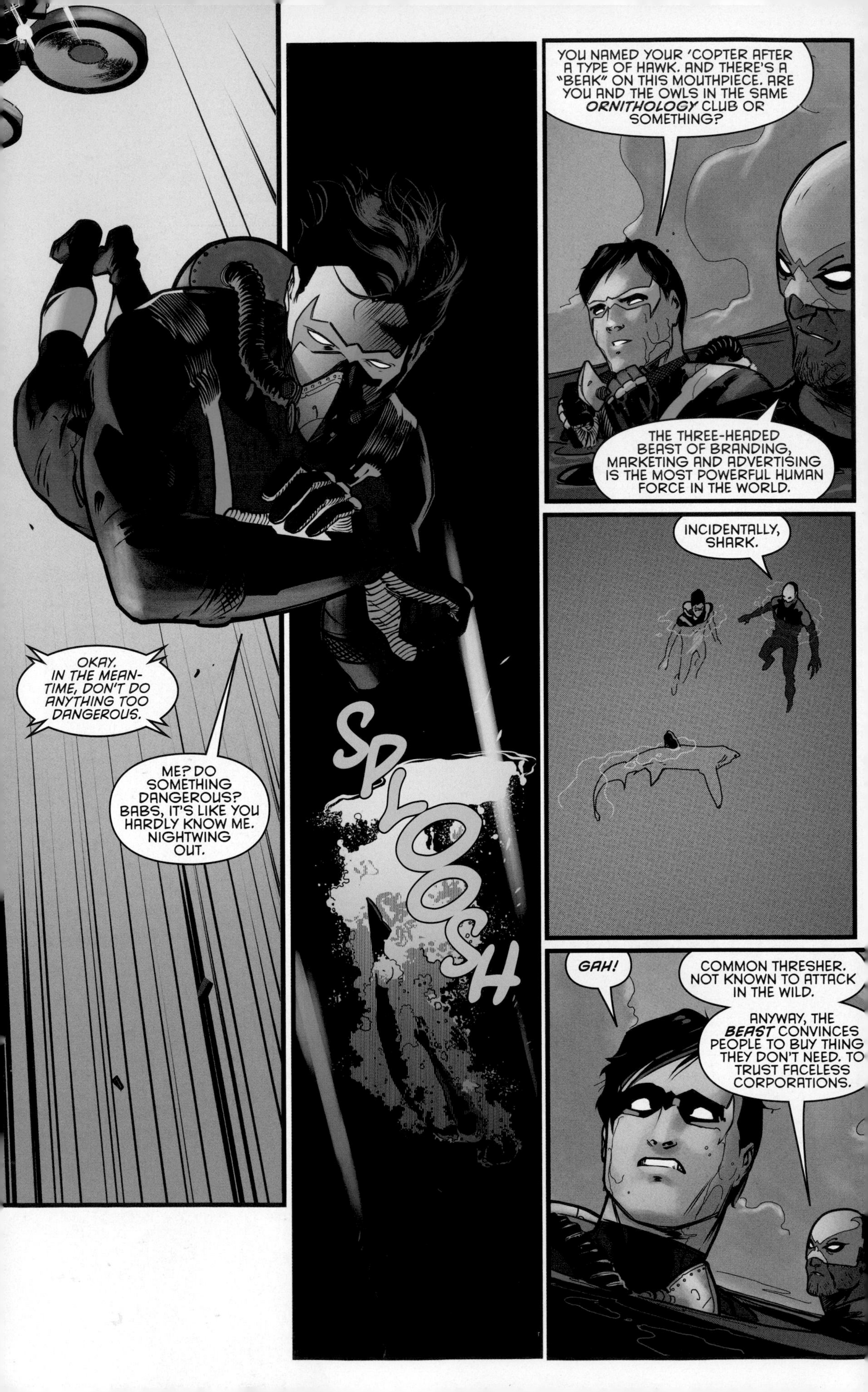
OKAY. IN THE MEAN-TIME, DON'T DO ANYTHING TOO DANGEROUS.
ME? DO SOMETHING DANGEROUS? BABS, IT'S LIKE YOU HARDLY KNOW ME. NIGHTWING OUT.
SPLOOSH
YOU NAMED YOUR 'COPTER AFTER A TYPE OF HAWK. AND THERE'S A "BEAK" ON THIS MOUTHPIECE. ARE YOU AND THE OWLS IN THE SAME *ORNITHOLOGY* CLUB OR SOMETHING?
THE THREE-HEADED BEAST OF BRANDING, MARKETING AND ADVERTISING IS THE MOST POWERFUL HUMAN FORCE IN THE WORLD.
INCIDENTALLY, SHARK.
GAH!
COMMON THRESHER. NOT KNOWN TO ATTACK IN THE WILD.
ANYWAY, THE *BEAST* CONVINCES PEOPLE TO BUY THING THEY DON'T NEED. TO TRUST FACELESS CORPORATIONS.

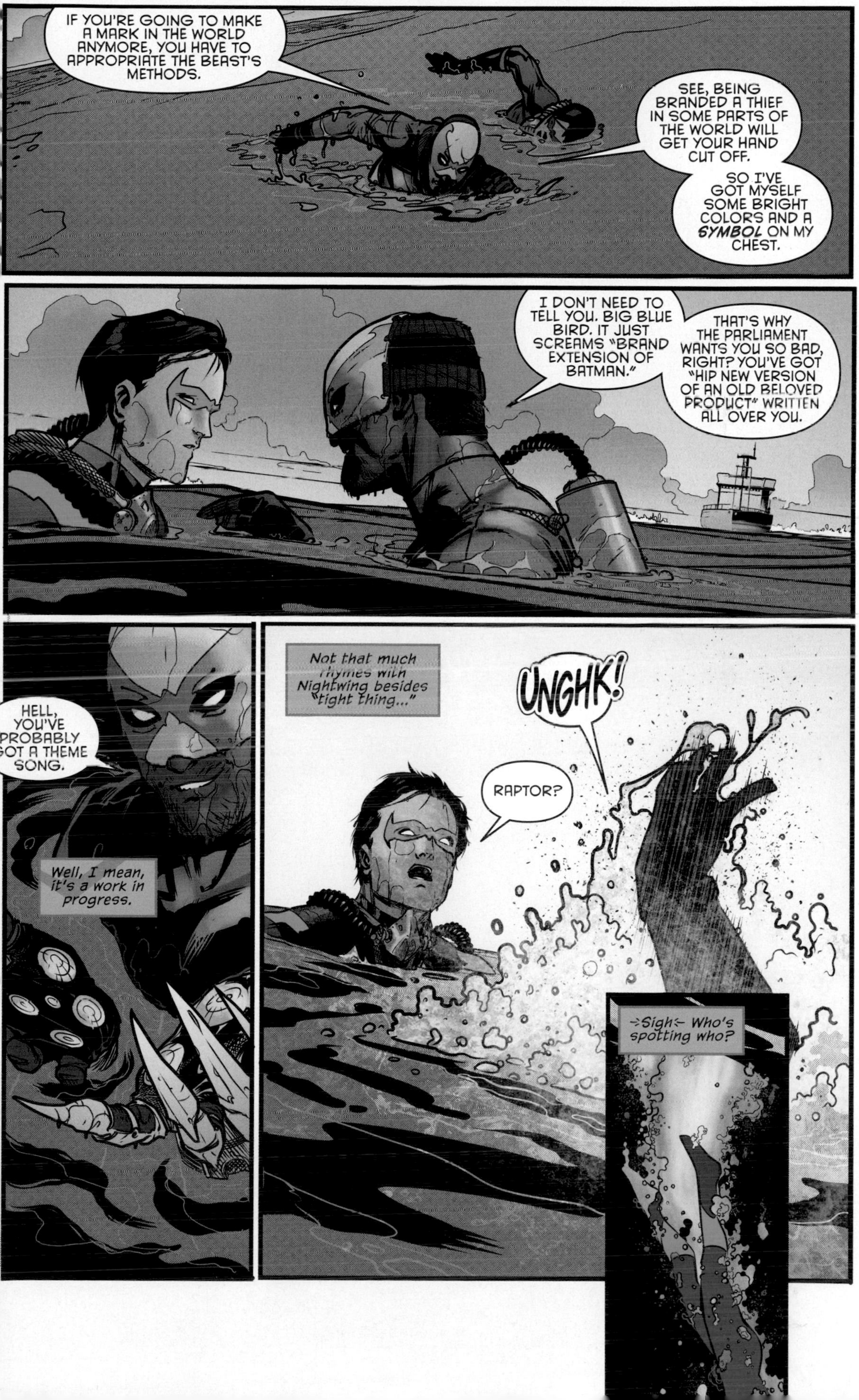
IF YOU'RE GOING TO MAKE A MARK IN THE WORLD ANYMORE, YOU HAVE TO APPROPRIATE THE BEAST'S METHODS.
SEE, BEING BRANDED A THIEF IN SOME PARTS OF THE WORLD WILL GET YOUR HAND CUT OFF.
SO I'VE GOT MYSELF SOME BRIGHT COLORS AND A SYMBOL ON MY CHEST.
I DON'T NEED TO TELL YOU. BIG BLUE BIRD. IT JUST SCREAMS "BRAND EXTENSION OF BATMAN."
THAT'S WHY THE PARLIAMENT WANTS YOU SO BAD, RIGHT? YOU'VE GOT "HIP NEW VERSION OF AN OLD BELOVED PRODUCT" WRITTEN ALL OVER YOU.
HELL, YOU'VE PROBABLY GOT A THEME SONG.
Well, I mean, it's a work in progress.
Not that much rhymes with Nightwing besides "tight thing..."
UNGHK!
RAPTOR?
Sigh Who's spotting who?

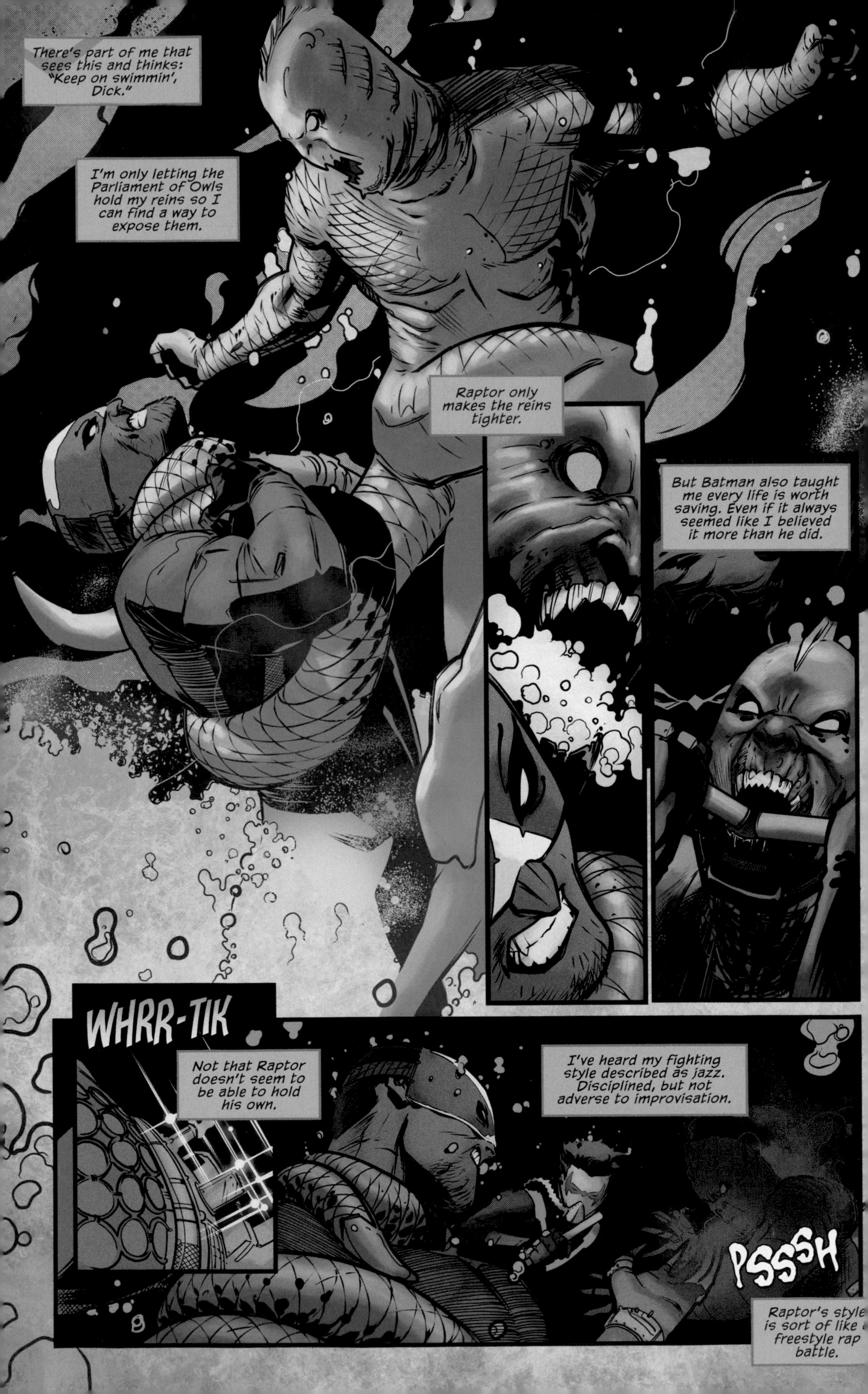

There's part of me that sees this and thinks: "Keep on swimmin', Dick."
I'm only letting the Parliament of Owls hold my reins so I can find a way to expose them.
Raptor only makes the reins tighter.
But Batman also taught me every life is worth saving. Even if it always seemed like I believed it more than he did.
WHRR-TIK
Not that Raptor doesn't seem to be able to hold his own.
I've heard my fighting style described as jazz. Disciplined, but not adverse to improvisation.
PSSSH
Raptor's style is sort of like freestyle rap battle.

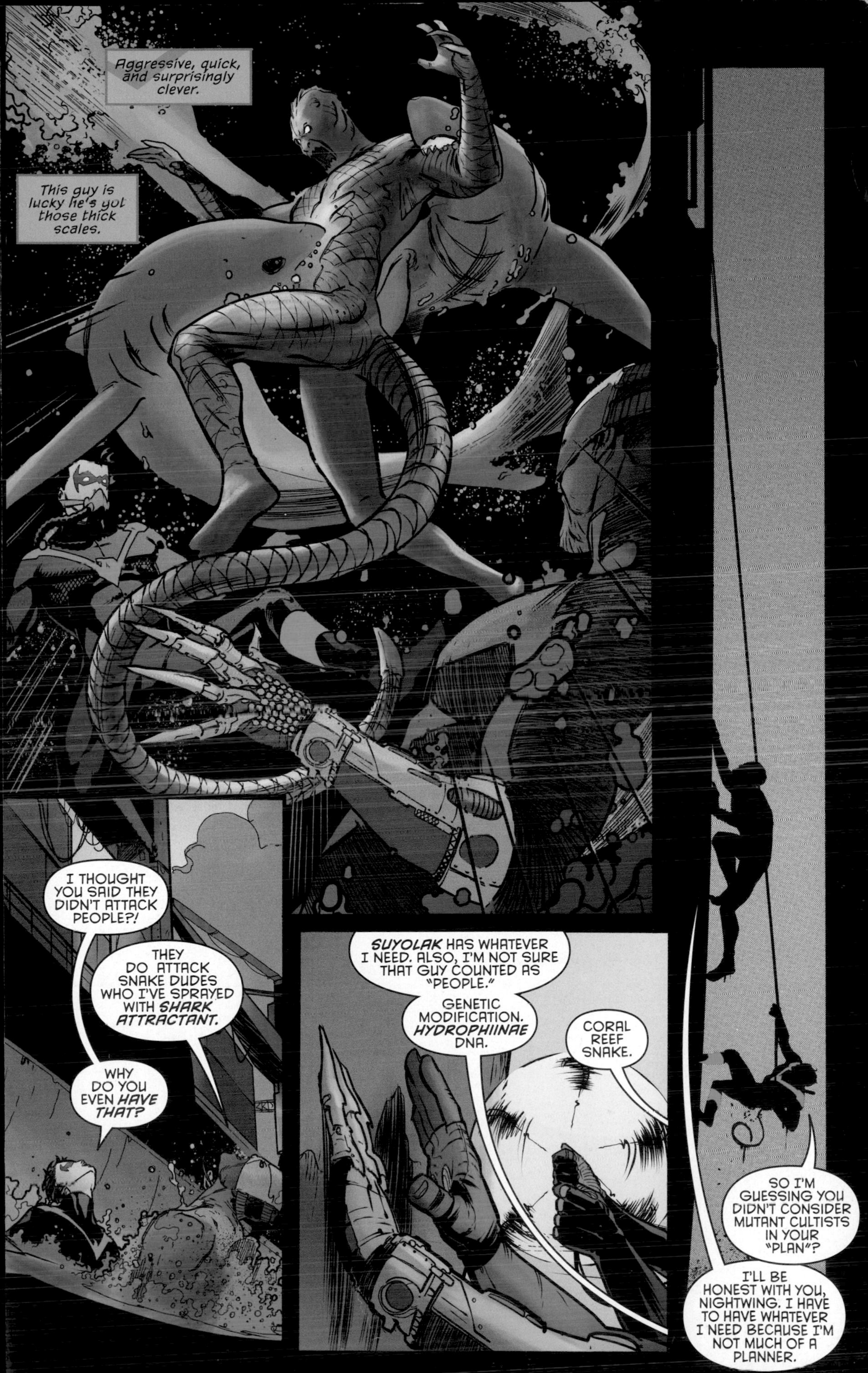
Aggressive, quick, and surprisingly clever.
This guy is lucky he's got those thick scales.
I THOUGHT YOU SAID THEY DIDN'T ATTACK PEOPLE?!
THEY DO ATTACK SNAKE DUDES WHO I'VE SPRAYED WITH SHARK ATTRACTANT.
WHY DO YOU EVEN HAVE THAT?
SUYOLAK HAS WHATEVER I NEED. ALSO, I'M NOT SURE THAT GUY COUNTED AS "PEOPLE."
GENETIC MODIFICATION. HYDROPHIINAE DNA.
CORAL REEF SNAKE.
SO I'M GUESSING YOU DIDN'T CONSIDER MUTANT CULTISTS IN YOUR "PLAN"?
I'LL BE HONEST WITH YOU, NIGHTWING. I HAVE TO HAVE WHATEVER I NEED BECAUSE I'M NOT MUCH OF A PLANNER.

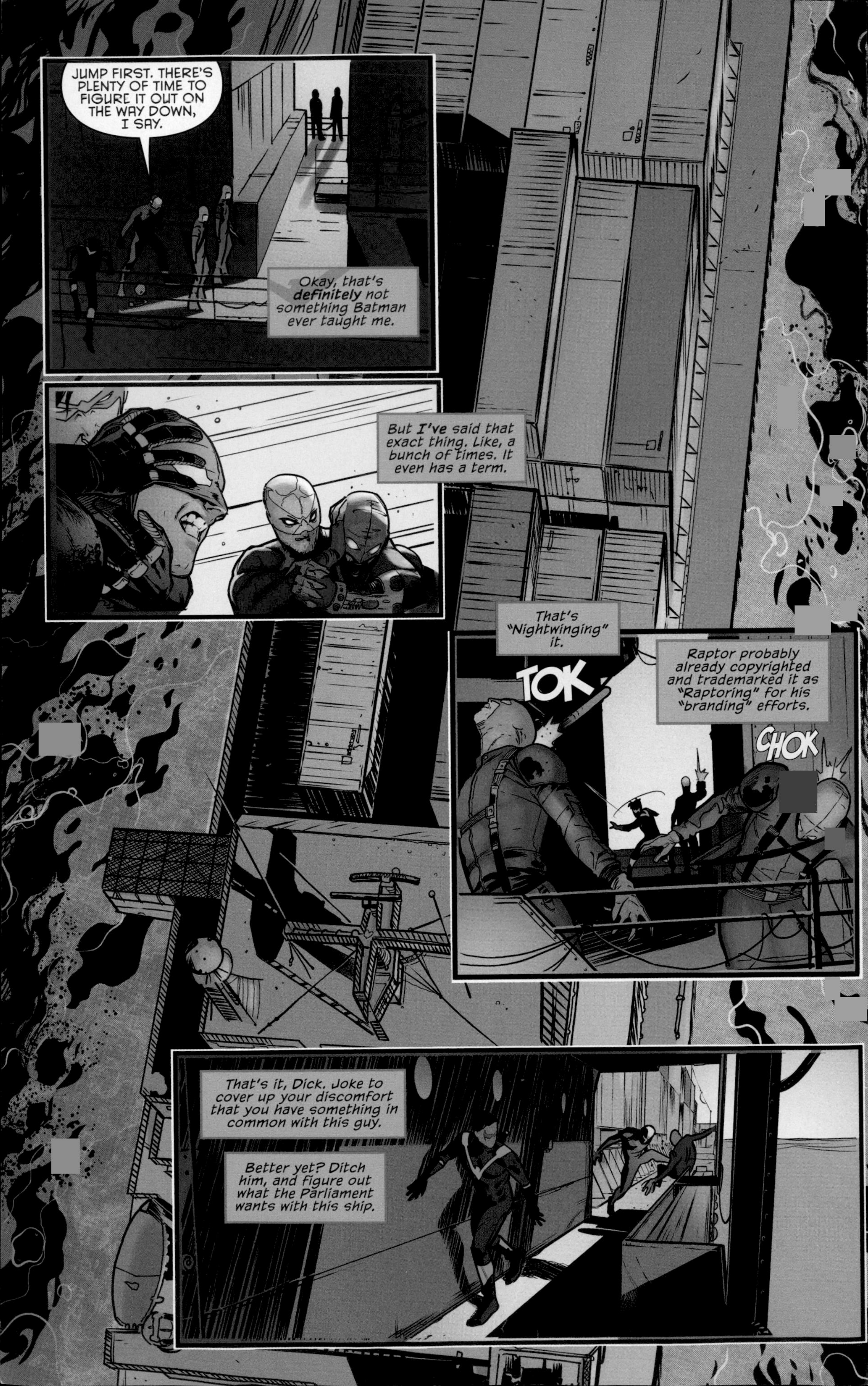
JUMP FIRST. THERE'S PLENTY OF TIME TO FIGURE IT OUT ON THE WAY DOWN, I SAY.
Okay, that's definitely not something Batman ever taught me.
But I've said that exact thing. Like, a bunch of times. It even has a term.
That's "Nightwinging" it.
TOK
Raptor probably already copyrighted and trademarked it as "Raptoring" for his "branding" efforts.
CHOK
That's it, Dick. Joke to cover up your discomfort that you have something in common with this guy.
Better yet? Ditch him, and figure out what the Parliament wants with this ship.

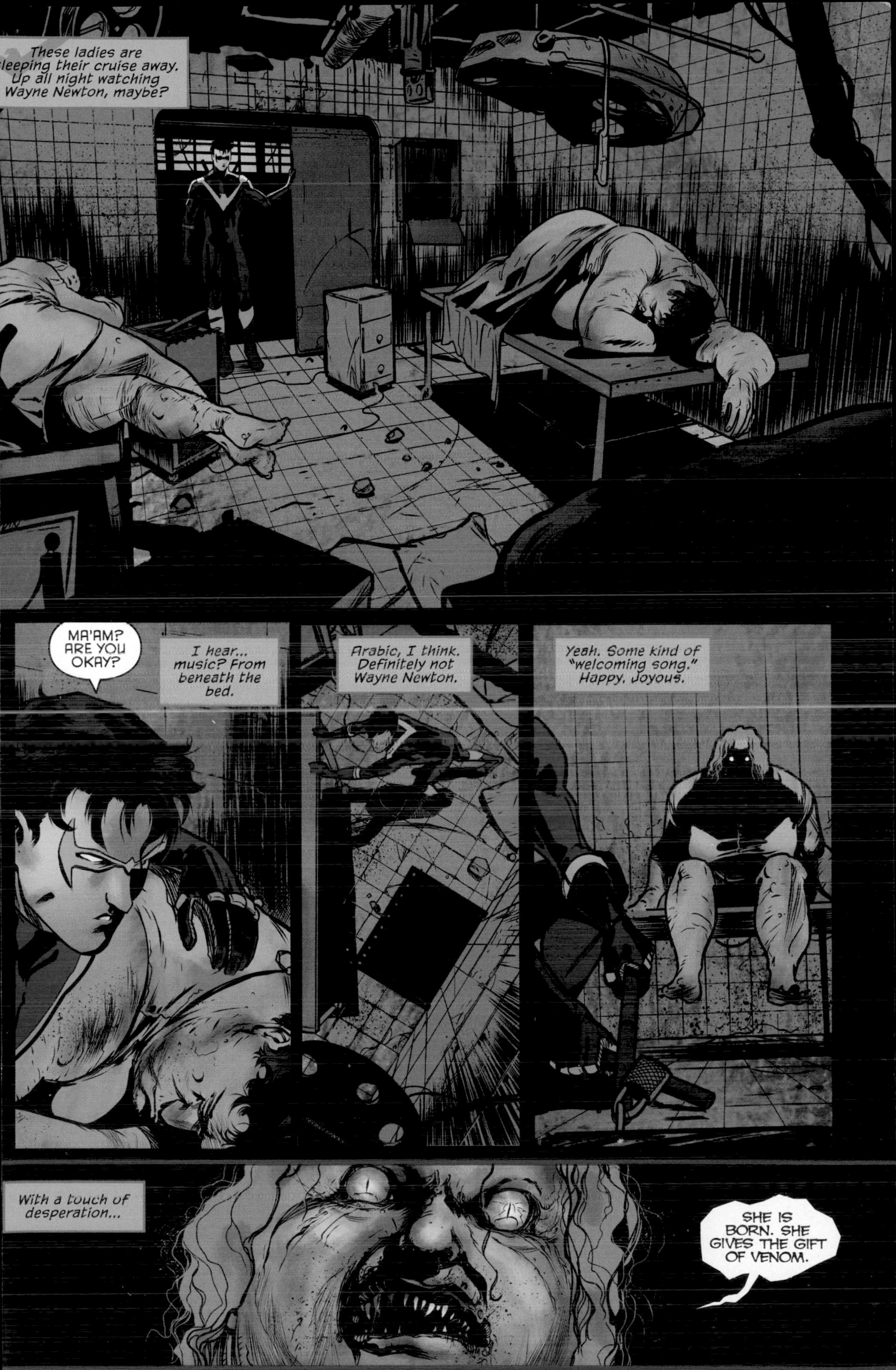
These ladies are sleeping their cruise away. Up all night watching Wayne Newton, maybe?
MA'AM? ARE YOU OKAY?
I hear... music? From beneath the bed.
Arabic, I think. Definitely not Wayne Newton.
Yeah. Some kind of "welcoming song." Happy. Joyous.
With a touch of desperation...
SHE IS BORN. SHE GIVES THE GIFT OF VENOM.

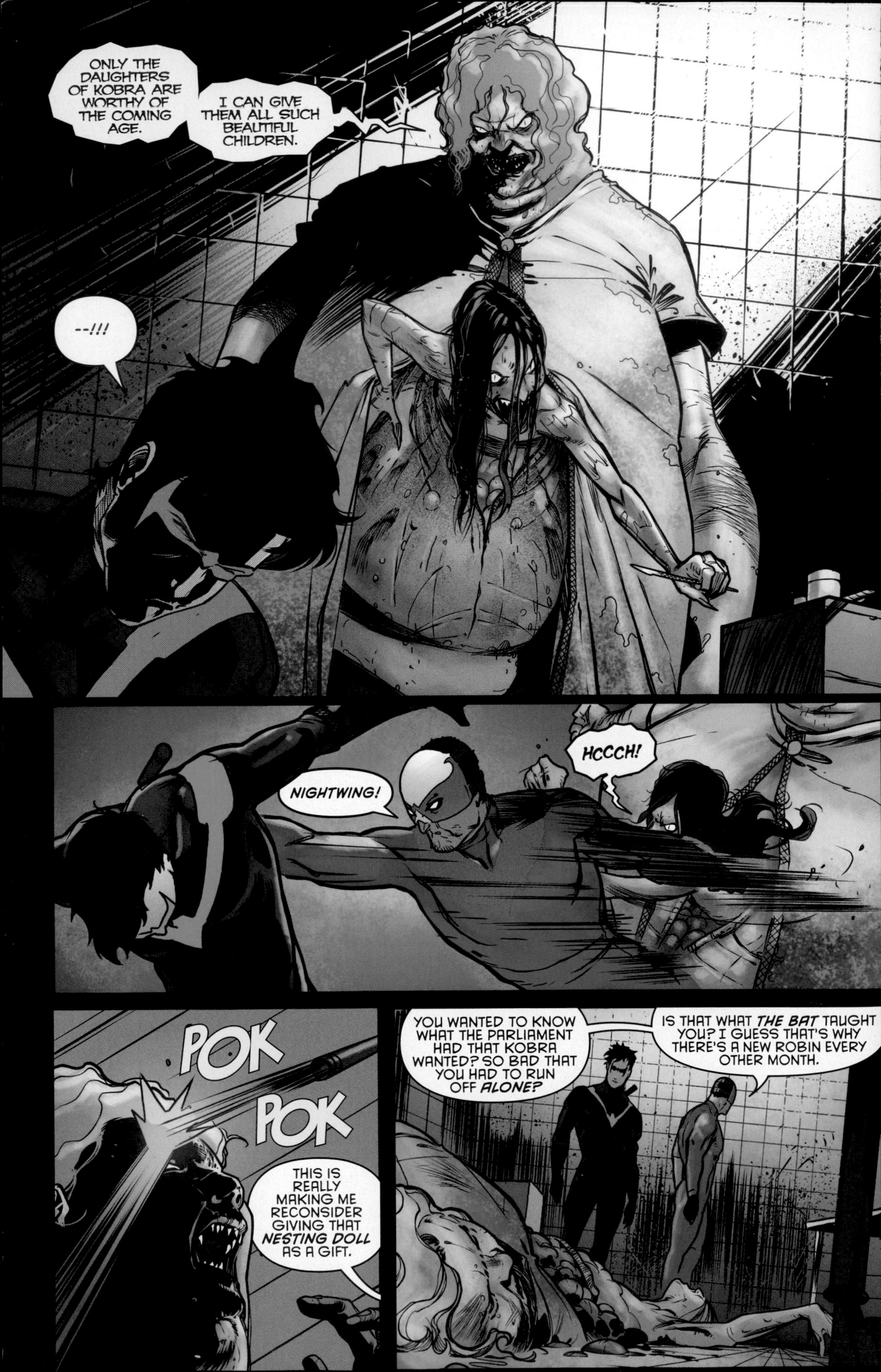
ONLY THE DAUGHTERS OF KOBRA ARE WORTHY OF THE COMING AGE.
I CAN GIVE THEM ALL SUCH BEAUTIFUL CHILDREN.
--!!!
NIGHTWING!
HCCCH!
POK
POK
THIS IS REALLY MAKING ME RECONSIDER GIVING THAT *NESTING DOLL* AS A GIFT.
YOU WANTED TO KNOW WHAT THE PARLIAMENT HAD THAT KOBRA WANTED? SO BAD THAT YOU HAD TO RUN OFF *ALONE?*
IS THAT WHAT *THE BAT* TAUGHT YOU? I GUESS THAT'S WHY THERE'S A NEW ROBIN EVERY OTHER MONTH.

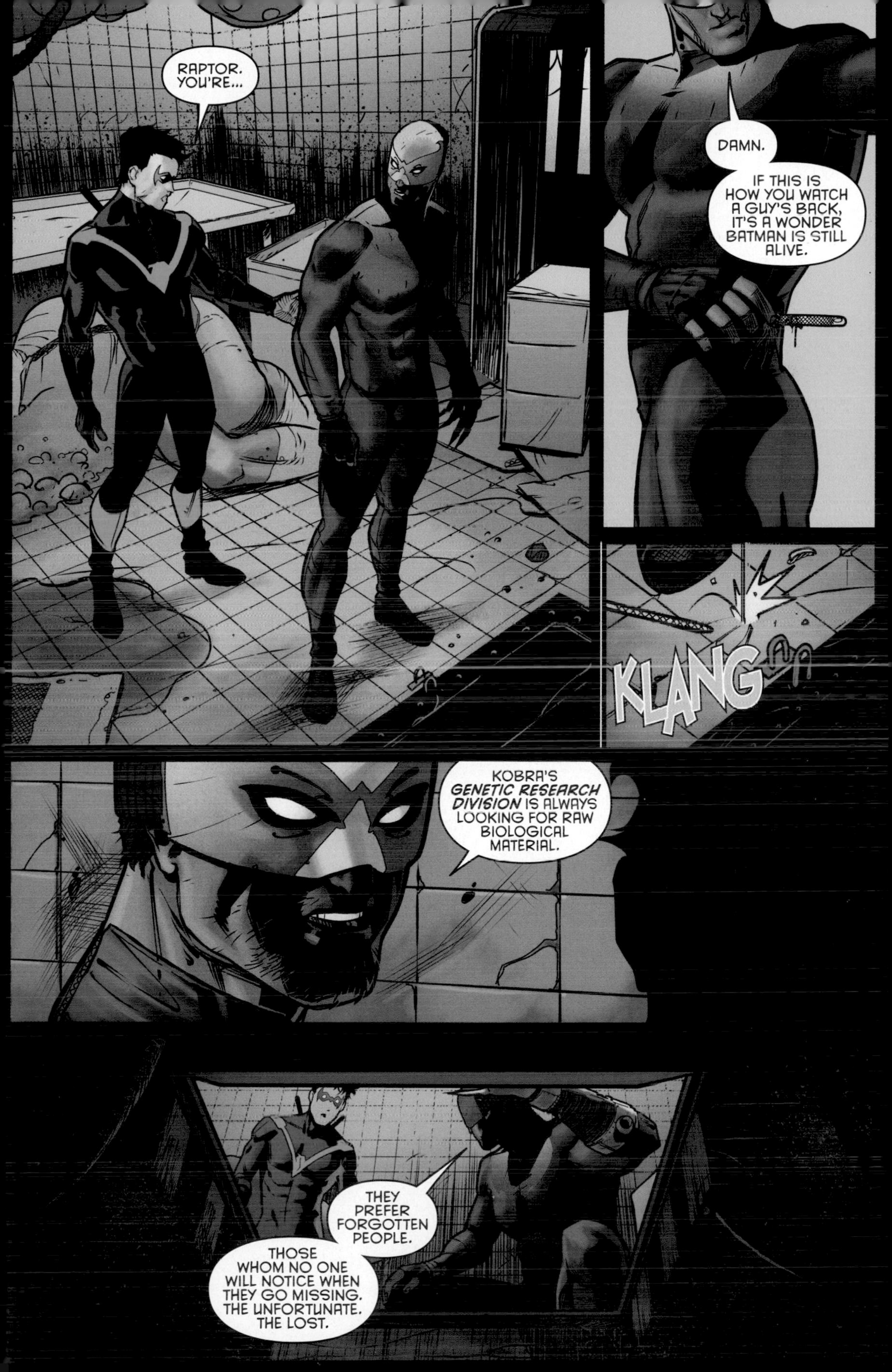
RAPTOR. YOU'RE...
DAMN.
IF THIS IS HOW YOU WATCH A GUY'S BACK, IT'S A WONDER BATMAN IS STILL ALIVE.
KLANG
KOBRA'S *GENETIC RESEARCH DIVISION* IS ALWAYS LOOKING FOR RAW BIOLOGICAL MATERIAL.
THEY PREFER FORGOTTEN PEOPLE.
THOSE WHOM NO ONE WILL NOTICE WHEN THEY GO MISSING. THE UNFORTUNATE. THE LOST.

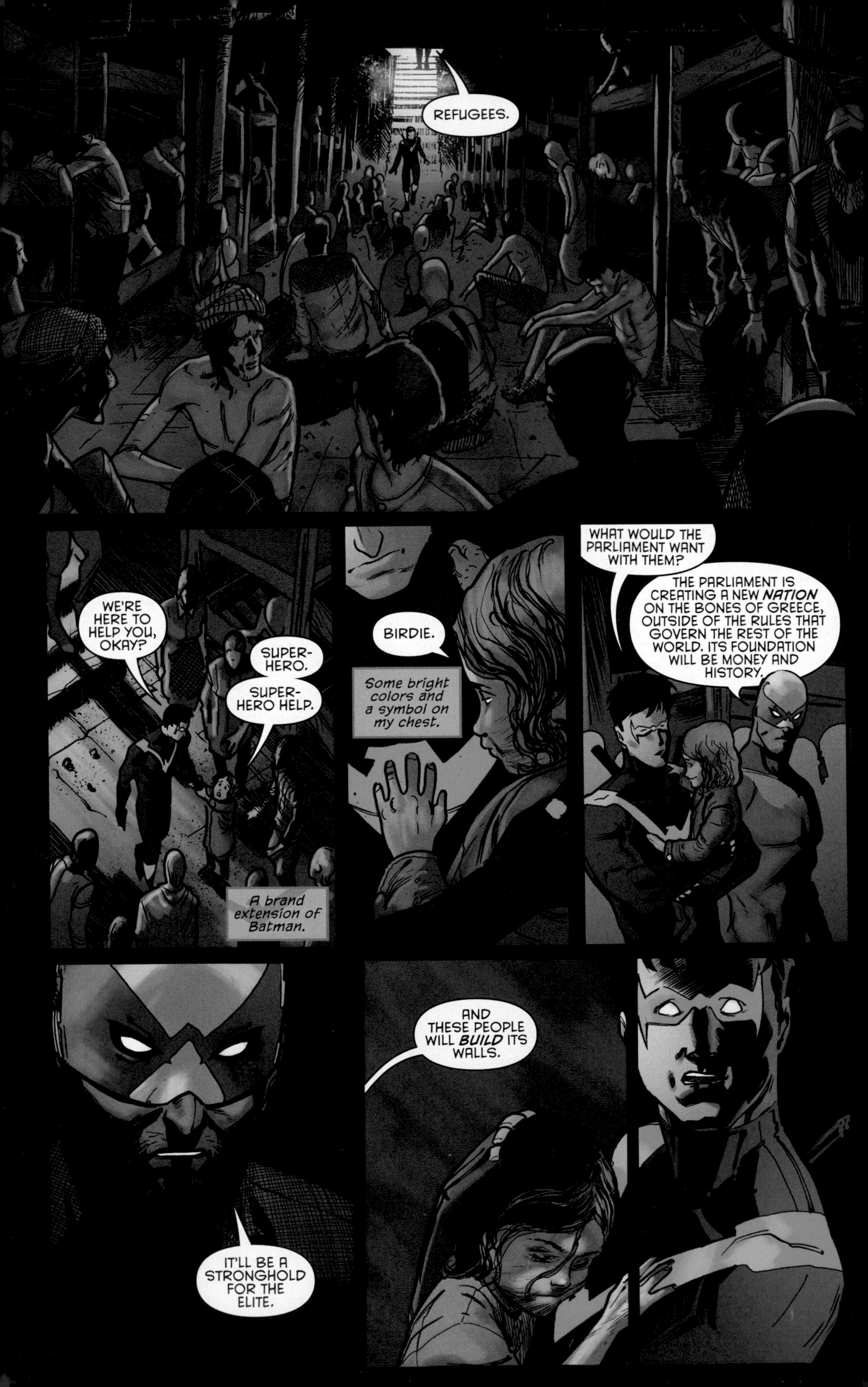
REFUGEES.
WE'RE HERE TO HELP YOU, OKAY?
SUPER-HERO.
SUPER-HERO HELP.
A brand extension of Batman.
BIRDIE.
Some bright colors and a symbol on my chest.
WHAT WOULD THE PARLIAMENT WANT WITH THEM?
THE PARLIAMENT IS CREATING A NEW NATION ON THE BONES OF GREECE, OUTSIDE OF THE RULES THAT GOVERN THE REST OF THE WORLD. ITS FOUNDATION WILL BE MONEY AND HISTORY.
IT'LL BE A STRONGHOLD FOR THE ELITE.
AND THESE PEOPLE WILL BUILD ITS WALLS.

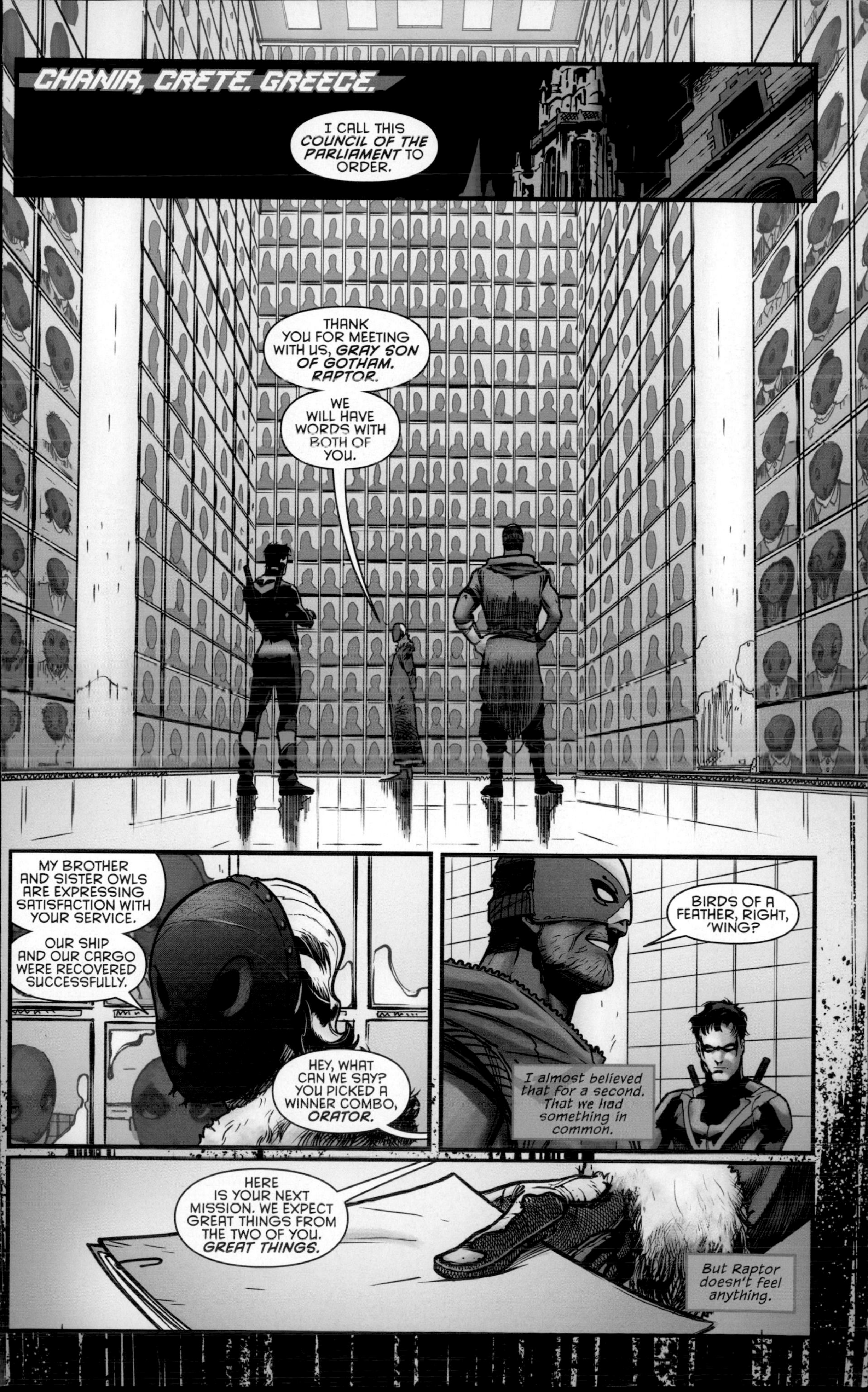
CHANIA, CRETE. GREECE.
I CALL THIS COUNCIL OF THE PARLIAMENT TO ORDER.
THANK YOU FOR MEETING WITH US, GRAY SON OF GOTHAM. RAPTOR.
WE WILL HAVE WORDS WITH BOTH OF YOU.
MY BROTHER AND SISTER OWLS ARE EXPRESSING SATISFACTION WITH YOUR SERVICE.
OUR SHIP AND OUR CARGO WERE RECOVERED SUCCESSFULLY.
HEY, WHAT CAN WE SAY? YOU PICKED A WINNER COMBO, ORATOR.
BIRDS OF A FEATHER, RIGHT, 'WING?
I almost believed that for a second. That we had something in common.
HERE IS YOUR NEXT MISSION. WE EXPECT GREAT THINGS FROM THE TWO OF YOU. GREAT THINGS.
But Raptor doesn't feel anything.

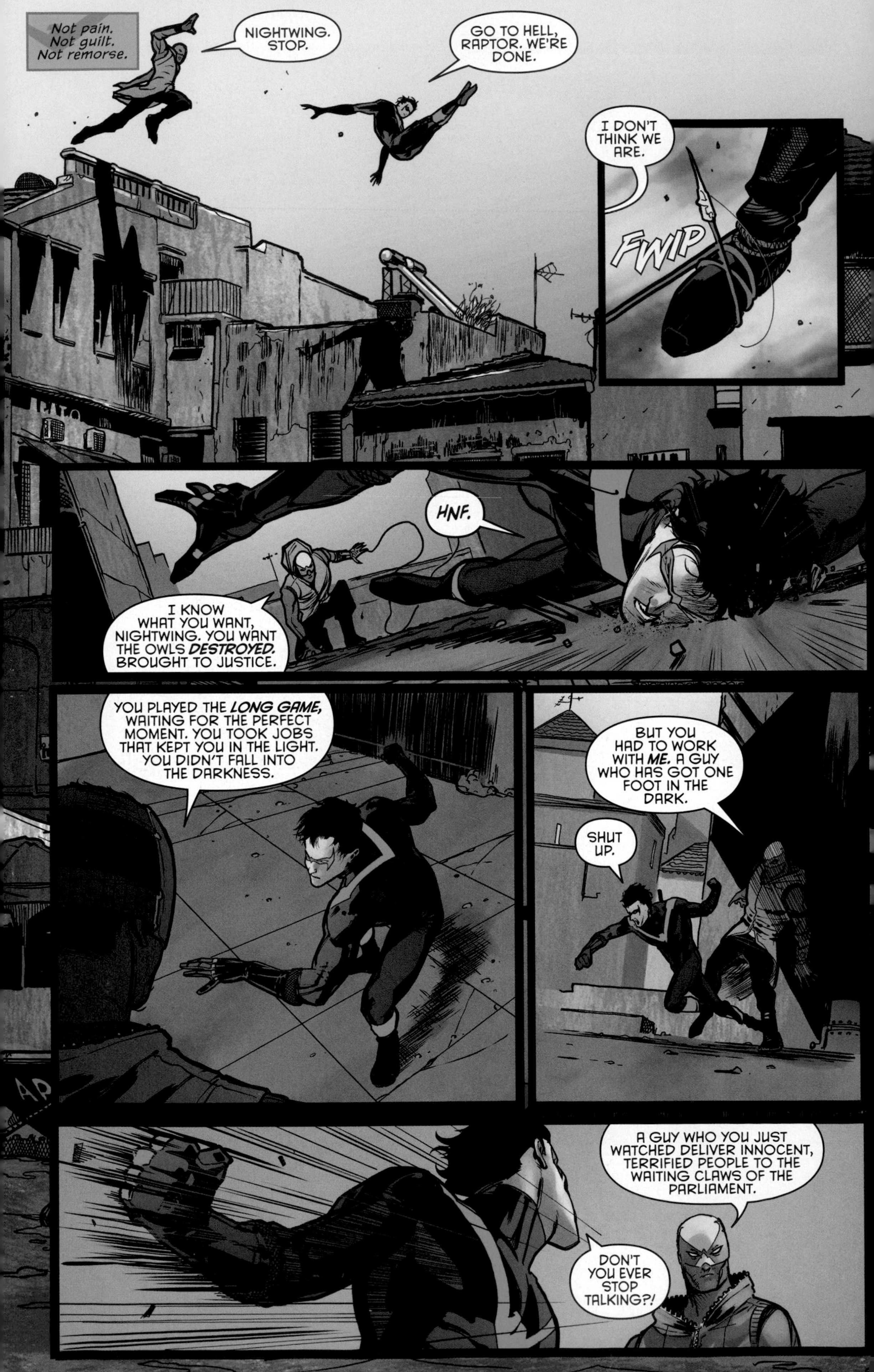

Not pain. Not guilt. Not remorse.
NIGHTWING. STOP.
GO TO HELL, RAPTOR. WE'RE DONE.
I DON'T THINK WE ARE.
FWIP
HNF.
I KNOW WHAT YOU WANT, NIGHTWING. YOU WANT THE OWLS DESTROYED. BROUGHT TO JUSTICE.
YOU PLAYED THE LONG GAME, WAITING FOR THE PERFECT MOMENT. YOU TOOK JOBS THAT KEPT YOU IN THE LIGHT. YOU DIDN'T FALL INTO THE DARKNESS.
BUT YOU HAD TO WORK WITH ME. A GUY WHO HAS GOT ONE FOOT IN THE DARK.
SHUT UP.
A GUY WHO YOU JUST WATCHED DELIVER INNOCENT, TERRIFIED PEOPLE TO THE WAITING CLAWS OF THE PARLIAMENT.
DON'T YOU EVER STOP TALKING?!

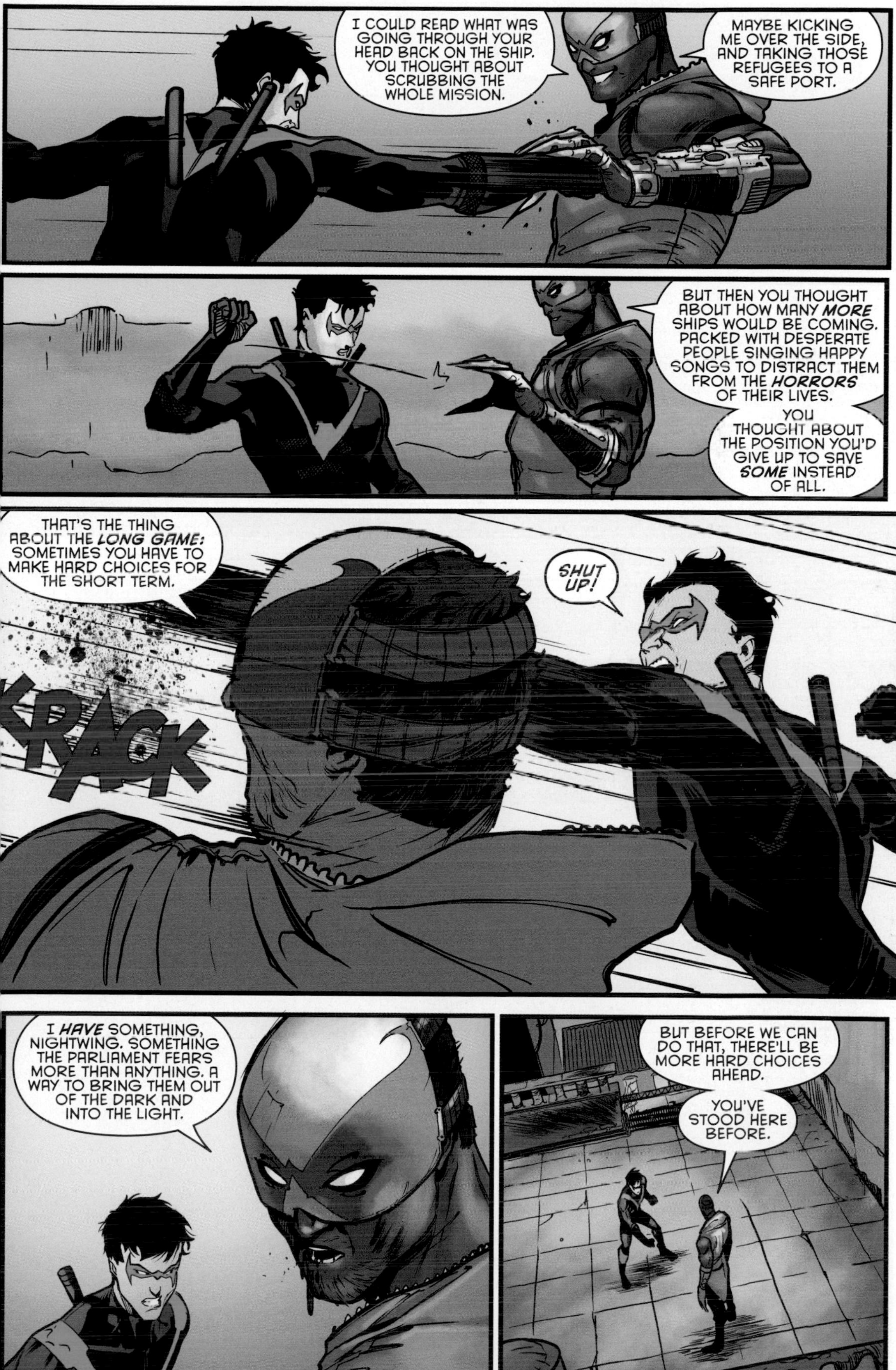
I COULD READ WHAT WAS GOING THROUGH YOUR HEAD BACK ON THE SHIP. YOU THOUGHT ABOUT SCRUBBING THE WHOLE MISSION.
MAYBE KICKING ME OVER THE SIDE, AND TAKING THOSE REFUGEES TO A SAFE PORT.
BUT THEN YOU THOUGHT ABOUT HOW MANY *MORE* SHIPS WOULD BE COMING. PACKED WITH DESPERATE PEOPLE SINGING HAPPY SONGS TO DISTRACT THEM FROM THE *HORRORS* OF THEIR LIVES.
YOU THOUGHT ABOUT THE POSITION YOU'D GIVE UP TO SAVE *SOME* INSTEAD OF ALL.
THAT'S THE THING ABOUT THE *LONG GAME:* SOMETIMES YOU HAVE TO MAKE HARD CHOICES FOR THE SHORT TERM.
SHUT UP!
KRACK
I *HAVE* SOMETHING, NIGHTWING. SOMETHING THE PARLIAMENT FEARS MORE THAN ANYTHING. A WAY TO BRING THEM OUT OF THE DARK AND INTO THE LIGHT.
BUT BEFORE WE CAN DO THAT, THERE'LL BE MORE HARD CHOICES AHEAD.
YOU'VE STOOD HERE BEFORE.

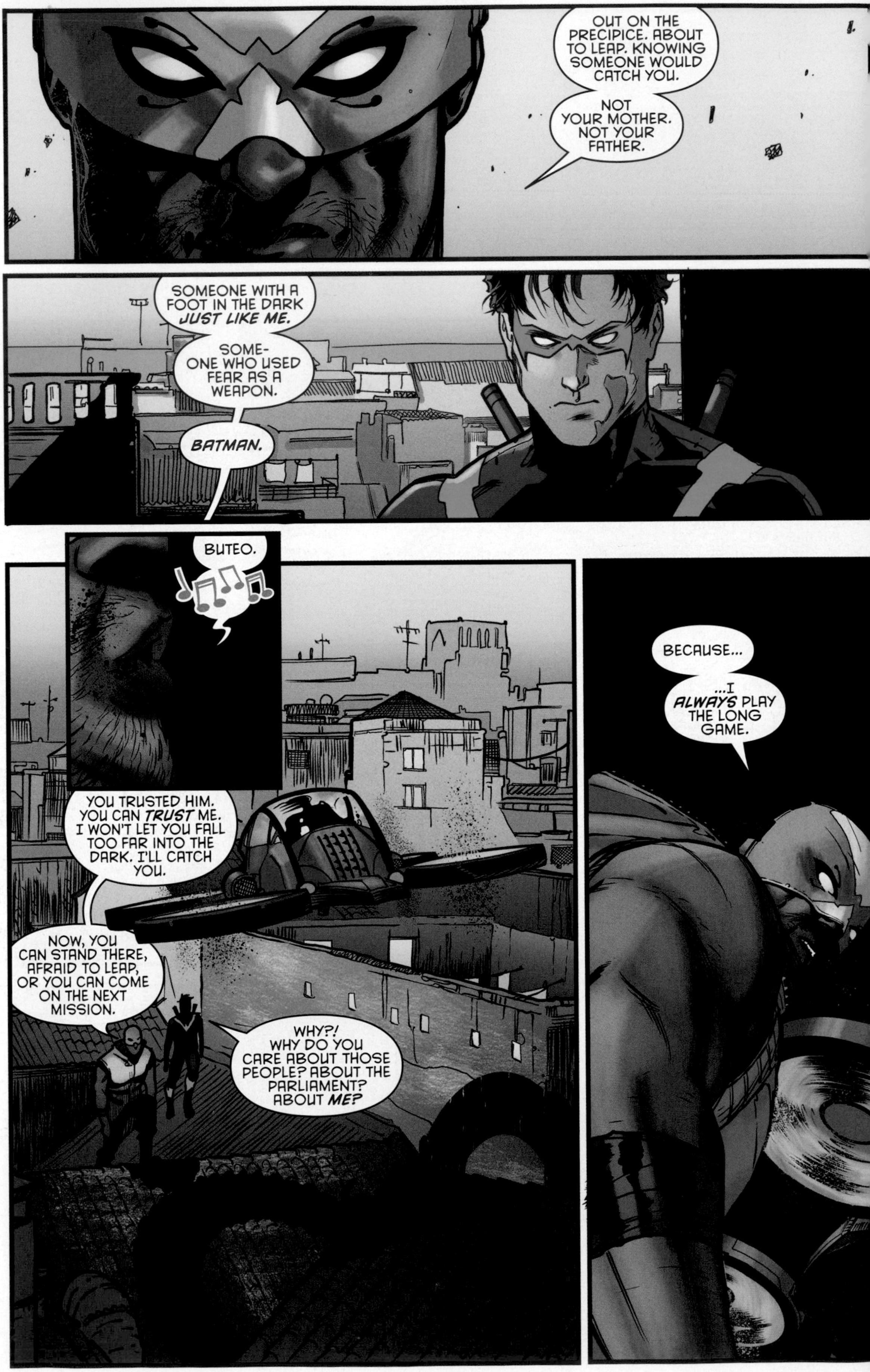
OUT ON THE PRECIPICE. ABOUT TO LEAP. KNOWING SOMEONE WOULD CATCH YOU.
NOT YOUR MOTHER. NOT YOUR FATHER.
SOMEONE WITH A FOOT IN THE DARK *JUST LIKE ME.*
SOME-ONE WHO USED FEAR AS A WEAPON.
BATMAN.
BUTEO.
YOU TRUSTED HIM. YOU CAN *TRUST* ME. I WON'T LET YOU FALL TOO FAR INTO THE DARK. I'LL CATCH YOU.
NOW, YOU CAN STAND THERE, AFRAID TO LEAP, OR YOU CAN COME ON THE NEXT MISSION.
WHY?! WHY DO YOU CARE ABOUT THOSE PEOPLE? ABOUT THE PARLIAMENT? ABOUT *ME?*
BECAUSE...
...I *ALWAYS* PLAY THE LONG GAME.

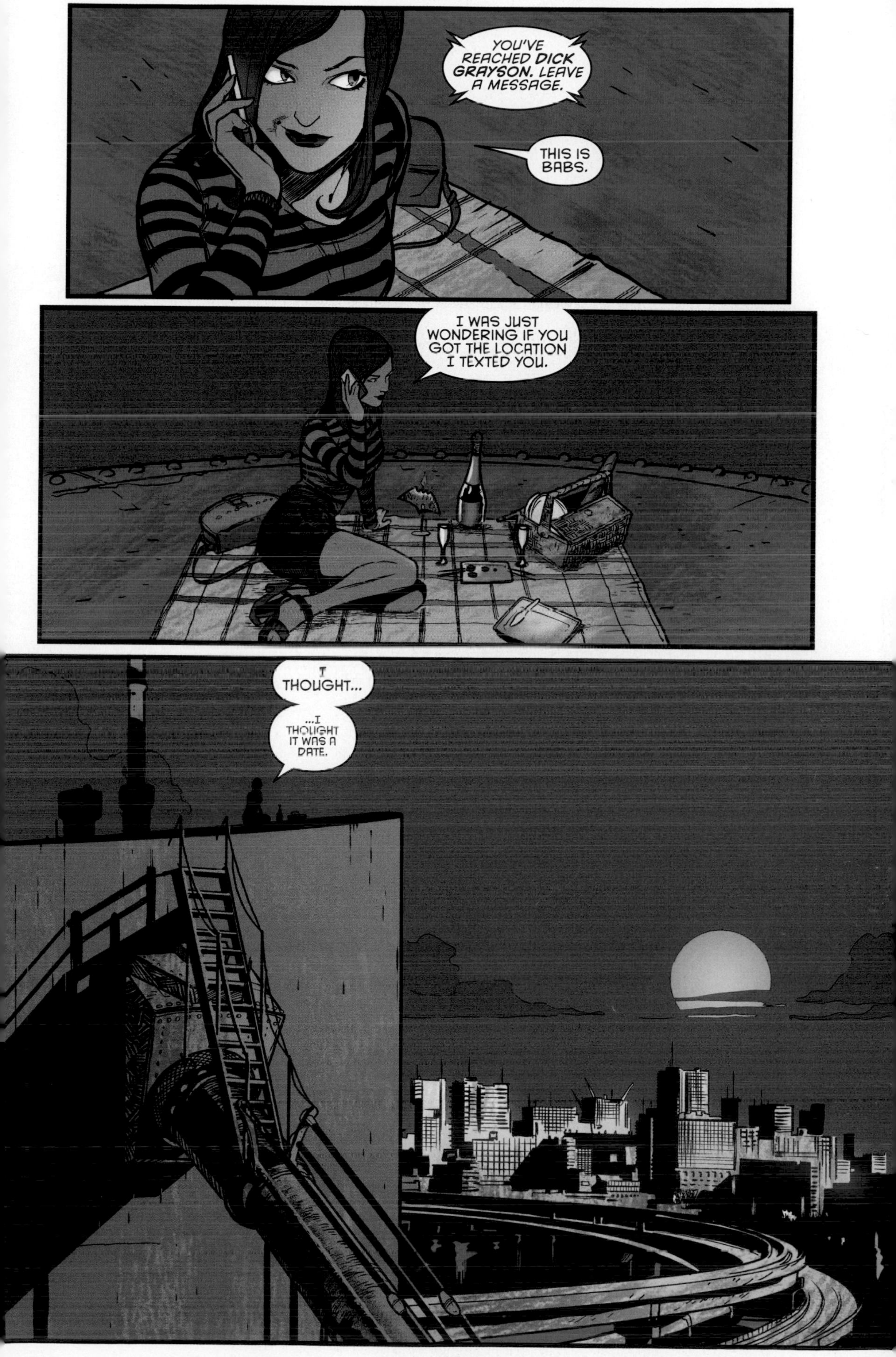
YOU'VE REACHED DICK GRAYSON. LEAVE A MESSAGE.
THIS IS BABS.
I WAS JUST WONDERING IF YOU GOT THE LOCATION I TEXTED YOU.
I THOUGHT...
...I THOUGHT IT WAS A DATE.

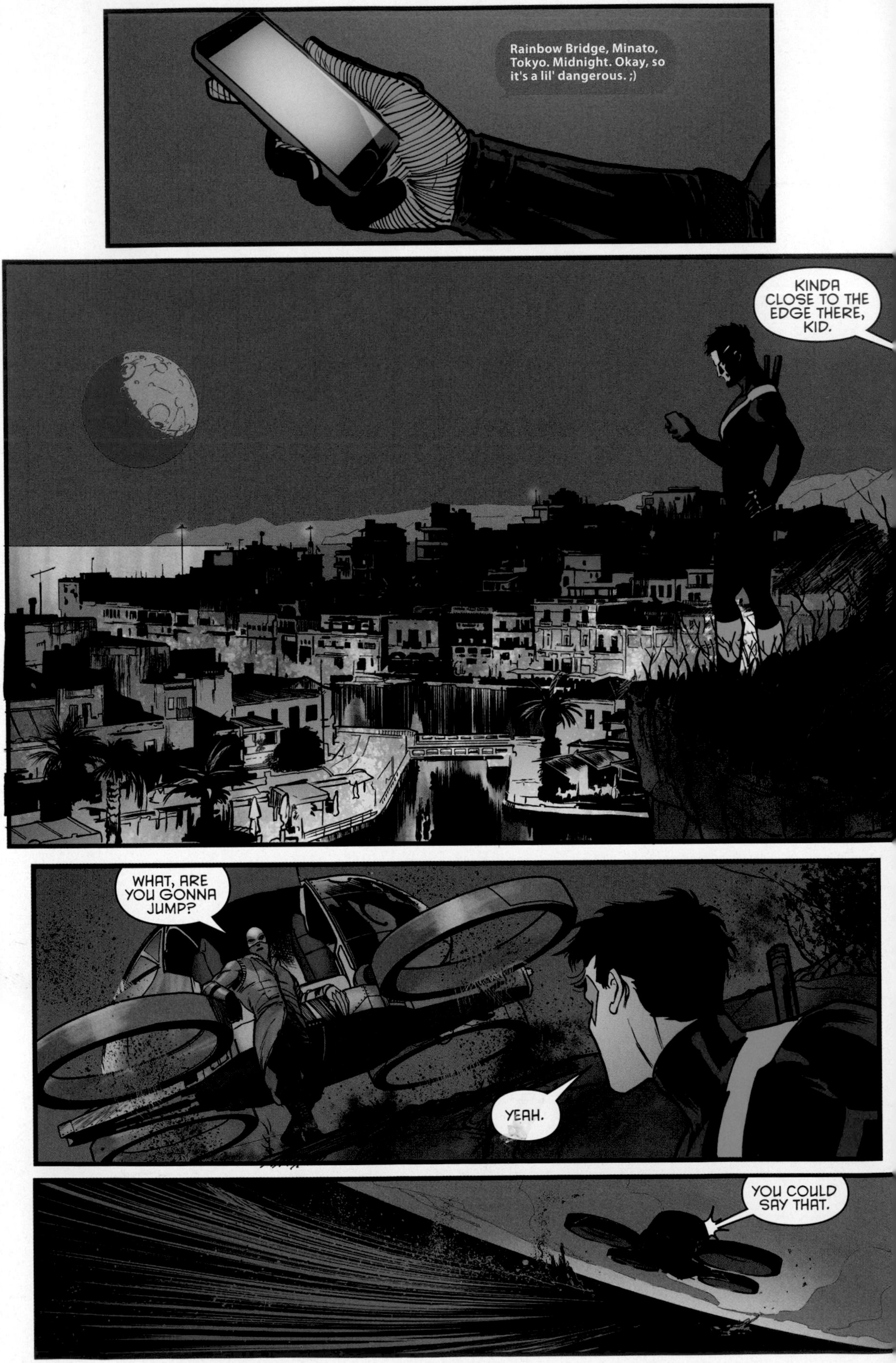
Rainbow Bridge, Minato, Tokyo. Midnight. Okay, so it's a lil' dangerous. ;)
KINDA CLOSE TO THE EDGE THERE, KID.
WHAT, ARE YOU GONNA JUMP?
YEAH.
YOU COULD SAY THAT.

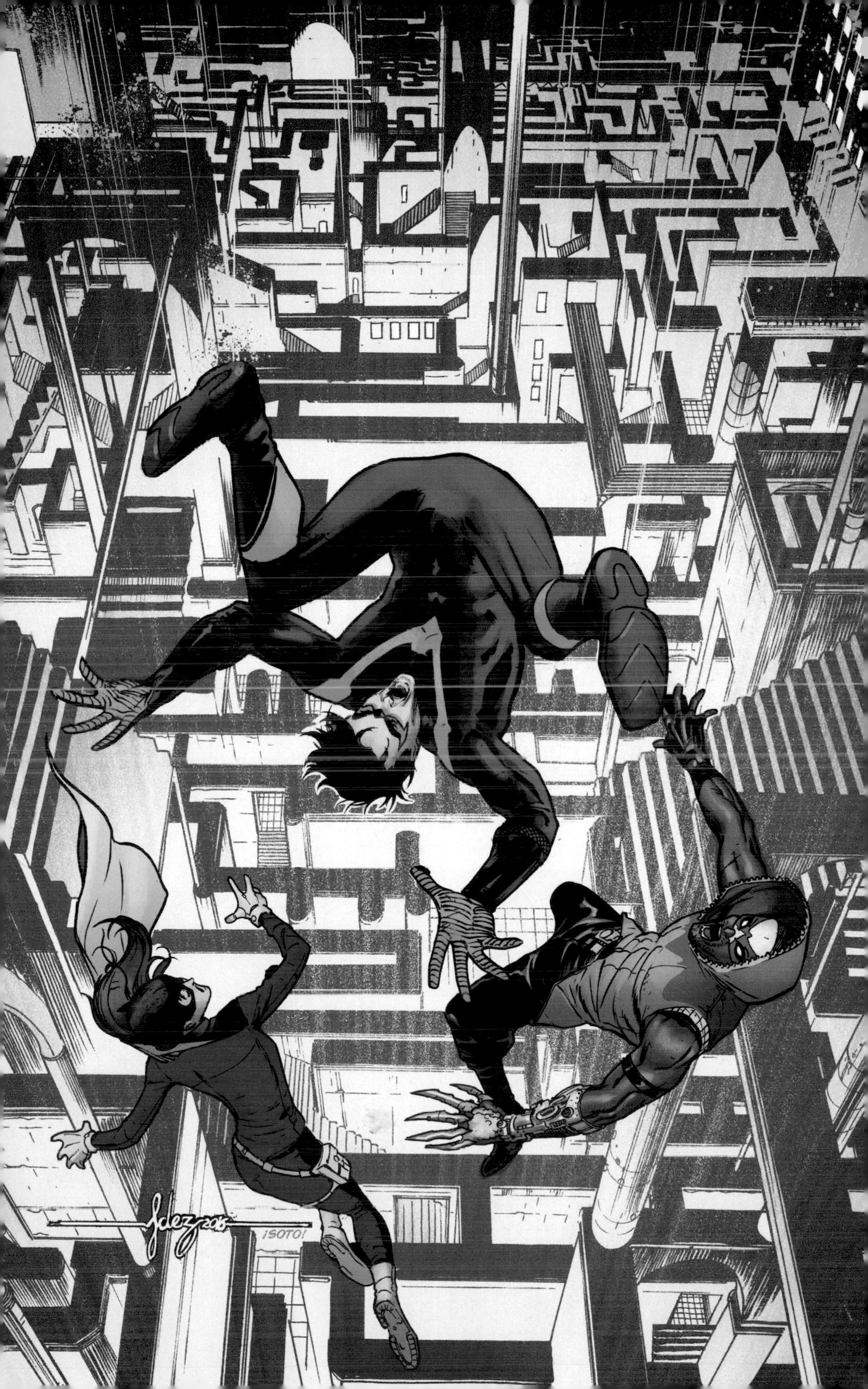
Fdez 2016
¡SOTO!

BETTER THAN BATMAN, PART 3

TIM SEELEY writer ∗ JAVIER FERNÁNDEZ artist ∗ CHRIS SOTOMAYOR colorist
CARLOS M. MANGUAL letterer ∗ JAVIER FERNÁNDEZ and CHRIS SOTOMAYOR cover artists

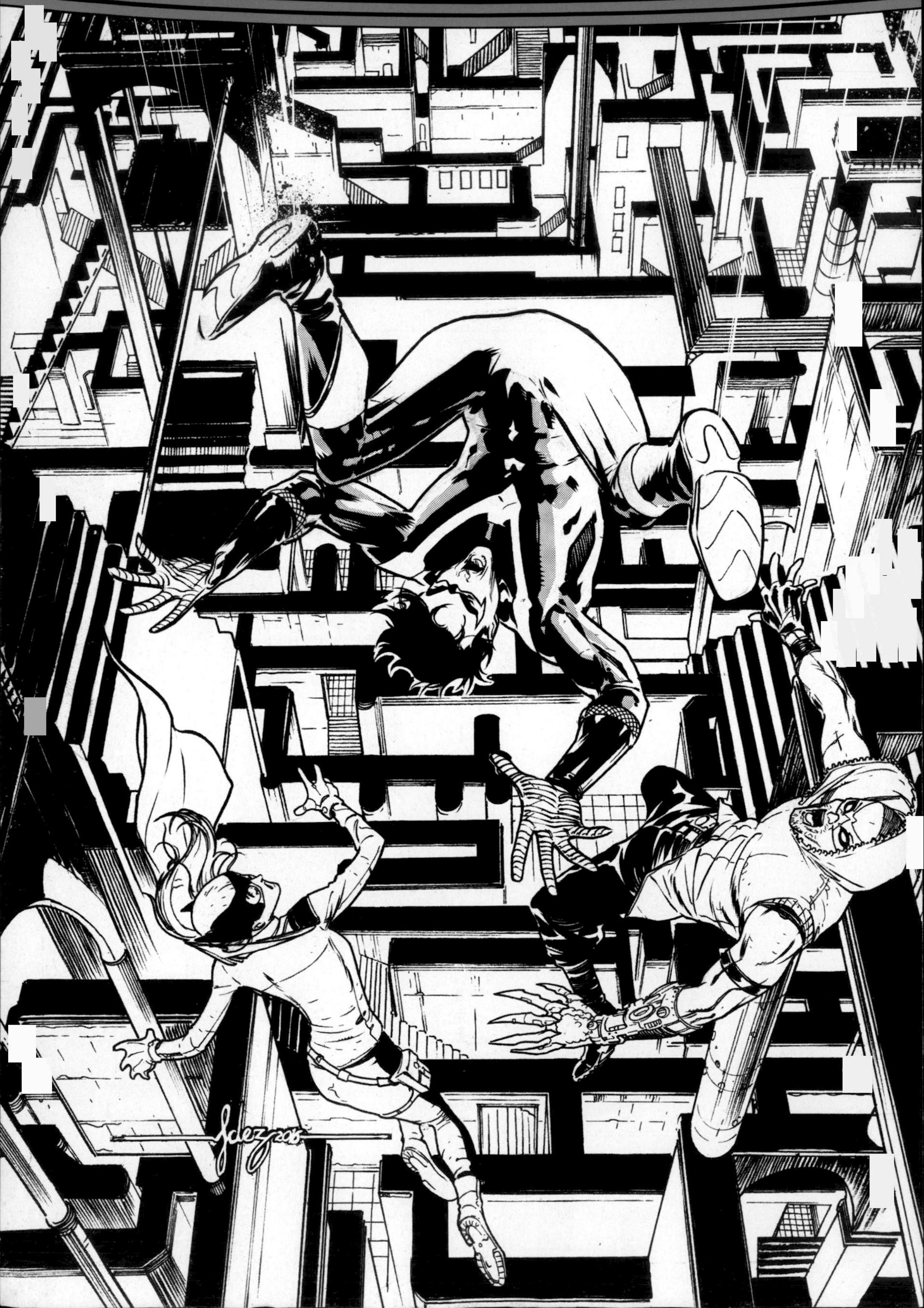

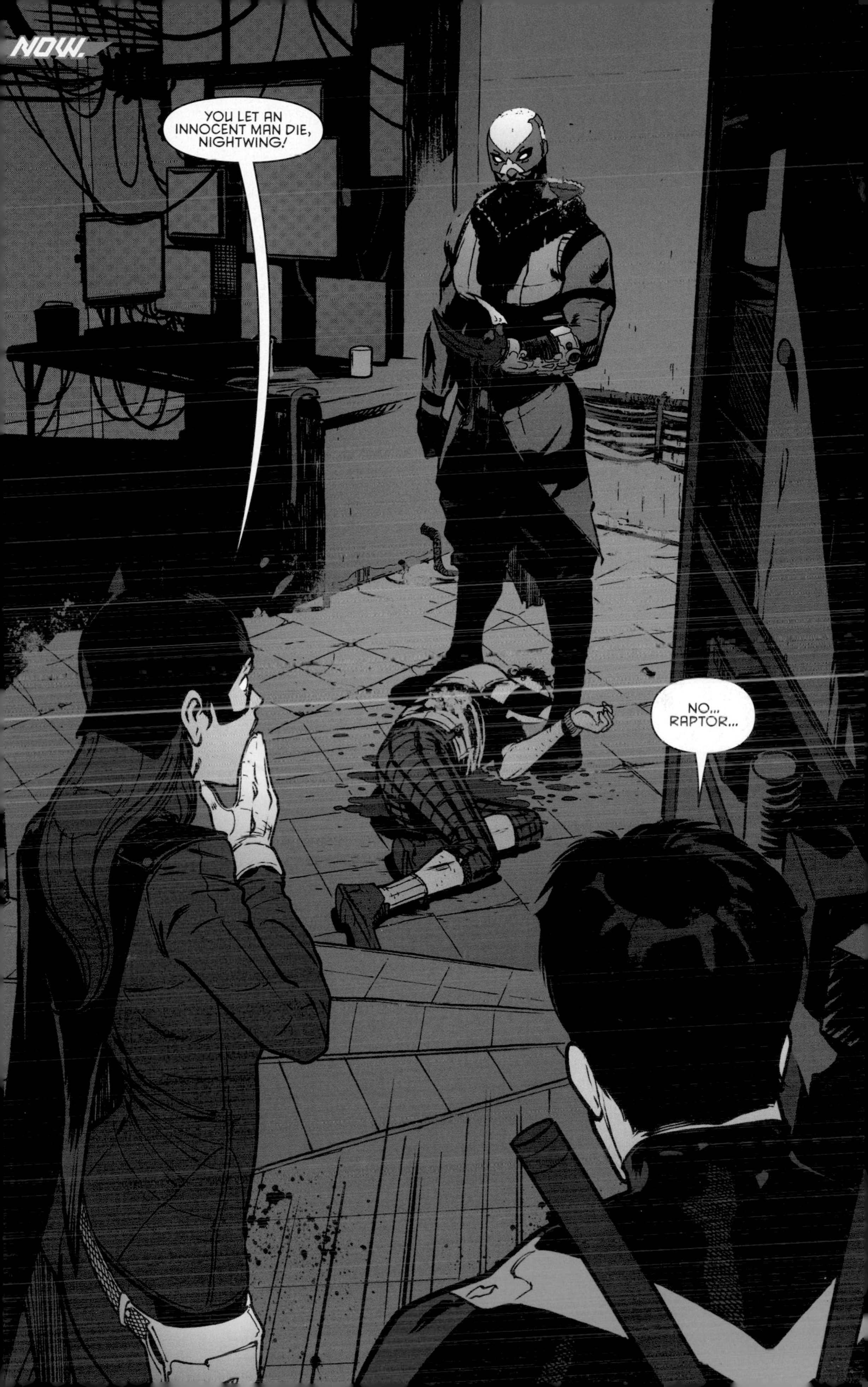
NOW.
YOU LET AN INNOCENT MAN DIE, NIGHTWING!
NO... RAPTOR...

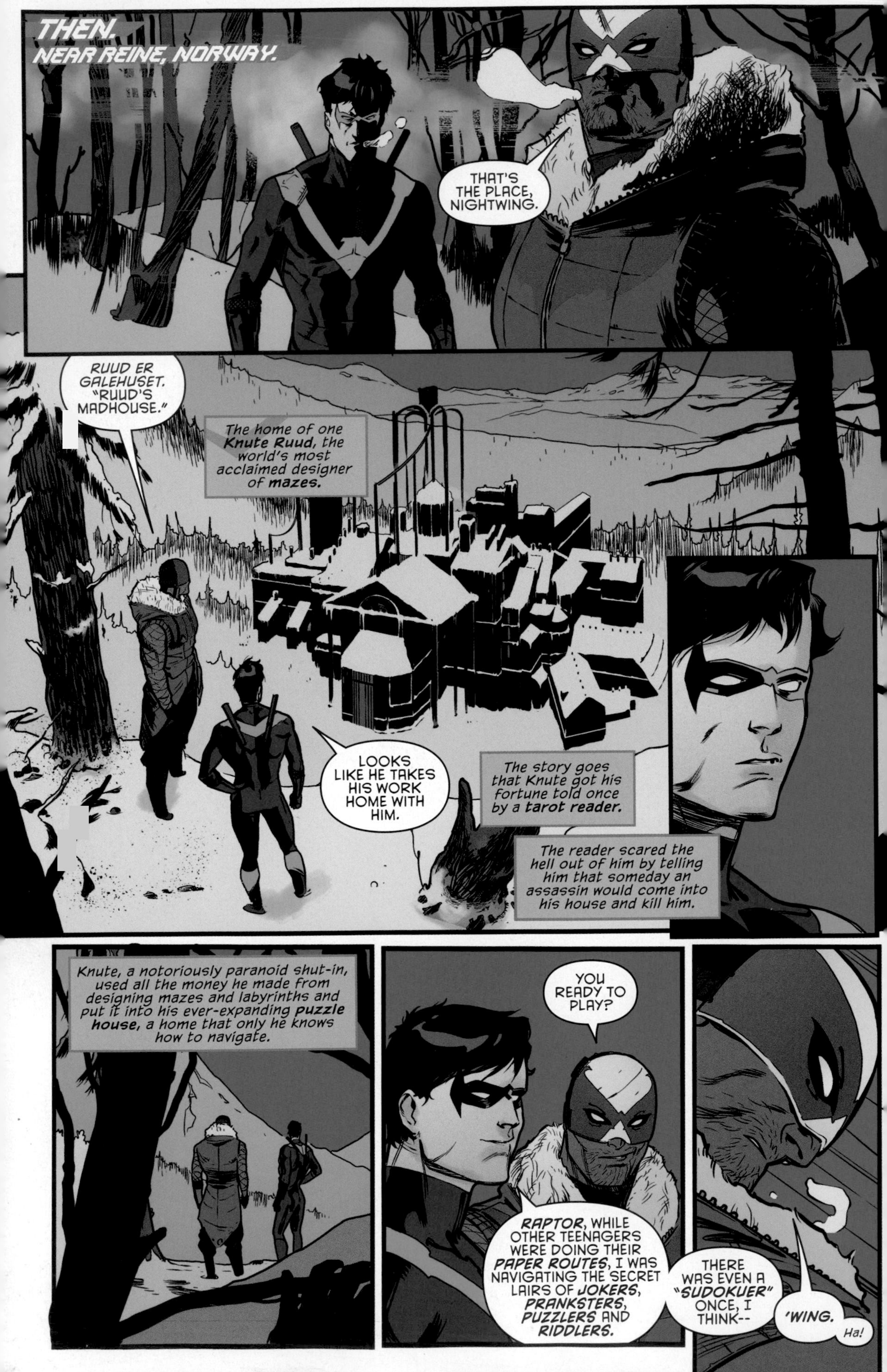
THEN.
NEAR REINE, NORWAY.
THAT'S THE PLACE, NIGHTWING.
RUUD ER GALEHUSET. "RUUD'S MADHOUSE."
The home of one Knute Ruud, the world's most acclaimed designer of mazes.
LOOKS LIKE HE TAKES HIS WORK HOME WITH HIM.
The story goes that Knute got his fortune told once by a tarot reader.
The reader scared the hell out of him by telling him that someday an assassin would come into his house and kill him.
Knute, a notoriously paranoid shut-in, used all the money he made from designing mazes and labyrinths and put it into his ever-expanding puzzle house, a home that only he knows how to navigate.
YOU READY TO PLAY?
RAPTOR, WHILE OTHER TEENAGERS WERE DOING THEIR PAPER ROUTES, I WAS NAVIGATING THE SECRET LAIRS OF JOKERS, PRANKSTERS, PUZZLERS AND RIDDLERS.
THERE WAS EVEN A "SUDOKUER" ONCE, I THINK--
'WING.
Ha!

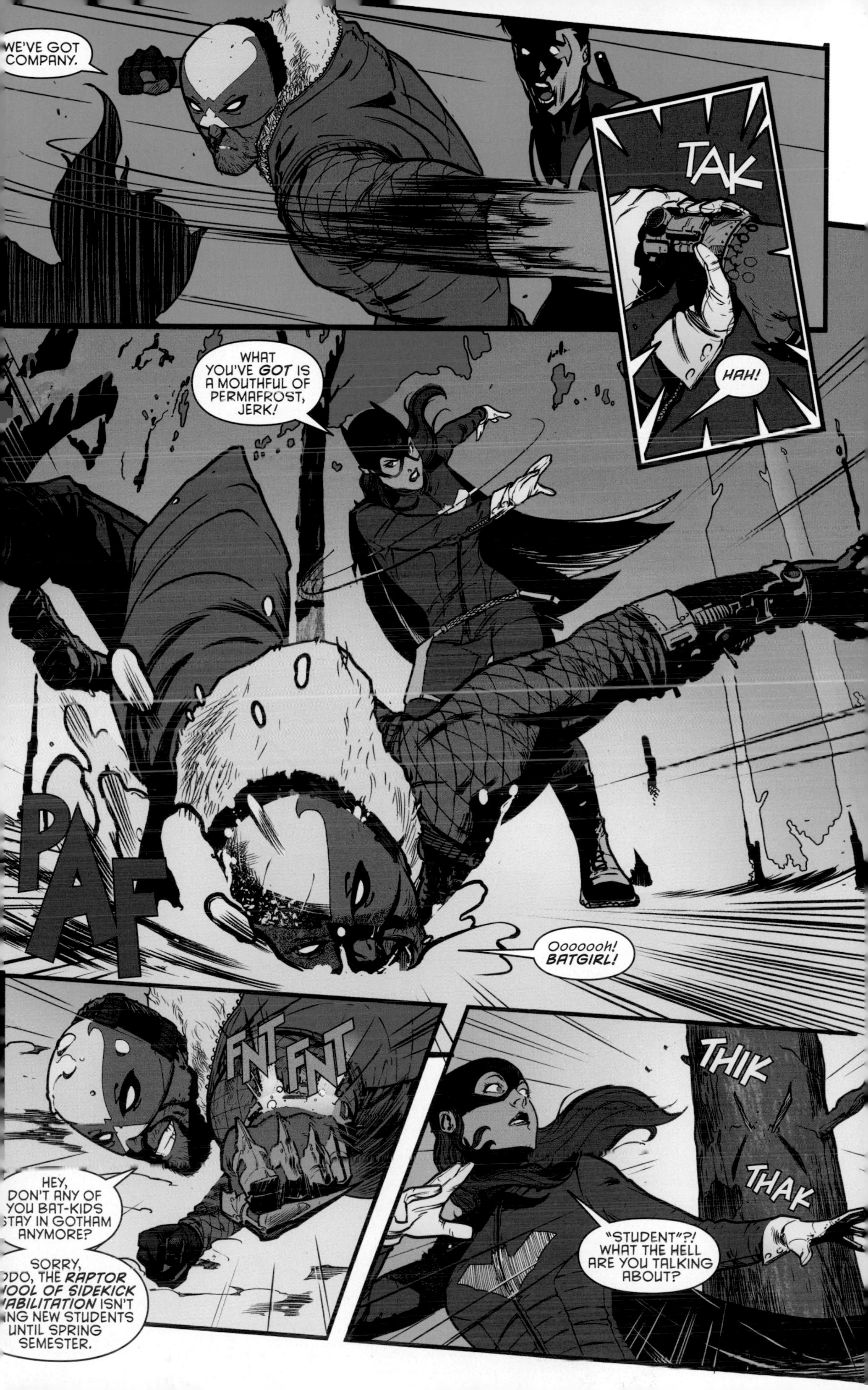
WE'VE GOT COMPANY.
TAK
HAH!
WHAT YOU'VE *GOT* IS A MOUTHFUL OF PERMAFROST, JERK!
PAF
Ooooooh! *BATGIRL!*
FNT FNT
HEY, DON'T ANY OF YOU BAT-KIDS STAY IN GOTHAM ANYMORE?
SORRY, DODO, THE *RAPTOR SCHOOL OF SIDEKICK REHABILITATION* ISN'T TAKING NEW STUDENTS UNTIL SPRING SEMESTER.
THIK
THAK
"STUDENT"?! WHAT THE HELL ARE YOU TALKING ABOUT?

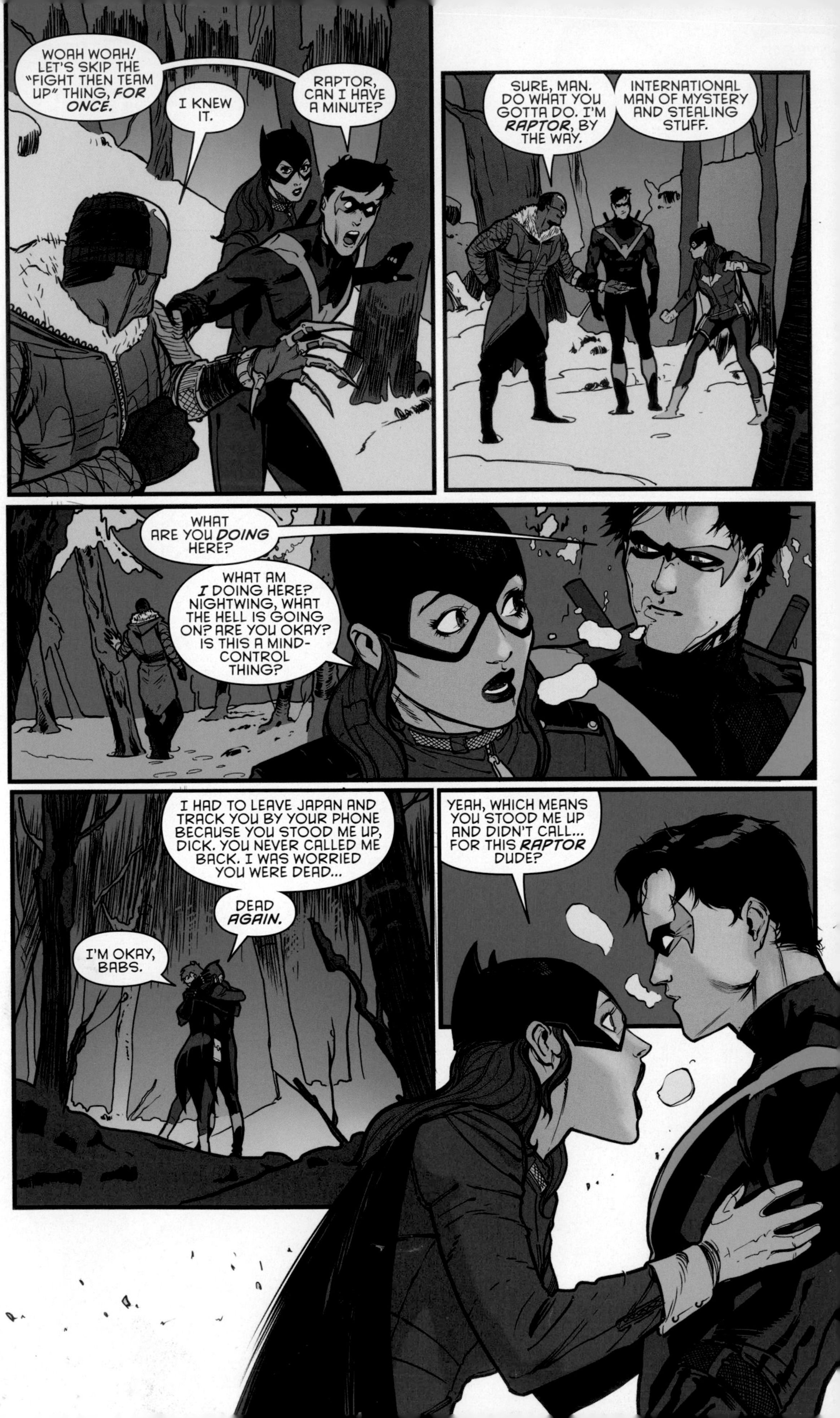
WOAH WOAH! LET'S SKIP THE "FIGHT THEN TEAM UP" THING, FOR ONCE.
I KNEW IT.
RAPTOR, CAN I HAVE A MINUTE?
SURE, MAN. DO WHAT YOU GOTTA DO. I'M RAPTOR, BY THE WAY.
INTERNATIONAL MAN OF MYSTERY AND STEALING STUFF.
WHAT ARE YOU DOING HERE?
WHAT AM I DOING HERE? NIGHTWING, WHAT THE HELL IS GOING ON? ARE YOU OKAY? IS THIS A MIND-CONTROL THING?
I HAD TO LEAVE JAPAN AND TRACK YOU BY YOUR PHONE BECAUSE YOU STOOD ME UP, DICK. YOU NEVER CALLED ME BACK. I WAS WORRIED YOU WERE DEAD...
DEAD AGAIN.
I'M OKAY, BABS.
YEAH, WHICH MEANS YOU STOOD ME UP AND DIDN'T CALL... FOR THIS RAPTOR DUDE?

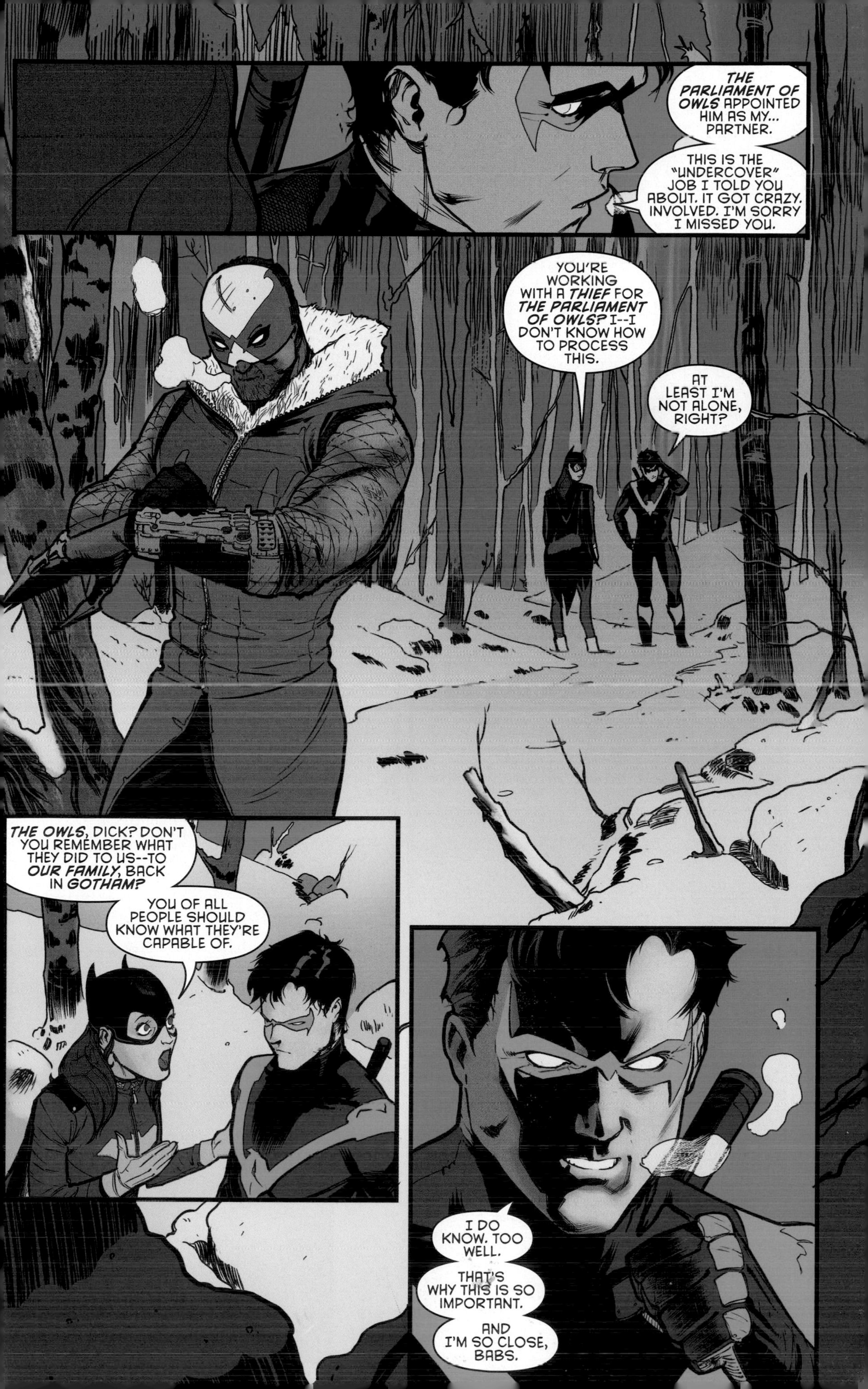
THE PARLIAMENT OF OWLS APPOINTED HIM AS MY... PARTNER.
THIS IS THE "UNDERCOVER" JOB I TOLD YOU ABOUT. IT GOT CRAZY. INVOLVED. I'M SORRY I MISSED YOU.
YOU'RE WORKING WITH A THIEF FOR THE PARLIAMENT OF OWLS? I--I DON'T KNOW HOW TO PROCESS THIS.
AT LEAST I'M NOT ALONE, RIGHT?
THE OWLS, DICK? DON'T YOU REMEMBER WHAT THEY DID TO US--TO OUR FAMILY, BACK IN GOTHAM?
YOU OF ALL PEOPLE SHOULD KNOW WHAT THEY'RE CAPABLE OF.
I DO KNOW. TOO WELL.
THAT'S WHY THIS IS SO IMPORTANT.
AND I'M SO CLOSE, BABS.

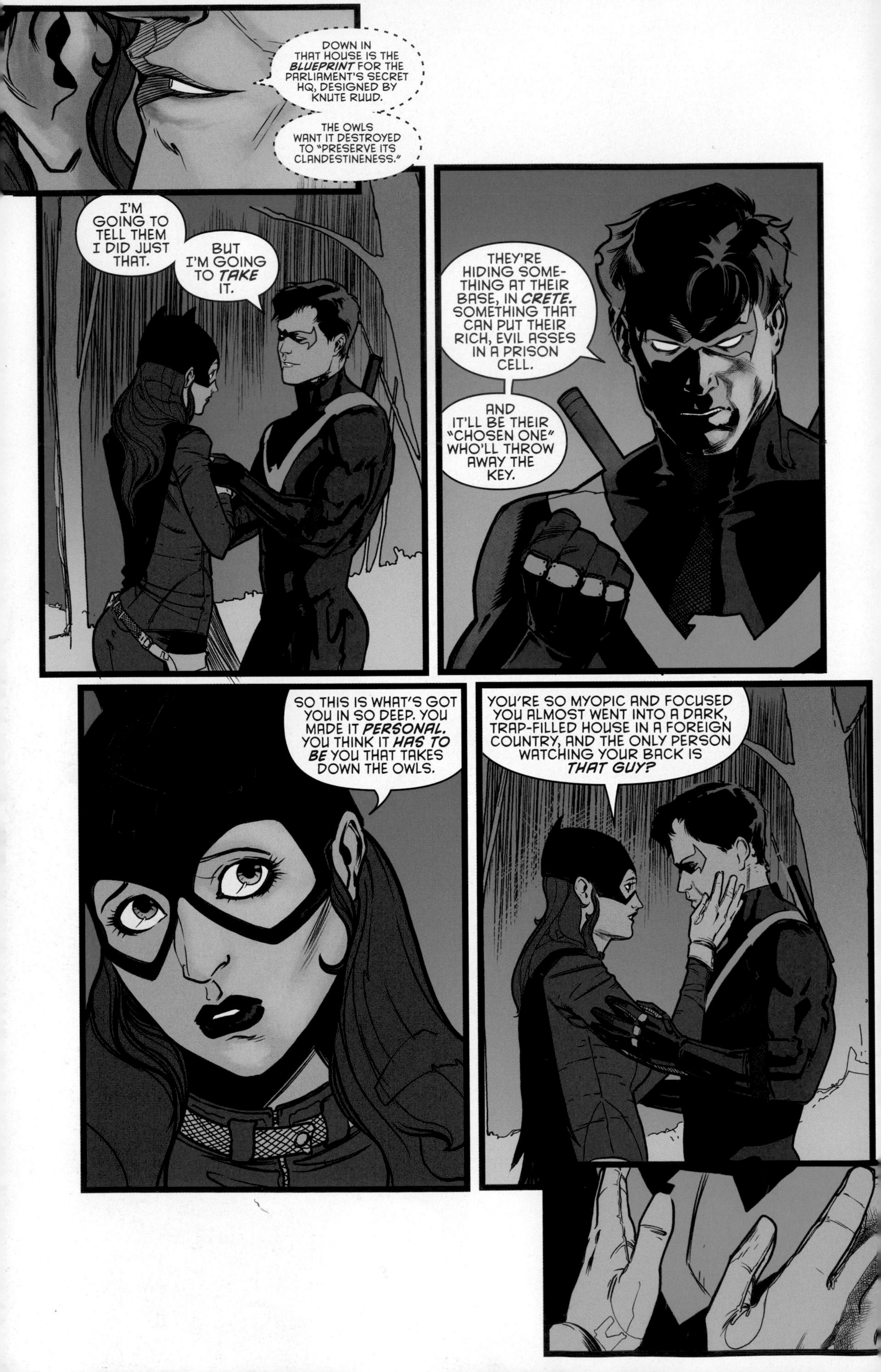
DOWN IN THAT HOUSE IS THE BLUEPRINT FOR THE PARLIAMENT'S SECRET HQ, DESIGNED BY KNUTE RUUD.
THE OWLS WANT IT DESTROYED TO "PRESERVE ITS CLANDESTINENESS."
I'M GOING TO TELL THEM I DID JUST THAT.
BUT I'M GOING TO TAKE IT.
THEY'RE HIDING SOMETHING AT THEIR BASE, IN CRETE. SOMETHING THAT CAN PUT THEIR RICH, EVIL ASSES IN A PRISON CELL.
AND IT'LL BE THEIR "CHOSEN ONE" WHO'LL THROW AWAY THE KEY.
SO THIS IS WHAT'S GOT YOU IN SO DEEP. YOU MADE IT PERSONAL. YOU THINK IT HAS TO BE YOU THAT TAKES DOWN THE OWLS.
YOU'RE SO MYOPIC AND FOCUSED YOU ALMOST WENT INTO A DARK, TRAP-FILLED HOUSE IN A FOREIGN COUNTRY, AND THE ONLY PERSON WATCHING YOUR BACK IS THAT GUY?

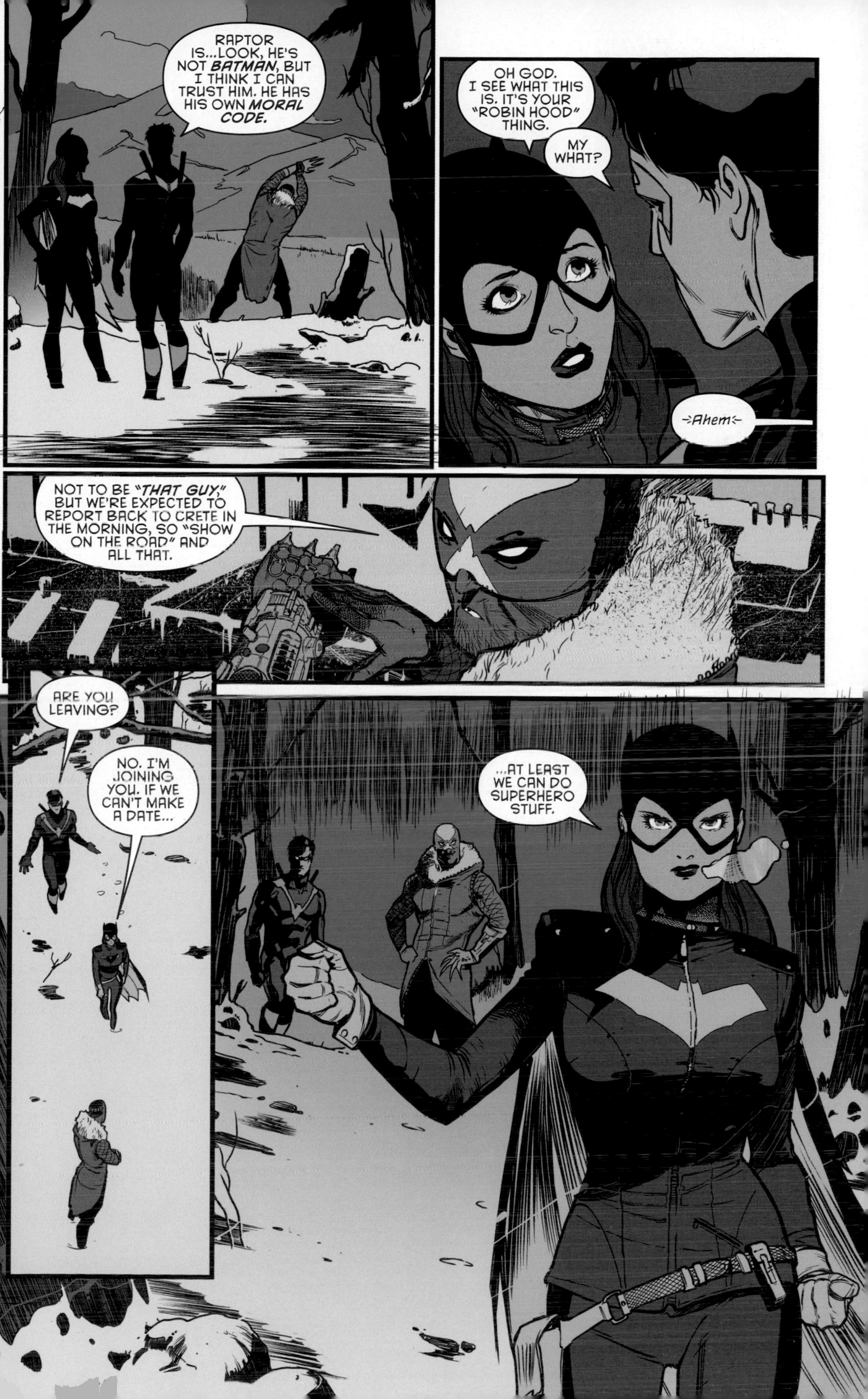
RAPTOR IS...LOOK, HE'S NOT BATMAN, BUT I THINK I CAN TRUST HIM. HE HAS HIS OWN MORAL CODE.
OH GOD. I SEE WHAT THIS IS. IT'S YOUR "ROBIN HOOD" THING.
MY WHAT?
-Ahem-
NOT TO BE "THAT GUY," BUT WE'RE EXPECTED TO REPORT BACK TO CRETE IN THE MORNING, SO "SHOW ON THE ROAD" AND ALL THAT.
ARE YOU LEAVING?
NO. I'M JOINING YOU. IF WE CAN'T MAKE A DATE...
...AT LEAST WE CAN DO SUPERHERO STUFF.

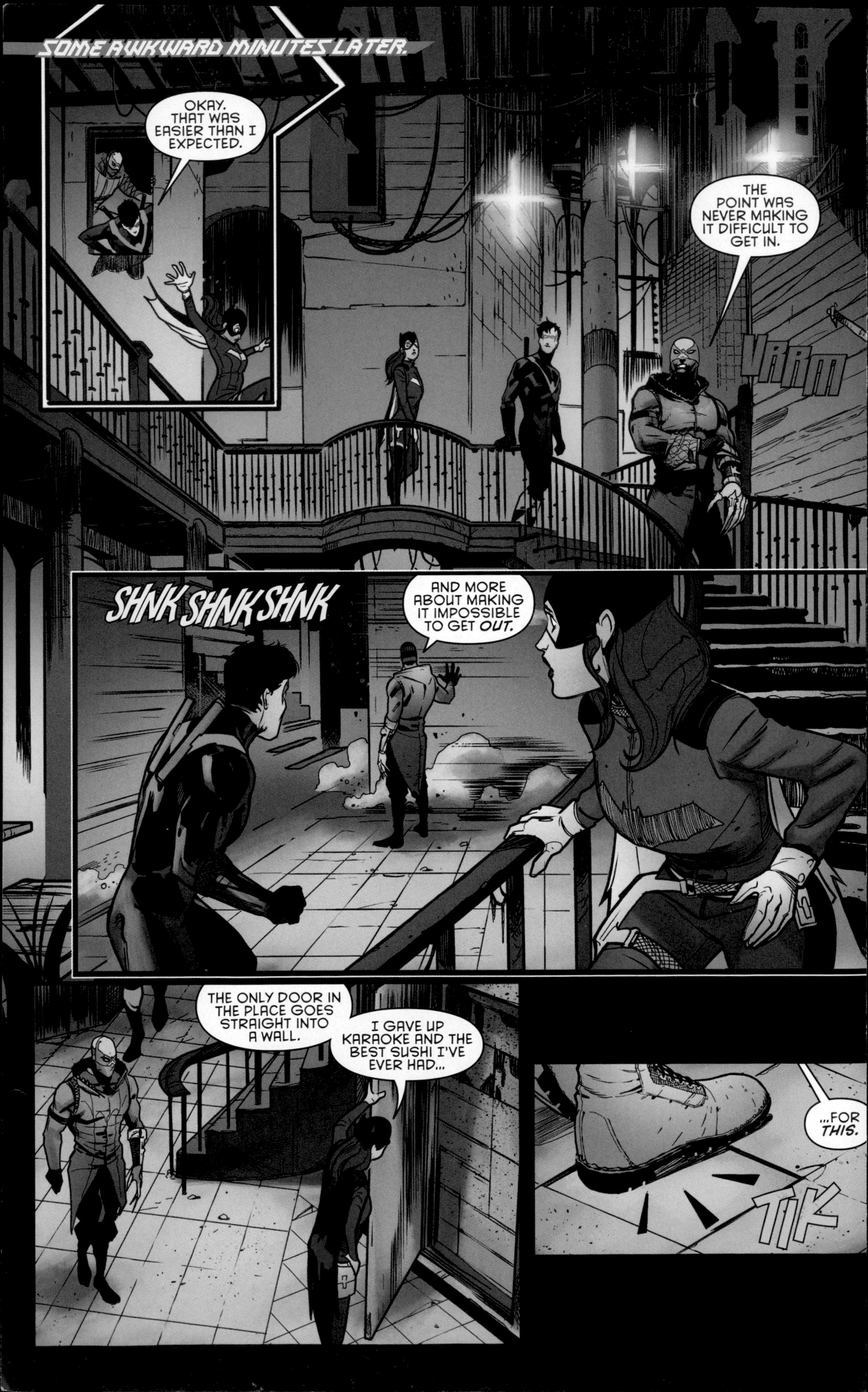
SOME AWKWARD MINUTES LATER.
OKAY. THAT WAS EASIER THAN I EXPECTED.
THE POINT WAS NEVER MAKING IT DIFFICULT TO GET IN.
VRRM
SHNK SHNK SHNK
AND MORE ABOUT MAKING IT IMPOSSIBLE TO GET OUT.
THE ONLY DOOR IN THE PLACE GOES STRAIGHT INTO A WALL.
I GAVE UP KARAOKE AND THE BEST SUSHI I'VE EVER HAD...
...FOR THIS.
TIK

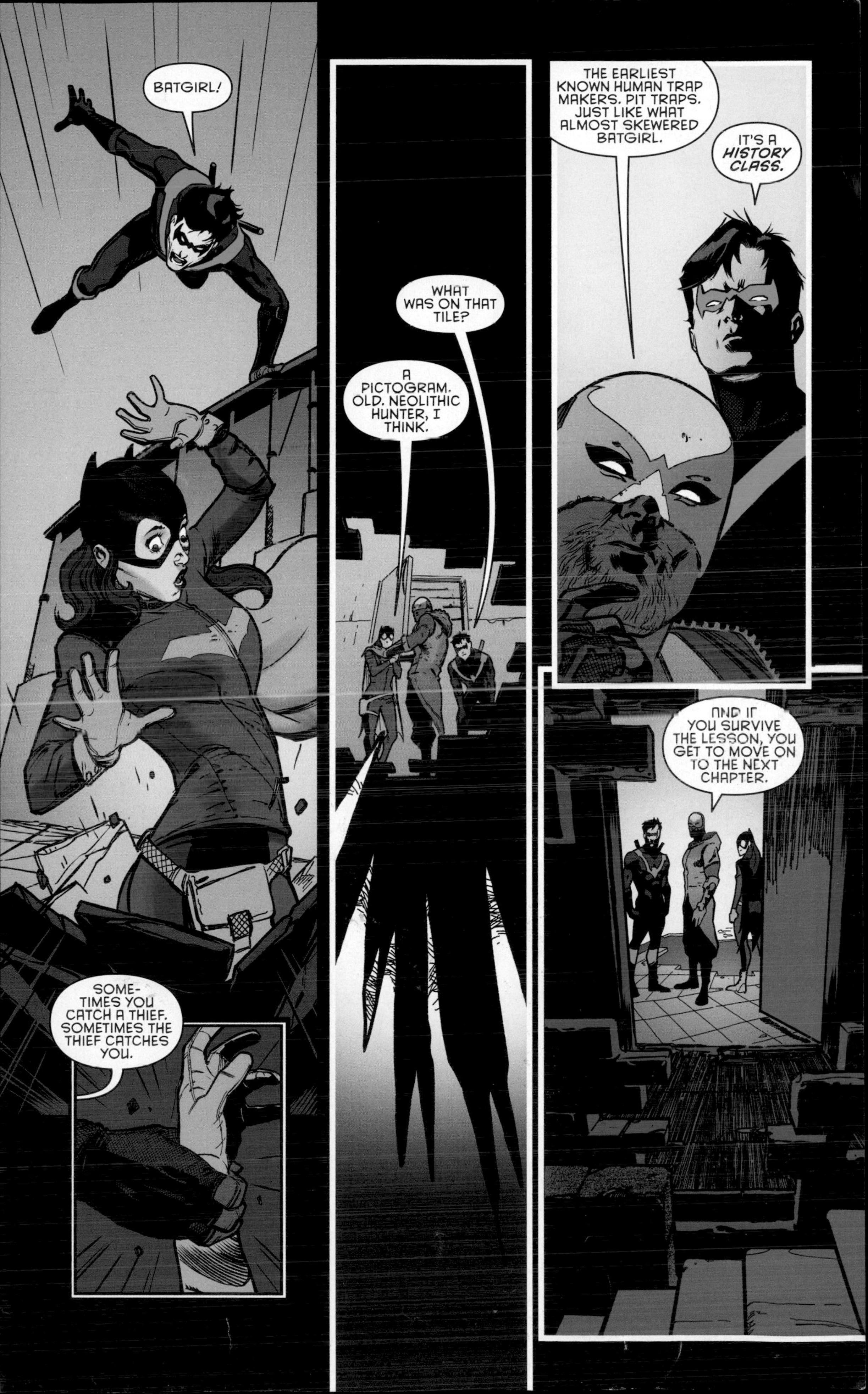
BATGIRL!
SOME-TIMES YOU CATCH A THIEF. SOMETIMES THE THIEF CATCHES YOU.
WHAT WAS ON THAT TILE?
A PICTOGRAM. OLD. NEOLITHIC HUNTER, I THINK.
THE EARLIEST KNOWN HUMAN TRAP MAKERS. PIT TRAPS. JUST LIKE WHAT ALMOST SKEWERED BATGIRL.
IT'S A *HISTORY CLASS.*
AND IF YOU SURVIVE THE LESSON, YOU GET TO MOVE ON TO THE NEXT CHAPTER.

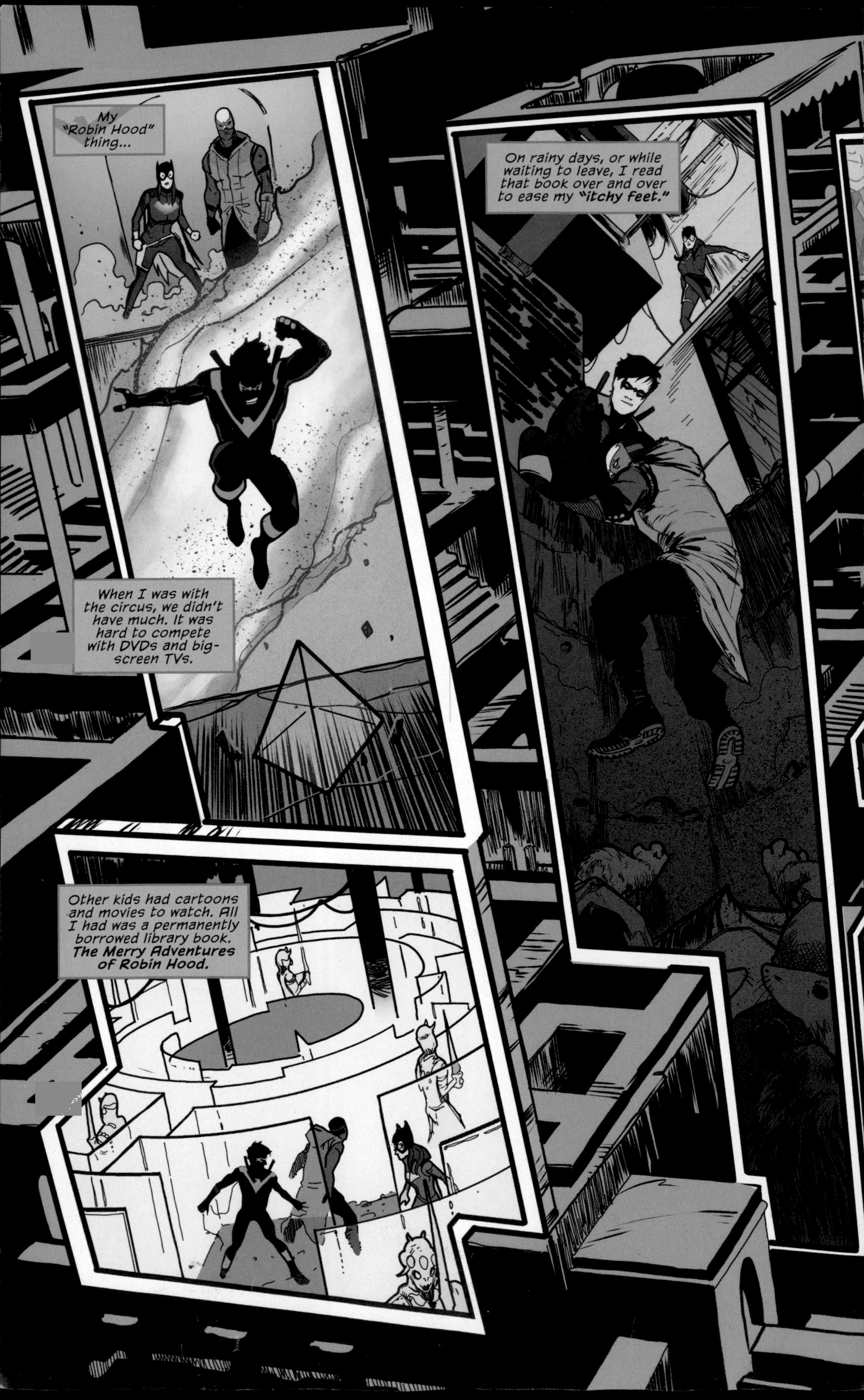
My "Robin Hood" thing...
When I was with the circus, we didn't have much. It was hard to compete with DVDs and big-screen TVs.
Other kids had cartoons and movies to watch. All I had was a permanently borrowed library book. The Merry Adventures of Robin Hood.
On rainy days, or while waiting to leave, I read that book over and over to ease my "itchy feet."

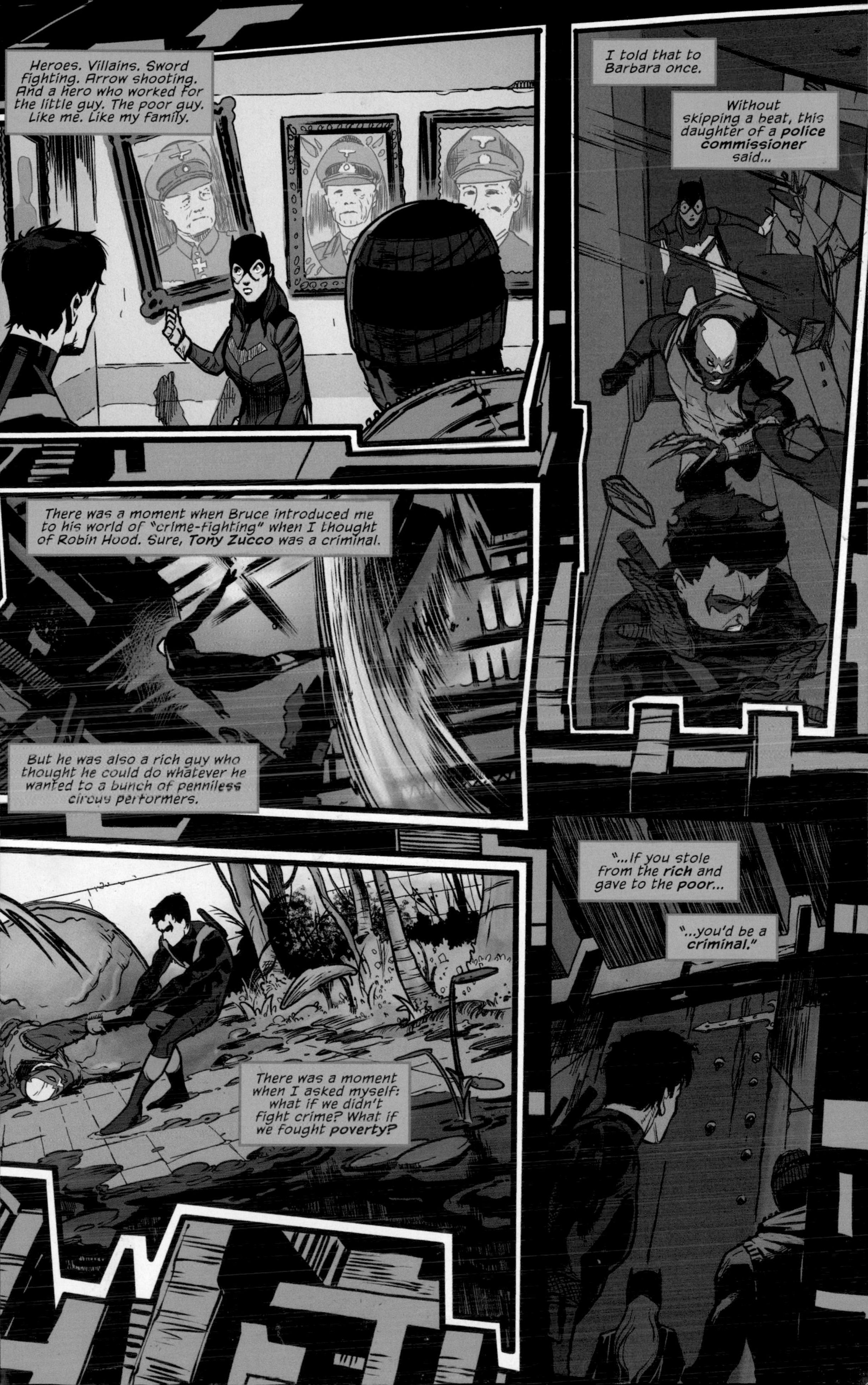

Heroes. Villains. Sword fighting. Arrow shooting. And a hero who worked for the little guy. The poor guy. Like me. Like my family.
I told that to Barbara once.
Without skipping a beat, this daughter of a **police commissioner** said...
There was a moment when Bruce introduced me to his world of "crime-fighting" when I thought of Robin Hood. Sure, **Tony Zucco** was a criminal.
But he was also a rich guy who thought he could do whatever he wanted to a bunch of penniless circus performers.
There was a moment when I asked myself: what if we didn't fight crime? What if we fought **poverty?**
"...If you stole from the **rich** and gave to the **poor**...
"...you'd be a **criminal.**"

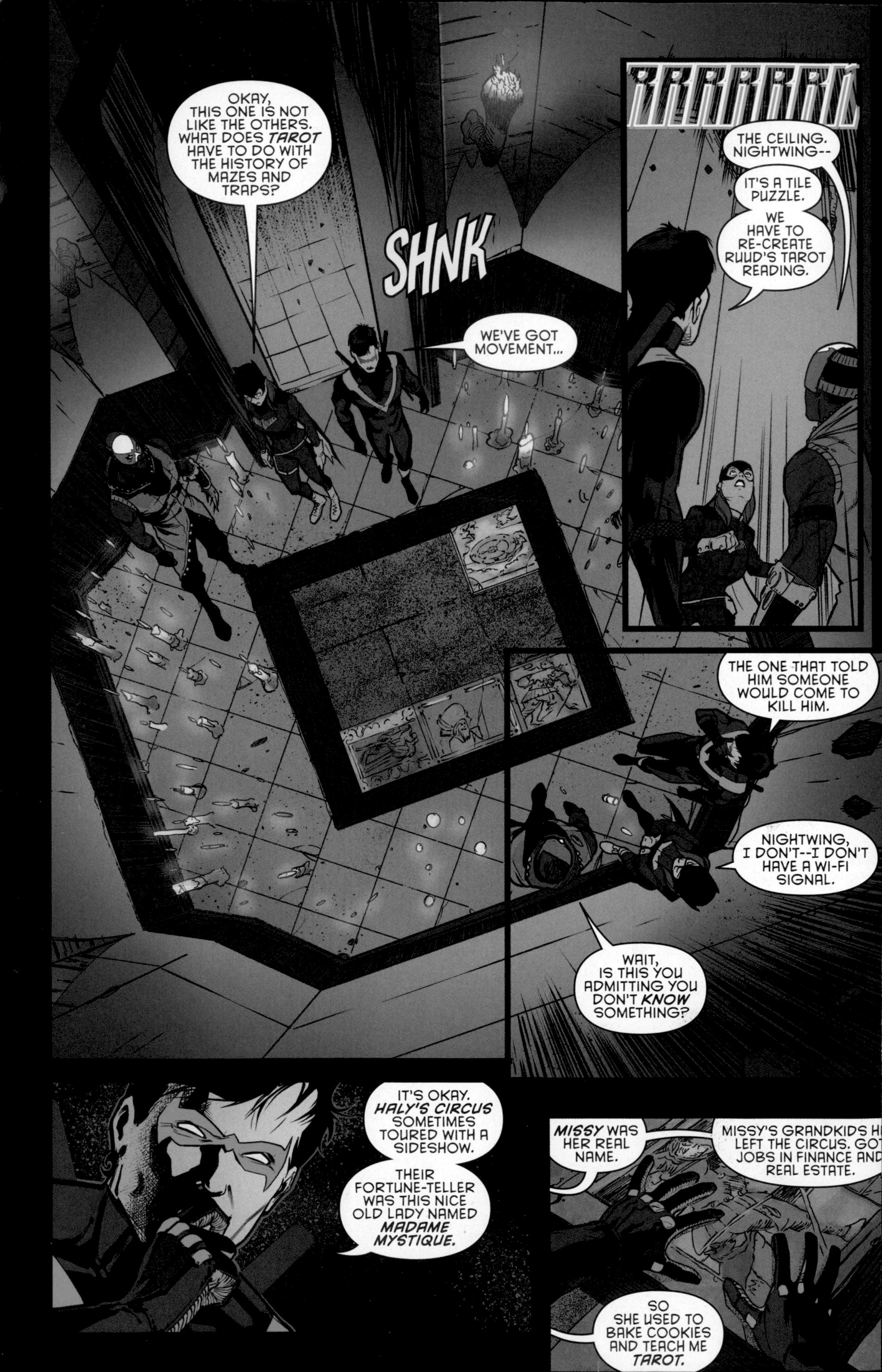
OKAY, THIS ONE IS NOT LIKE THE OTHERS. WHAT DOES TAROT HAVE TO DO WITH THE HISTORY OF MAZES AND TRAPS?
SHNK
WE'VE GOT MOVEMENT...
RRRRRR
THE CEILING. NIGHTWING--
IT'S A TILE PUZZLE.
WE HAVE TO RE-CREATE RUUD'S TAROT READING.
THE ONE THAT TOLD HIM SOMEONE WOULD COME TO KILL HIM.
NIGHTWING, I DON'T--I DON'T HAVE A WI-FI SIGNAL.
WAIT, IS THIS YOU ADMITTING YOU DON'T KNOW SOMETHING?
IT'S OKAY. HALY'S CIRCUS SOMETIMES TOURED WITH A SIDESHOW.
THEIR FORTUNE-TELLER WAS THIS NICE OLD LADY NAMED MADAME MYSTIQUE.
MISSY WAS HER REAL NAME.
MISSY'S GRANDKIDS H LEFT THE CIRCUS. GOT JOBS IN FINANCE AND REAL ESTATE.
SO SHE USED TO BAKE COOKIES AND TEACH ME TAROT.

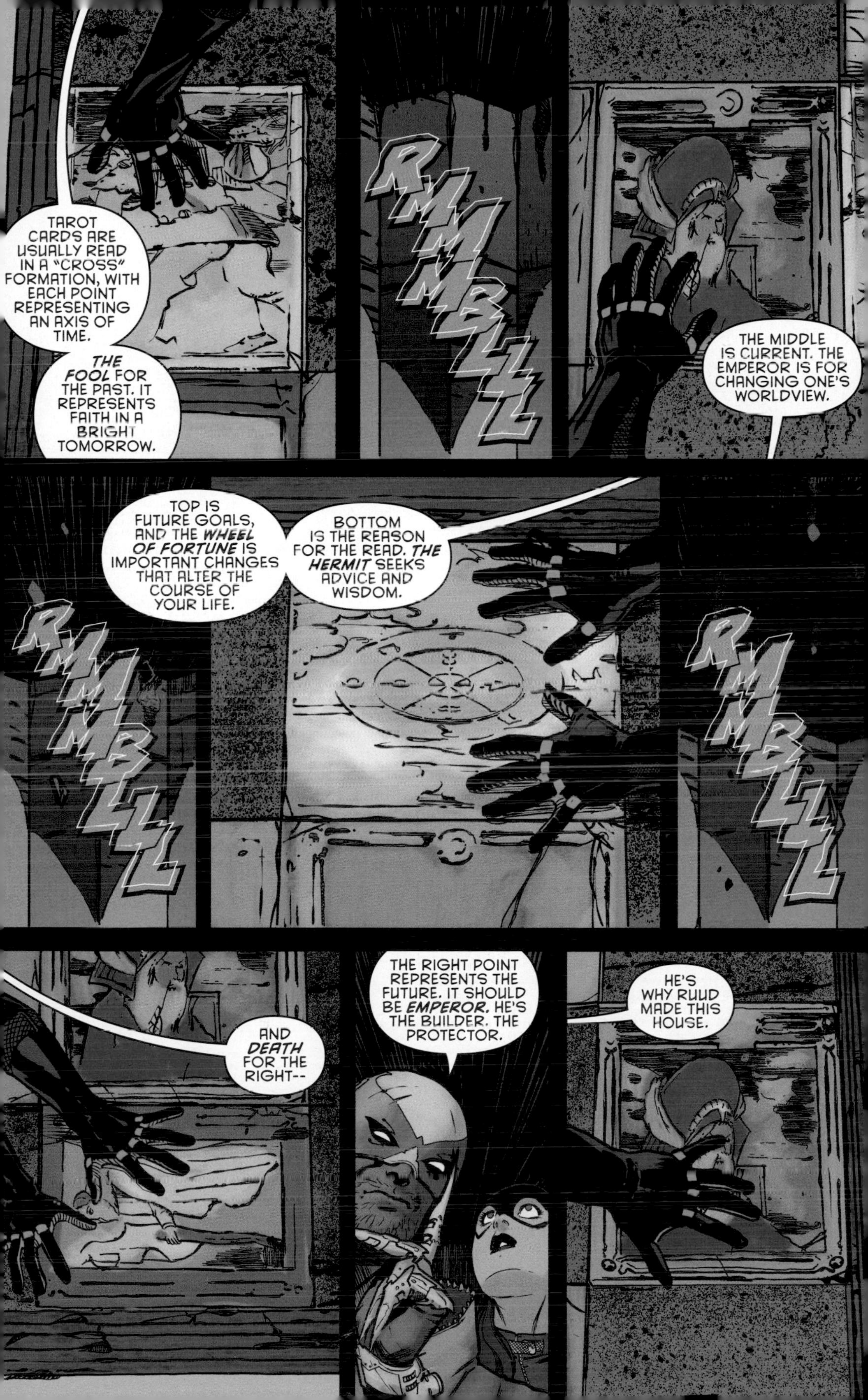
TAROT CARDS ARE USUALLY READ IN A "CROSS" FORMATION, WITH EACH POINT REPRESENTING AN AXIS OF TIME.
THE FOOL FOR THE PAST. IT REPRESENTS FAITH IN A BRIGHT TOMORROW.
RMMMBLLL
THE MIDDLE IS CURRENT. THE EMPEROR IS FOR CHANGING ONE'S WORLDVIEW.
TOP IS FUTURE GOALS, AND THE WHEEL OF FORTUNE IS IMPORTANT CHANGES THAT ALTER THE COURSE OF YOUR LIFE.
BOTTOM IS THE REASON FOR THE READ. THE HERMIT SEEKS ADVICE AND WISDOM.
RMMMBLLL
RMMMBLLL
AND DEATH FOR THE RIGHT--
THE RIGHT POINT REPRESENTS THE FUTURE. IT SHOULD BE EMPEROR. HE'S THE BUILDER. THE PROTECTOR.
HE'S WHY RUUD MADE THIS HOUSE.

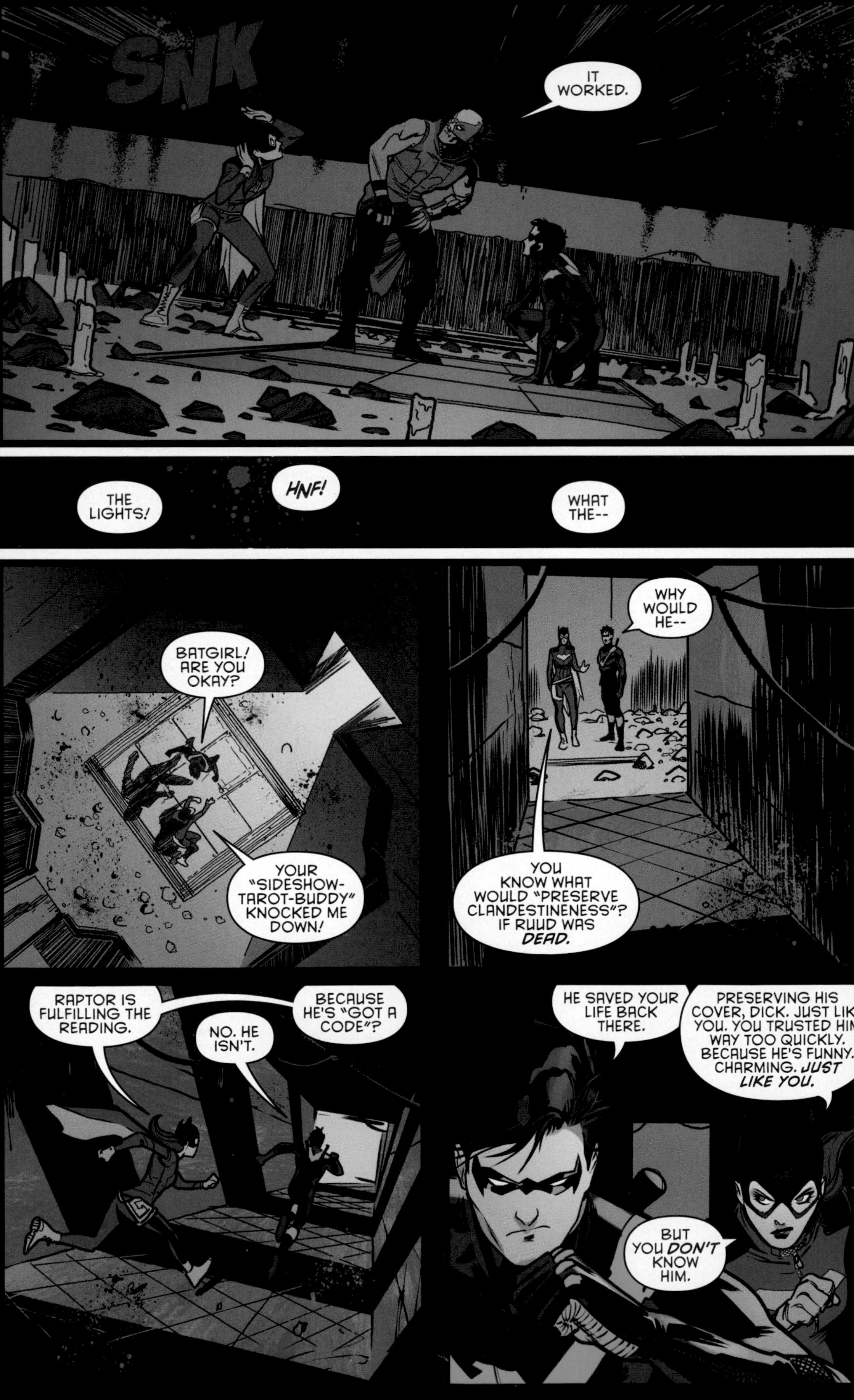
SNK
IT WORKED.
THE LIGHTS!
HNF!
WHAT THE--
BATGIRL! ARE YOU OKAY?
YOUR "SIDESHOW-TAROT-BUDDY" KNOCKED ME DOWN!
WHY WOULD HE--
YOU KNOW WHAT WOULD "PRESERVE CLANDESTINENESS"? IF RUUD WAS DEAD.
RAPTOR IS FULFILLING THE READING.
BECAUSE HE'S "GOT A CODE"?
NO. HE ISN'T.
HE SAVED YOUR LIFE BACK THERE.
PRESERVING HIS COVER, DICK. JUST LIKE YOU. YOU TRUSTED HIM WAY TOO QUICKLY. BECAUSE HE'S FUNNY. CHARMING. JUST LIKE YOU.
BUT YOU DON'T KNOW HIM.

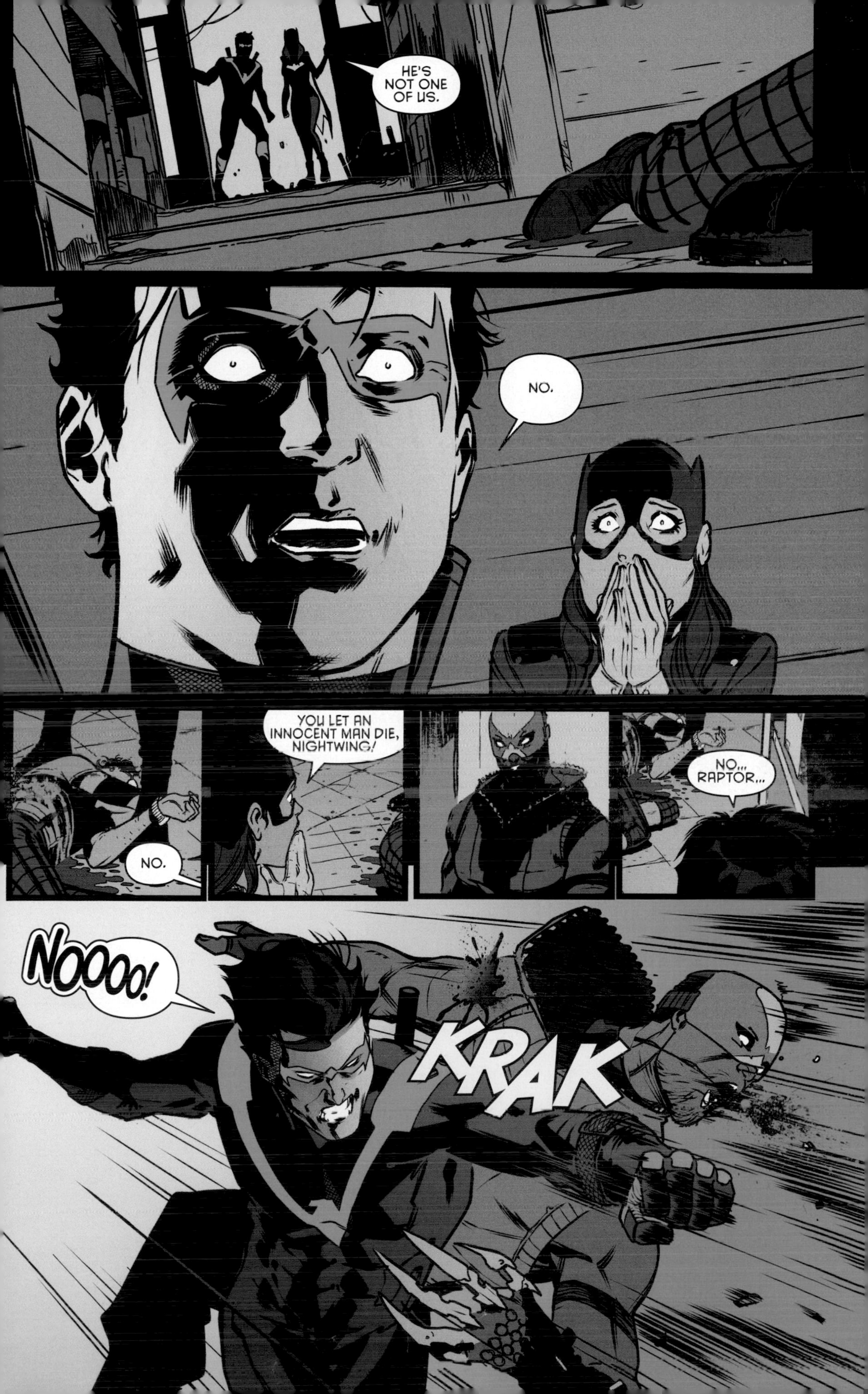
HE'S NOT ONE OF US.
NO.
NO.
YOU LET AN INNOCENT MAN DIE, NIGHTWING!
NO... RAPTOR...
NOOOO!
KRAK

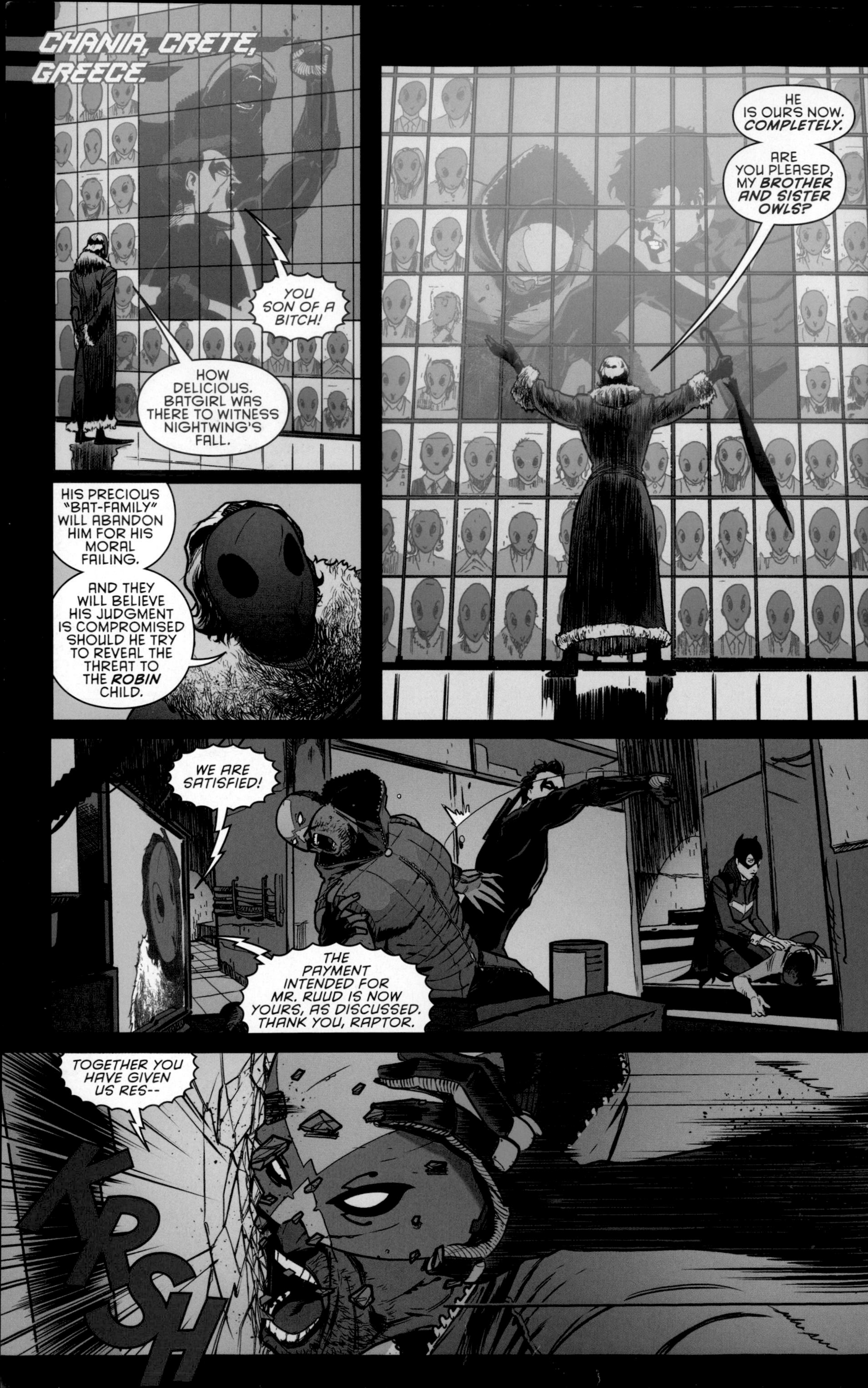
CHANIA, CRETE, GREECE.
YOU SON OF A BITCH!
HOW DELICIOUS. BATGIRL WAS THERE TO WITNESS NIGHTWING'S FALL.
HE IS OURS NOW. COMPLETELY.
ARE YOU PLEASED, MY BROTHER AND SISTER OWLS?
HIS PRECIOUS "BAT-FAMILY" WILL ABANDON HIM FOR HIS MORAL FAILING.
AND THEY WILL BELIEVE HIS JUDGMENT IS COMPROMISED SHOULD HE TRY TO REVEAL THE THREAT TO THE ROBIN CHILD.
WE ARE SATISFIED!
THE PAYMENT INTENDED FOR MR. RUUD IS NOW YOURS, AS DISCUSSED. THANK YOU, RAPTOR.
TOGETHER YOU HAVE GIVEN US RES--
KRSH

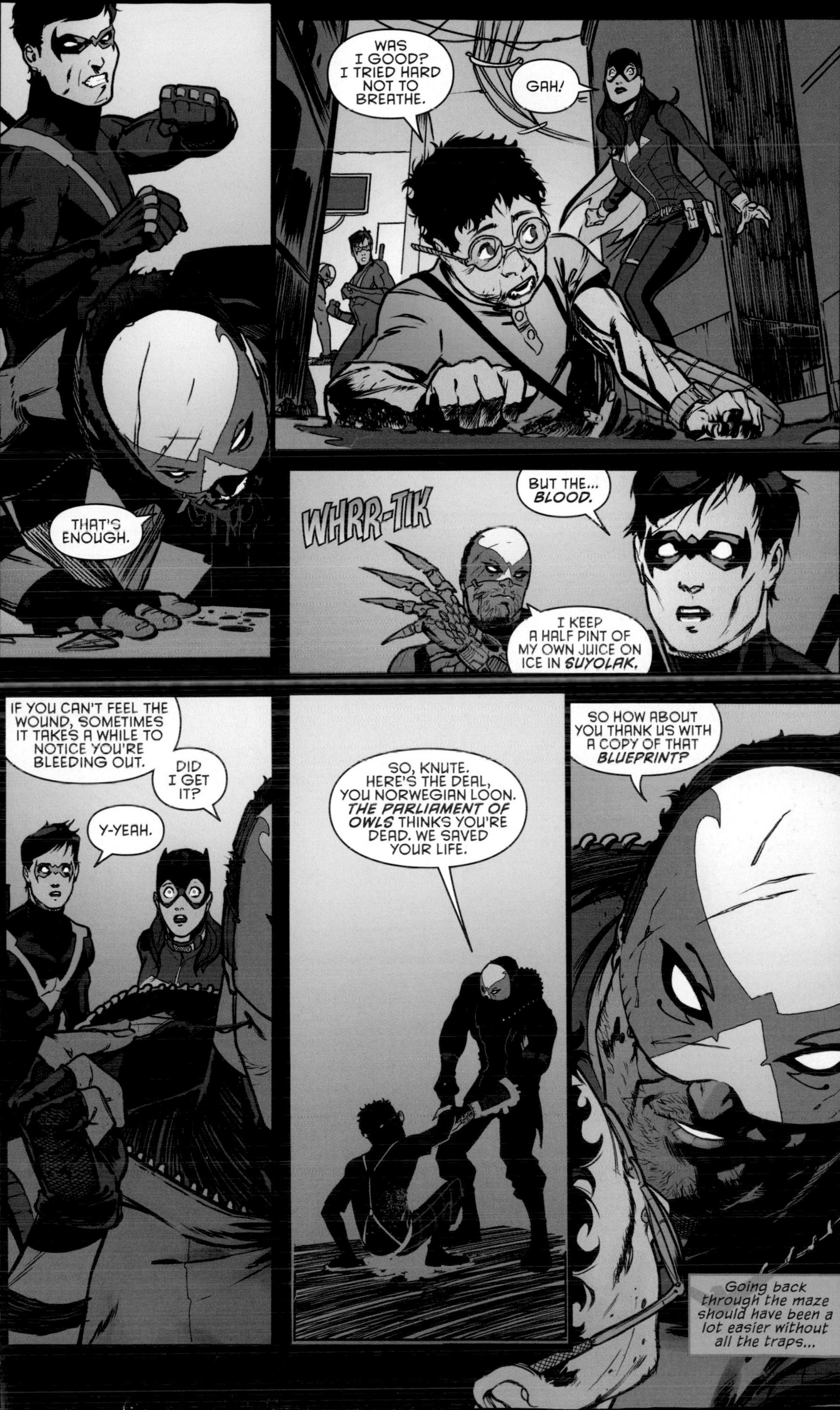
WAS I GOOD? I TRIED HARD NOT TO BREATHE.
GAH!
THAT'S ENOUGH.
WHRR-TIK
BUT THE... *BLOOD.*
I KEEP A HALF PINT OF MY OWN JUICE ON ICE IN *SUYOLAK.*
IF YOU CAN'T FEEL THE WOUND, SOMETIMES IT TAKES A WHILE TO NOTICE YOU'RE BLEEDING OUT.
DID I GET IT?
Y-YEAH.
SO, KNUTE. HERE'S THE DEAL, YOU NORWEGIAN LOON. *THE PARLIAMENT OF OWLS* THINKS YOU'RE DEAD. WE SAVED YOUR LIFE.
SO HOW ABOUT YOU THANK US WITH A COPY OF THAT *BLUEPRINT?*
Going back through the maze should have been a lot easier without all the traps...

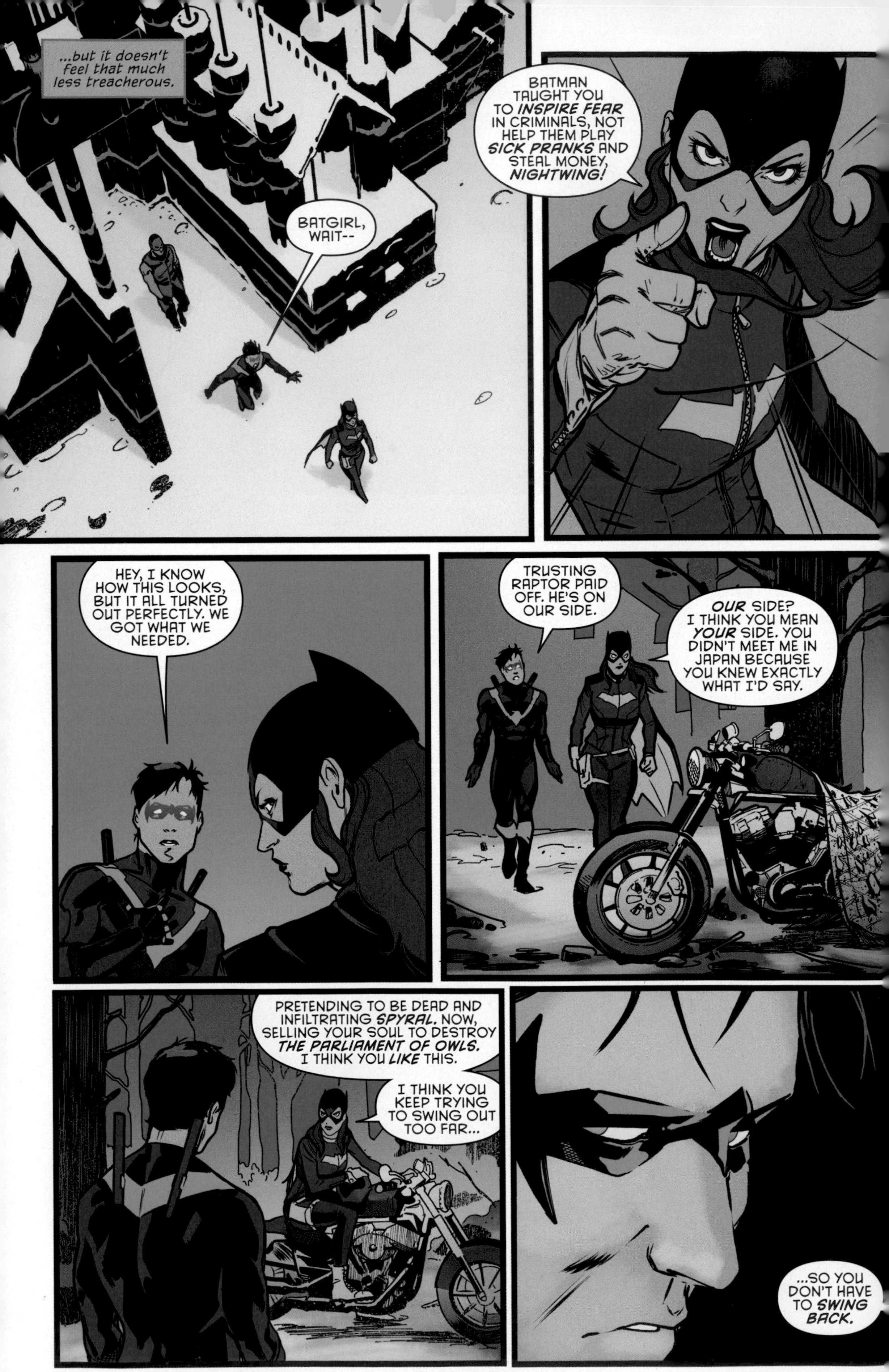

...but it doesn't feel that much less treacherous.
BATGIRL, WAIT--
BATMAN TAUGHT YOU TO INSPIRE FEAR IN CRIMINALS, NOT HELP THEM PLAY SICK PRANKS AND STEAL MONEY, NIGHTWING!
HEY, I KNOW HOW THIS LOOKS, BUT IT ALL TURNED OUT PERFECTLY. WE GOT WHAT WE NEEDED.
TRUSTING RAPTOR PAID OFF. HE'S ON OUR SIDE.
OUR SIDE? I THINK YOU MEAN YOUR SIDE. YOU DIDN'T MEET ME IN JAPAN BECAUSE YOU KNEW EXACTLY WHAT I'D SAY.
PRETENDING TO BE DEAD AND INFILTRATING SPYRAL. NOW, SELLING YOUR SOUL TO DESTROY THE PARLIAMENT OF OWLS. I THINK YOU LIKE THIS.
I THINK YOU KEEP TRYING TO SWING OUT TOO FAR...
...SO YOU DON'T HAVE TO SWING BACK.

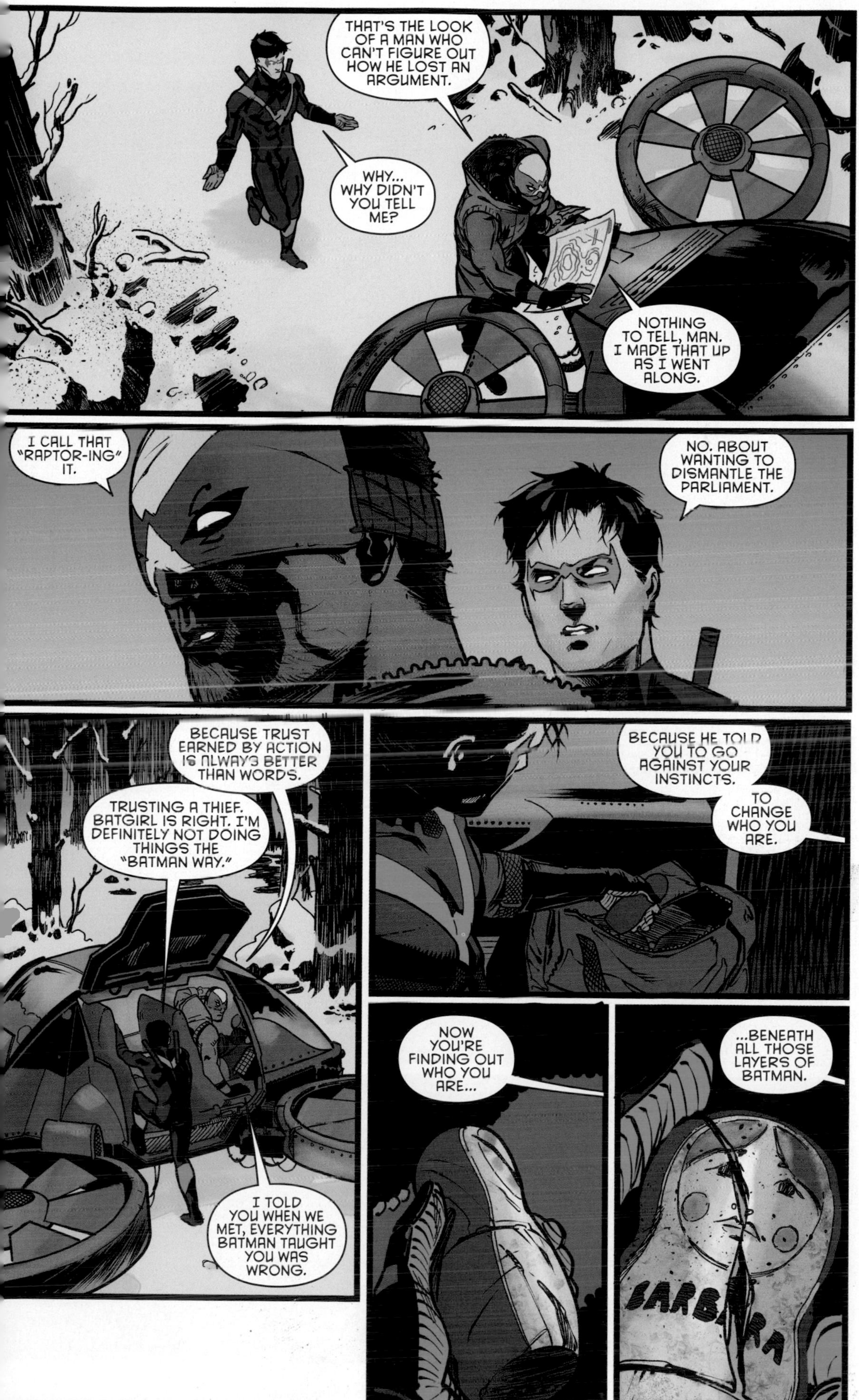
THAT'S THE LOOK OF A MAN WHO CAN'T FIGURE OUT HOW HE LOST AN ARGUMENT.
WHY... WHY DIDN'T YOU TELL ME?
NOTHING TO TELL, MAN. I MADE THAT UP AS I WENT ALONG.
I CALL THAT "RAPTOR-ING" IT.
NO. ABOUT WANTING TO DISMANTLE THE PARLIAMENT.
BECAUSE TRUST EARNED BY ACTION IS ALWAYS BETTER THAN WORDS.
TRUSTING A THIEF. BATGIRL IS RIGHT. I'M DEFINITELY NOT DOING THINGS THE "BATMAN WAY."
I TOLD YOU WHEN WE MET, EVERYTHING BATMAN TAUGHT YOU WAS WRONG.
BECAUSE HE TOLD YOU TO GO AGAINST YOUR INSTINCTS.
TO CHANGE WHO YOU ARE.
NOW YOU'RE FINDING OUT WHO YOU ARE...
...BENEATH ALL THOSE LAYERS OF BATMAN.
BARBARA

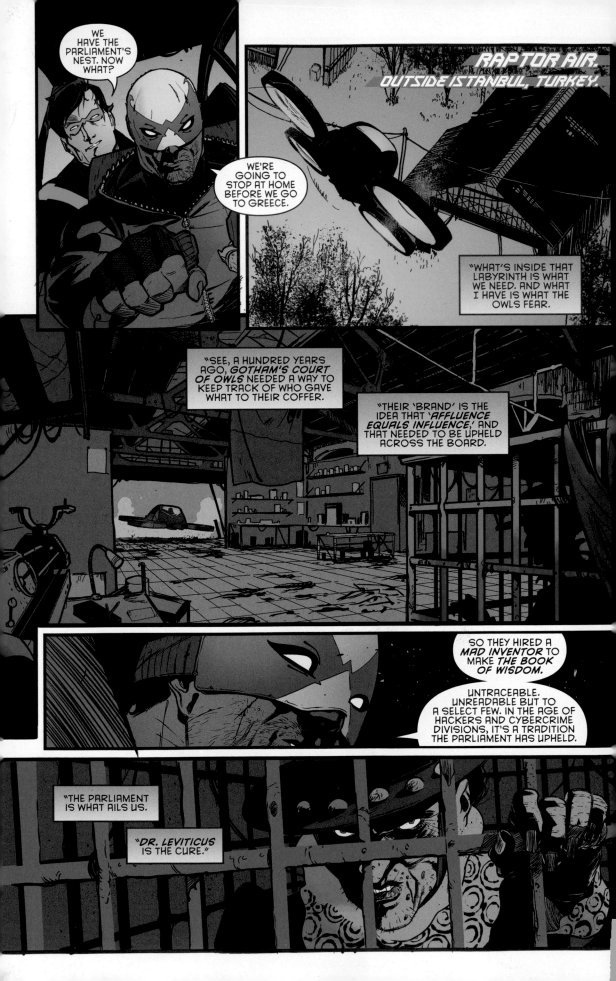

WE HAVE THE PARLIAMENT'S NEST. NOW WHAT?

WE'RE GOING TO STOP AT HOME BEFORE WE GO TO GREECE.

RAPTOR AIR. OUTSIDE ISTANBUL, TURKEY.

"WHAT'S INSIDE THAT LABYRINTH IS WHAT WE NEED. AND WHAT I HAVE IS WHAT THE OWLS FEAR."

"SEE, A HUNDRED YEARS AGO, *GOTHAM'S COURT OF OWLS* NEEDED A WAY TO KEEP TRACK OF WHO GAVE WHAT TO THEIR COFFER.

"THEIR 'BRAND' IS THE IDEA THAT *'AFFLUENCE EQUALS INFLUENCE,'* AND THAT NEEDED TO BE UPHELD ACROSS THE BOARD.

SO THEY HIRED A *MAD INVENTOR* TO MAKE *THE BOOK OF WISDOM.*

UNTRACEABLE. UNREADABLE BUT TO A SELECT FEW. IN THE AGE OF HACKERS AND CYBERCRIME DIVISIONS, IT'S A TRADITION THE PARLIAMENT HAS UPHELD.

"THE PARLIAMENT IS WHAT AILS US.

"*DR. LEVITICUS* IS THE CURE."

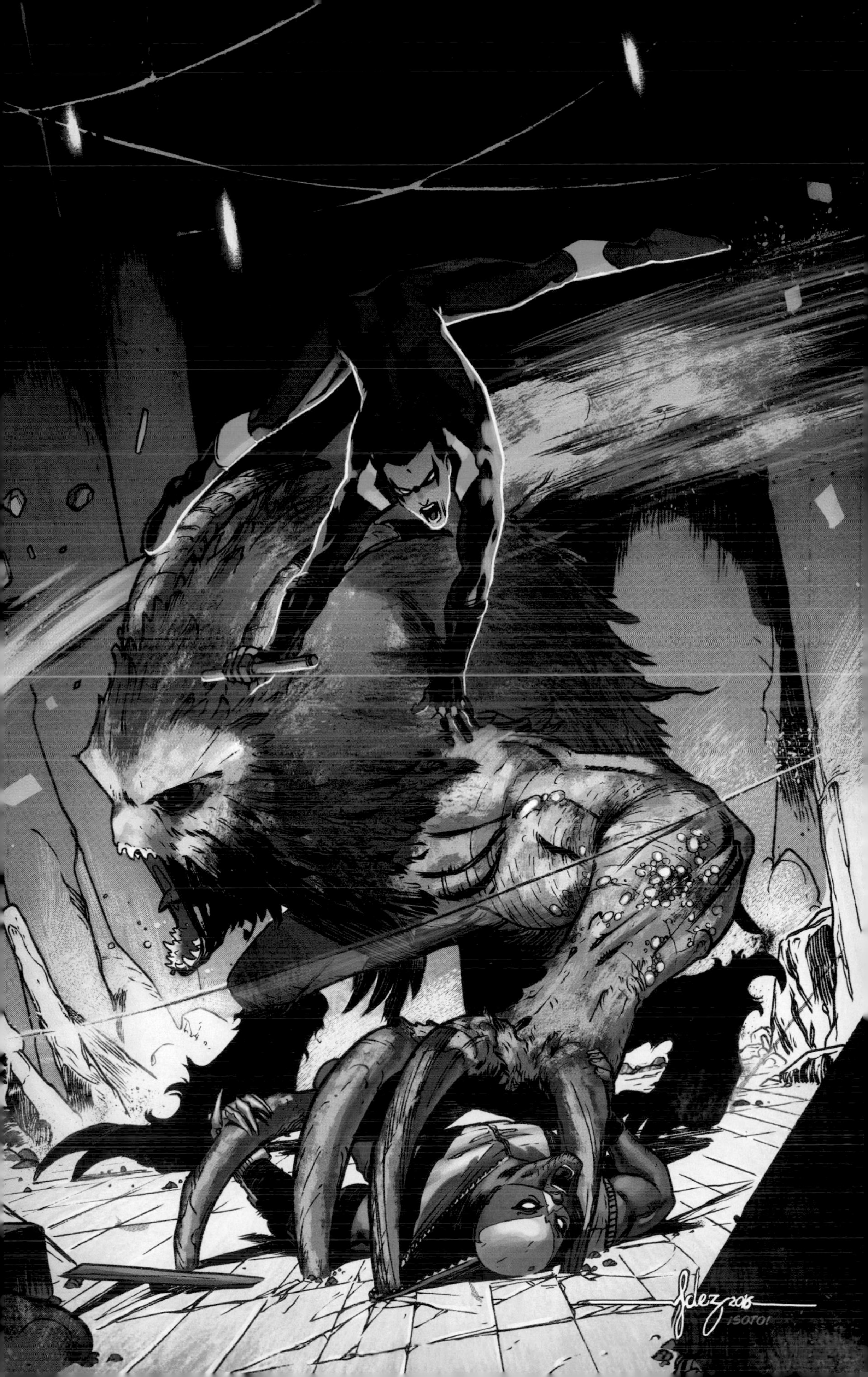
fdez 2015

BETTER THAN BATMAN, PART 4

TIM SEELEY writer * JAVIER FERNÁNDEZ artist * CHRIS SOTOMAYOR colorist
CARLOS M. MANGUAL letterer * JAVIER FERNÁNDEZ and CHRIS SOTOMAYOR cover artists

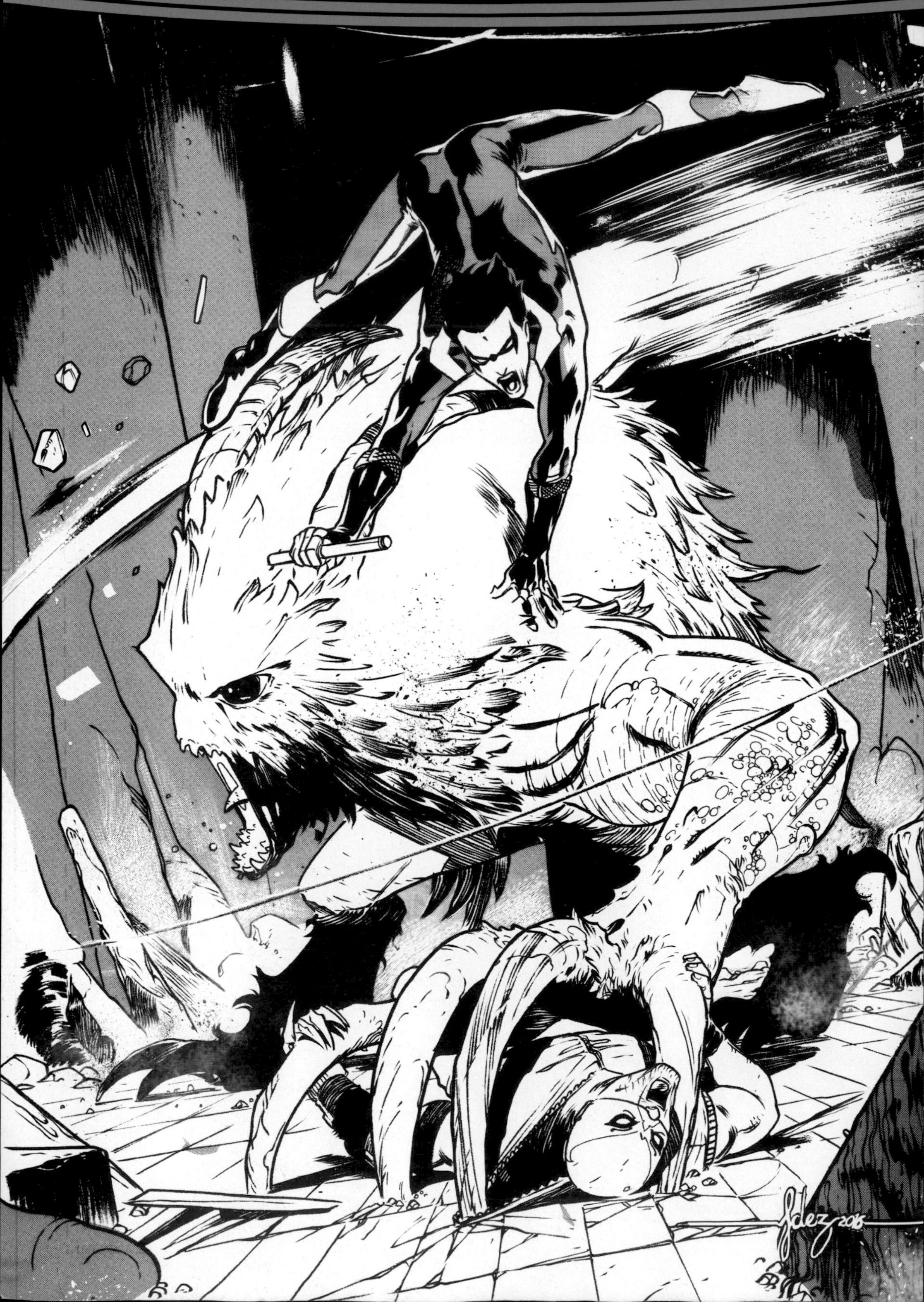
fdez 2016

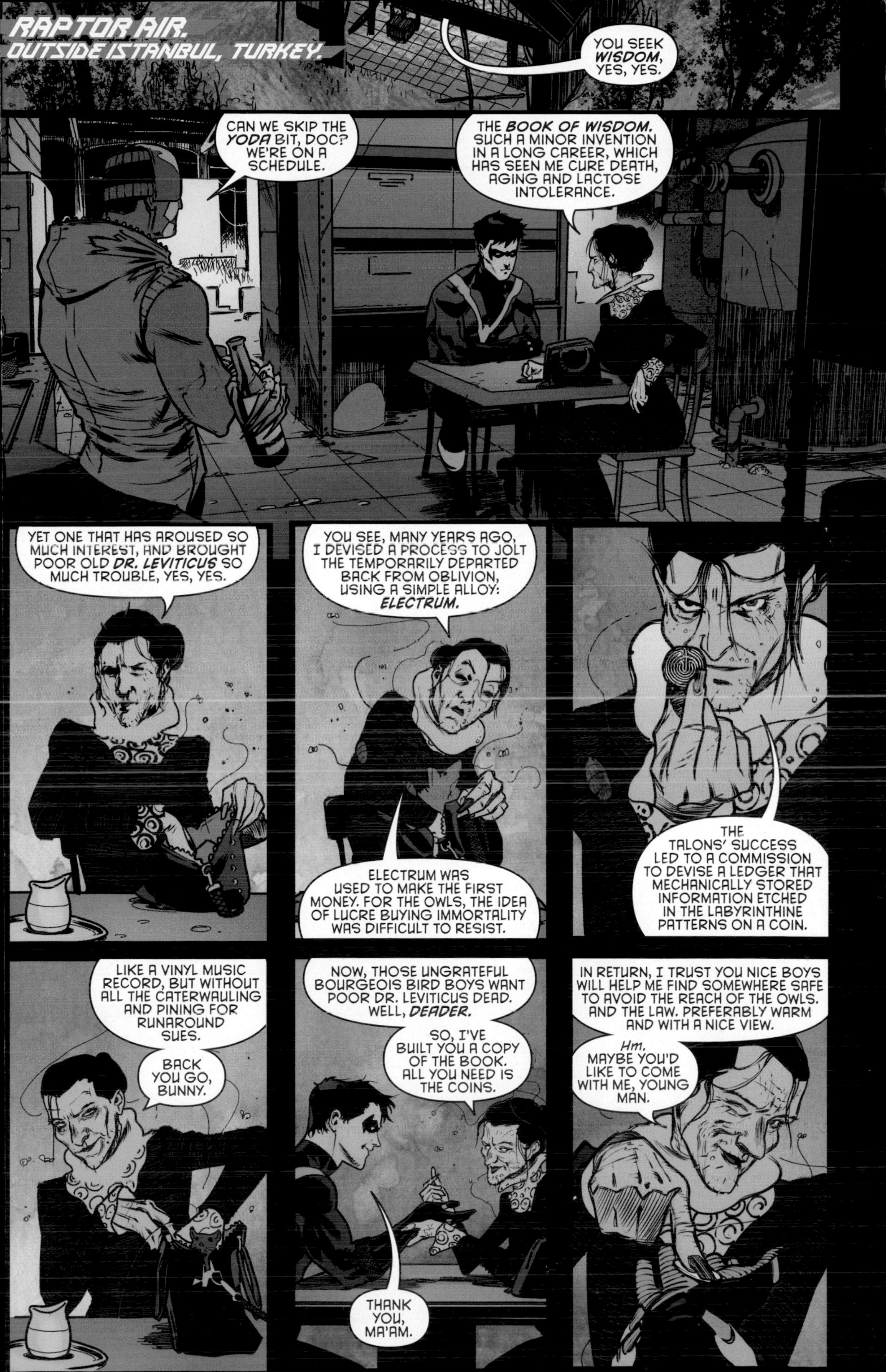
RAPTOR AIR.
OUTSIDE ISTANBUL, TURKEY.
YOU SEEK WISDOM, YES, YES.
CAN WE SKIP THE YODA BIT, DOC? WE'RE ON A SCHEDULE.
THE BOOK OF WISDOM. SUCH A MINOR INVENTION IN A LONG CAREER, WHICH HAS SEEN ME CURE DEATH, AGING AND LACTOSE INTOLERANCE.
YET ONE THAT HAS AROUSED SO MUCH INTEREST, AND BROUGHT POOR OLD DR. LEVITICUS SO MUCH TROUBLE, YES, YES.
YOU SEE, MANY YEARS AGO, I DEVISED A PROCESS TO JOLT THE TEMPORARILY DEPARTED BACK FROM OBLIVION, USING A SIMPLE ALLOY: ELECTRUM.
ELECTRUM WAS USED TO MAKE THE FIRST MONEY. FOR THE OWLS, THE IDEA OF LUCRE BUYING IMMORTALITY WAS DIFFICULT TO RESIST.
THE TALONS' SUCCESS LED TO A COMMISSION TO DEVISE A LEDGER THAT MECHANICALLY STORED INFORMATION ETCHED IN THE LABYRINTHINE PATTERNS ON A COIN.
LIKE A VINYL MUSIC RECORD, BUT WITHOUT ALL THE CATERWAULING AND PINING FOR RUNAROUND SUES.
BACK YOU GO, BUNNY.
NOW, THOSE UNGRATEFUL BOURGEOIS BIRD BOYS WANT POOR DR. LEVITICUS DEAD. WELL, DEADER.
SO, I'VE BUILT YOU A COPY OF THE BOOK. ALL YOU NEED IS THE COINS.
THANK YOU, MA'AM.
IN RETURN, I TRUST YOU NICE BOYS WILL HELP ME FIND SOMEWHERE SAFE TO AVOID THE REACH OF THE OWLS. AND THE LAW. PREFERABLY WARM AND WITH A NICE VIEW.
Hm. MAYBE YOU'D LIKE TO COME WITH ME, YOUNG MAN.

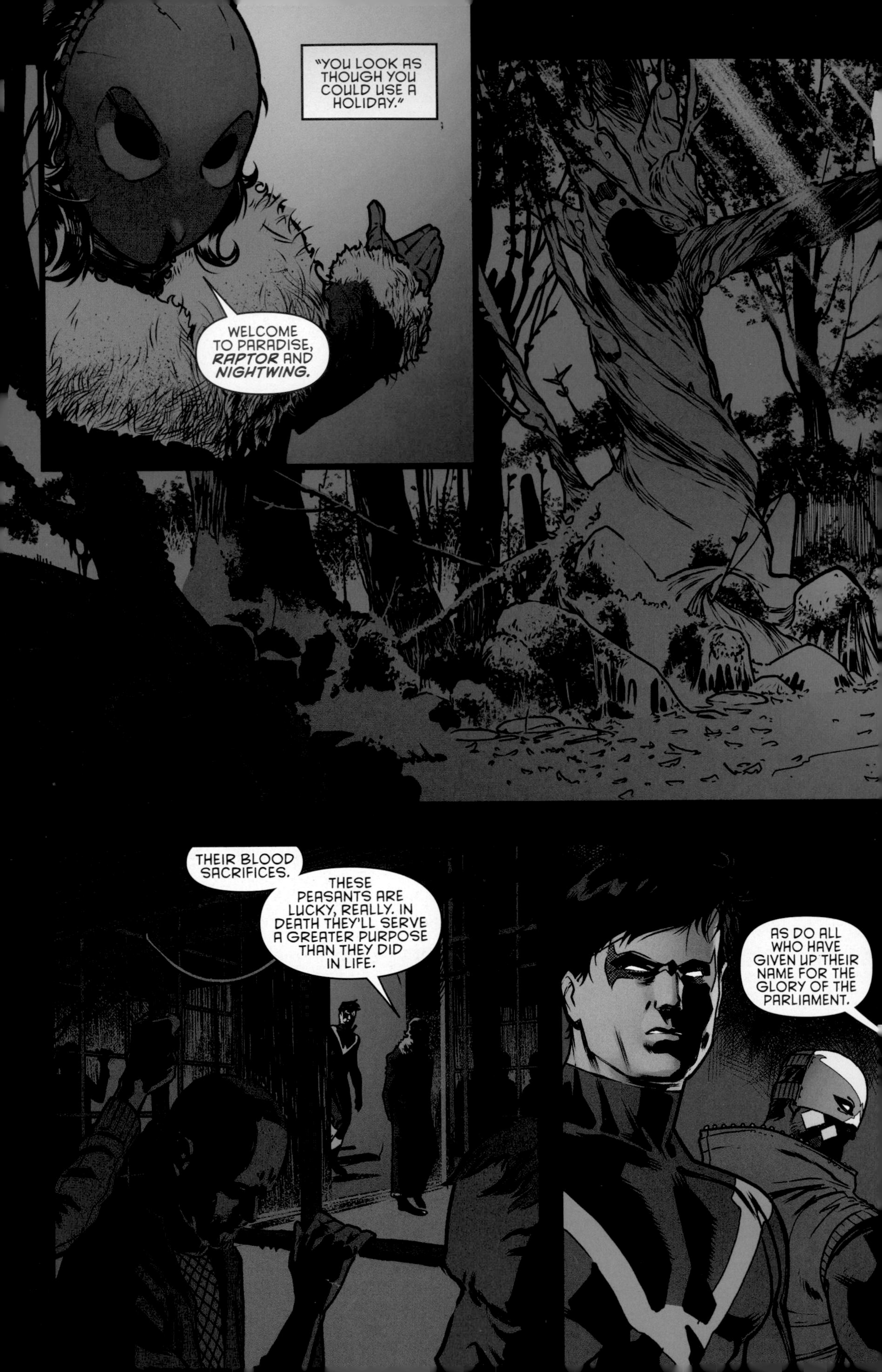

"YOU LOOK AS THOUGH YOU COULD USE A HOLIDAY."
WELCOME TO PARADISE, *RAPTOR* AND *NIGHTWING.*
THEIR BLOOD SACRIFICES.
THESE PEASANTS ARE LUCKY, REALLY. IN DEATH THEY'LL SERVE A GREATER PURPOSE THAN THEY DID IN LIFE.
AS DO ALL WHO HAVE GIVEN UP THEIR NAME FOR THE GLORY OF THE PARLIAMENT.

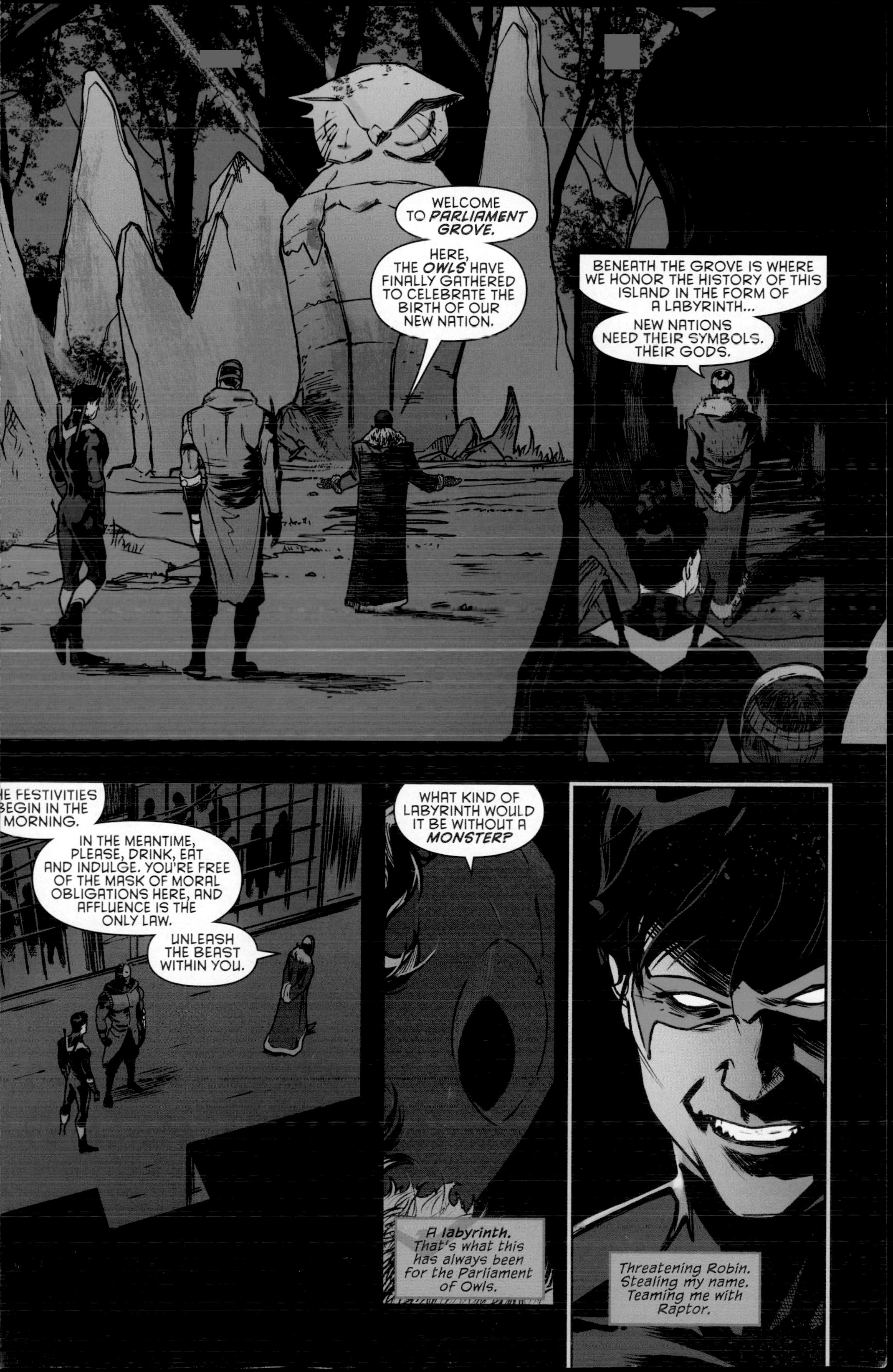
WELCOME TO PARLIAMENT GROVE.
HERE, THE OWLS' HAVE FINALLY GATHERED TO CELEBRATE THE BIRTH OF OUR NEW NATION.
BENEATH THE GROVE IS WHERE WE HONOR THE HISTORY OF THIS ISLAND IN THE FORM OF A LABYRINTH...
NEW NATIONS NEED THEIR SYMBOLS. THEIR GODS.
HE FESTIVITIES BEGIN IN THE MORNING.
IN THE MEANTIME, PLEASE, DRINK, EAT AND INDULGE. YOU'RE FREE OF THE MASK OF MORAL OBLIGATIONS HERE, AND AFFLUENCE IS THE ONLY LAW.
UNLEASH THE BEAST WITHIN YOU.
WHAT KIND OF LABYRINTH WOULD IT BE WITHOUT A MONSTER?
A labyrinth. That's what this has always been for the Parliament of Owls.
Threatening Robin. Stealing my name. Teaming me with Raptor.

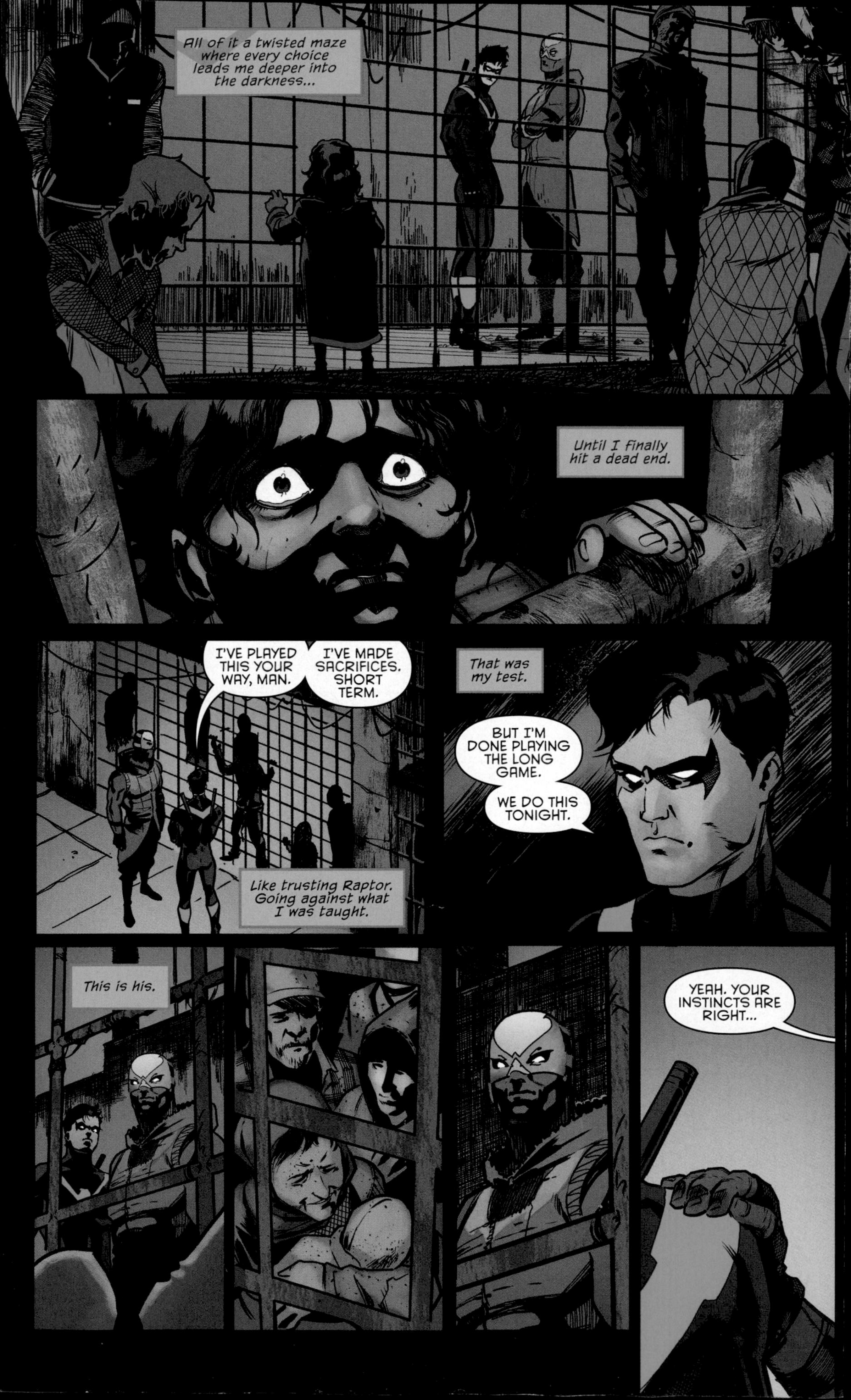
All of it a twisted maze where every choice leads me deeper into the darkness...
Until I finally hit a dead end.
I'VE PLAYED THIS YOUR WAY, MAN.
I'VE MADE SACRIFICES. SHORT TERM.
Like trusting Raptor. Going against what I was taught.
That was my test.
BUT I'M DONE PLAYING THE LONG GAME.
WE DO THIS TONIGHT.
This is his.
YEAH. YOUR INSTINCTS ARE RIGHT...

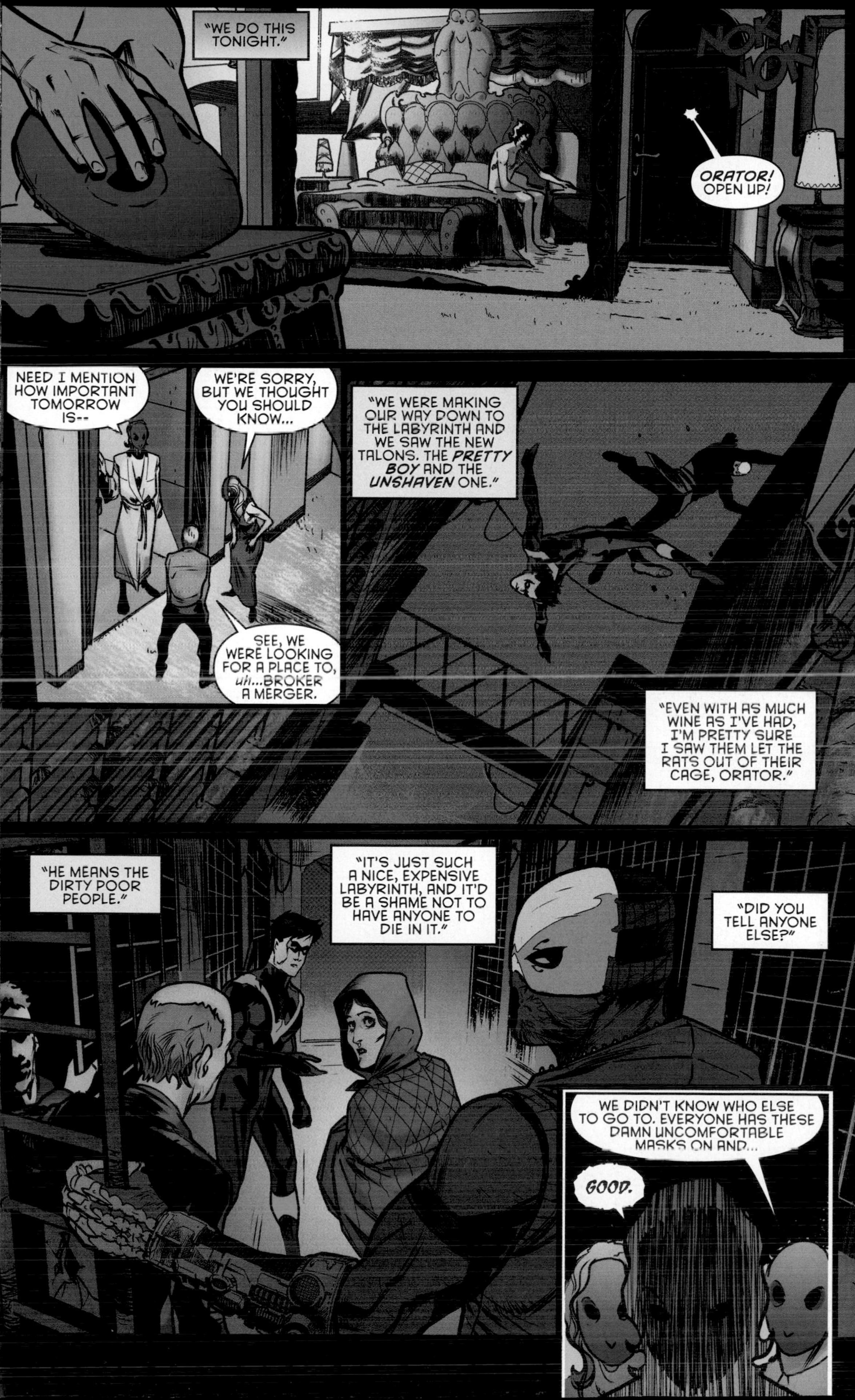
"WE DO THIS TONIGHT."
NOK NOK
ORATOR! OPEN UP!
NEED I MENTION HOW IMPORTANT TOMORROW IS--
WE'RE SORRY, BUT WE THOUGHT YOU SHOULD KNOW...
SEE, WE WERE LOOKING FOR A PLACE TO, *uh*...BROKER A MERGER.
"WE WERE MAKING OUR WAY DOWN TO THE LABYRINTH AND WE SAW THE NEW TALONS. THE *PRETTY BOY* AND THE *UNSHAVEN* ONE."
"EVEN WITH AS MUCH WINE AS I'VE HAD, I'M PRETTY SURE I SAW THEM LET THE RATS OUT OF THEIR CAGE, ORATOR."
"HE MEANS THE DIRTY POOR PEOPLE."
"IT'S JUST SUCH A NICE, EXPENSIVE LABYRINTH, AND IT'D BE A SHAME NOT TO HAVE ANYONE TO DIE IN IT."
"DID YOU TELL ANYONE ELSE?"
WE DIDN'T KNOW WHO ELSE TO GO TO. EVERYONE HAS THESE DAMN UNCOMFORTABLE MASKS ON AND...
GOOD.

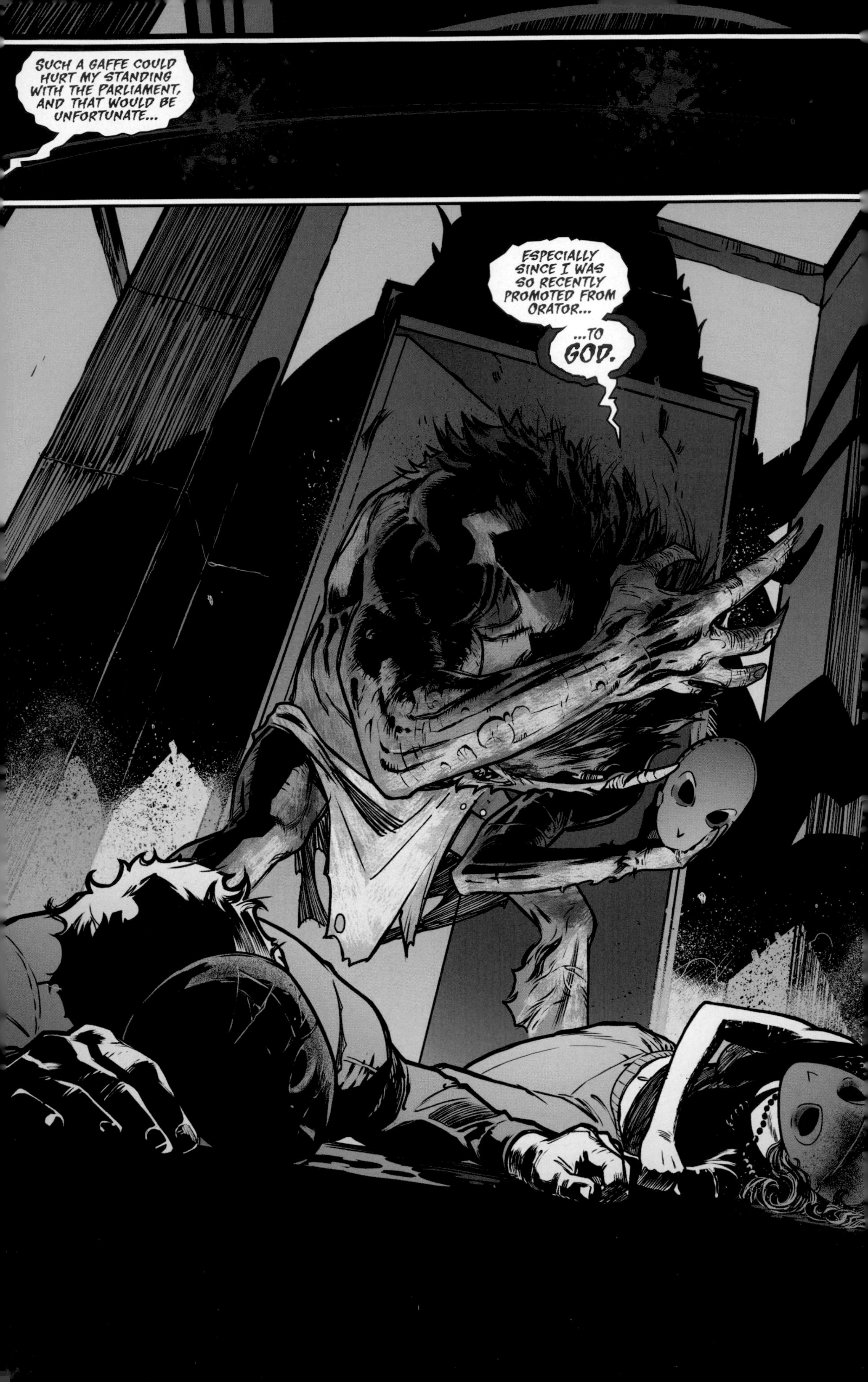
SUCH A GAFFE COULD HURT MY STANDING WITH THE PARLIAMENT, AND THAT WOULD BE UNFORTUNATE...
ESPECIALLY SINCE I WAS SO RECENTLY PROMOTED FROM ORATOR...
...TO GOD.

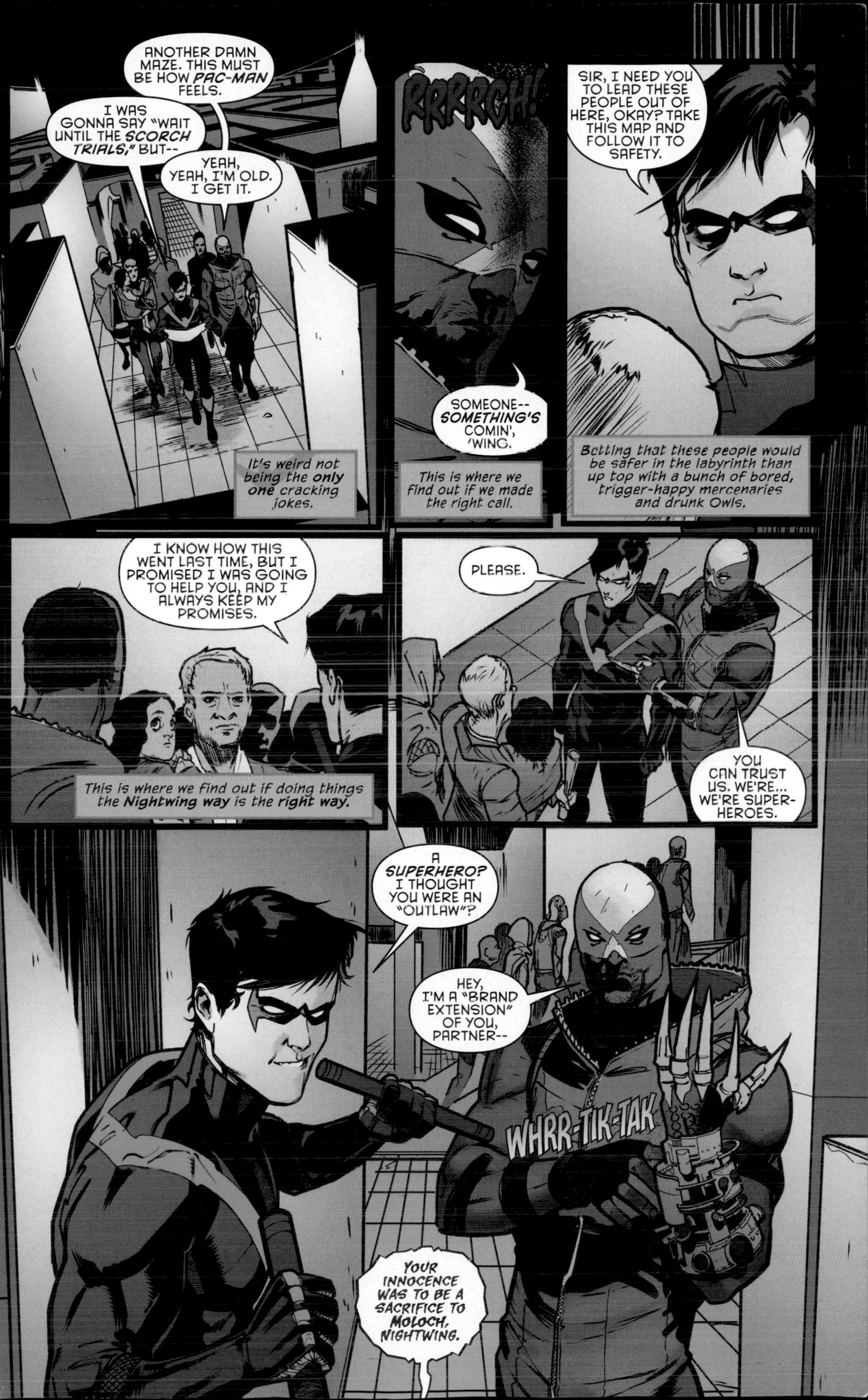
ANOTHER DAMN MAZE. THIS MUST BE HOW PAC-MAN FEELS.
I WAS GONNA SAY "WAIT UNTIL THE SCORCH TRIALS," BUT--
YEAH, YEAH, I'M OLD. I GET IT.
It's weird not being the only one cracking jokes.
RRRRCH!
SOMEONE-- SOMETHING'S COMIN', 'WING.
This is where we find out if we made the right call.
SIR, I NEED YOU TO LEAD THESE PEOPLE OUT OF HERE, OKAY? TAKE THIS MAP AND FOLLOW IT TO SAFETY.
Betting that these people would be safer in the labyrinth than up top with a bunch of bored, trigger-happy mercenaries and drunk Owls.
I KNOW HOW THIS WENT LAST TIME, BUT I PROMISED I WAS GOING TO HELP YOU, AND I ALWAYS KEEP MY PROMISES.
This is where we find out if doing things the Nightwing way is the right way.
PLEASE.
YOU CAN TRUST US. WE'RE... WE'RE SUPER-HEROES.
A SUPERHERO? I THOUGHT YOU WERE AN "OUTLAW"?
HEY, I'M A "BRAND EXTENSION" OF YOU, PARTNER--
WHRR-TIK-TAK
YOUR INNOCENCE WAS TO BE A SACRIFICE TO MOLOCH, NIGHTWING.

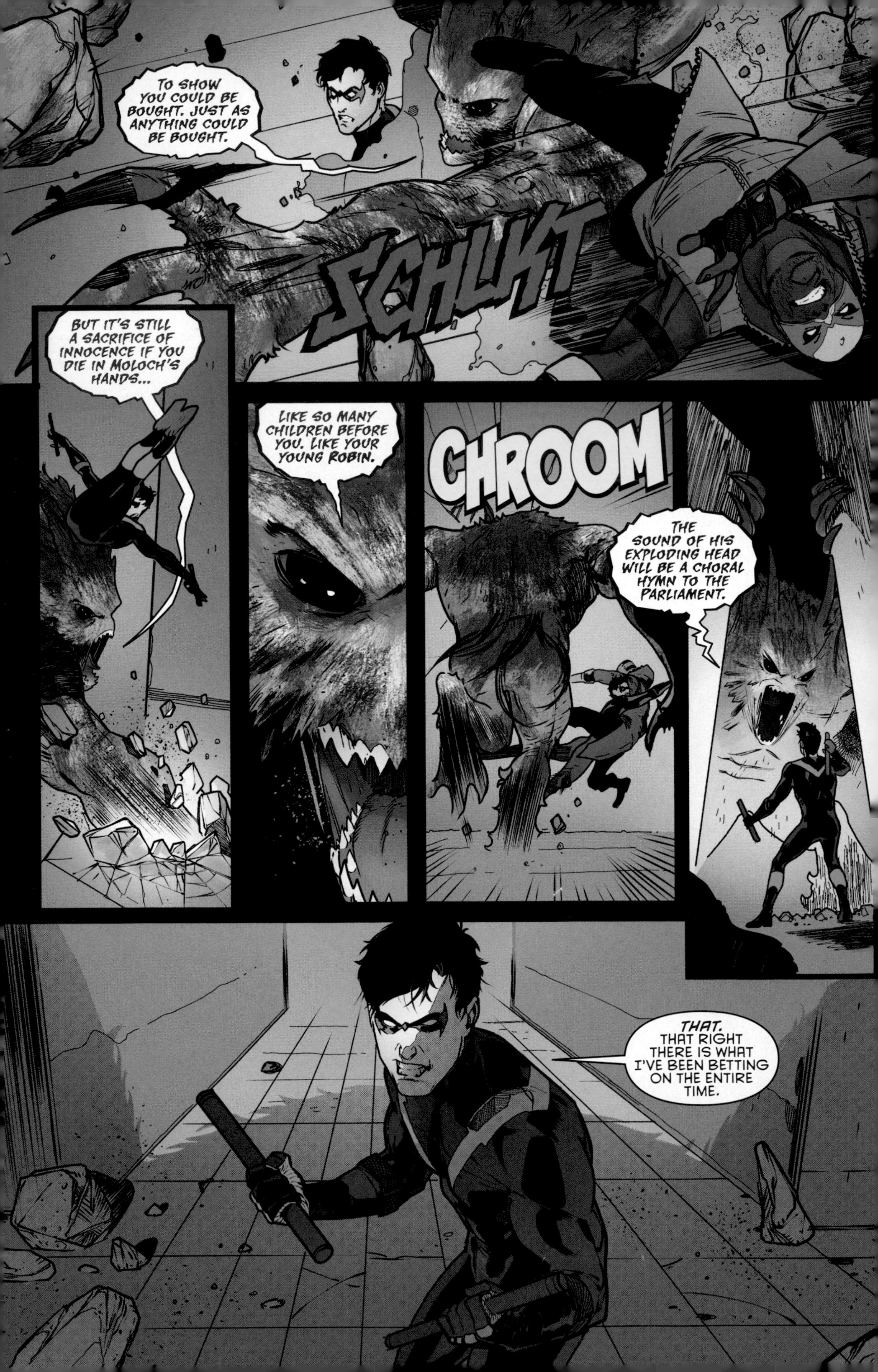
TO SHOW YOU COULD BE BOUGHT. JUST AS ANYTHING COULD BE BOUGHT.
SCHLUKT
BUT IT'S STILL A SACRIFICE OF INNOCENCE IF YOU DIE IN MOLOCH'S HANDS...
LIKE SO MANY CHILDREN BEFORE YOU. LIKE YOUR YOUNG ROBIN.
CHROOM
THE SOUND OF HIS EXPLODING HEAD WILL BE A CHORAL HYMN TO THE PARLIAMENT.
THAT. THAT RIGHT THERE IS WHAT I'VE BEEN BETTING ON THE ENTIRE TIME.

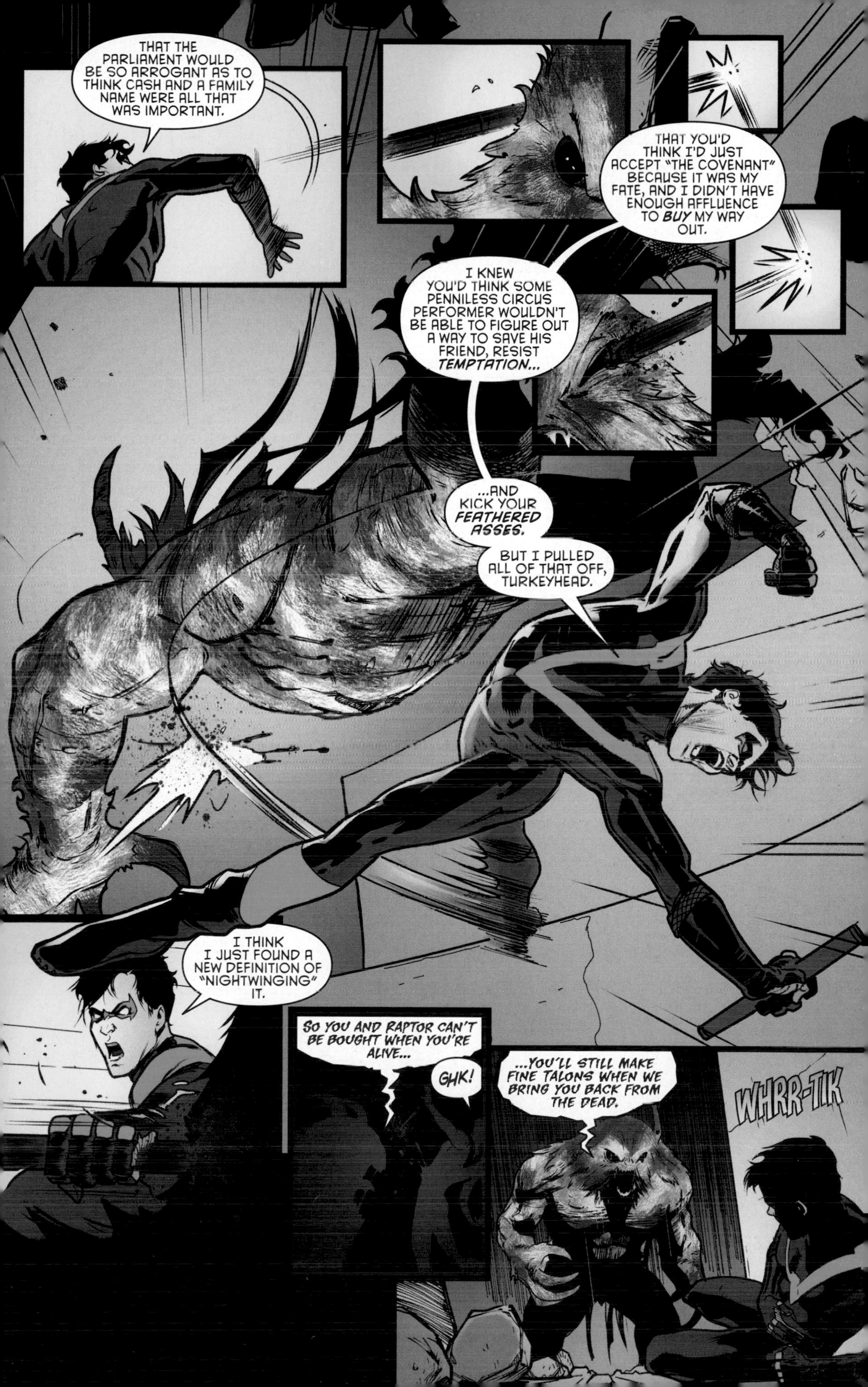
THAT THE PARLIAMENT WOULD BE SO ARROGANT AS TO THINK CASH AND A FAMILY NAME WERE ALL THAT WAS IMPORTANT.
THAT YOU'D THINK I'D JUST ACCEPT "THE COVENANT" BECAUSE IT WAS MY FATE, AND I DIDN'T HAVE ENOUGH AFFLUENCE TO BUY MY WAY OUT.
I KNEW YOU'D THINK SOME PENNILESS CIRCUS PERFORMER WOULDN'T BE ABLE TO FIGURE OUT A WAY TO SAVE HIS FRIEND, RESIST TEMPTATION...
...AND KICK YOUR FEATHERED ASSES.
BUT I PULLED ALL OF THAT OFF, TURKEYHEAD.
I THINK I JUST FOUND A NEW DEFINITION OF "NIGHTWINGING" IT.
SO YOU AND RAPTOR CAN'T BE BOUGHT WHEN YOU'RE ALIVE...
GHK!
...YOU'LL STILL MAKE FINE TALONS WHEN WE BRING YOU BACK FROM THE DEAD.
WHRR-TIK

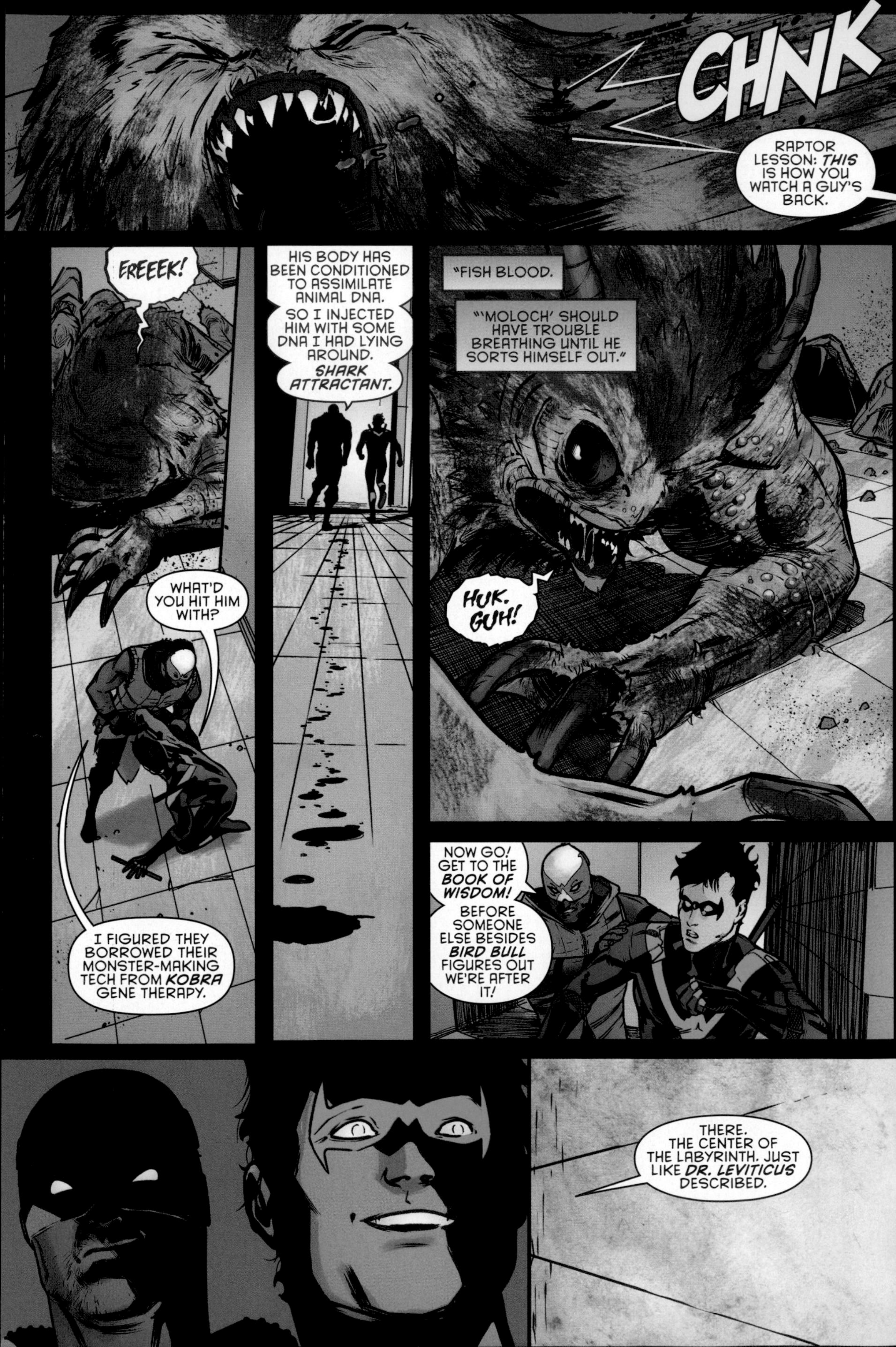
CHNK
RAPTOR LESSON: THIS IS HOW YOU WATCH A GUY'S BACK.
EREEEK!
WHAT'D YOU HIT HIM WITH?
I FIGURED THEY BORROWED THEIR MONSTER-MAKING TECH FROM KOBRA GENE THERAPY.
HIS BODY HAS BEEN CONDITIONED TO ASSIMILATE ANIMAL DNA.
SO I INJECTED HIM WITH SOME DNA I HAD LYING AROUND. SHARK ATTRACTANT.
"FISH BLOOD.
"'MOLOCH' SHOULD HAVE TROUBLE BREATHING UNTIL HE SORTS HIMSELF OUT."
HUK. GUH!
NOW GO! GET TO THE BOOK OF WISDOM!
BEFORE SOMEONE ELSE BESIDES BIRD BULL FIGURES OUT WE'RE AFTER IT!
THERE. THE CENTER OF THE LABYRINTH. JUST LIKE DR. LEVITICUS DESCRIBED.

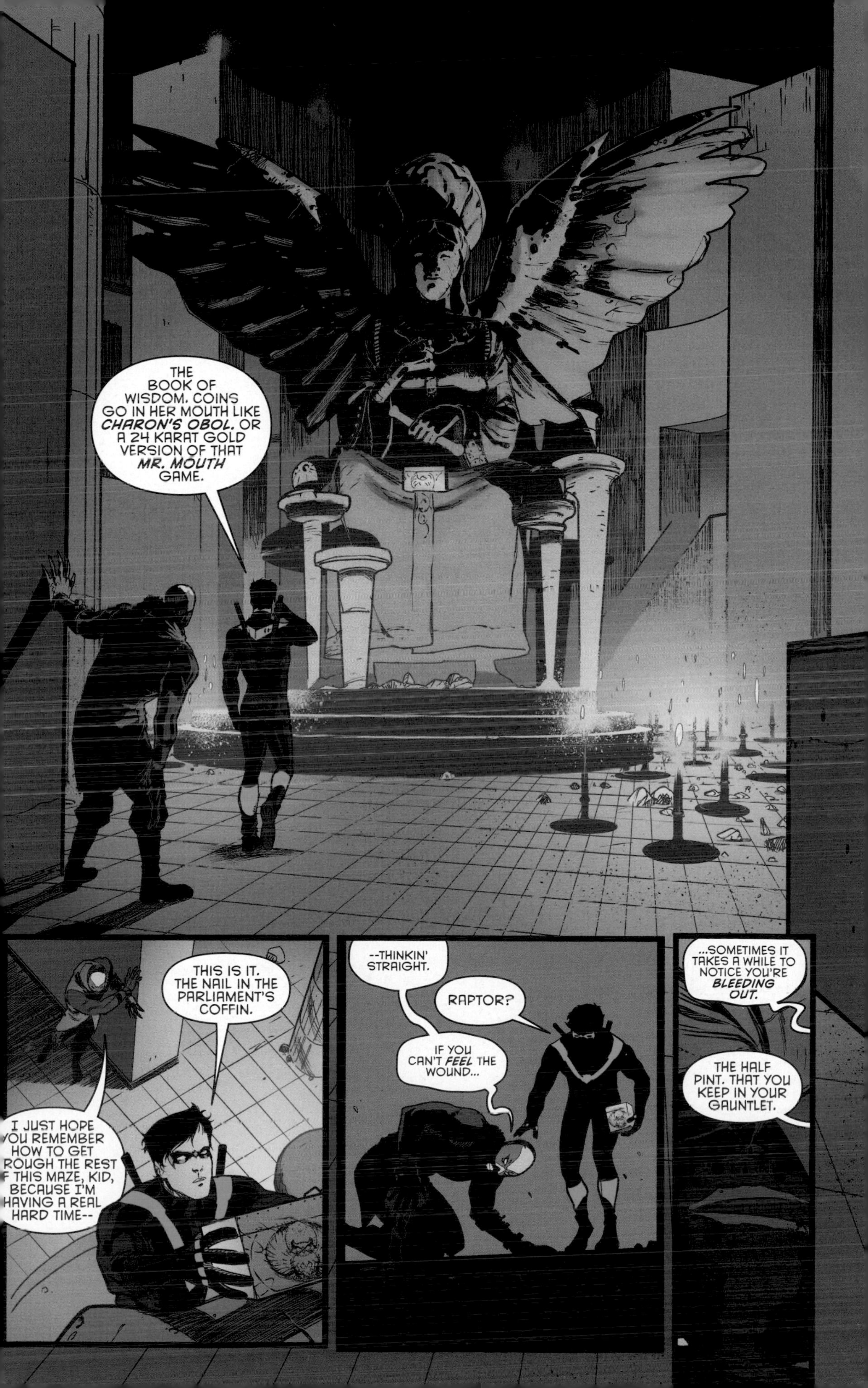
THE BOOK OF WISDOM. COINS GO IN HER MOUTH LIKE CHARON'S OBOL. OR A 24 KARAT GOLD VERSION OF THAT MR. MOUTH GAME.
THIS IS IT. THE NAIL IN THE PARLIAMENT'S COFFIN.
I JUST HOPE YOU REMEMBER HOW TO GET ROUGH THE REST F THIS MAZE, KID, BECAUSE I'M HAVING A REAL HARD TIME--
--THINKIN' STRAIGHT.
RAPTOR?
IF YOU CAN'T FEEL THE WOUND...
...SOMETIMES IT TAKES A WHILE TO NOTICE YOU'RE BLEEDING OUT.
THE HALF PINT. THAT YOU KEEP IN YOUR GAUNTLET.

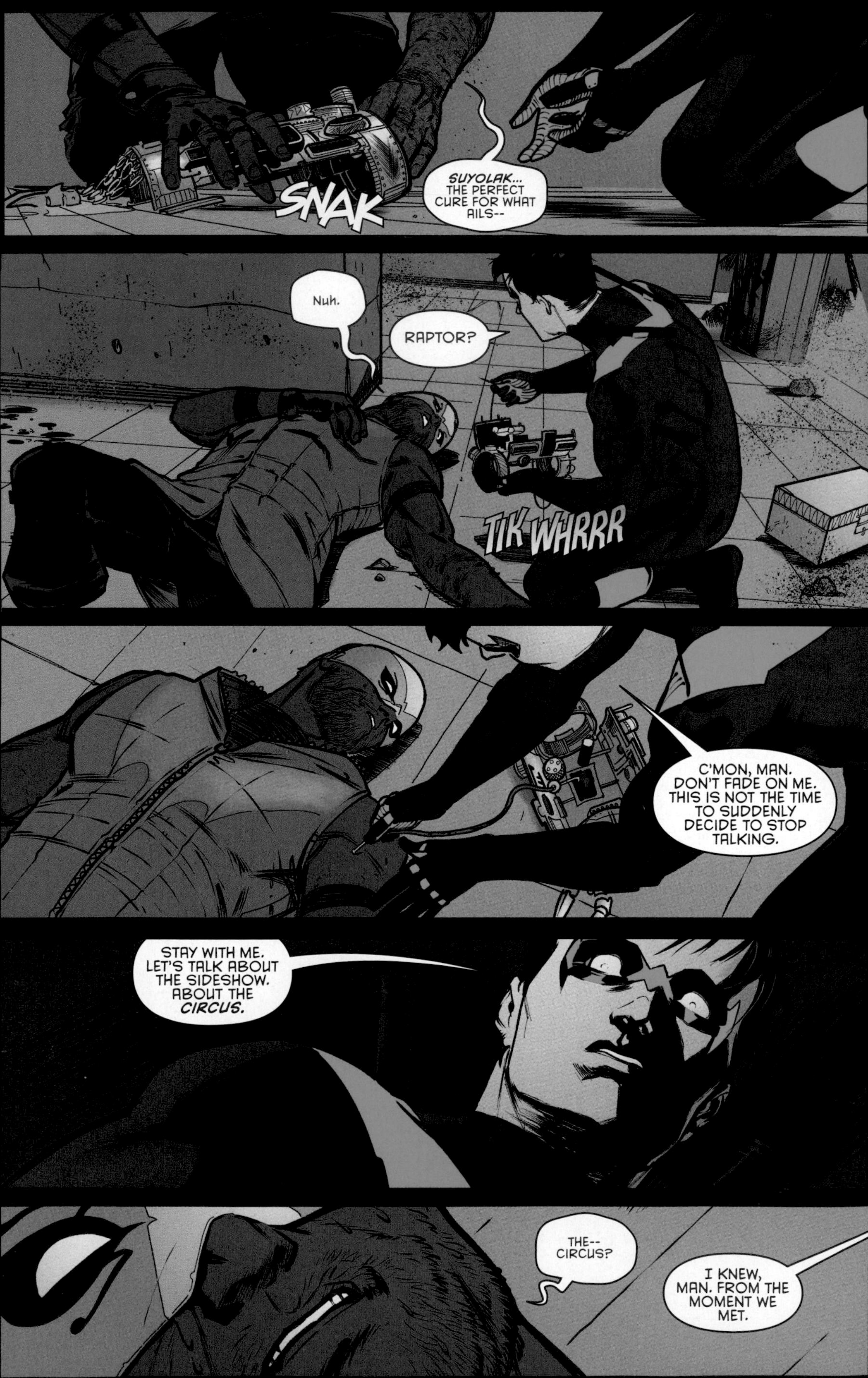
SNAK
SUYOLAK... THE PERFECT CURE FOR WHAT AILS--
Nuh.
RAPTOR?
TIK WHRRR
C'MON, MAN. DON'T FADE ON ME. THIS IS NOT THE TIME TO SUDDENLY DECIDE TO STOP TALKING.
STAY WITH ME. LET'S TALK ABOUT THE SIDESHOW. ABOUT THE CIRCUS.
THE-- CIRCUS?
I KNEW, MAN. FROM THE MOMENT WE MET.

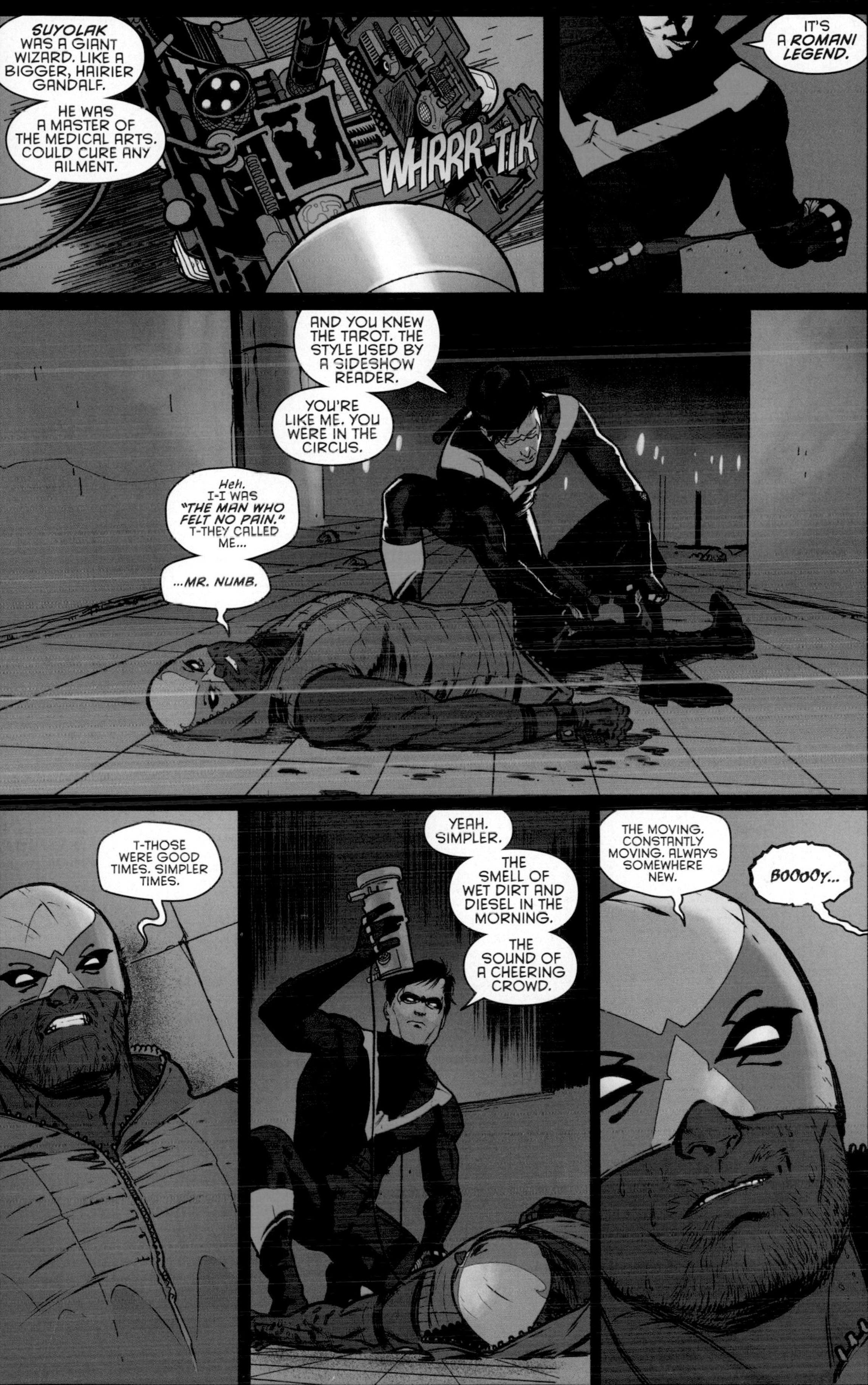
SUYOLAK WAS A GIANT WIZARD. LIKE A BIGGER, HAIRIER GANDALF.
HE WAS A MASTER OF THE MEDICAL ARTS. COULD CURE ANY AILMENT.
WHRRR-TIK
IT'S A ROMANI LEGEND.
AND YOU KNEW THE TAROT. THE STYLE USED BY A SIDESHOW READER.
YOU'RE LIKE ME. YOU WERE IN THE CIRCUS.
Heh. I-I WAS "THE MAN WHO FELT NO PAIN." T-THEY CALLED ME...
...MR. NUMB.
T-THOSE WERE GOOD TIMES. SIMPLER TIMES.
YEAH. SIMPLER.
THE SMELL OF WET DIRT AND DIESEL IN THE MORNING.
THE SOUND OF A CHEERING CROWD.
THE MOVING. CONSTANTLY MOVING. ALWAYS SOMEWHERE NEW.
BOOOOY...

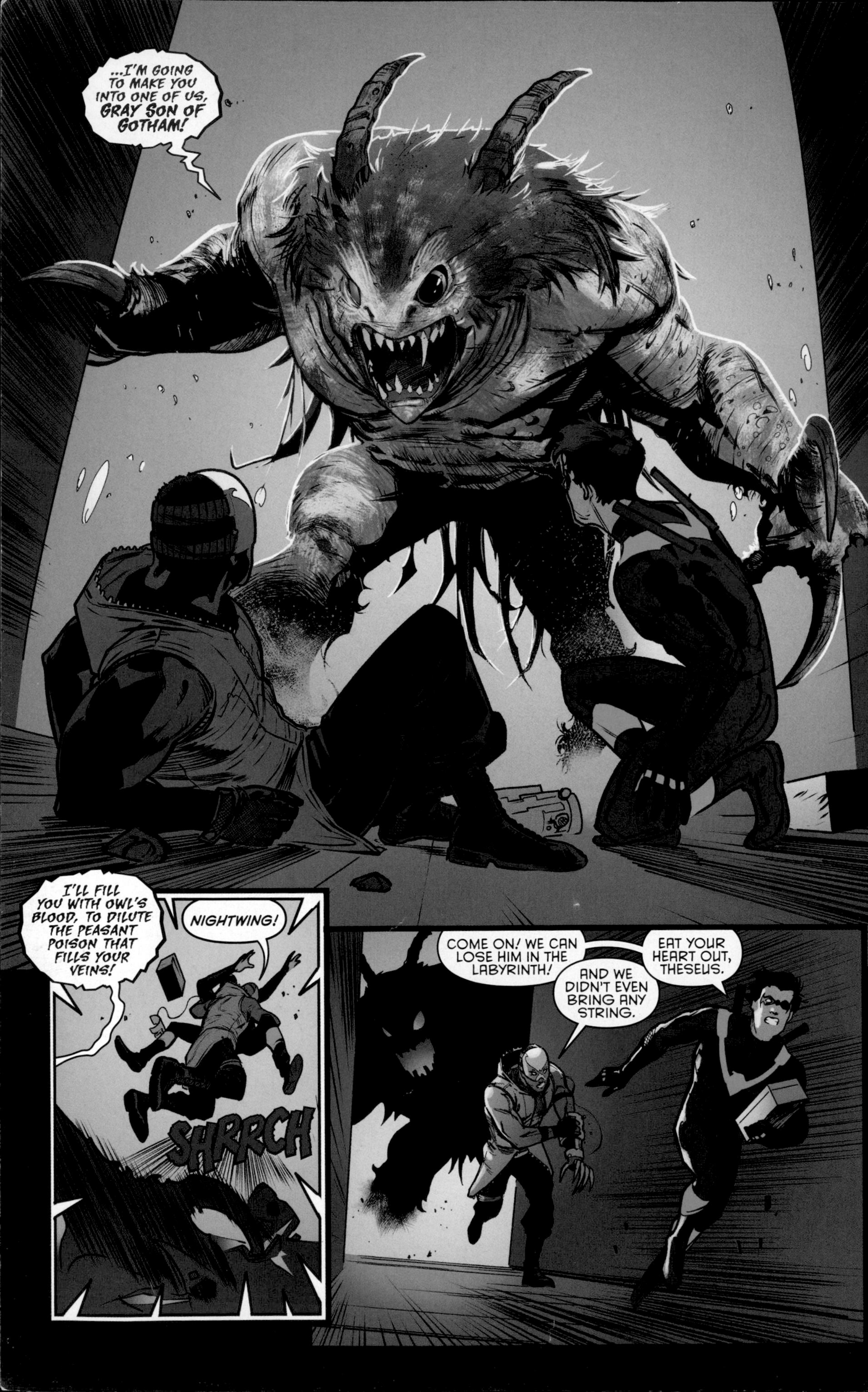
...I'M GOING TO MAKE YOU INTO ONE OF US, GRAY SON OF GOTHAM!
I'LL FILL YOU WITH OWL'S BLOOD, TO DILUTE THE PEASANT POISON THAT FILLS YOUR VEINS!
NIGHTWING!
SHRRCH
COME ON! WE CAN LOSE HIM IN THE LABYRINTH!
AND WE DIDN'T EVEN BRING ANY STRING.
EAT YOUR HEART OUT, THESEUS.

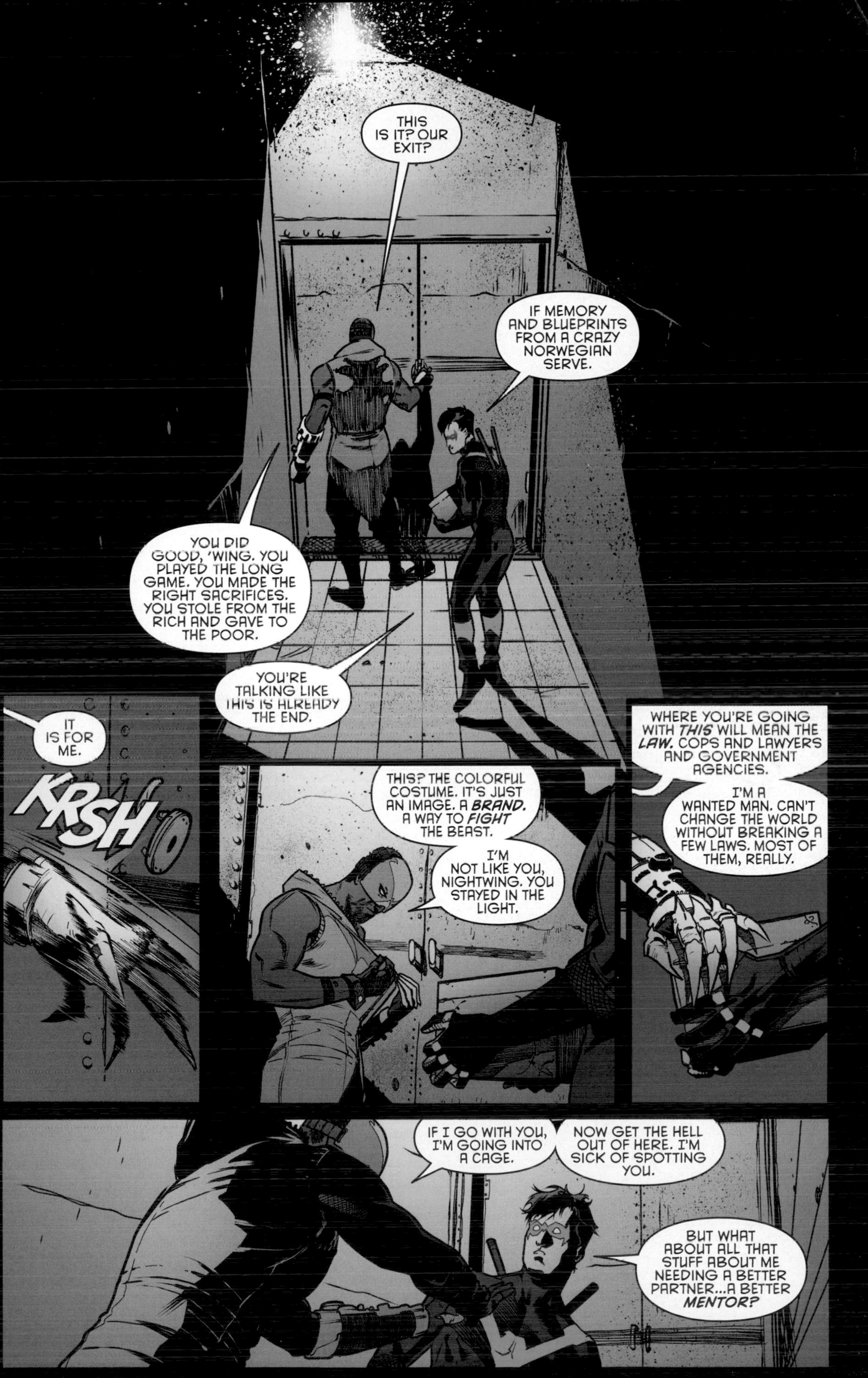
THIS IS IT? OUR EXIT?
IF MEMORY AND BLUEPRINTS FROM A CRAZY NORWEGIAN SERVE.
YOU DID GOOD, 'WING. YOU PLAYED THE LONG GAME. YOU MADE THE RIGHT SACRIFICES. YOU STOLE FROM THE RICH AND GAVE TO THE POOR.
YOU'RE TALKING LIKE THIS IS ALREADY THE END.
IT IS FOR ME.
KRSH
THIS? THE COLORFUL COSTUME. IT'S JUST AN IMAGE. A BRAND. A WAY TO FIGHT THE BEAST.
I'M NOT LIKE YOU, NIGHTWING. YOU STAYED IN THE LIGHT.
WHERE YOU'RE GOING WITH THIS WILL MEAN THE LAW. COPS AND LAWYERS AND GOVERNMENT AGENCIES.
I'M A WANTED MAN. CAN'T CHANGE THE WORLD WITHOUT BREAKING A FEW LAWS. MOST OF THEM, REALLY.
IF I GO WITH YOU, I'M GOING INTO A CAGE.
NOW GET THE HELL OUT OF HERE. I'M SICK OF SPOTTING YOU.
BUT WHAT ABOUT ALL THAT STUFF ABOUT ME NEEDING A BETTER PARTNER...A BETTER MENTOR?

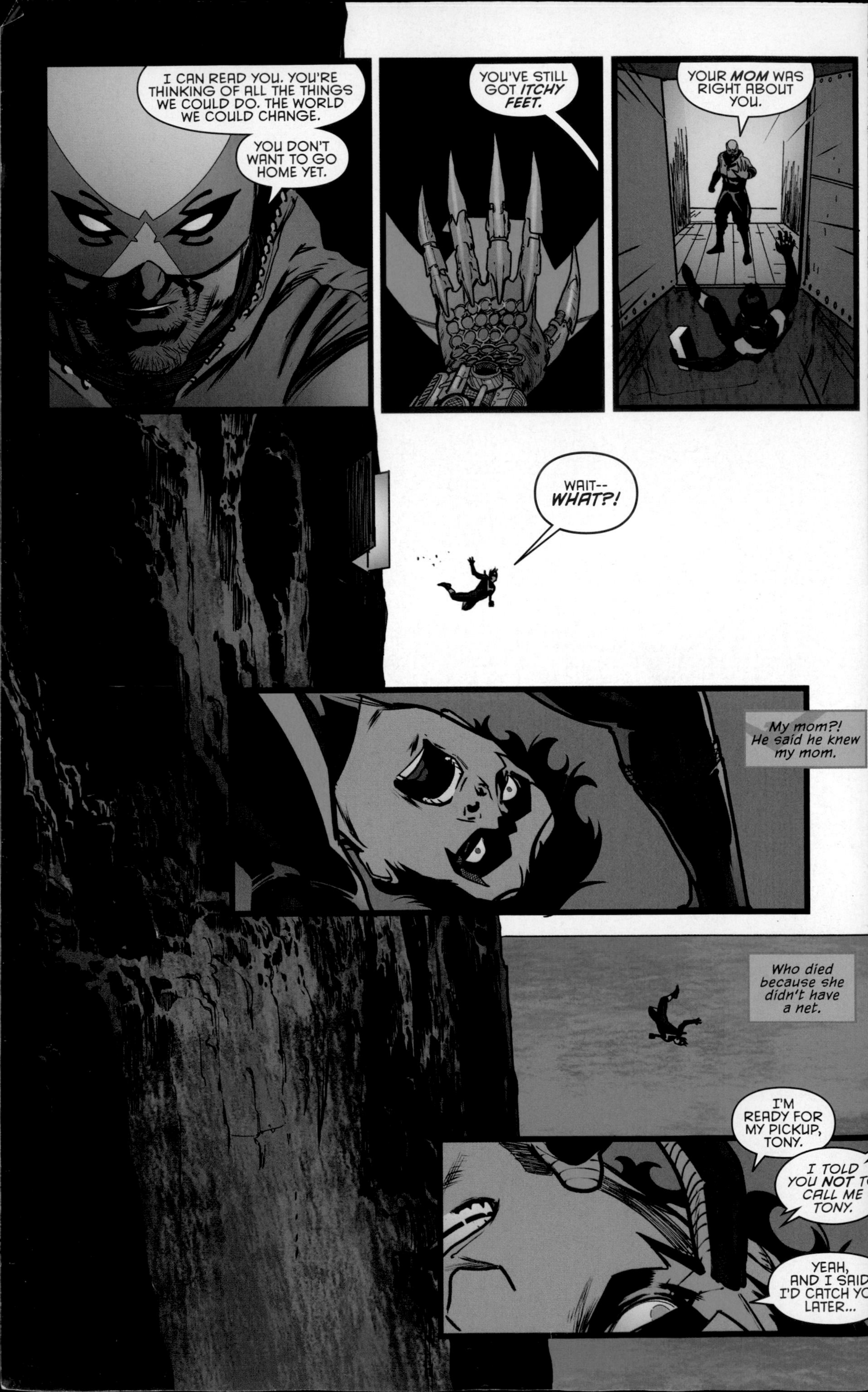
I CAN READ YOU. YOU'RE THINKING OF ALL THE THINGS WE COULD DO. THE WORLD WE COULD CHANGE.
YOU DON'T WANT TO GO HOME YET.
YOU'VE STILL GOT *ITCHY FEET.*
YOUR **MOM** WAS RIGHT ABOUT YOU.
WAIT-- *WHAT?!*
My mom?! He said he knew my mom.
Who died because she didn't have a net.
I'M READY FOR MY PICKUP, TONY.
I TOLD YOU **NOT** TO CALL ME TONY.
YEAH, AND I SAID I'D CATCH YOU LATER...

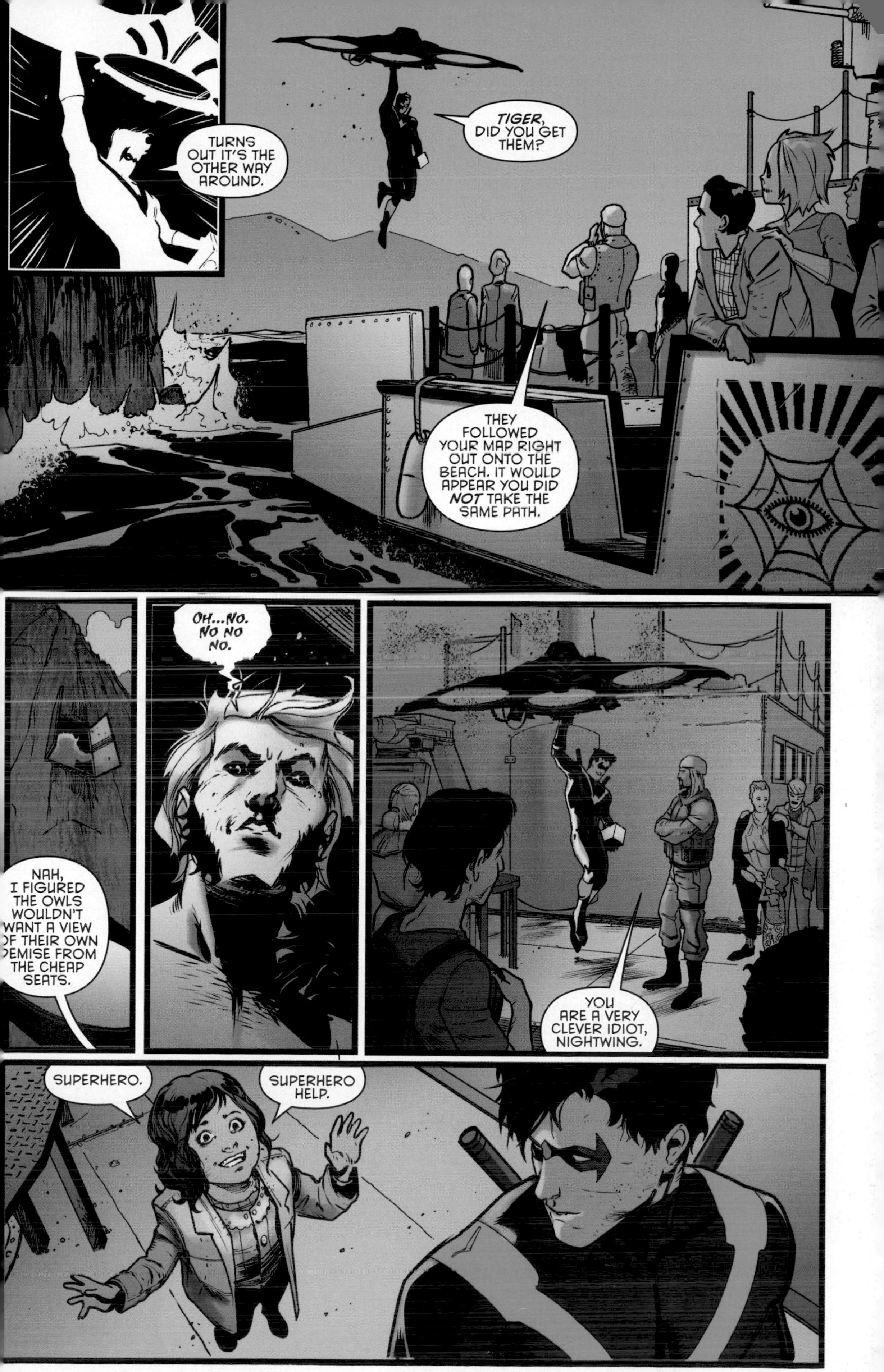
TURNS OUT IT'S THE OTHER WAY AROUND.
TIGER, DID YOU GET THEM?
THEY FOLLOWED YOUR MAP RIGHT OUT ONTO THE BEACH. IT WOULD APPEAR YOU DID NOT TAKE THE SAME PATH.
NAH, I FIGURED THE OWLS WOULDN'T WANT A VIEW OF THEIR OWN DEMISE FROM THE CHEAP SEATS.
OH...NO. NO NO NO.
YOU ARE A VERY CLEVER IDIOT, NIGHTWING.
SUPERHERO.
SUPERHERO HELP.

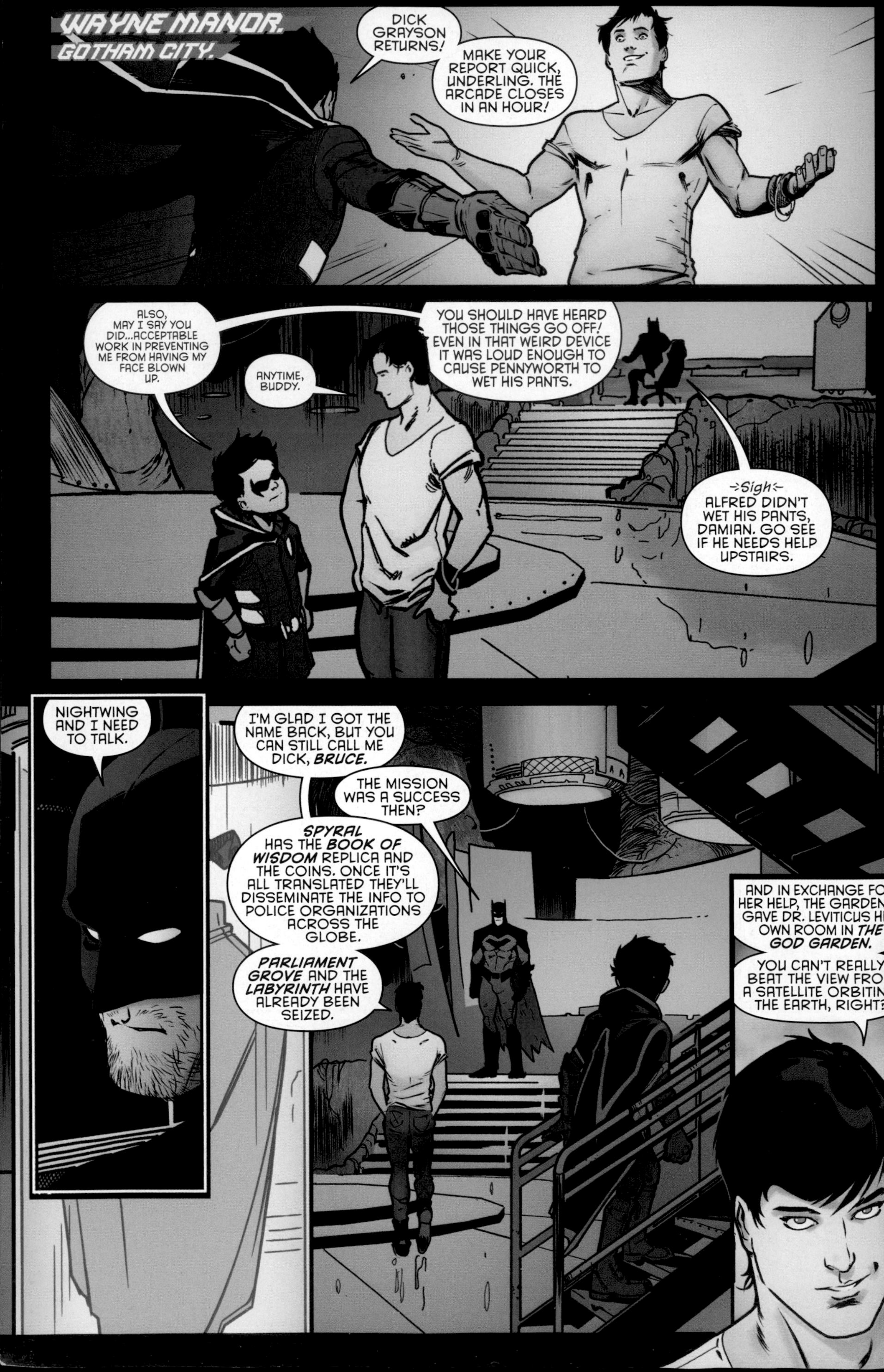
WAYNE MANOR. GOTHAM CITY.
DICK GRAYSON RETURNS!
MAKE YOUR REPORT QUICK, UNDERLING. THE ARCADE CLOSES IN AN HOUR!
ALSO, MAY I SAY YOU DID...ACCEPTABLE WORK IN PREVENTING ME FROM HAVING MY FACE BLOWN UP.
ANYTIME, BUDDY.
YOU SHOULD HAVE HEARD THOSE THINGS GO OFF! EVEN IN THAT WEIRD DEVICE IT WAS LOUD ENOUGH TO CAUSE PENNYWORTH TO WET HIS PANTS.
Sigh
ALFRED DIDN'T WET HIS PANTS, DAMIAN. GO SEE IF HE NEEDS HELP UPSTAIRS.
NIGHTWING AND I NEED TO TALK.
I'M GLAD I GOT THE NAME BACK, BUT YOU CAN STILL CALL ME DICK, BRUCE.
THE MISSION WAS A SUCCESS THEN?
SPYRAL HAS THE BOOK OF WISDOM REPLICA AND THE COINS. ONCE IT'S ALL TRANSLATED THEY'LL DISSEMINATE THE INFO TO POLICE ORGANIZATIONS ACROSS THE GLOBE.
PARLIAMENT GROVE AND THE LABYRINTH HAVE ALREADY BEEN SEIZED.
AND IN EXCHANGE FO HER HELP, THE GARDEN GAVE DR. LEVITICUS H OWN ROOM IN THE GOD GARDEN.
YOU CAN'T REALLY BEAT THE VIEW FRO A SATELLITE ORBITIN THE EARTH, RIGHT?

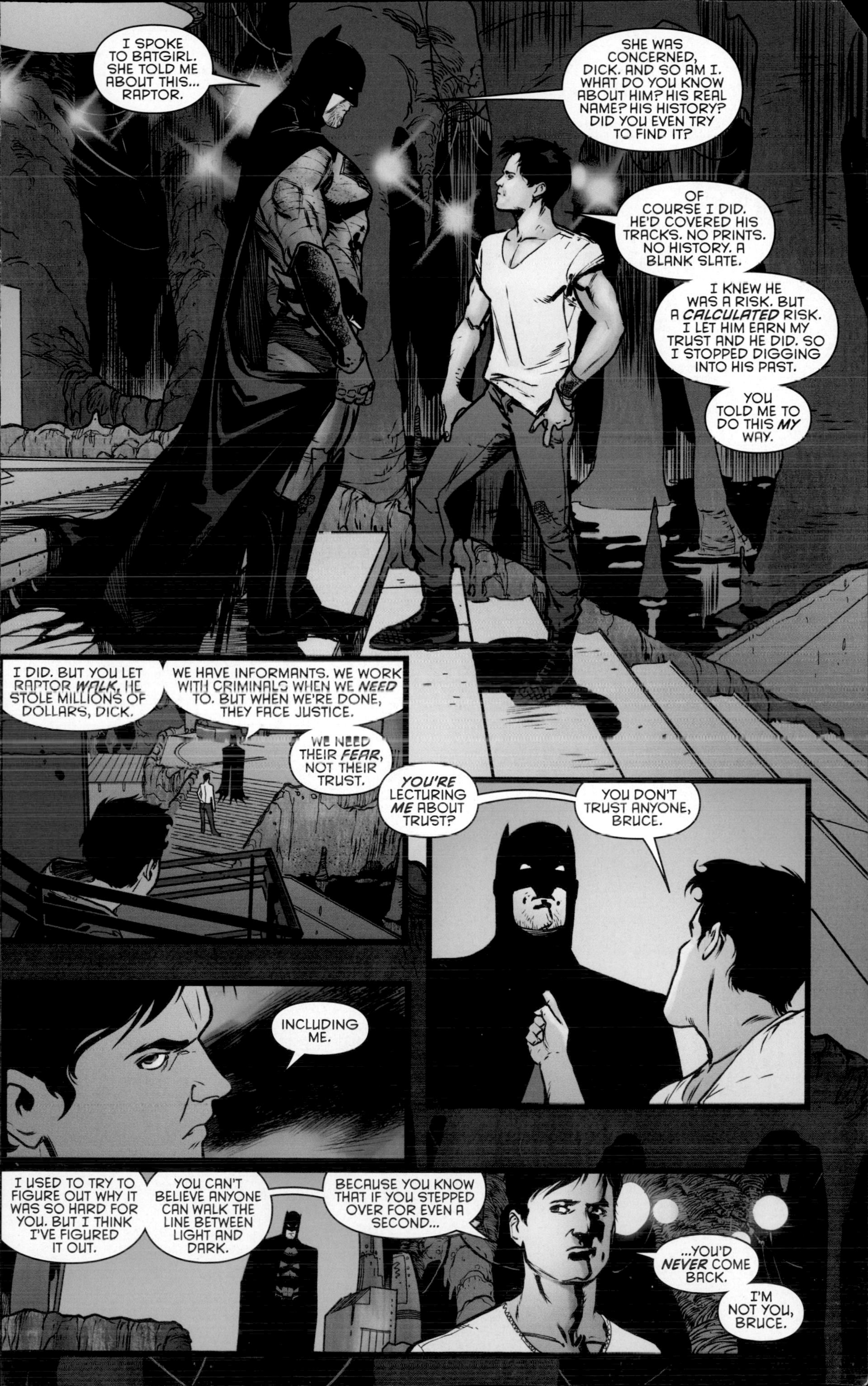

I SPOKE TO BATGIRL. SHE TOLD ME ABOUT THIS... RAPTOR.
SHE WAS CONCERNED, DICK. AND SO AM I. WHAT DO YOU KNOW ABOUT HIM? HIS REAL NAME? HIS HISTORY? DID YOU EVEN TRY TO FIND IT?
OF COURSE I DID. HE'D COVERED HIS TRACKS. NO PRINTS. NO HISTORY. A BLANK SLATE.
I KNEW HE WAS A RISK. BUT A CALCULATED RISK. I LET HIM EARN MY TRUST AND HE DID. SO I STOPPED DIGGING INTO HIS PAST.
YOU TOLD ME TO DO THIS MY WAY.
I DID. BUT YOU LET RAPTOR WALK. HE STOLE MILLIONS OF DOLLARS, DICK.
WE HAVE INFORMANTS. WE WORK WITH CRIMINALS WHEN WE NEED TO. BUT WHEN WE'RE DONE, THEY FACE JUSTICE.
WE NEED THEIR FEAR, NOT THEIR TRUST.
YOU'RE LECTURING ME ABOUT TRUST?
YOU DON'T TRUST ANYONE, BRUCE.
INCLUDING ME.
I USED TO TRY TO FIGURE OUT WHY IT WAS SO HARD FOR YOU. BUT I THINK I'VE FIGURED IT OUT.
YOU CAN'T BELIEVE ANYONE CAN WALK THE LINE BETWEEN LIGHT AND DARK.
BECAUSE YOU KNOW THAT IF YOU STEPPED OVER FOR EVEN A SECOND...
...YOU'D NEVER COME BACK.
I'M NOT YOU, BRUCE.

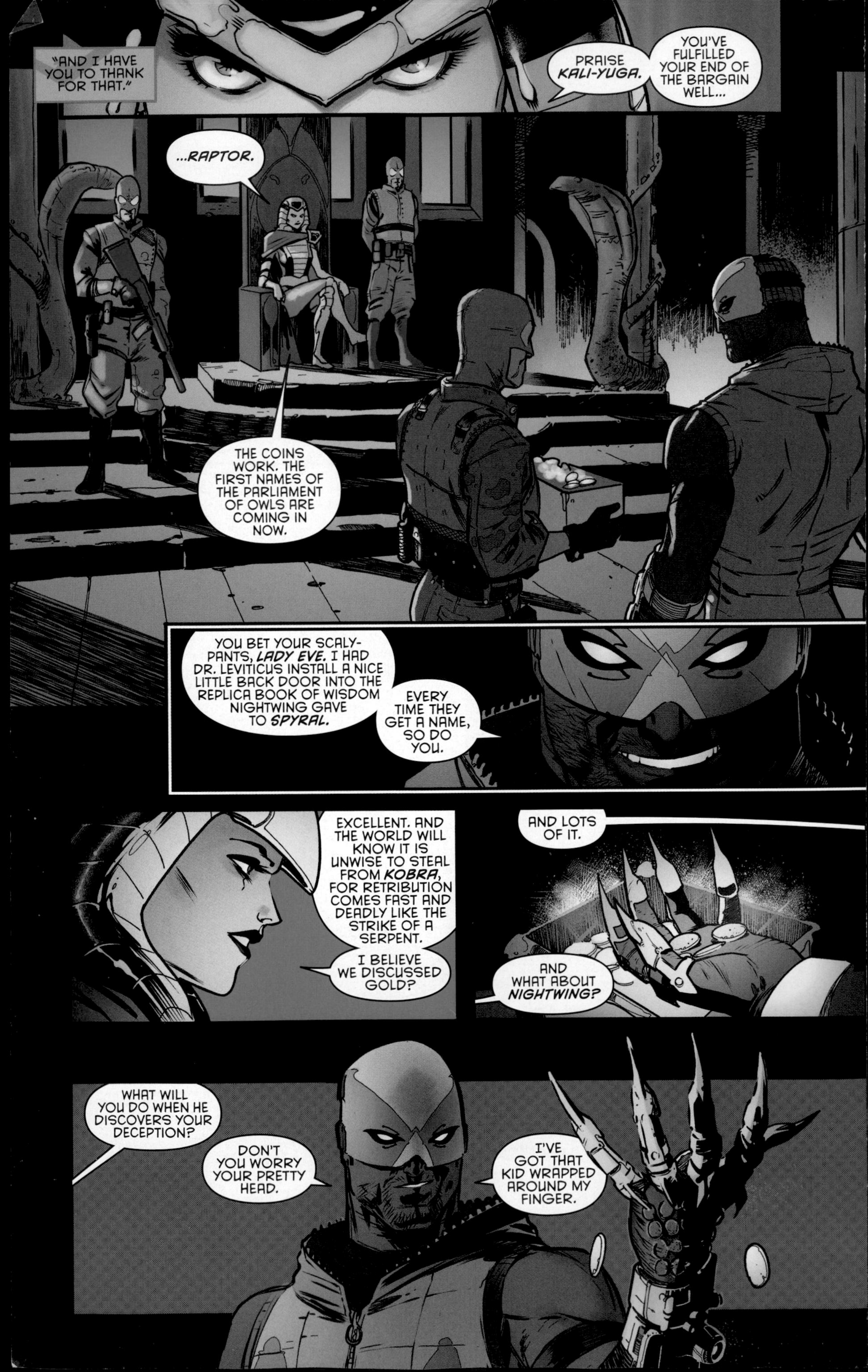
"AND I HAVE YOU TO THANK FOR THAT."
PRAISE KALI-YUGA.
YOU'VE FULFILLED YOUR END OF THE BARGAIN WELL...
...RAPTOR.
THE COINS WORK. THE FIRST NAMES OF THE PARLIAMENT OF OWLS ARE COMING IN NOW.
YOU BET YOUR SCALY-PANTS, LADY EVE. I HAD DR. LEVITICUS INSTALL A NICE LITTLE BACK DOOR INTO THE REPLICA BOOK OF WISDOM NIGHTWING GAVE TO SPYRAL.
EVERY TIME THEY GET A NAME, SO DO YOU.
EXCELLENT. AND THE WORLD WILL KNOW IT IS UNWISE TO STEAL FROM KOBRA, FOR RETRIBUTION COMES FAST AND DEADLY LIKE THE STRIKE OF A SERPENT.
I BELIEVE WE DISCUSSED GOLD?
AND LOTS OF IT.
AND WHAT ABOUT NIGHTWING?
WHAT WILL YOU DO WHEN HE DISCOVERS YOUR DECEPTION?
DON'T YOU WORRY YOUR PRETTY HEAD.
I'VE GOT THAT KID WRAPPED AROUND MY FINGER.

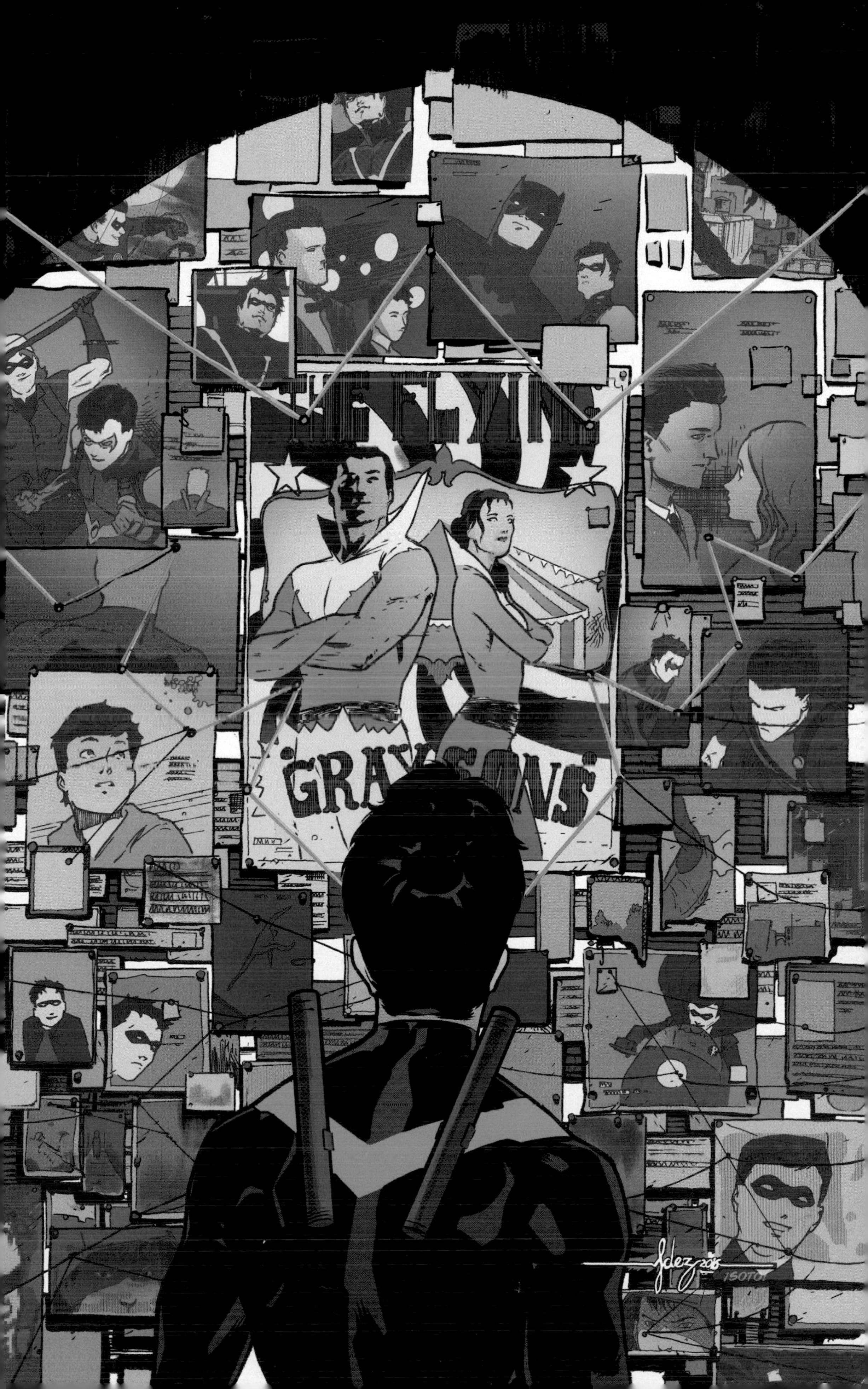
THE FLYING
GRAYSONS

RISE OF RAPTOR, PART 1

TIM SEELEY writer ∗ JAVIER FERNÁNDEZ artist ∗ CHRIS SOTOMAYOR colorist
CARLOS M. MANGUAL letterer ∗ JAVIER FERNÁNDEZ and CHRIS SOTOMAYOR cover artists

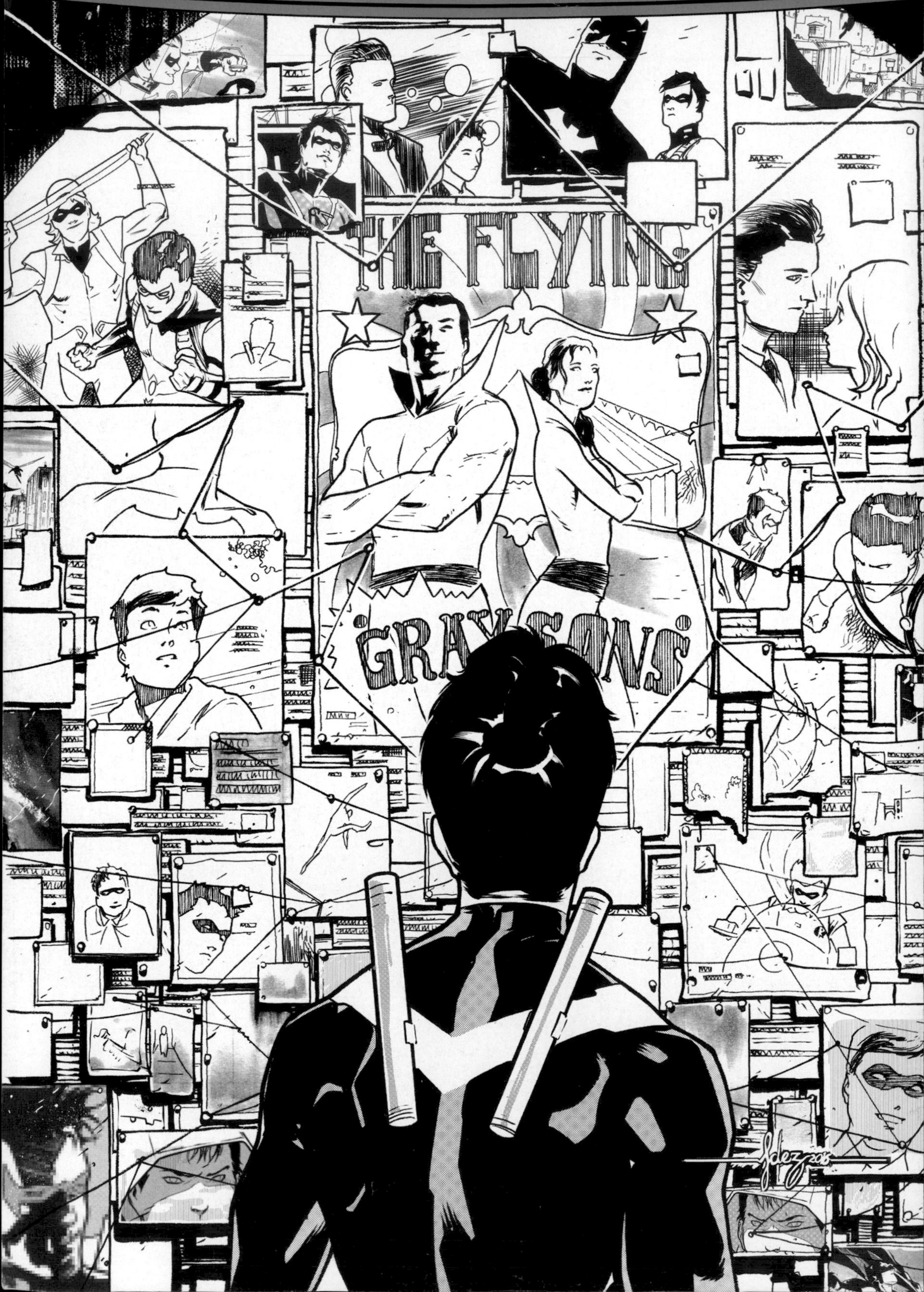
THE FLYING

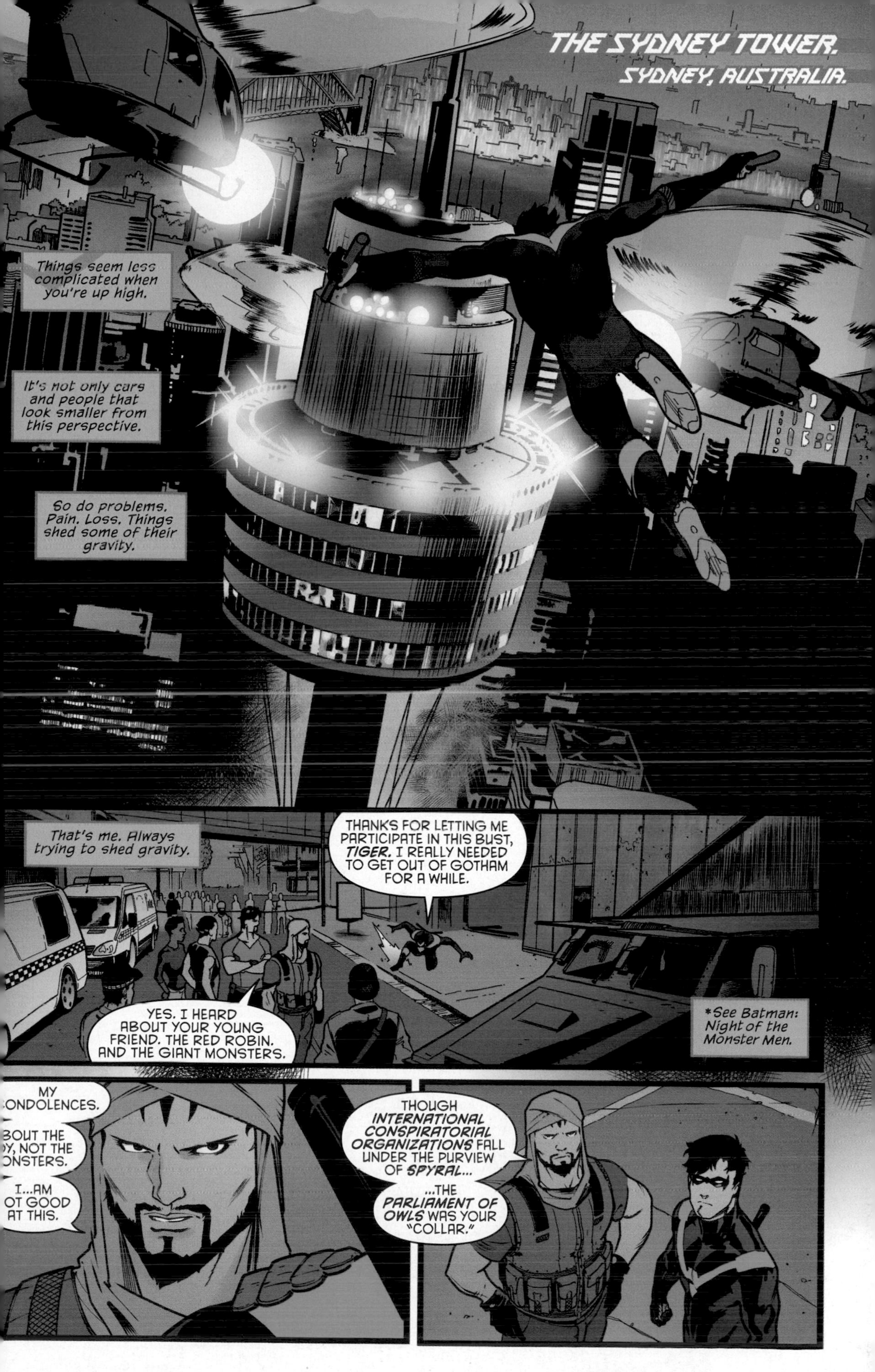

THE SYDNEY TOWER.
SYDNEY, AUSTRALIA.
Things seem less complicated when you're up high.
It's not only cars and people that look smaller from this perspective.
So do problems. Pain. Loss. Things shed some of their gravity.
That's me. Always trying to shed gravity.
THANKS FOR LETTING ME PARTICIPATE IN THIS BUST, TIGER. I REALLY NEEDED TO GET OUT OF GOTHAM FOR A WHILE.
YES. I HEARD ABOUT YOUR YOUNG FRIEND. THE RED ROBIN. AND THE GIANT MONSTERS.
*See Batman: Night of the Monster Men.
MY CONDOLENCES.
ABOUT THE BOY, NOT THE MONSTERS.
I...AM NOT GOOD AT THIS.
THOUGH INTERNATIONAL CONSPIRATORIAL ORGANIZATIONS FALL UNDER THE PURVIEW OF SPYRAL...
...THE PARLIAMENT OF OWLS WAS YOUR "COLLAR."

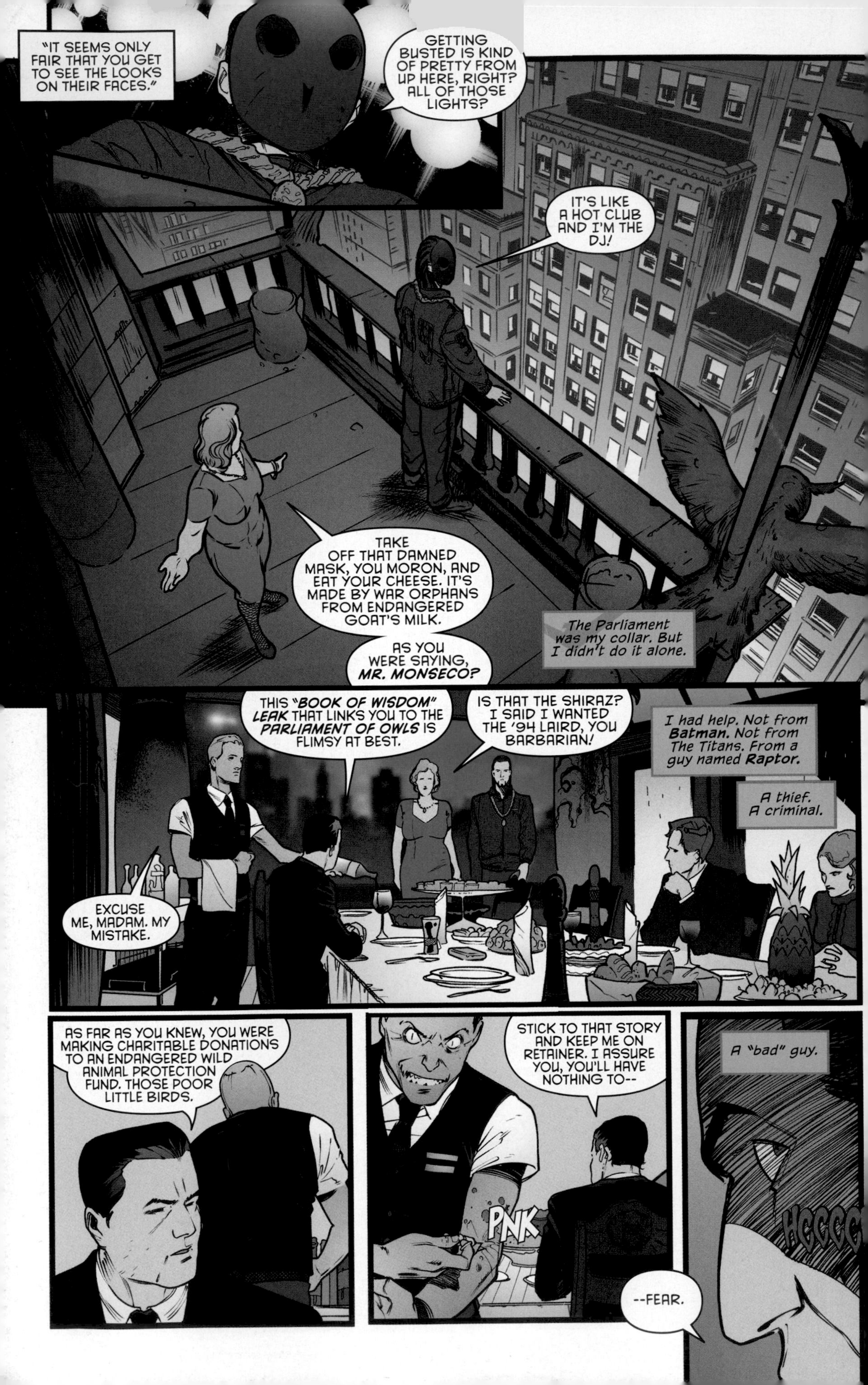
"IT SEEMS ONLY FAIR THAT YOU GET TO SEE THE LOOKS ON THEIR FACES."
GETTING BUSTED IS KIND OF PRETTY FROM UP HERE, RIGHT? ALL OF THOSE LIGHTS?
IT'S LIKE A HOT CLUB AND I'M THE DJ!
TAKE OFF THAT DAMNED MASK, YOU MORON, AND EAT YOUR CHEESE. IT'S MADE BY WAR ORPHANS FROM ENDANGERED GOAT'S MILK.
AS YOU WERE SAYING, MR. MONSECO?
The Parliament was my collar. But I didn't do it alone.
THIS "BOOK OF WISDOM" LEAK THAT LINKS YOU TO THE PARLIAMENT OF OWLS IS FLIMSY AT BEST.
IS THAT THE SHIRAZ? I SAID I WANTED THE '94 LAIRD, YOU BARBARIAN!
I had help. Not from Batman. Not from The Titans. From a guy named Raptor.
A thief. A criminal.
EXCUSE ME, MADAM. MY MISTAKE.
AS FAR AS YOU KNEW, YOU WERE MAKING CHARITABLE DONATIONS TO AN ENDANGERED WILD ANIMAL PROTECTION FUND. THOSE POOR LITTLE BIRDS.
STICK TO THAT STORY AND KEEP ME ON RETAINER. I ASSURE YOU, YOU'LL HAVE NOTHING TO--
PNK
A "bad" guy.
HCCCC
--FEAR.

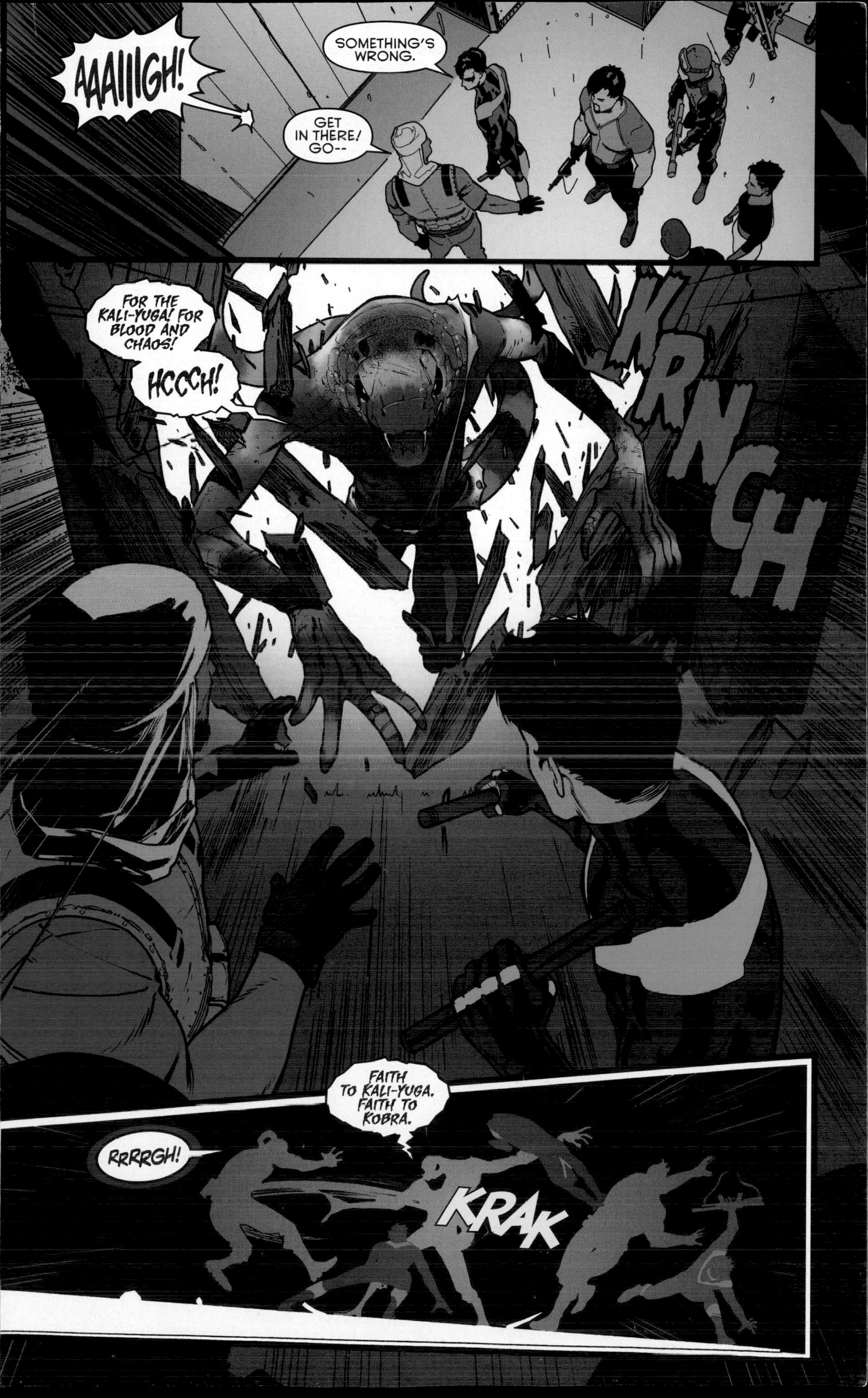
AAAIIIGH!
SOMETHING'S WRONG.
GET IN THERE! GO--
FOR THE KALI-YUGA! FOR BLOOD AND CHAOS!
HCCCH!
KRNCH
FAITH TO KALI-YUGA. FAITH TO KOBRA.
RRRRGH!
KRAK

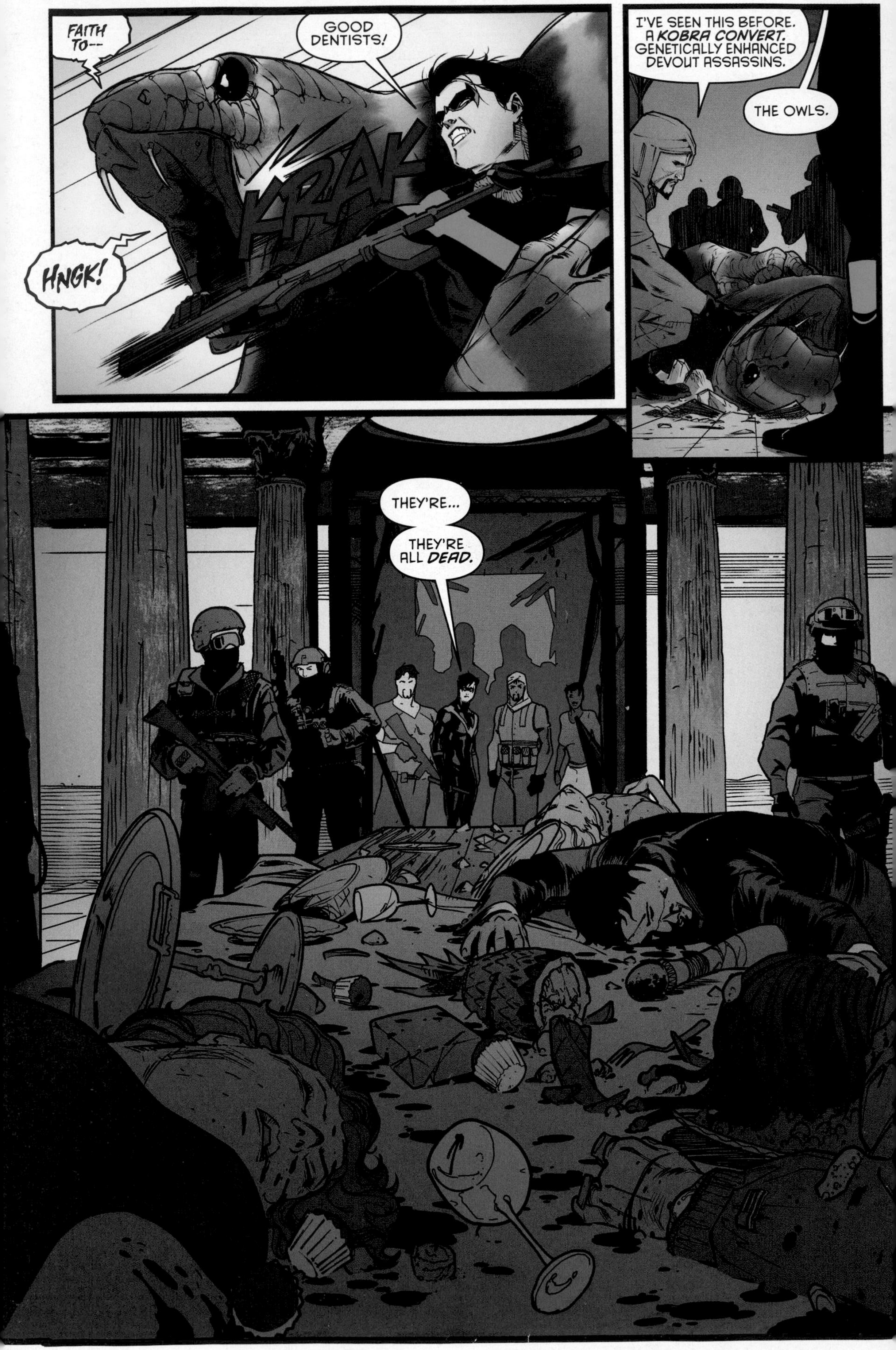
FAITH TO--
GOOD DENTISTS!
KRAK
HNGK!
I'VE SEEN THIS BEFORE. A KOBRA CONVERT. GENETICALLY ENHANCED DEVOUT ASSASSINS.
THE OWLS.
THEY'RE...
THEY'RE ALL DEAD.

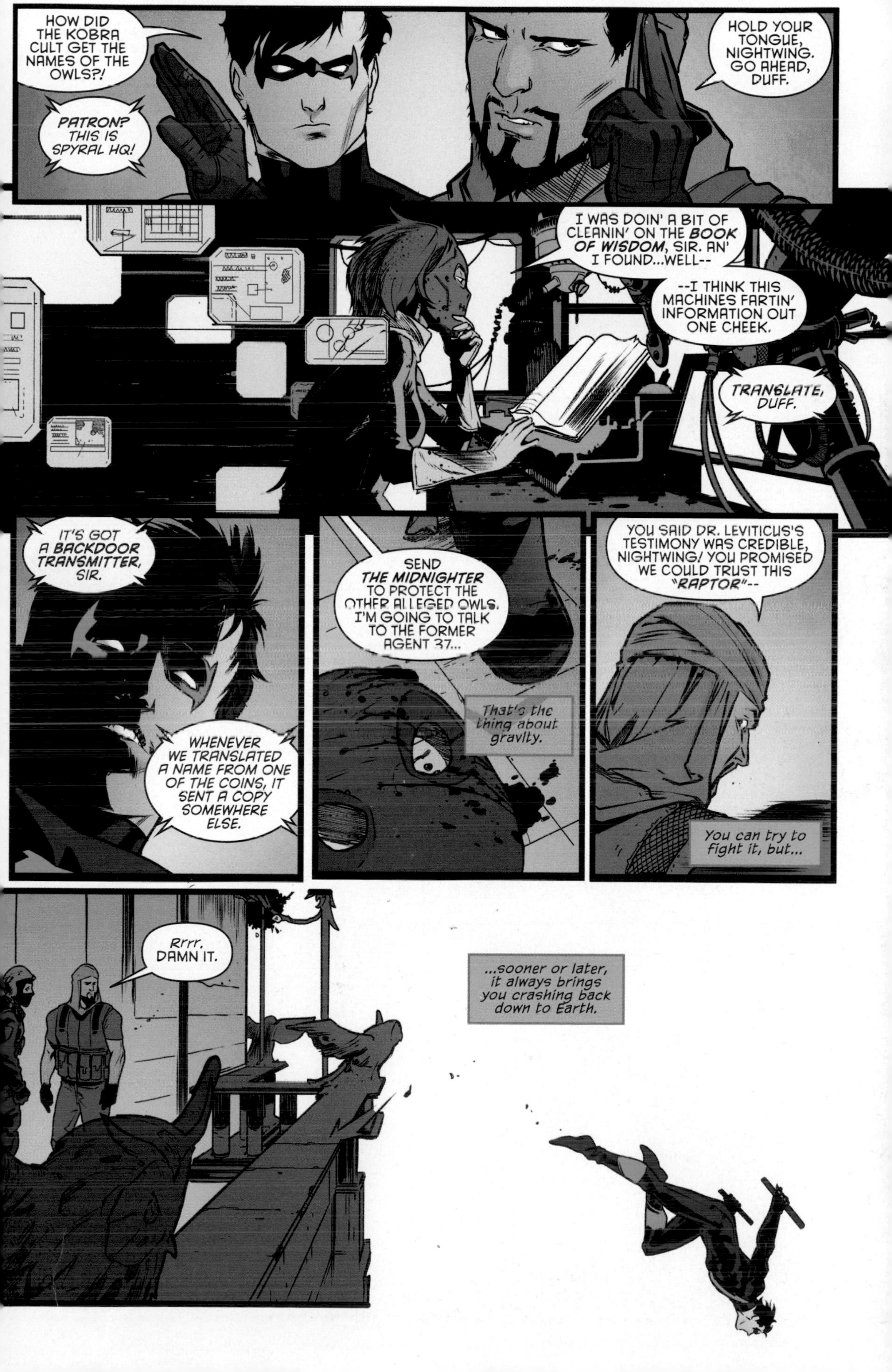
HOW DID THE KOBRA CULT GET THE NAMES OF THE OWLS?!
PATRON? THIS IS SPYRAL HQ!
HOLD YOUR TONGUE, NIGHTWING. GO AHEAD, DUFF.
I WAS DOIN' A BIT OF CLEANIN' ON THE BOOK OF WISDOM, SIR. AN' I FOUND...WELL--
--I THINK THIS MACHINES FARTIN' INFORMATION OUT ONE CHEEK.
TRANSLATE, DUFF.
IT'S GOT A BACKDOOR TRANSMITTER, SIR.
WHENEVER WE TRANSLATED A NAME FROM ONE OF THE COINS, IT SENT A COPY SOMEWHERE ELSE.
SEND THE MIDNIGHTER TO PROTECT THE OTHER ALLEGED OWLS. I'M GOING TO TALK TO THE FORMER AGENT 37...
That's the thing about gravity.
YOU SAID DR. LEVITICUS'S TESTIMONY WAS CREDIBLE, NIGHTWING! YOU PROMISED WE COULD TRUST THIS "RAPTOR"--
You can try to fight it, but...
Rrrr. DAMN IT.
...sooner or later, it always brings you crashing back down to Earth.

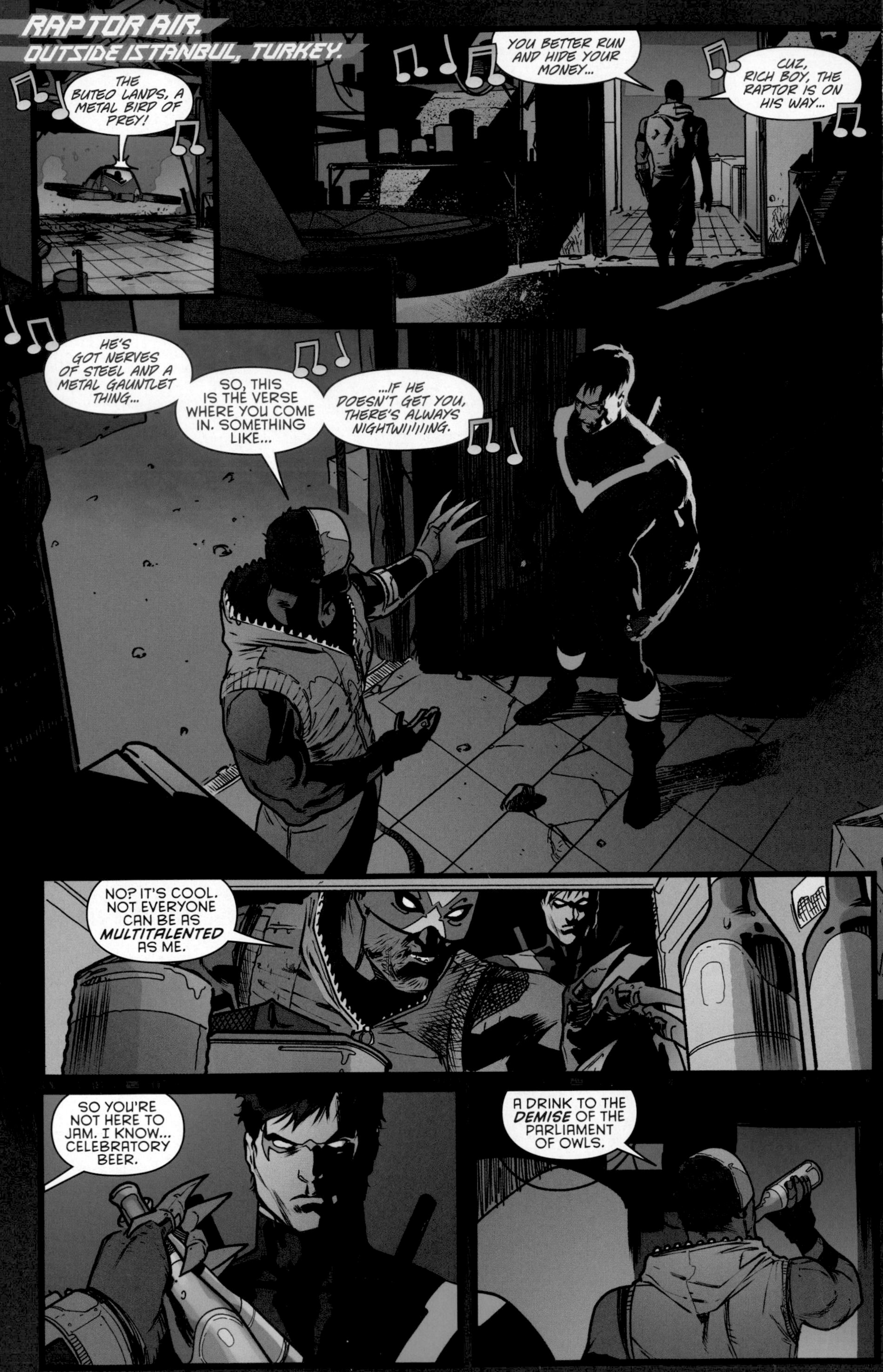
RAPTOR AIR.
OUTSIDE ISTANBUL, TURKEY.
THE BUTEO LANDS, A METAL BIRD OF PREY!
YOU BETTER RUN AND HIDE YOUR MONEY...
CUZ, RICH BOY, THE RAPTOR IS ON HIS WAY...
HE'S GOT NERVES OF STEEL AND A METAL GAUNTLET THING...
SO, THIS IS THE VERSE WHERE YOU COME IN. SOMETHING LIKE...
...IF HE DOESN'T GET YOU, THERE'S ALWAYS NIGHTWIIIIIING.
NO? IT'S COOL. NOT EVERYONE CAN BE AS MULTITALENTED AS ME.
SO YOU'RE NOT HERE TO JAM. I KNOW... CELEBRATORY BEER.
A DRINK TO THE DEMISE OF THE PARLIAMENT OF OWLS.

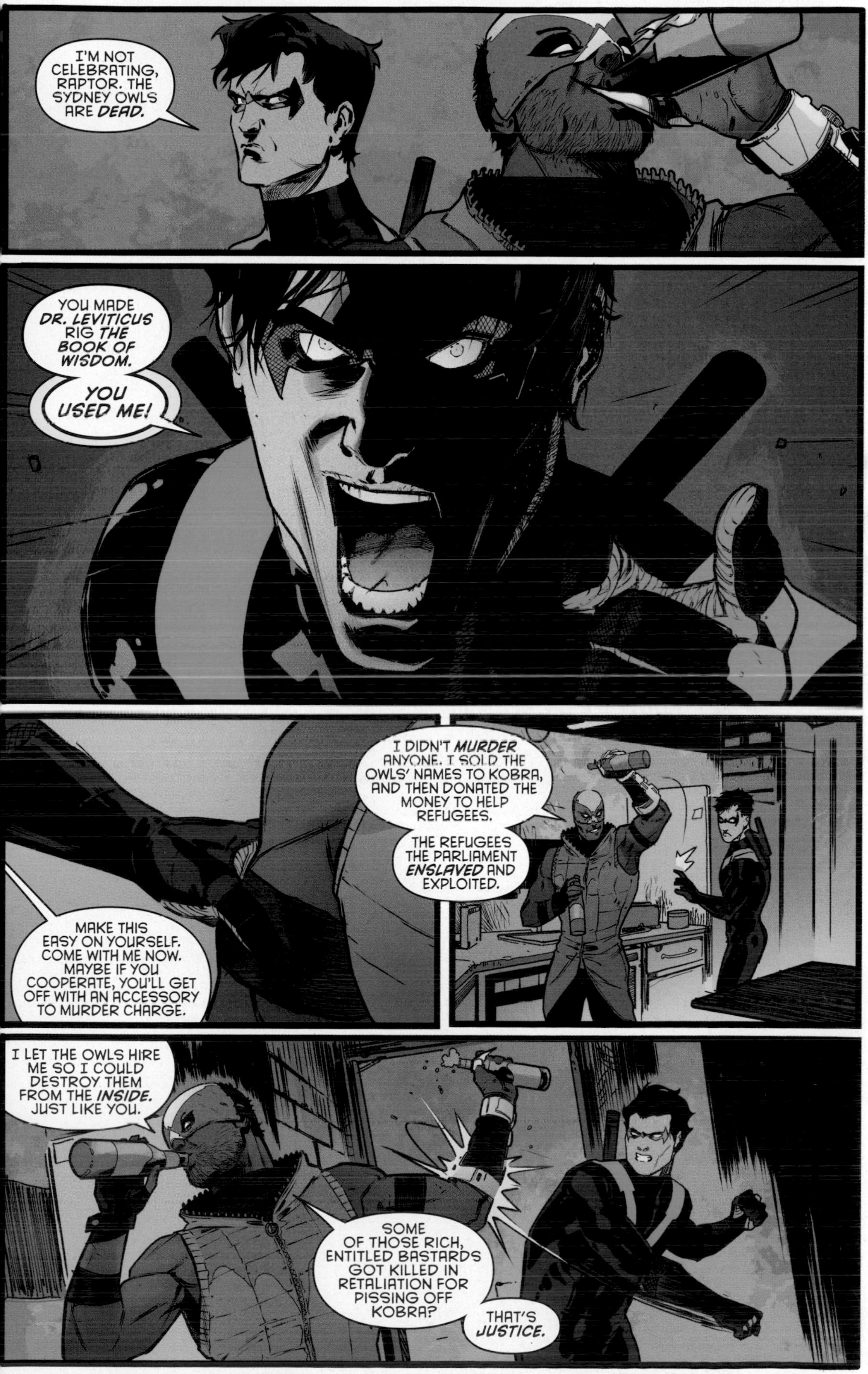
I'M NOT CELEBRATING, RAPTOR. THE SYDNEY OWLS ARE *DEAD.*
YOU MADE *DR. LEVITICUS* RIG *THE BOOK OF WISDOM.*
YOU USED ME!
MAKE THIS EASY ON YOURSELF. COME WITH ME NOW. MAYBE IF YOU COOPERATE, YOU'LL GET OFF WITH AN ACCESSORY TO MURDER CHARGE.
I DIDN'T *MURDER* ANYONE. I SOLD THE OWLS' NAMES TO KOBRA, AND THEN DONATED THE MONEY TO HELP REFUGEES.
THE REFUGEES THE PARLIAMENT *ENSLAVED* AND EXPLOITED.
I LET THE OWLS HIRE ME SO I COULD DESTROY THEM FROM THE *INSIDE.* JUST LIKE YOU.
SOME OF THOSE RICH, ENTITLED BASTARDS GOT KILLED IN RETALIATION FOR PISSING OFF KOBRA?
THAT'S *JUSTICE.*

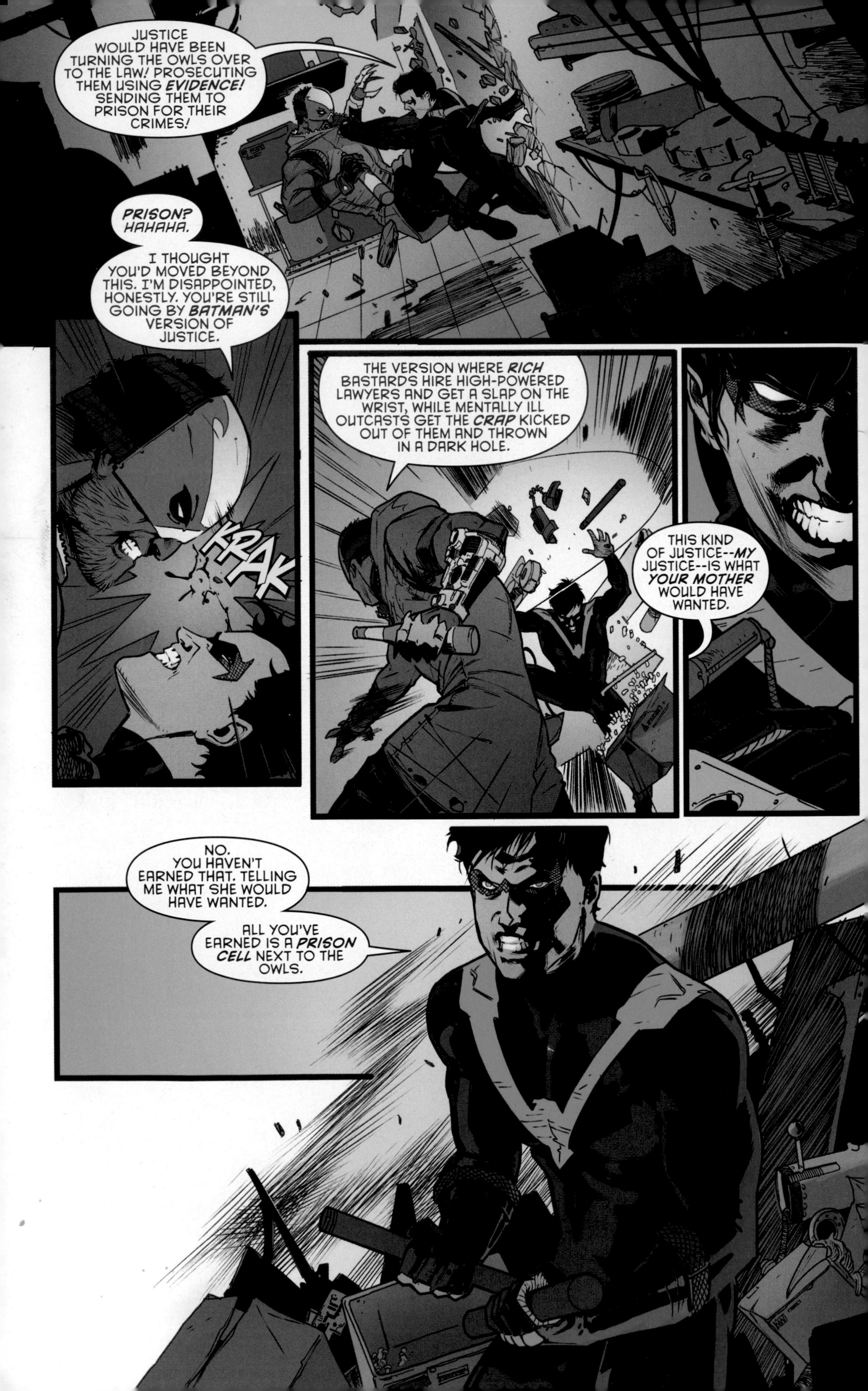
JUSTICE WOULD HAVE BEEN TURNING THE OWLS OVER TO THE LAW! PROSECUTING THEM USING EVIDENCE! SENDING THEM TO PRISON FOR THEIR CRIMES!
PRISON? HAHAHA.
I THOUGHT YOU'D MOVED BEYOND THIS. I'M DISAPPOINTED, HONESTLY. YOU'RE STILL GOING BY BATMAN'S VERSION OF JUSTICE.
KRAK
THE VERSION WHERE RICH BASTARDS HIRE HIGH-POWERED LAWYERS AND GET A SLAP ON THE WRIST, WHILE MENTALLY ILL OUTCASTS GET THE CRAP KICKED OUT OF THEM AND THROWN IN A DARK HOLE.
THIS KIND OF JUSTICE--MY JUSTICE--IS WHAT YOUR MOTHER WOULD HAVE WANTED.
NO. YOU HAVEN'T EARNED THAT. TELLING ME WHAT SHE WOULD HAVE WANTED.
ALL YOU'VE EARNED IS A PRISON CELL NEXT TO THE OWLS.

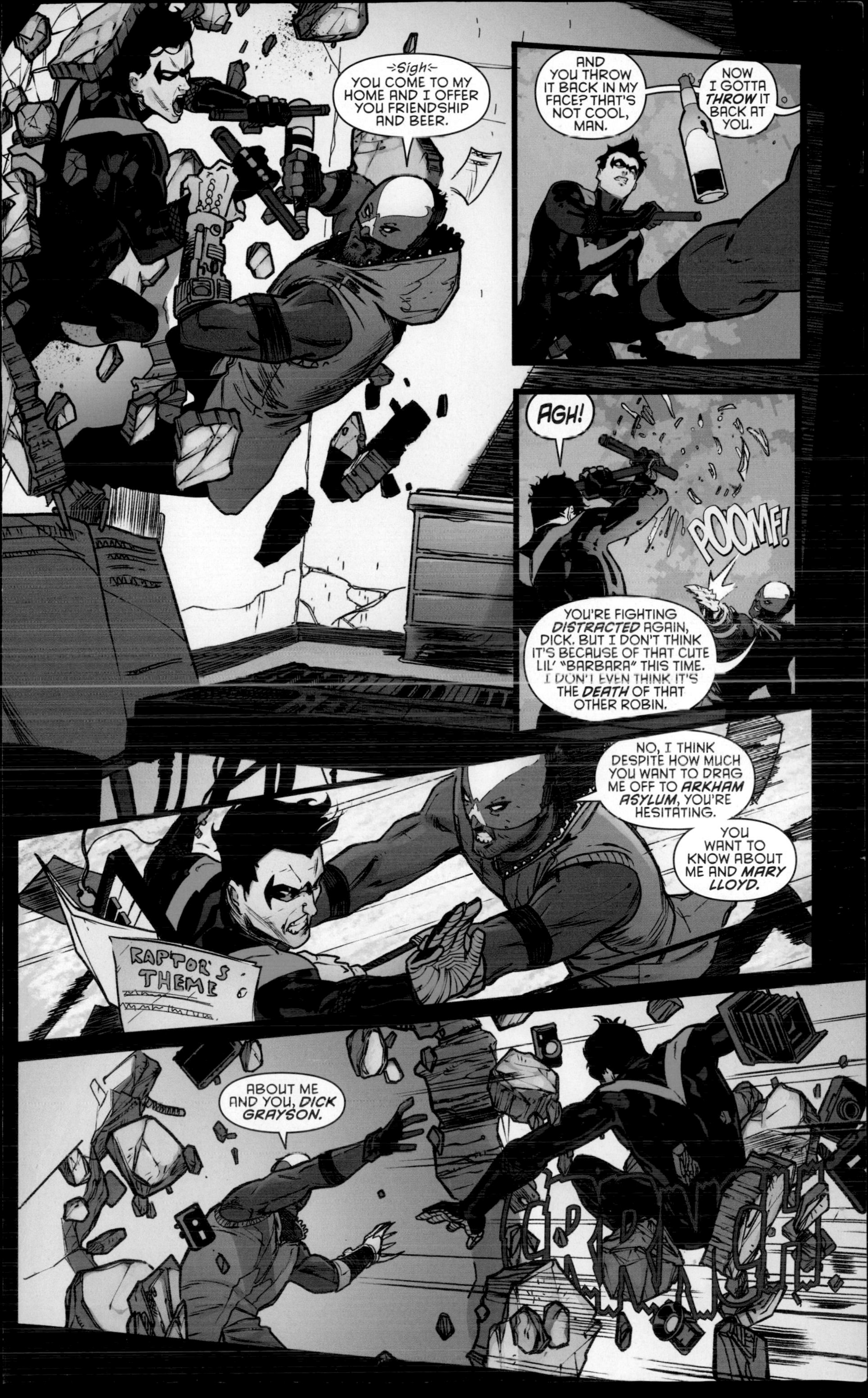
-Sigh-
YOU COME TO MY HOME AND I OFFER YOU FRIENDSHIP AND BEER.
AND YOU THROW IT BACK IN MY FACE? THAT'S NOT COOL, MAN.
NOW I GOTTA THROW IT BACK AT YOU.
AGH!
POOMF!
YOU'RE FIGHTING DISTRACTED AGAIN, DICK. BUT I DON'T THINK IT'S BECAUSE OF THAT CUTE LIL' "BARBARA" THIS TIME. I DON'T EVEN THINK IT'S THE DEATH OF THAT OTHER ROBIN.
NO, I THINK DESPITE HOW MUCH YOU WANT TO DRAG ME OFF TO ARKHAM ASYLUM, YOU'RE HESITATING.
YOU WANT TO KNOW ABOUT ME AND MARY LLOYD.
RAPTOR'S THEME
ABOUT ME AND YOU, DICK GRAYSON.

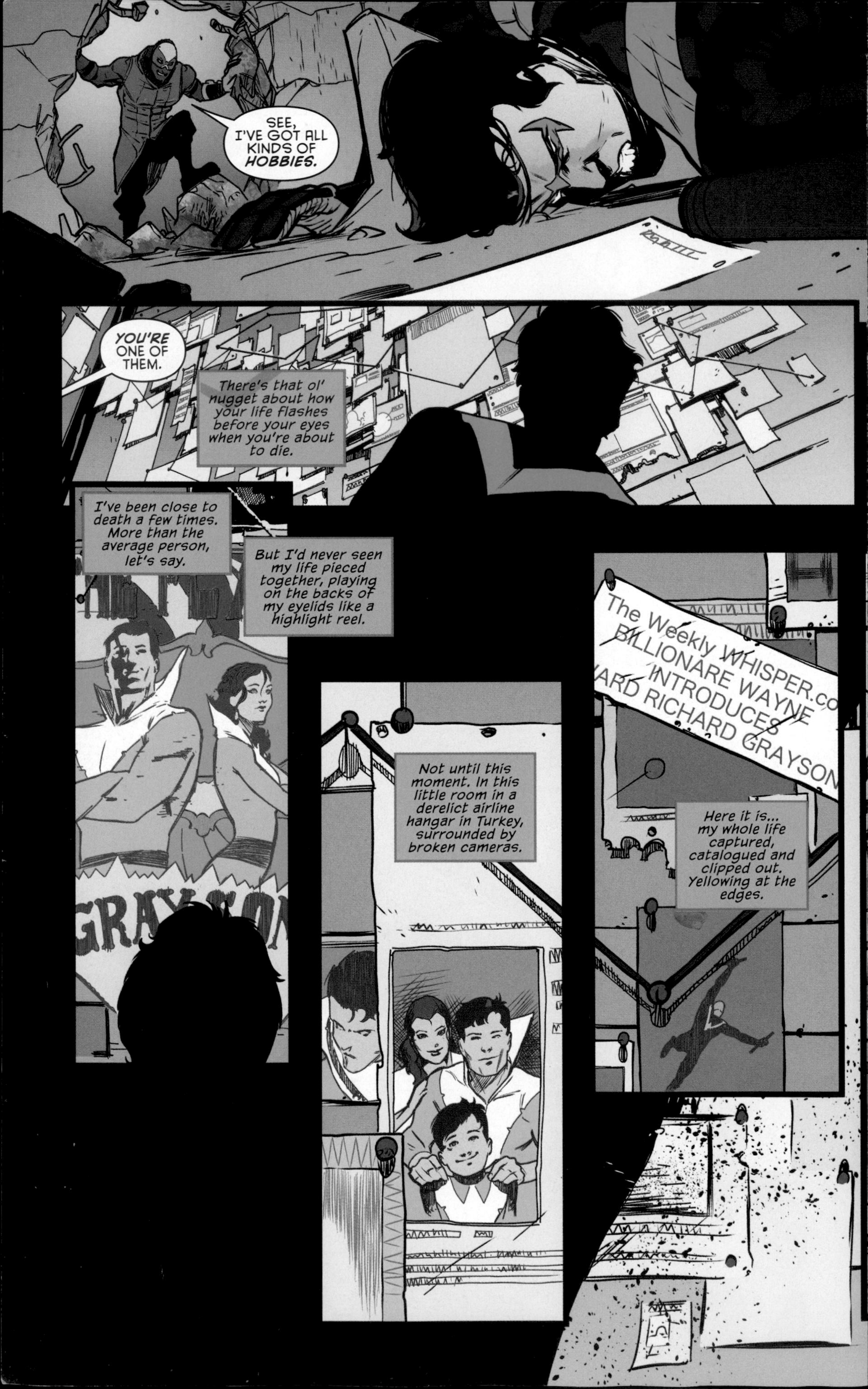
SEE, I'VE GOT ALL KINDS OF HOBBIES.
YOU'RE ONE OF THEM.
There's that ol' nugget about how your life flashes before your eyes when you're about to die.
I've been close to death a few times. More than the average person, let's say.
But I'd never seen my life pieced together, playing on the backs of my eyelids like a highlight reel.
The Weekly WHISPER.co
BILLIONARE WAYNE INTRODUCES
ARD RICHARD GRAYSON
GRAYSON
Not until this moment. In this little room in a derelict airline hangar in Turkey, surrounded by broken cameras.
Here it is... my whole life captured, catalogued and clipped out. Yellowing at the edges.

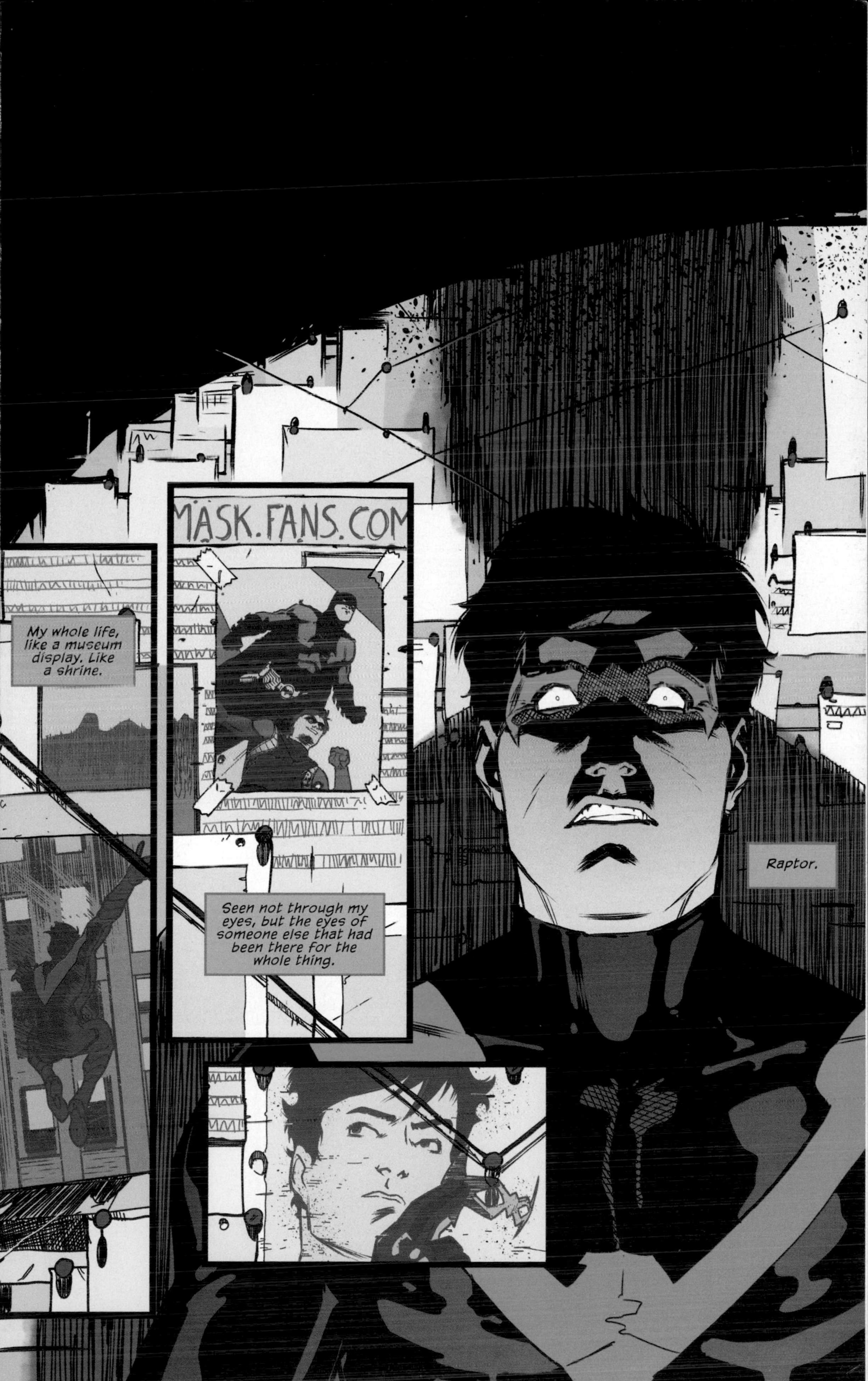
My whole life, like a museum display. Like a shrine.
MASK.FANS.COM
Seen not through my eyes, but the eyes of someone else that had been there for the whole thing.
Raptor.

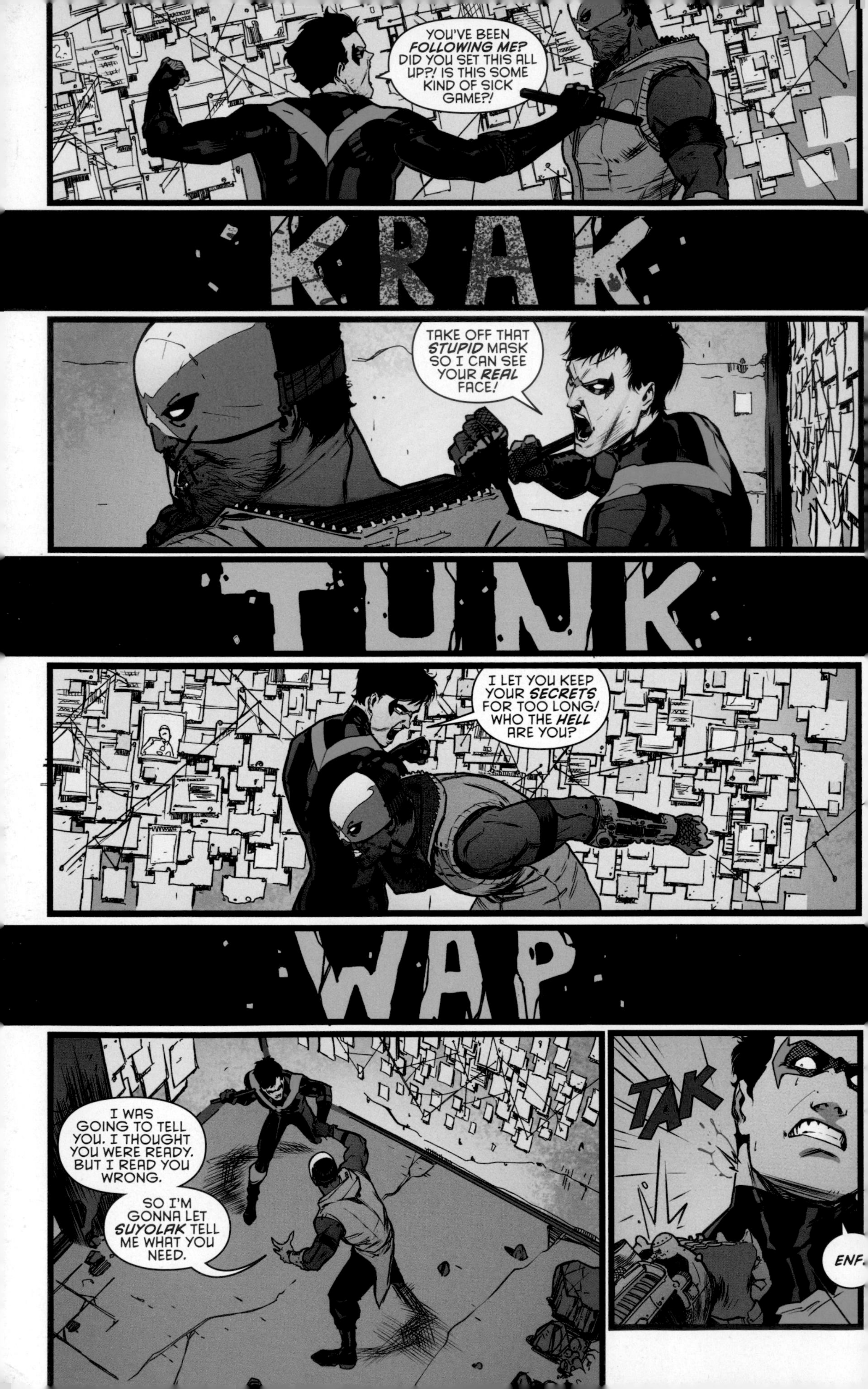
YOU'VE BEEN FOLLOWING ME? DID YOU SET THIS ALL UP?! IS THIS SOME KIND OF SICK GAME?!
KRAK
TAKE OFF THAT STUPID MASK SO I CAN SEE YOUR REAL FACE!
TUNK
I LET YOU KEEP YOUR SECRETS FOR TOO LONG! WHO THE HELL ARE YOU?
WAP
I WAS GOING TO TELL YOU. I THOUGHT YOU WERE READY. BUT I READ YOU WRONG.
SO I'M GONNA LET SUYOLAK TELL ME WHAT YOU NEED.
TAK
ENF.

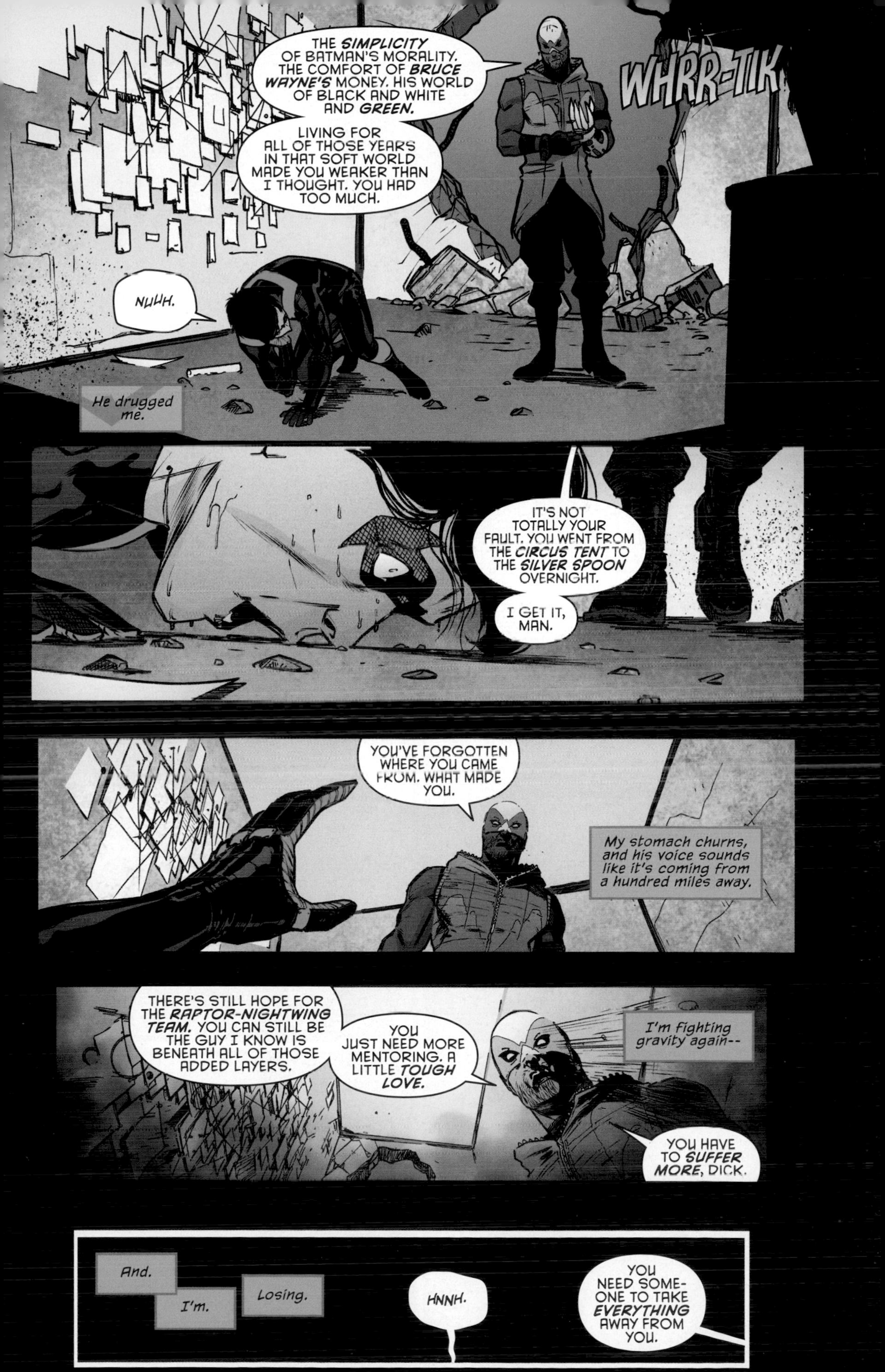

THE SIMPLICITY OF BATMAN'S MORALITY. THE COMFORT OF BRUCE WAYNE'S MONEY. HIS WORLD OF BLACK AND WHITE AND GREEN.
LIVING FOR ALL OF THOSE YEARS IN THAT SOFT WORLD MADE YOU WEAKER THAN I THOUGHT. YOU HAD TOO MUCH.
WHRR-TIK
NUUH.
He drugged me.
IT'S NOT TOTALLY YOUR FAULT. YOU WENT FROM THE CIRCUS TENT TO THE SILVER SPOON OVERNIGHT.
I GET IT, MAN.
YOU'VE FORGOTTEN WHERE YOU CAME FROM. WHAT MADE YOU.
My stomach churns, and his voice sounds like it's coming from a hundred miles away.
THERE'S STILL HOPE FOR THE RAPTOR-NIGHTWING TEAM. YOU CAN STILL BE THE GUY I KNOW IS BENEATH ALL OF THOSE ADDED LAYERS.
YOU JUST NEED MORE MENTORING. A LITTLE TOUGH LOVE.
I'm fighting gravity again--
YOU HAVE TO SUFFER MORE, DICK.
And.
I'm.
Losing.
HNNH.
YOU NEED SOMEONE TO TAKE EVERYTHING AWAY FROM YOU.

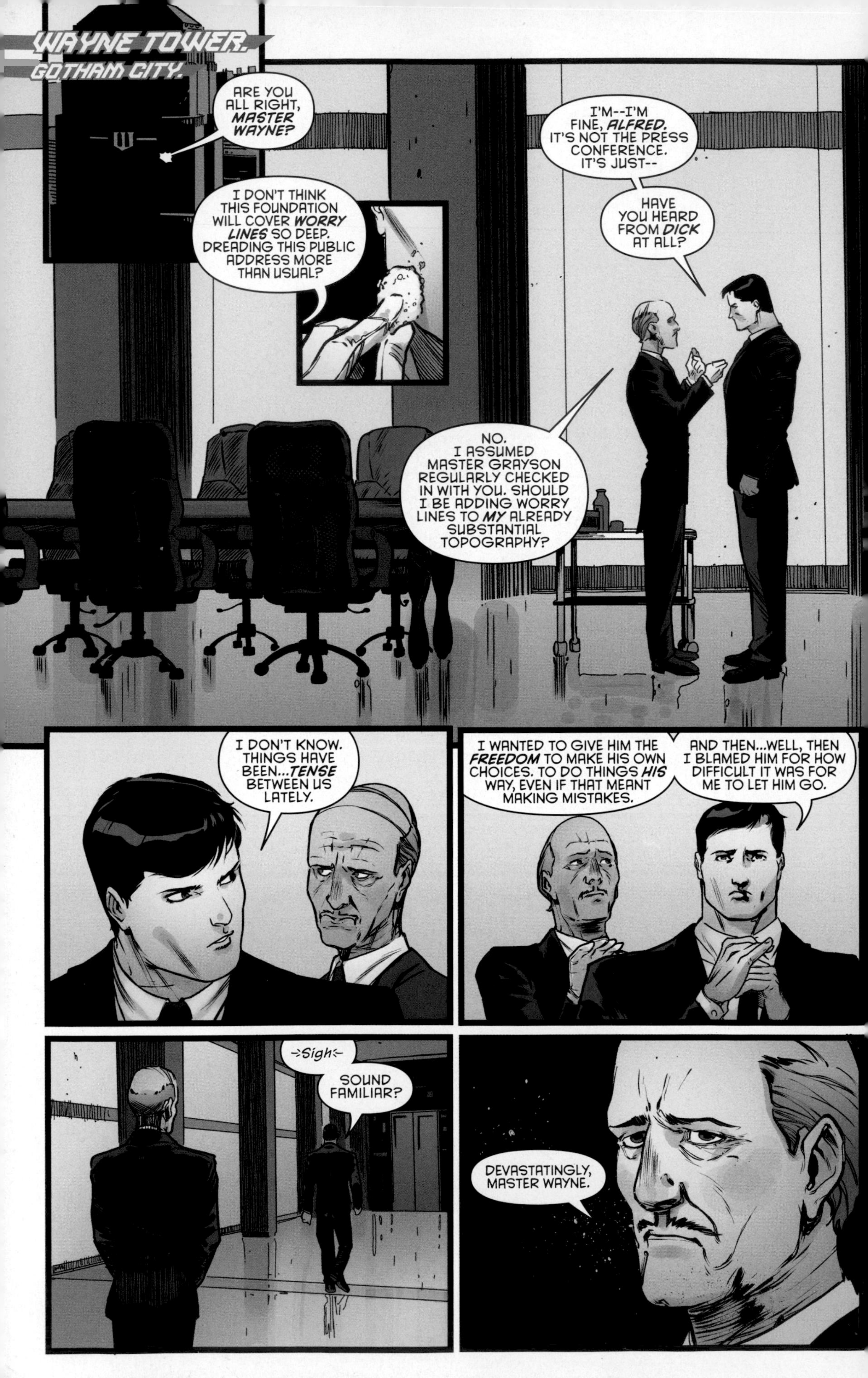
WAYNE TOWER. GOTHAM CITY.
ARE YOU ALL RIGHT, MASTER WAYNE?
I DON'T THINK THIS FOUNDATION WILL COVER WORRY LINES SO DEEP. DREADING THIS PUBLIC ADDRESS MORE THAN USUAL?
I'M--I'M FINE, ALFRED. IT'S NOT THE PRESS CONFERENCE. IT'S JUST--
HAVE YOU HEARD FROM DICK AT ALL?
NO. I ASSUMED MASTER GRAYSON REGULARLY CHECKED IN WITH YOU. SHOULD I BE ADDING WORRY LINES TO MY ALREADY SUBSTANTIAL TOPOGRAPHY?
I DON'T KNOW. THINGS HAVE BEEN...TENSE BETWEEN US LATELY.
I WANTED TO GIVE HIM THE FREEDOM TO MAKE HIS OWN CHOICES. TO DO THINGS HIS WAY, EVEN IF THAT MEANT MAKING MISTAKES.
AND THEN...WELL, THEN I BLAMED HIM FOR HOW DIFFICULT IT WAS FOR ME TO LET HIM GO.
-Sigh-
SOUND FAMILIAR?
DEVASTATINGLY, MASTER WAYNE.

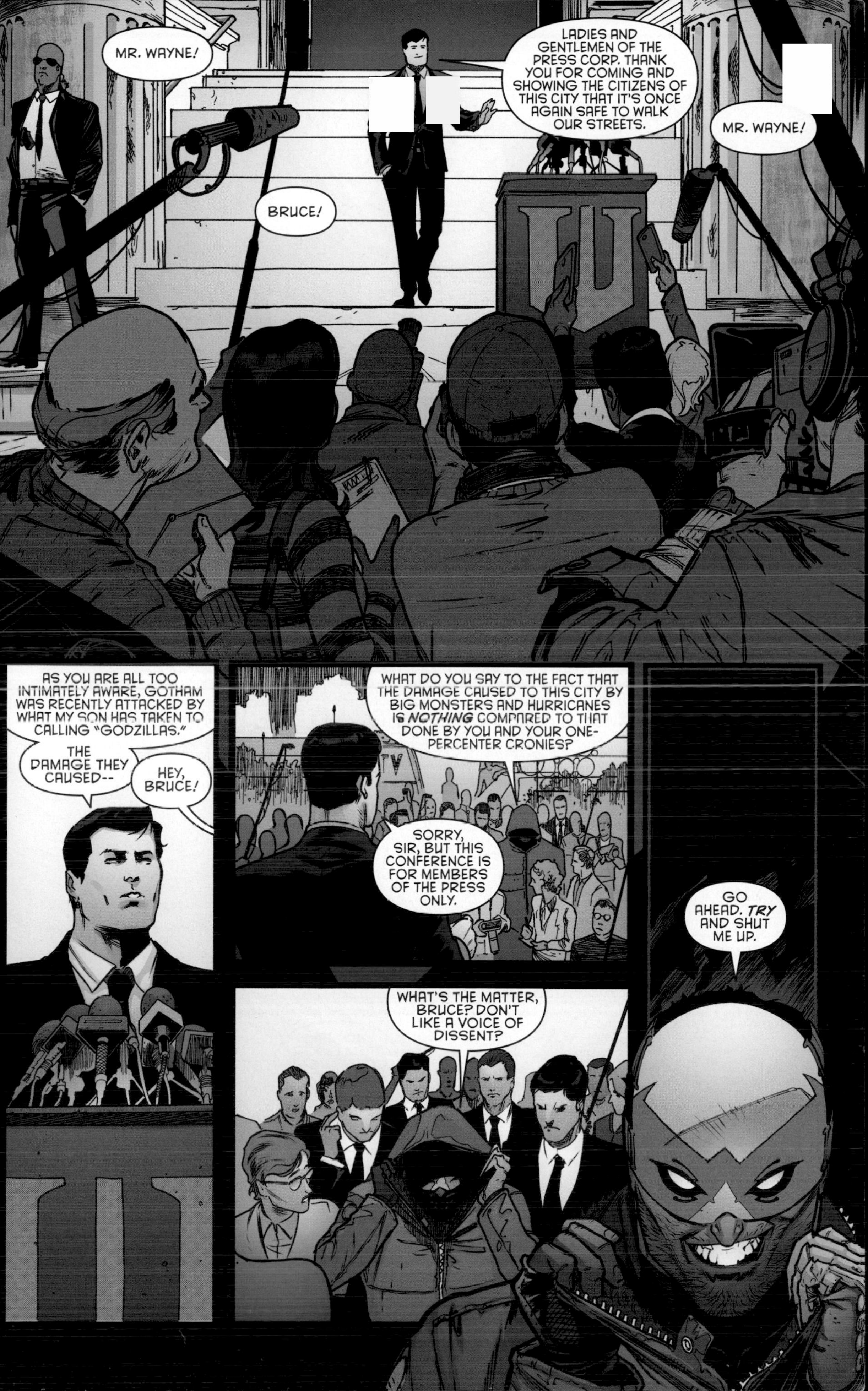
MR. WAYNE!
LADIES AND GENTLEMEN OF THE PRESS CORP. THANK YOU FOR COMING AND SHOWING THE CITIZENS OF THIS CITY THAT IT'S ONCE AGAIN SAFE TO WALK OUR STREETS.
MR. WAYNE!
BRUCE!
AS YOU ARE ALL TOO INTIMATELY AWARE, GOTHAM WAS RECENTLY ATTACKED BY WHAT MY SON HAS TAKEN TO CALLING "GODZILLAS."
THE DAMAGE THEY CAUSED--
HEY, BRUCE!
WHAT DO YOU SAY TO THE FACT THAT THE DAMAGE CAUSED TO THIS CITY BY BIG MONSTERS AND HURRICANES IS *NOTHING* COMPARED TO THAT DONE BY YOU AND YOUR ONE-PERCENTER CRONIES?
SORRY, SIR, BUT THIS CONFERENCE IS FOR MEMBERS OF THE PRESS ONLY.
GO AHEAD. ***TRY*** AND SHUT ME UP.
WHAT'S THE MATTER, BRUCE? DON'T LIKE A VOICE OF DISSENT?

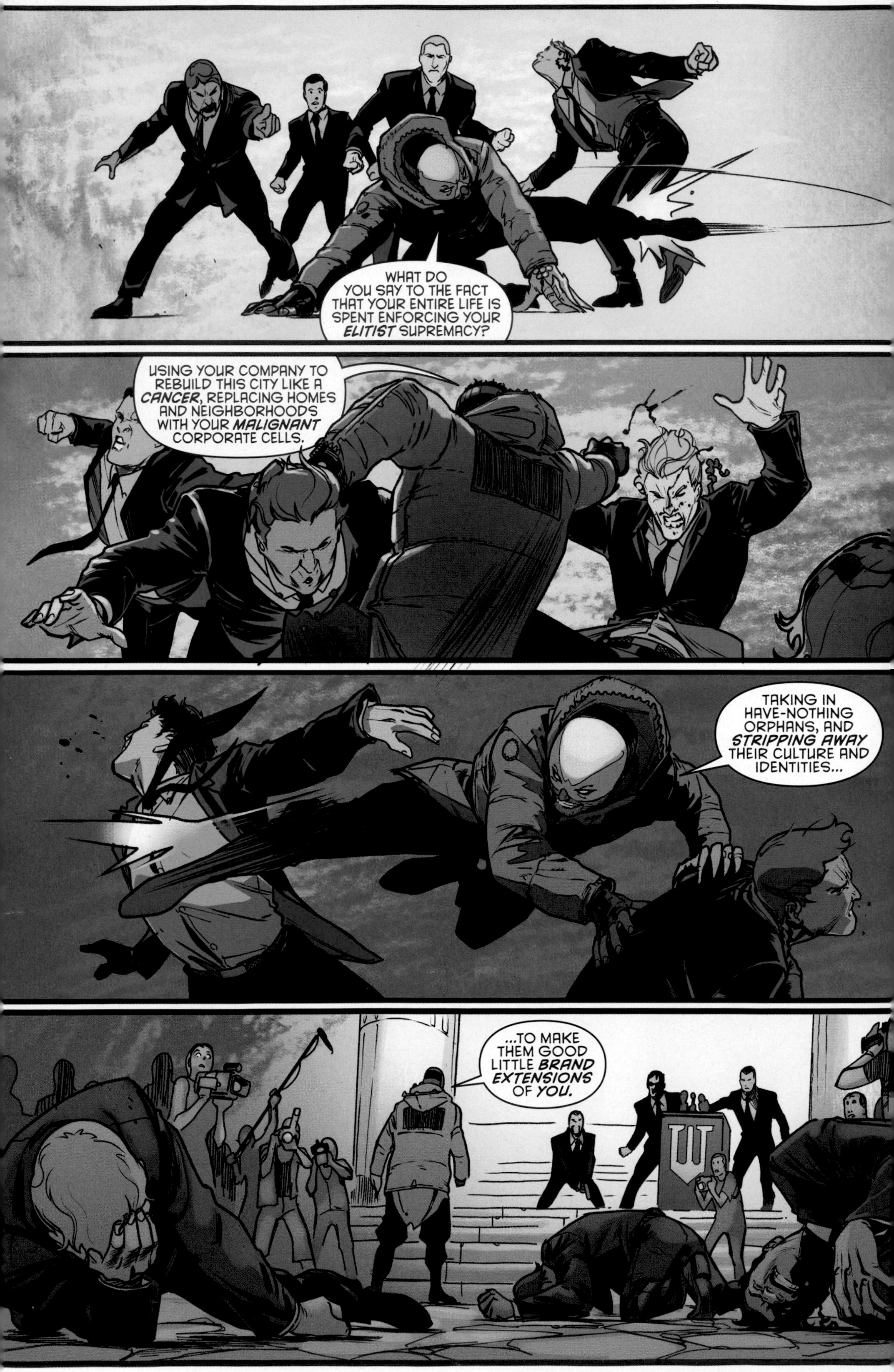
WHAT DO YOU SAY TO THE FACT THAT YOUR ENTIRE LIFE IS SPENT ENFORCING YOUR *ELITIST* SUPREMACY?
USING YOUR COMPANY TO REBUILD THIS CITY LIKE A *CANCER*, REPLACING HOMES AND NEIGHBORHOODS WITH YOUR *MALIGNANT* CORPORATE CELLS.
TAKING IN HAVE-NOTHING ORPHANS, AND *STRIPPING AWAY* THEIR CULTURE AND IDENTITIES...
...TO MAKE THEM GOOD LITTLE *BRAND EXTENSIONS* OF *YOU*.

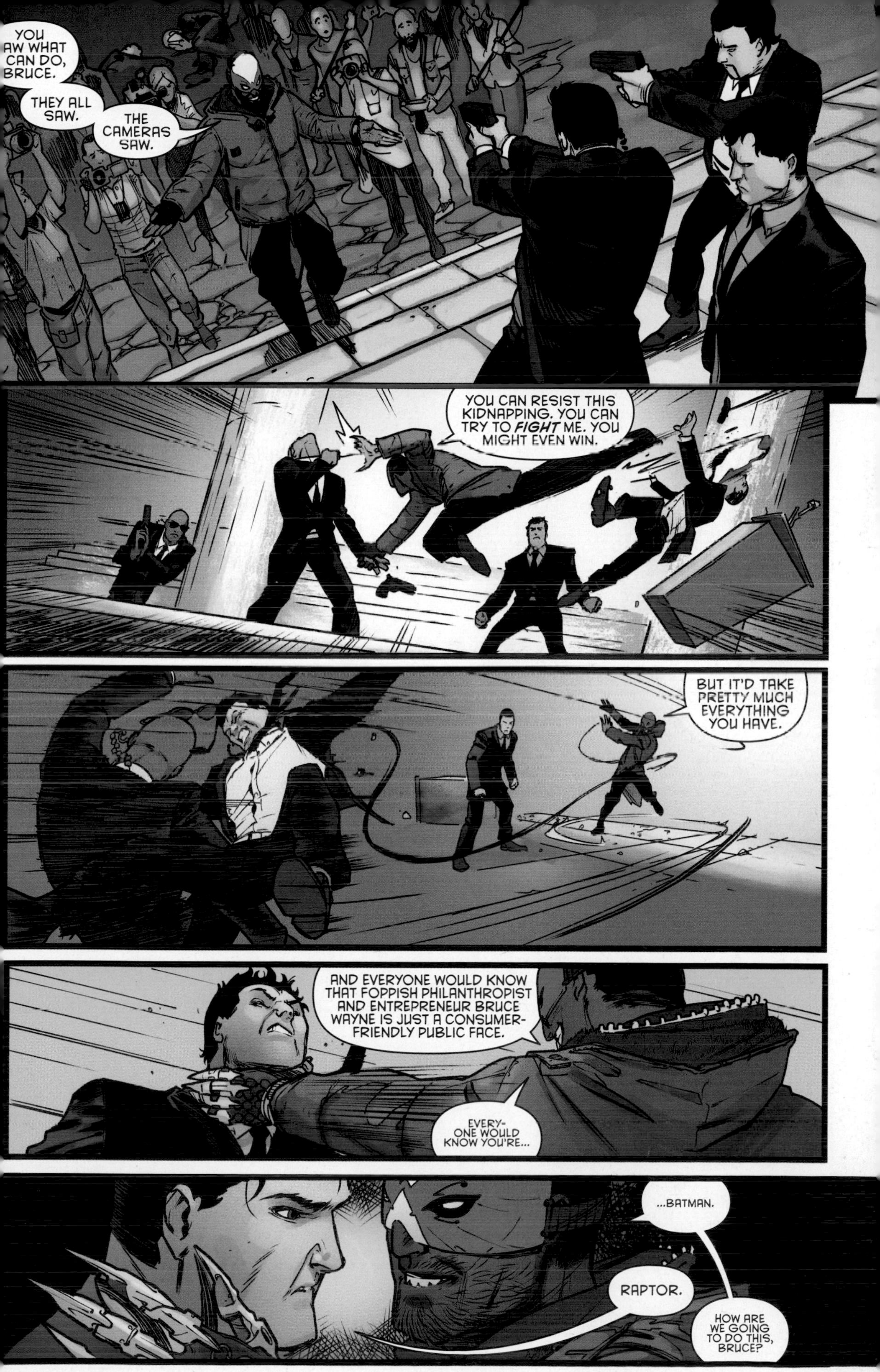
YOU AW WHAT CAN DO, BRUCE.
THEY ALL SAW.
THE CAMERAS SAW.
YOU CAN RESIST THIS KIDNAPPING. YOU CAN TRY TO FIGHT ME. YOU MIGHT EVEN WIN.
BUT IT'D TAKE PRETTY MUCH EVERYTHING YOU HAVE.
AND EVERYONE WOULD KNOW THAT FOPPISH PHILANTHROPIST AND ENTREPRENEUR BRUCE WAYNE IS JUST A CONSUMER-FRIENDLY PUBLIC FACE.
EVERY-ONE WOULD KNOW YOU'RE...
...BATMAN.
RAPTOR.
HOW ARE WE GOING TO DO THIS, BRUCE?

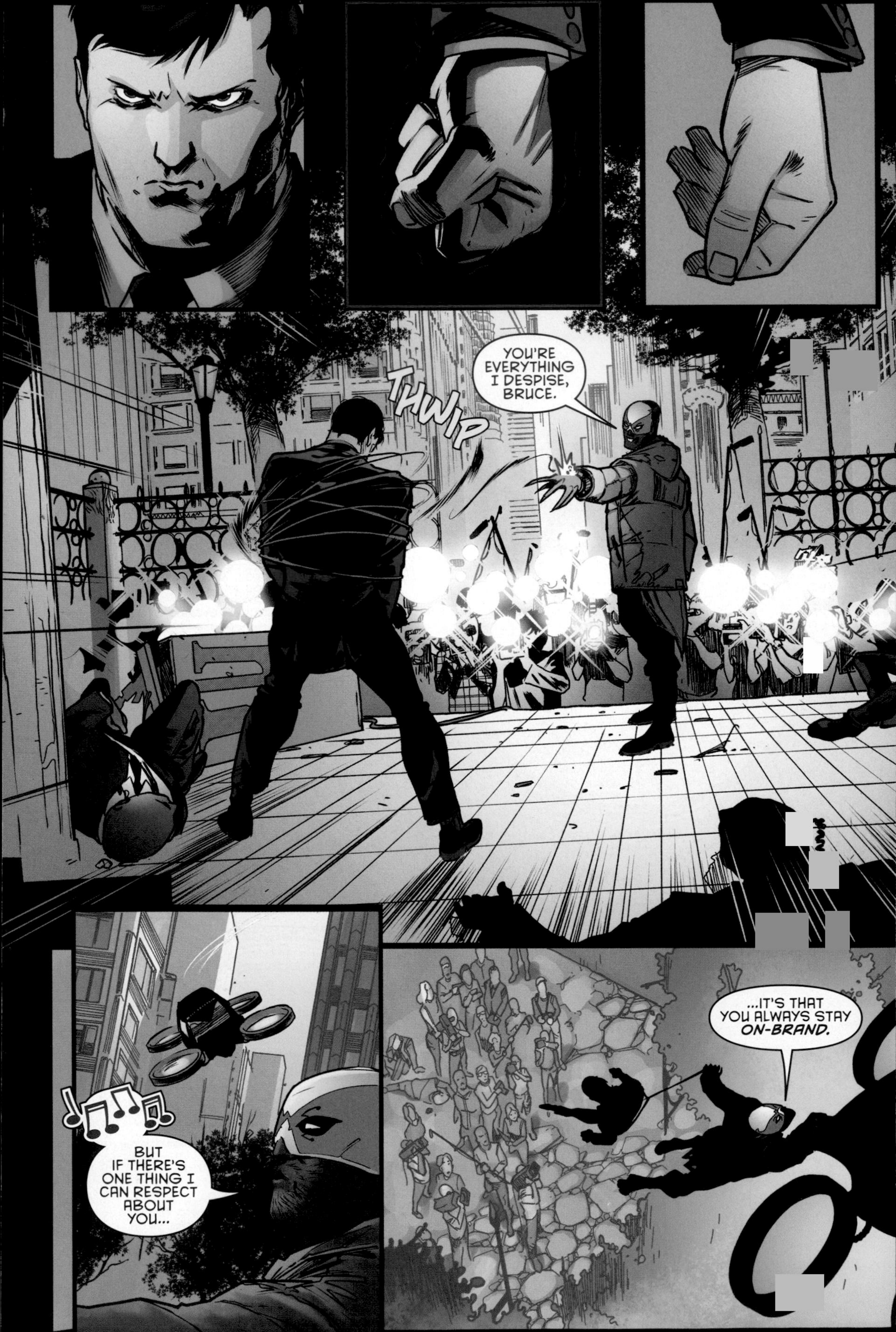
THWIP
YOU'RE EVERYTHING I DESPISE, BRUCE.
BUT IF THERE'S ONE THING I CAN RESPECT ABOUT YOU...
...IT'S THAT YOU ALWAYS STAY *ON-BRAND.*

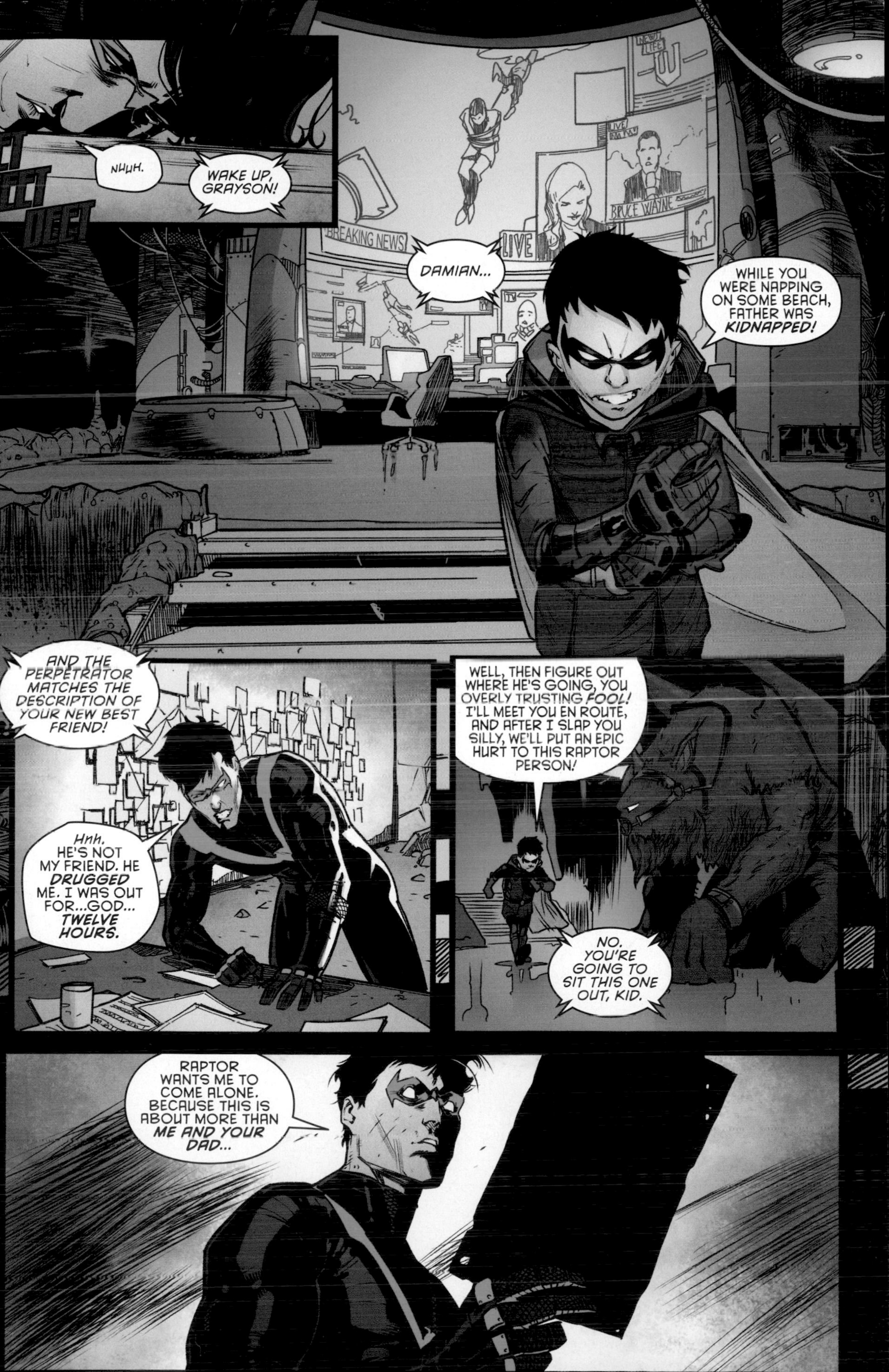
DEET DEET DEET
NUUH.
WAKE UP, GRAYSON!
BREAKING NEWS
LIVE
BRUCE WAYNE
DAMIAN...
WHILE YOU WERE NAPPING ON SOME BEACH, FATHER WAS *KIDNAPPED!*
AND THE PERPETRATOR MATCHES THE DESCRIPTION OF YOUR NEW BEST FRIEND!
Hnh. HE'S NOT MY FRIEND. HE ***DRUGGED*** ME. I WAS OUT FOR...GOD... ***TWELVE HOURS.***
WELL, THEN FIGURE OUT WHERE HE'S GOING, YOU OVERLY TRUSTING *FOOL!* I'LL MEET YOU EN ROUTE, AND AFTER I SLAP YOU SILLY, WE'LL PUT AN EPIC HURT TO THIS RAPTOR PERSON!
NO. YOU'RE GOING TO SIT THIS ONE OUT, KID.
RAPTOR WANTS ME TO COME ALONE. BECAUSE THIS IS ABOUT MORE THAN ***ME AND YOUR DAD...***

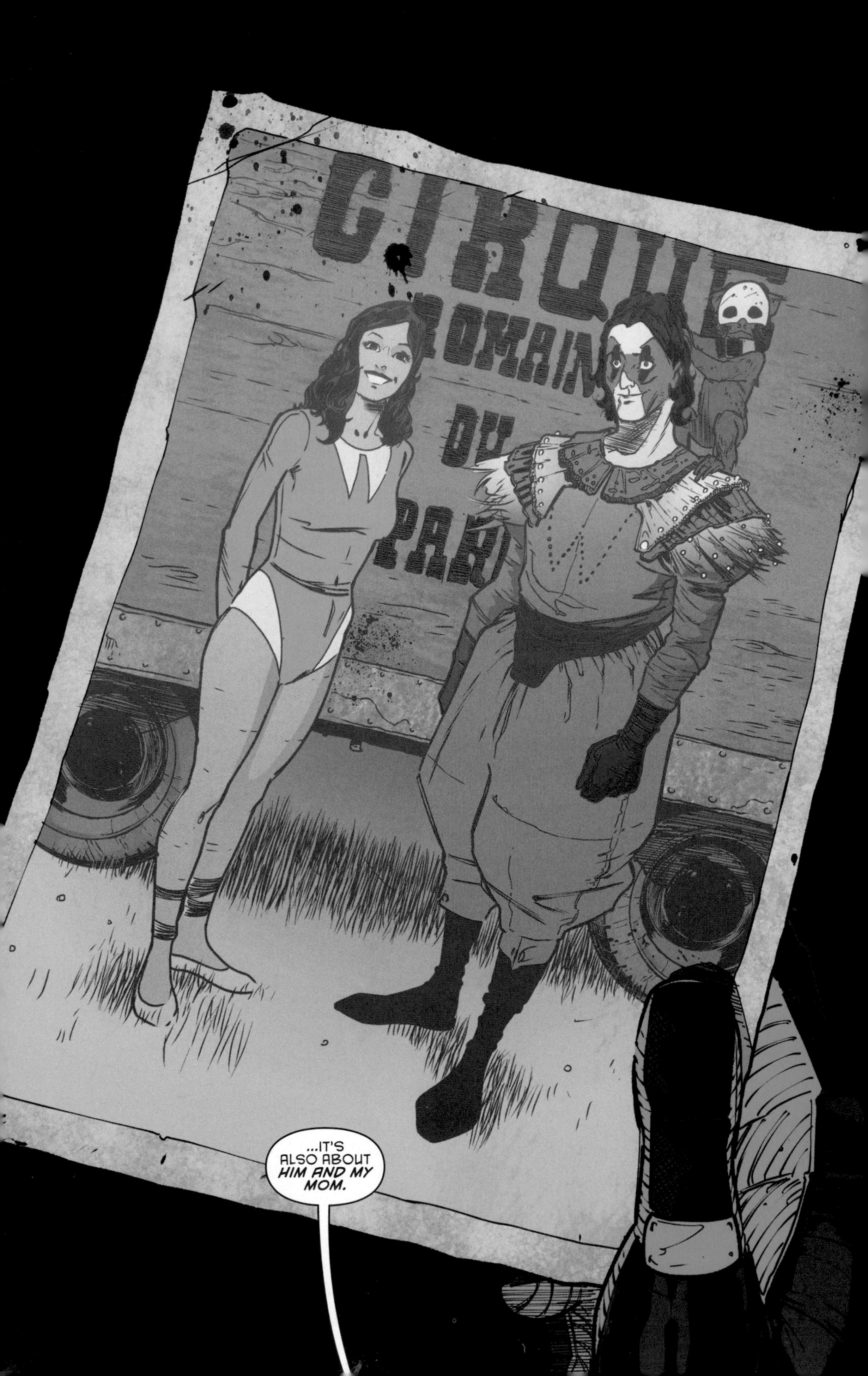

CIRQUE
...IT'S ALSO ABOUT *HIM AND MY MOM.*

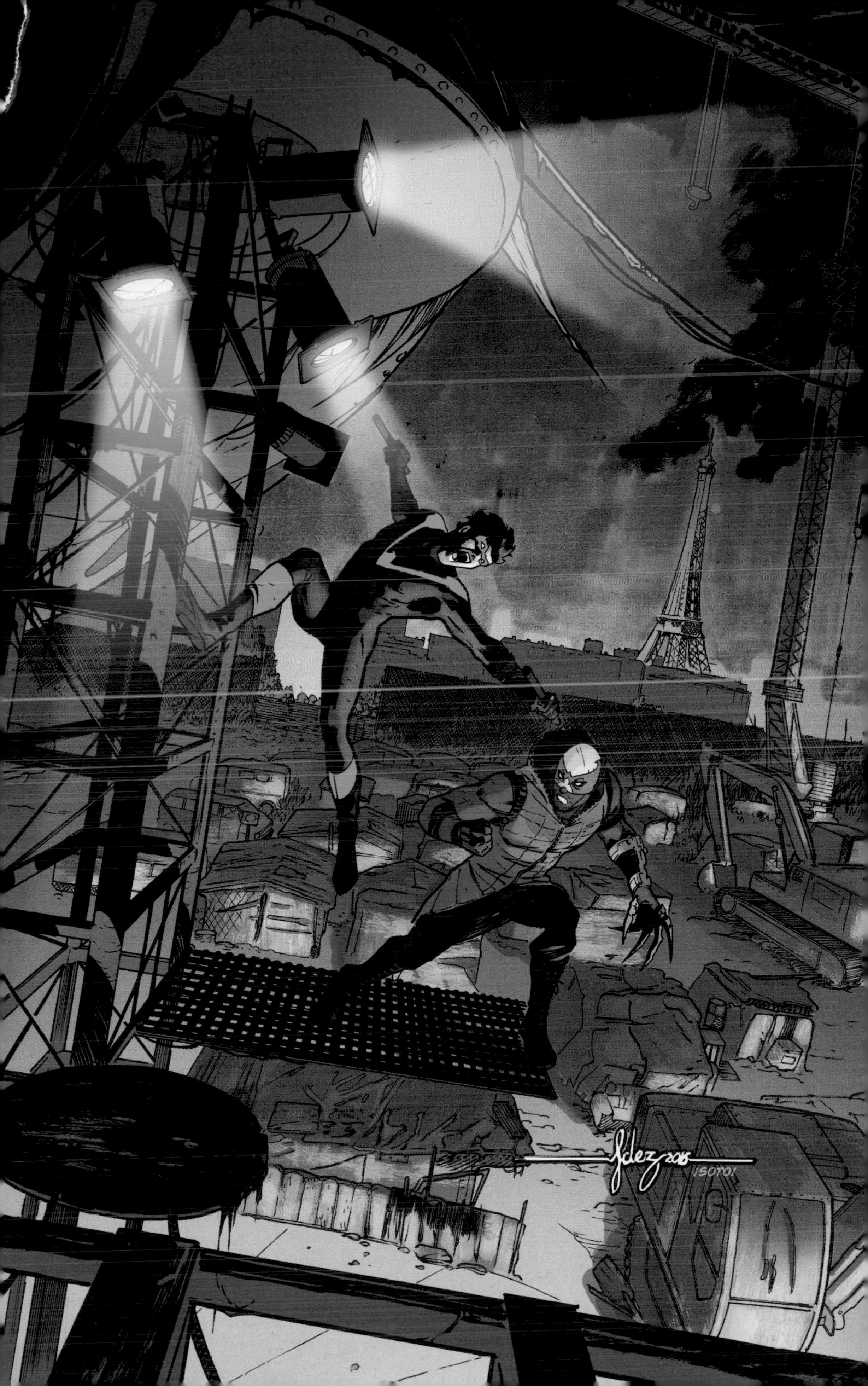
fdez 2018
¡SOTO!

RISE OF RAPTOR, PART 2

TIM SEELEY writer * JAVIER FERNÁNDEZ artist * CHRIS SOTOMAYOR colorist
CARLOS M. MANGUAL letterer * JAVIER FERNÁNDEZ and CHRIS SOTOMAYOR cover artists

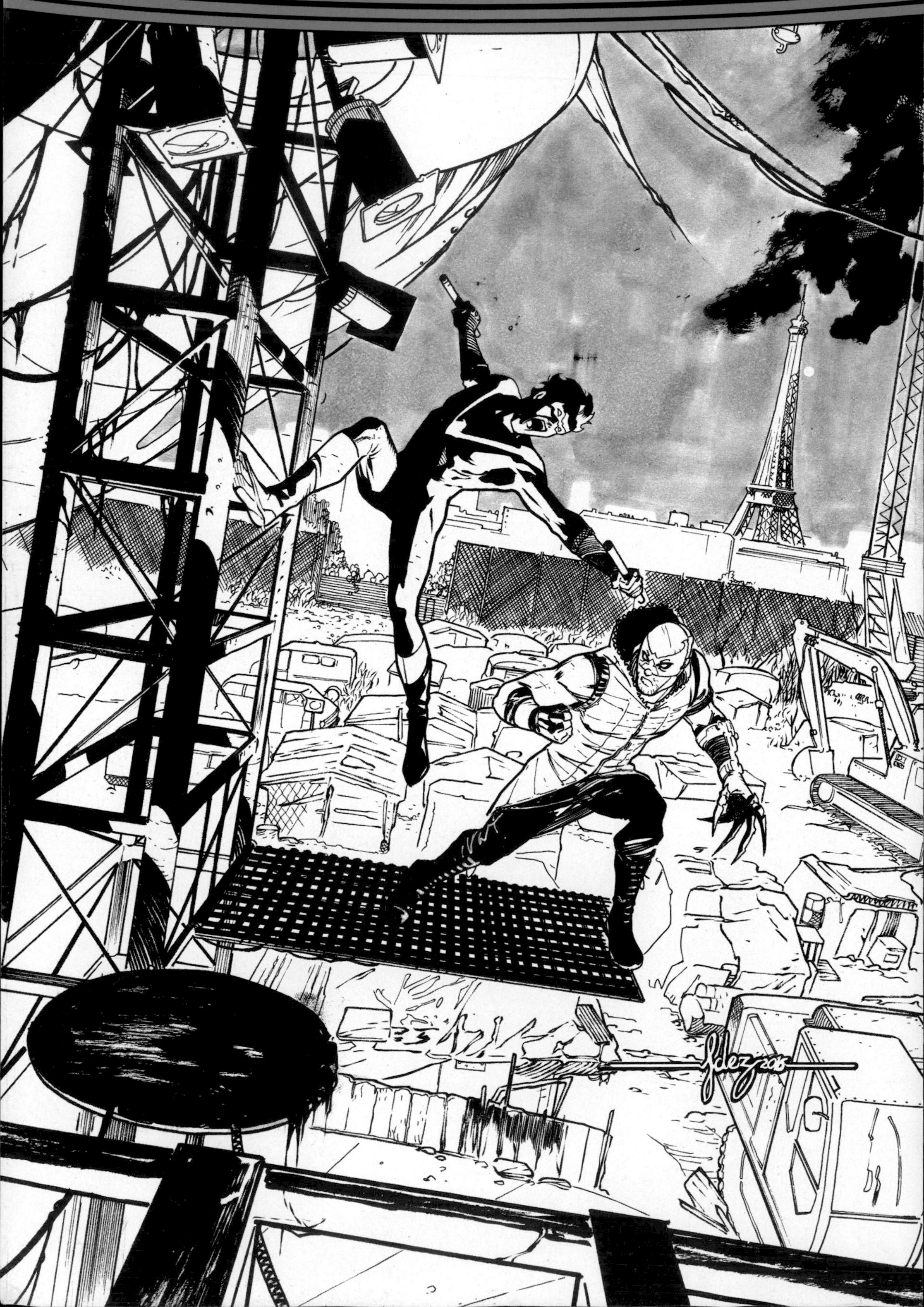

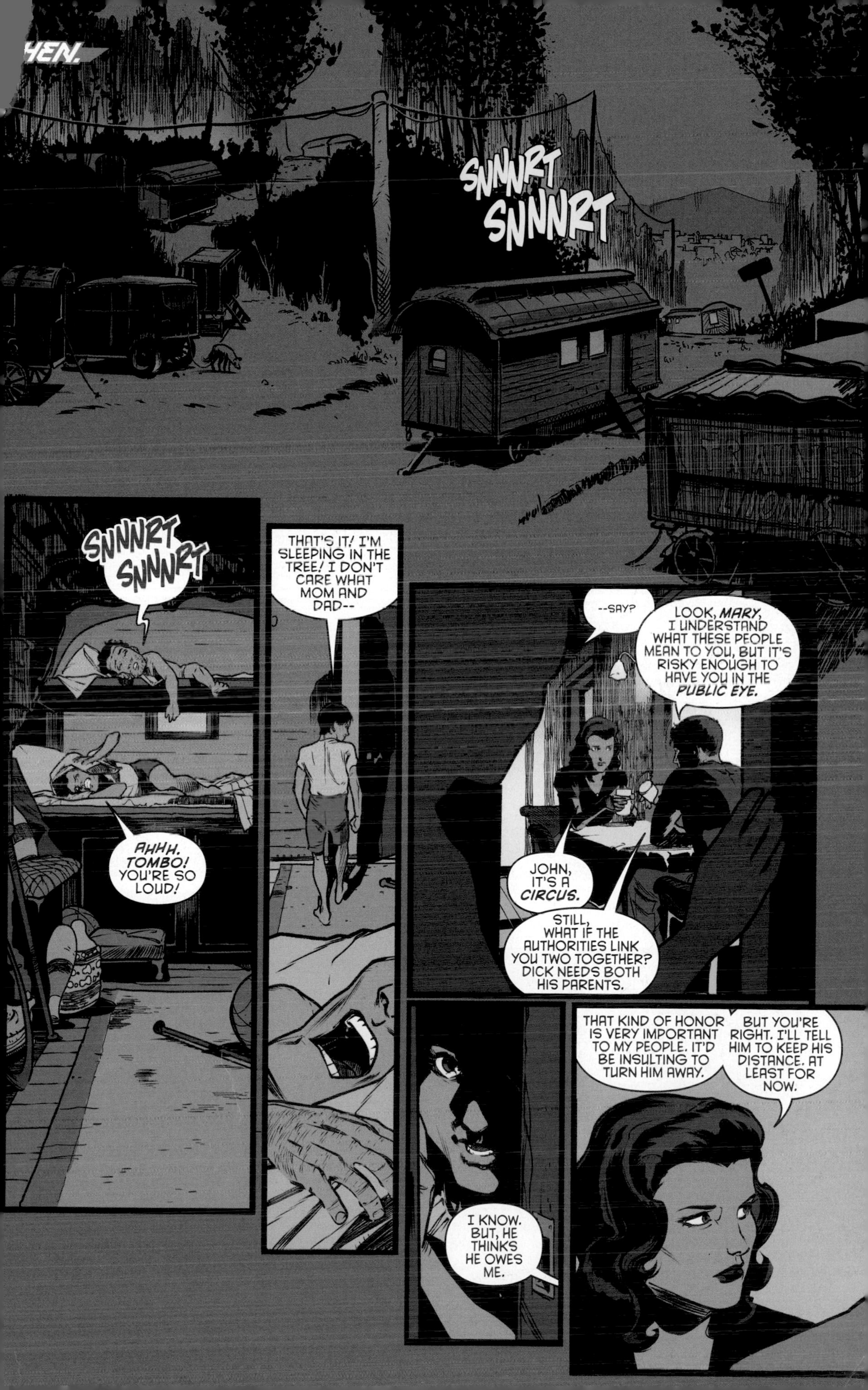

...HEN.
SNNNRT SNNNRT
SNNNRT SNNNRT
AHHH. TOMBO! YOU'RE SO LOUD!
THAT'S IT! I'M SLEEPING IN THE TREE! I DON'T CARE WHAT MOM AND DAD--
--SAY?
LOOK, MARY, I UNDERSTAND WHAT THESE PEOPLE MEAN TO YOU, BUT IT'S RISKY ENOUGH TO HAVE YOU IN THE PUBLIC EYE.
JOHN, IT'S A CIRCUS.
STILL, WHAT IF THE AUTHORITIES LINK YOU TWO TOGETHER? DICK NEEDS BOTH HIS PARENTS.
I KNOW. BUT, HE THINKS HE OWES ME.
THAT KIND OF HONOR IS VERY IMPORTANT TO MY PEOPLE. IT'D BE INSULTING TO TURN HIM AWAY.
BUT YOU'RE RIGHT. I'LL TELL HIM TO KEEP HIS DISTANCE. AT LEAST FOR NOW.

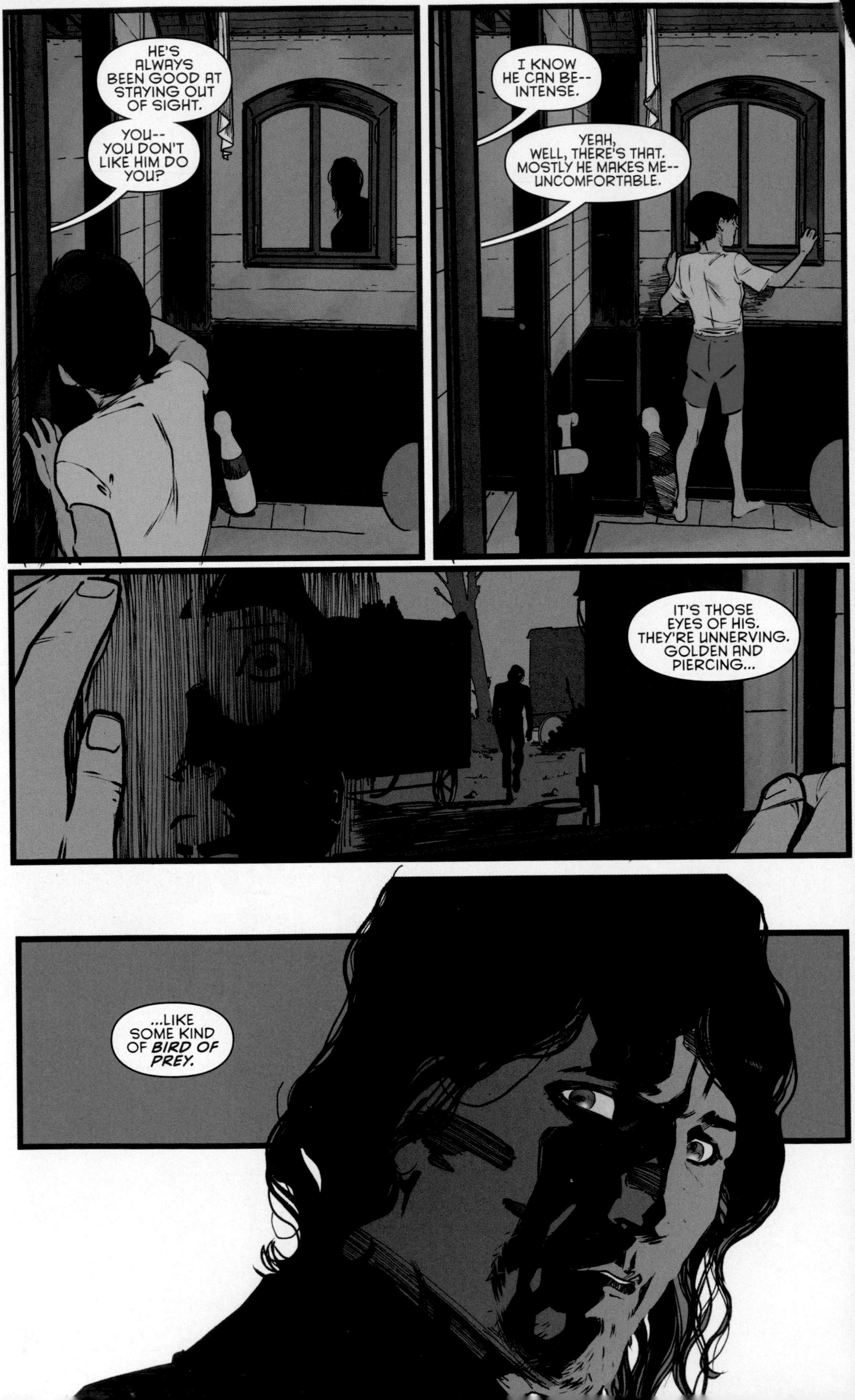
HE'S ALWAYS BEEN GOOD AT STAYING OUT OF SIGHT.
YOU-- YOU DON'T LIKE HIM DO YOU?
I KNOW HE CAN BE-- INTENSE.
YEAH, WELL, THERE'S THAT. MOSTLY HE MAKES ME-- UNCOMFORTABLE.
IT'S THOSE EYES OF HIS. THEY'RE UNNERVING. GOLDEN AND PIERCING...
...LIKE SOME KIND OF *BIRD OF PREY.*

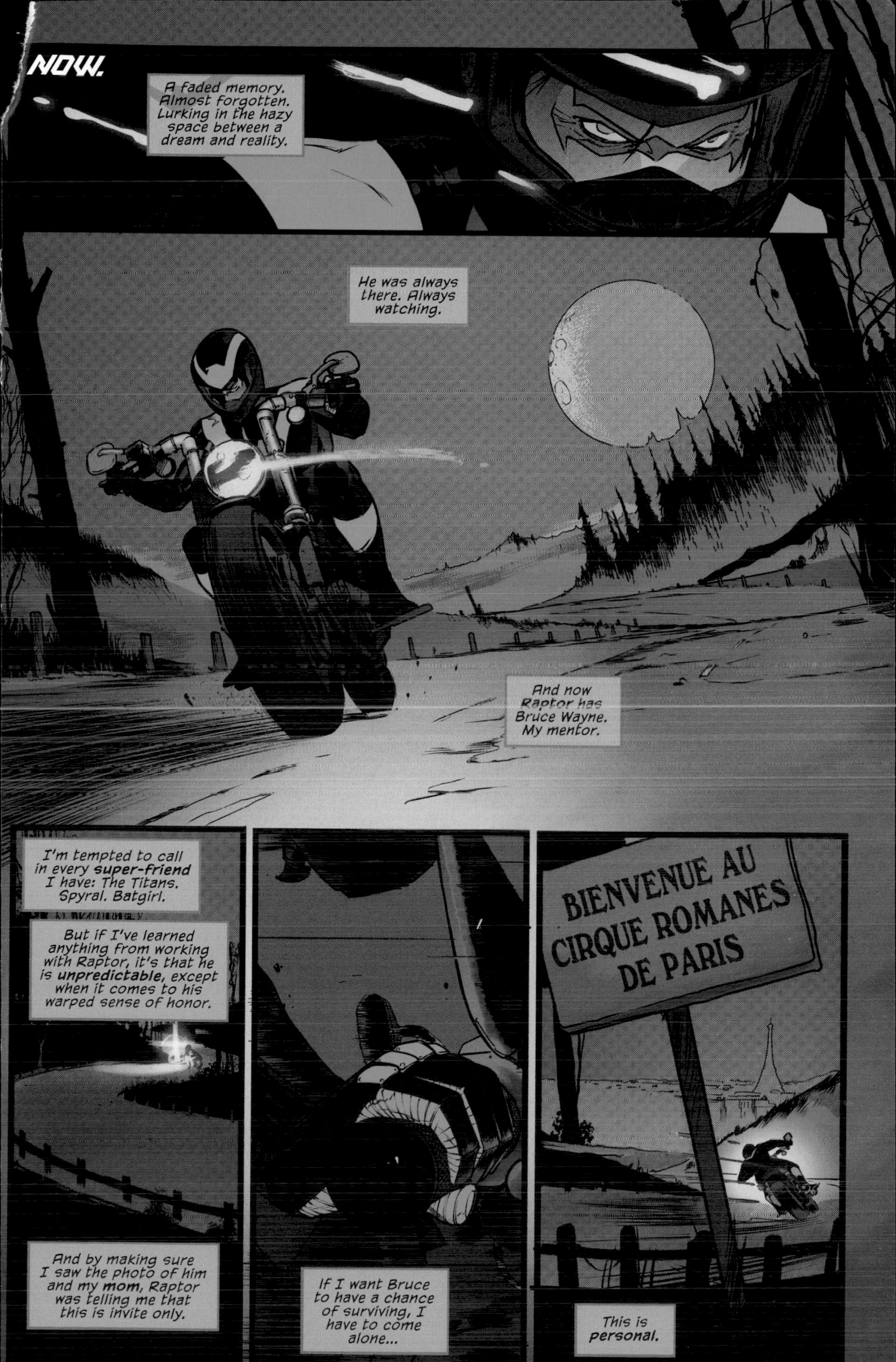
NOW.
A faded memory. Almost forgotten. Lurking in the hazy space between a dream and reality.
He was always there. Always watching.
And now Raptor has Bruce Wayne. My mentor.
I'm tempted to call in every super-friend I have: The Titans. Spyral. Batgirl.
But if I've learned anything from working with Raptor, it's that he is unpredictable, except when it comes to his warped sense of honor.
And by making sure I saw the photo of him and my mom, Raptor was telling me that this is invite only.
If I want Bruce to have a chance of surviving, I have to come alone...
BIENVENUE AU CIRQUE ROMANES DE PARIS
This is personal.

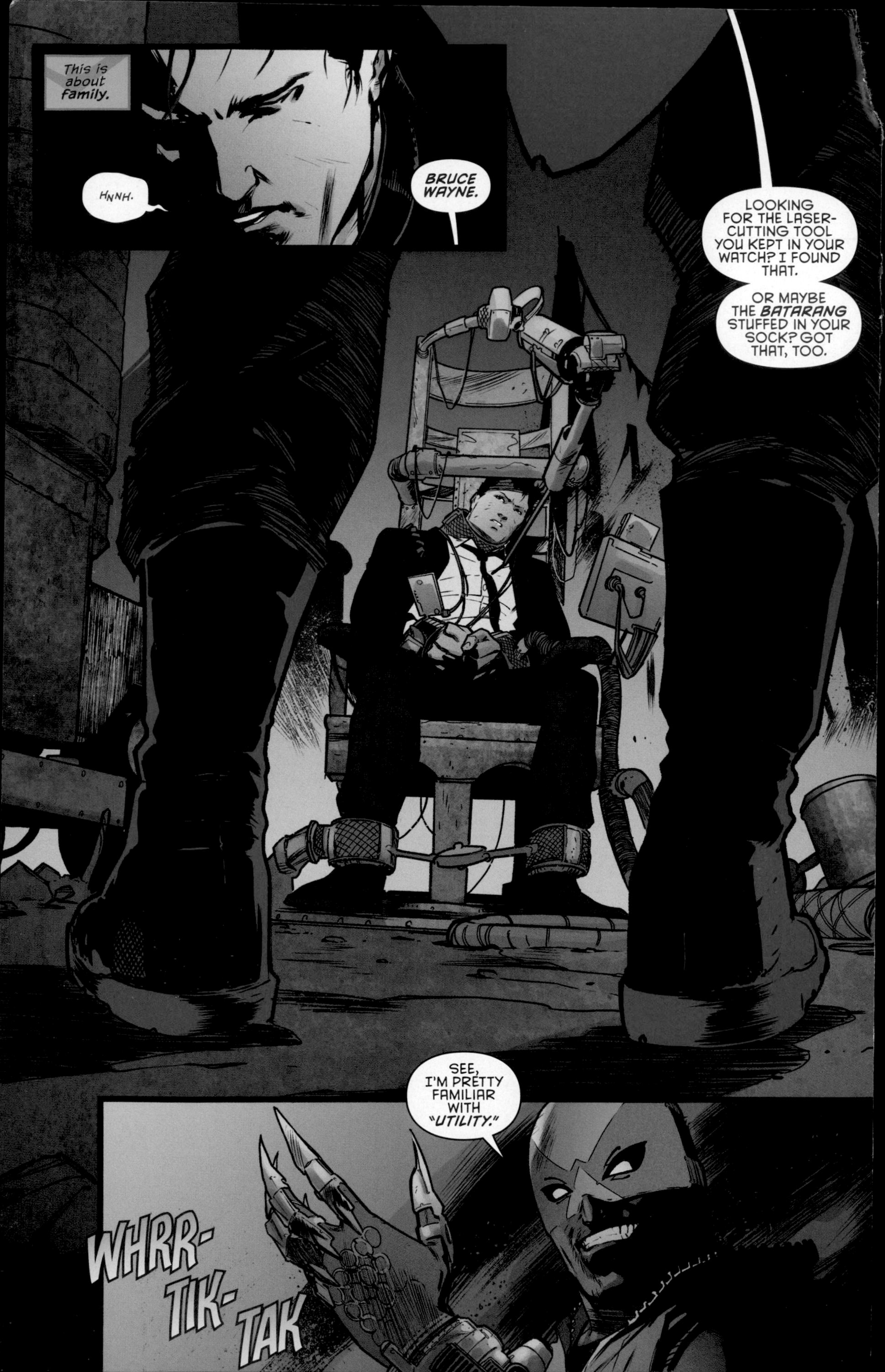
This is about family.
HNNH.
BRUCE WAYNE.
LOOKING FOR THE LASER-CUTTING TOOL YOU KEPT IN YOUR WATCH? I FOUND THAT.
OR MAYBE THE BATARANG STUFFED IN YOUR SOCK? GOT THAT, TOO.
SEE, I'M PRETTY FAMILIAR WITH "UTILITY."
WHRR-TIK-TAK

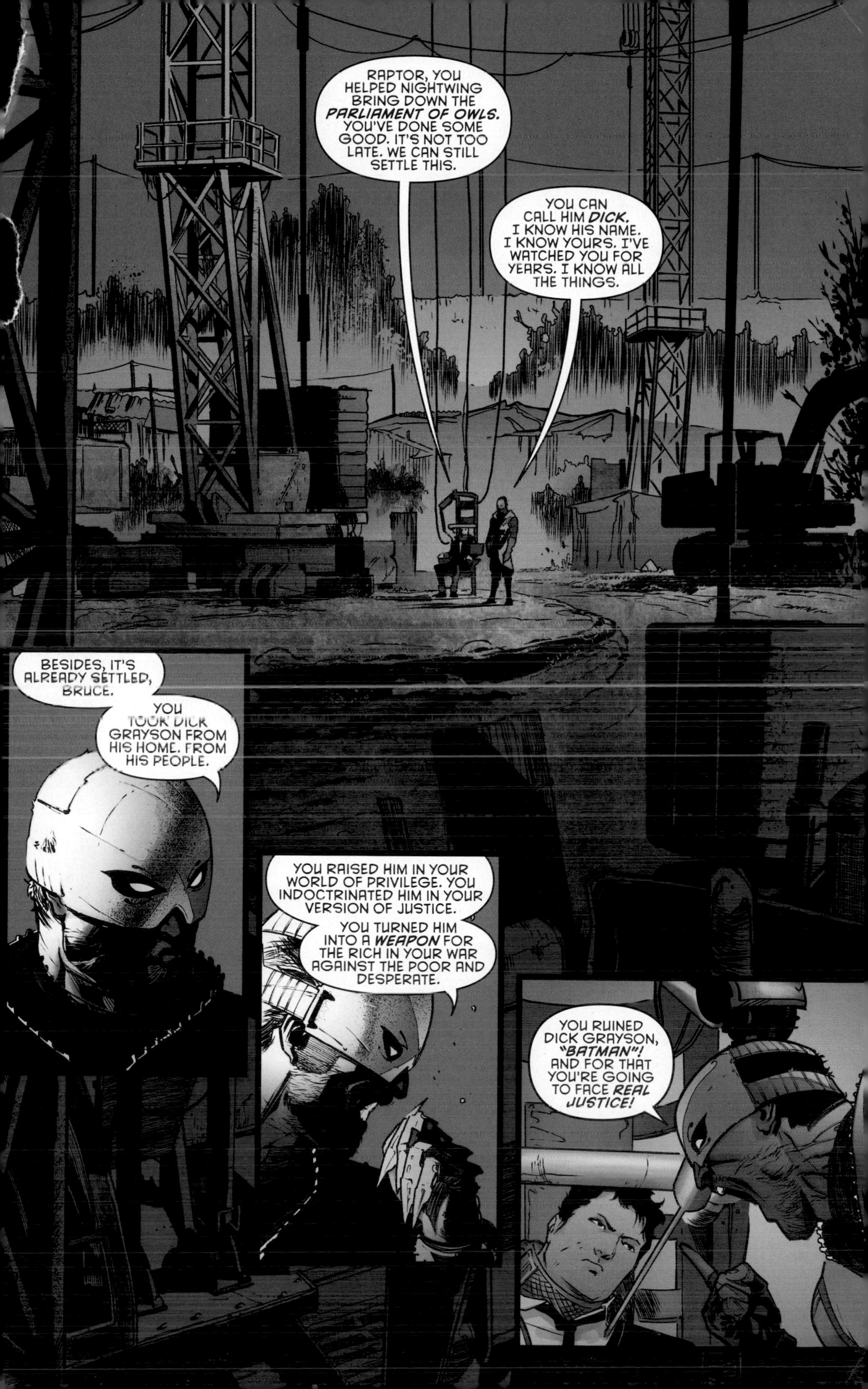
RAPTOR, YOU HELPED NIGHTWING BRING DOWN THE *PARLIAMENT OF OWLS.* YOU'VE DONE SOME GOOD. IT'S NOT TOO LATE. WE CAN STILL SETTLE THIS.
YOU CAN CALL HIM *DICK.* I KNOW HIS NAME. I KNOW YOURS. I'VE WATCHED YOU FOR YEARS. I KNOW ALL THE THINGS.
BESIDES, IT'S ALREADY SETTLED, BRUCE.
YOU TOOK DICK GRAYSON FROM HIS HOME. FROM HIS PEOPLE.
YOU RAISED HIM IN YOUR WORLD OF PRIVILEGE. YOU INDOCTRINATED HIM IN YOUR VERSION OF JUSTICE.
YOU TURNED HIM INTO A *WEAPON* FOR THE RICH IN YOUR WAR AGAINST THE POOR AND DESPERATE.
YOU RUINED DICK GRAYSON, *"BATMAN"!* AND FOR THAT YOU'RE GOING TO FACE *REAL JUSTICE!*

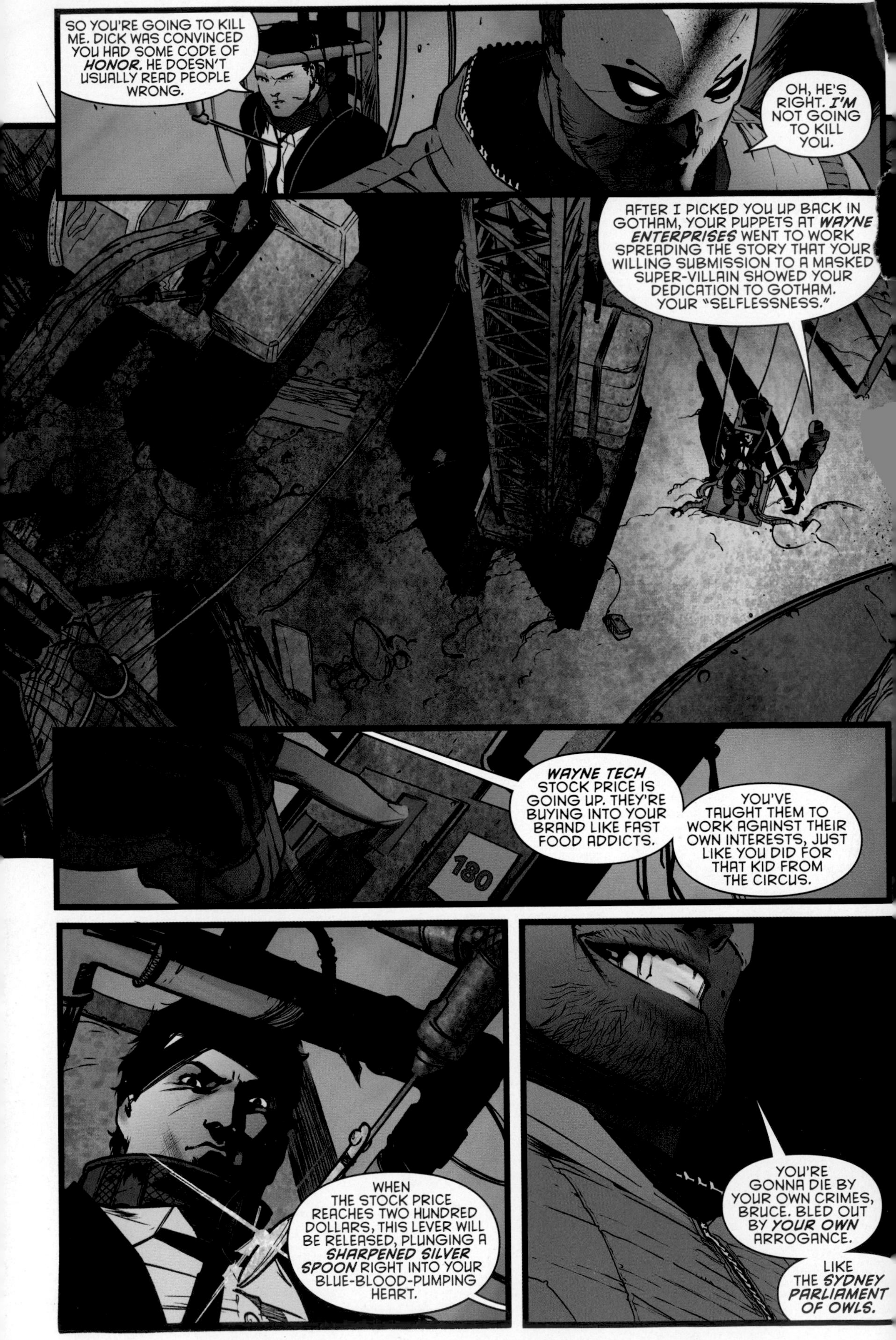
SO YOU'RE GOING TO KILL ME. DICK WAS CONVINCED YOU HAD SOME CODE OF *HONOR.* HE DOESN'T USUALLY READ PEOPLE WRONG.
OH, HE'S RIGHT. *I'M* NOT GOING TO KILL YOU.
AFTER I PICKED YOU UP BACK IN GOTHAM, YOUR PUPPETS AT *WAYNE ENTERPRISES* WENT TO WORK SPREADING THE STORY THAT YOUR WILLING SUBMISSION TO A MASKED SUPER-VILLAIN SHOWED YOUR DEDICATION TO GOTHAM. YOUR "SELFLESSNESS."
WAYNE TECH STOCK PRICE IS GOING UP. THEY'RE BUYING INTO YOUR BRAND LIKE FAST FOOD ADDICTS.
YOU'VE TAUGHT THEM TO WORK AGAINST THEIR OWN INTERESTS, JUST LIKE YOU DID FOR THAT KID FROM THE CIRCUS.
180
WHEN THE STOCK PRICE REACHES TWO HUNDRED DOLLARS, THIS LEVER WILL BE RELEASED, PLUNGING A *SHARPENED SILVER SPOON* RIGHT INTO YOUR BLUE-BLOOD-PUMPING HEART.
YOU'RE GONNA DIE BY YOUR OWN CRIMES, BRUCE. BLED OUT BY *YOUR OWN* ARROGANCE.
LIKE THE *SYDNEY PARLIAMENT OF OWLS.*

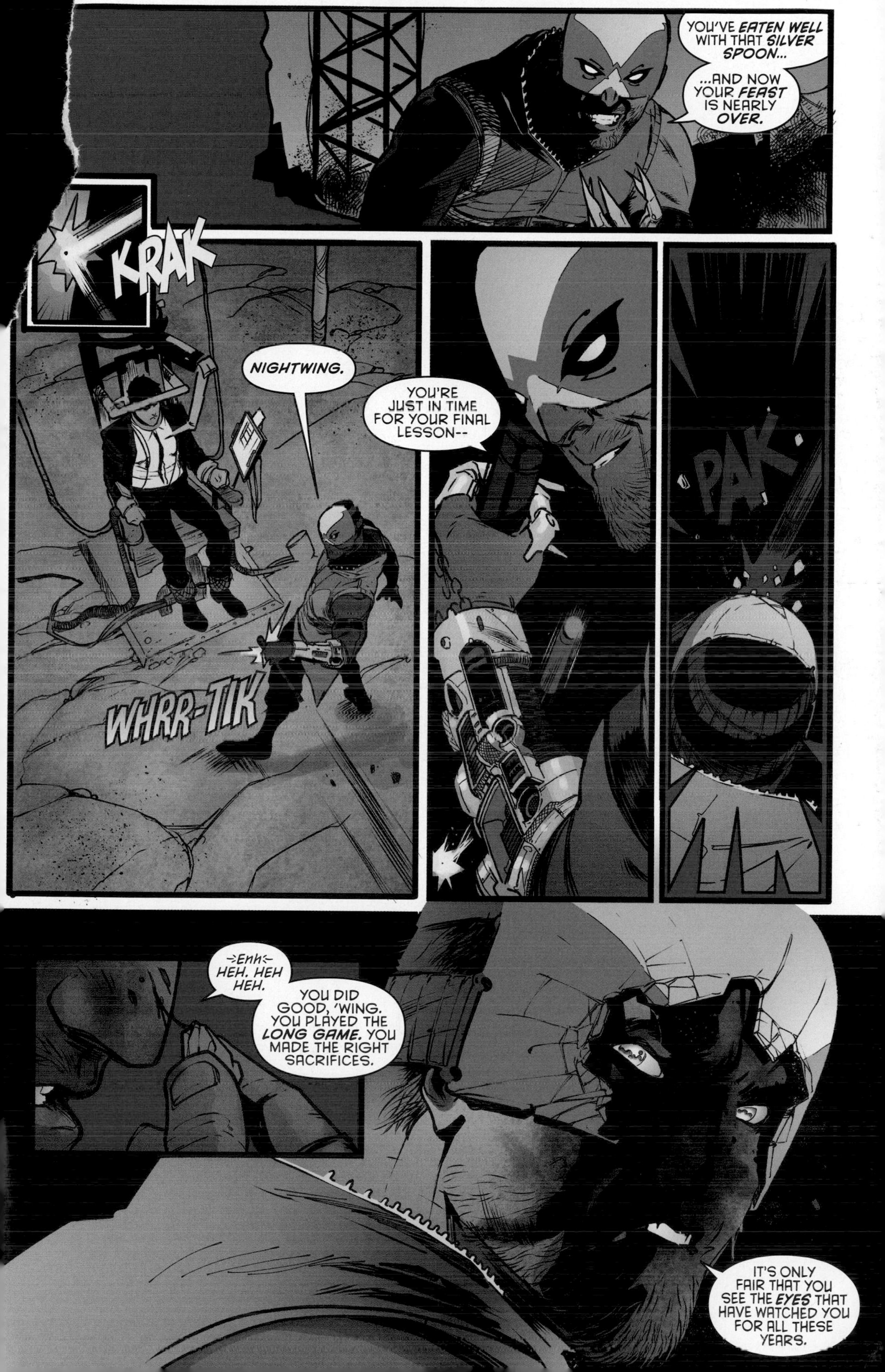
YOU'VE EATEN WELL WITH THAT SILVER SPOON...
...AND NOW YOUR FEAST IS NEARLY OVER.
KRAK
NIGHTWING.
YOU'RE JUST IN TIME FOR YOUR FINAL LESSON--
WHRR-TIK
PAK
-Enh- HEH. HEH HEH.
YOU DID GOOD, 'WING. YOU PLAYED THE LONG GAME. YOU MADE THE RIGHT SACRIFICES.
IT'S ONLY FAIR THAT YOU SEE THE EYES THAT HAVE WATCHED YOU FOR ALL THESE YEARS.

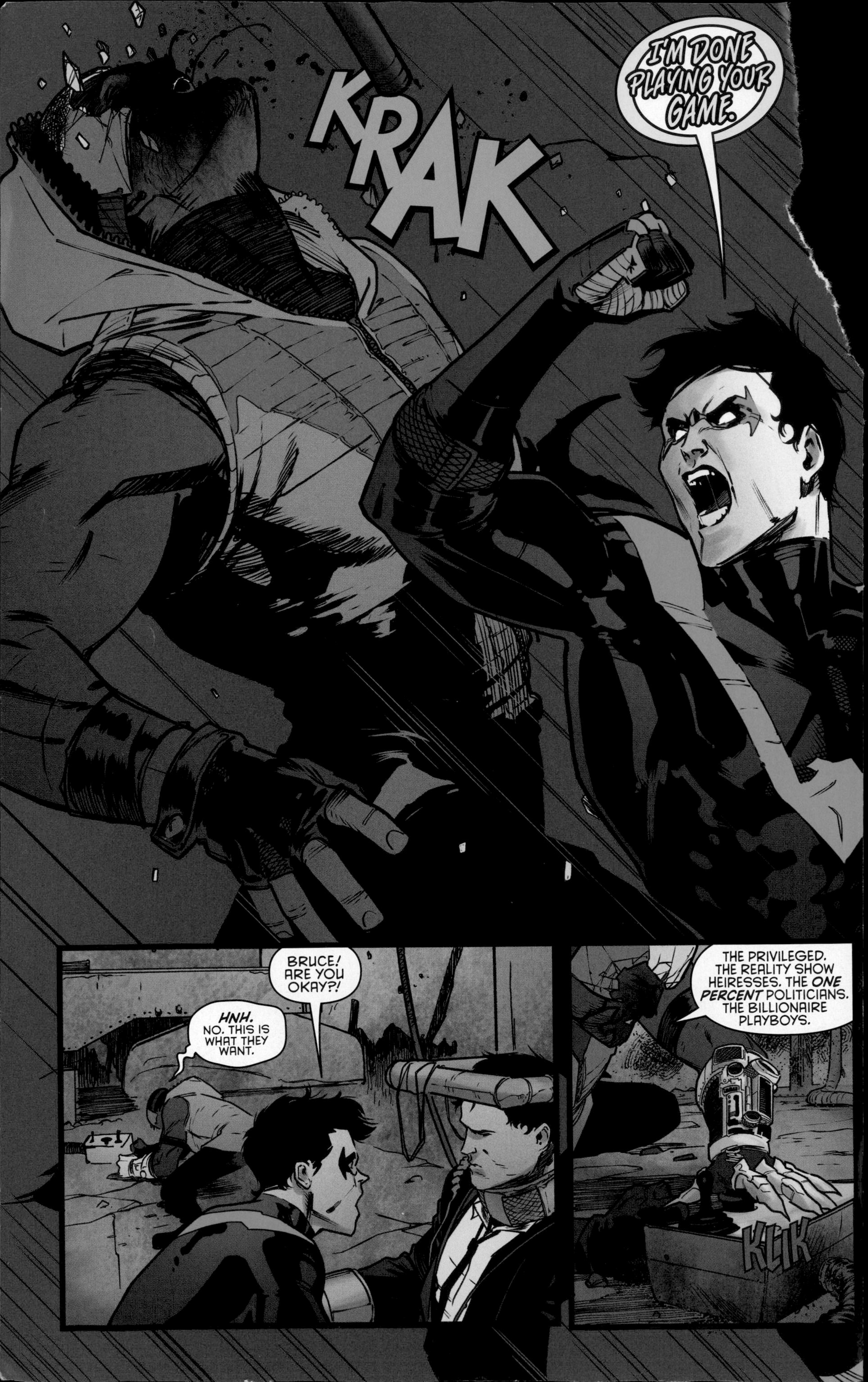
KRAK
I'M DONE PLAYING YOUR GAME.
BRUCE! ARE YOU OKAY?!
HNH. NO. THIS IS WHAT THEY WANT.
THE PRIVILEGED. THE REALITY SHOW HEIRESSES. THE ONE PERCENT POLITICIANS. THE BILLIONAIRE PLAYBOYS.
KLIK

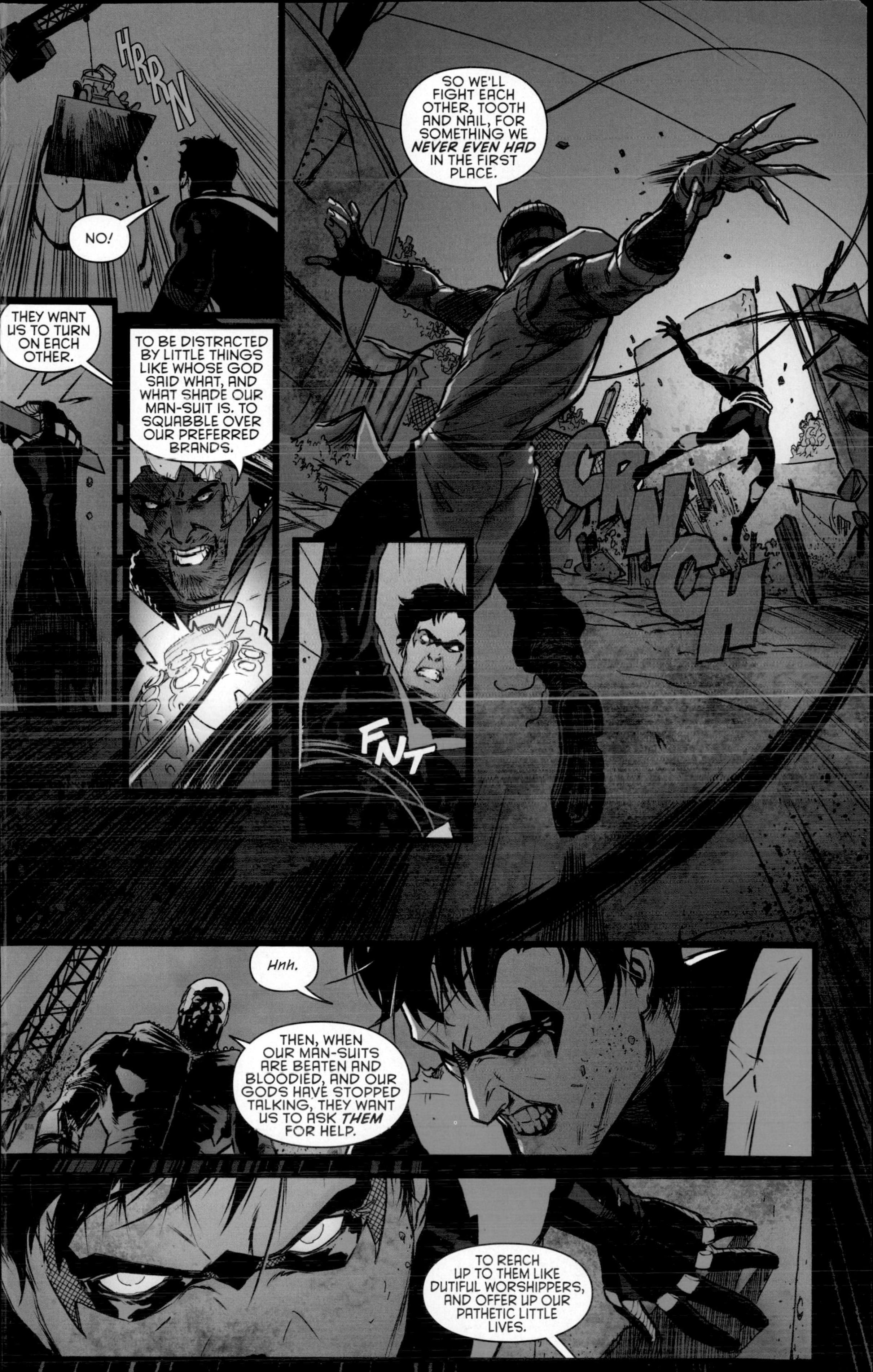

HRRRN
NO!
THEY WANT US TO TURN ON EACH OTHER.
TO BE DISTRACTED BY LITTLE THINGS LIKE WHOSE GOD SAID WHAT, AND WHAT SHADE OUR MAN-SUIT IS. TO SQUABBLE OVER OUR PREFERRED BRANDS.
SO WE'LL FIGHT EACH OTHER, TOOTH AND NAIL, FOR SOMETHING WE NEVER EVEN HAD IN THE FIRST PLACE.
CRNCH
FNT
Hnh.
THEN, WHEN OUR MAN-SUITS ARE BEATEN AND BLOODIED, AND OUR GODS HAVE STOPPED TALKING, THEY WANT US TO ASK THEM FOR HELP.
TO REACH UP TO THEM LIKE DUTIFUL WORSHIPPERS, AND OFFER UP OUR PATHETIC LITTLE LIVES.

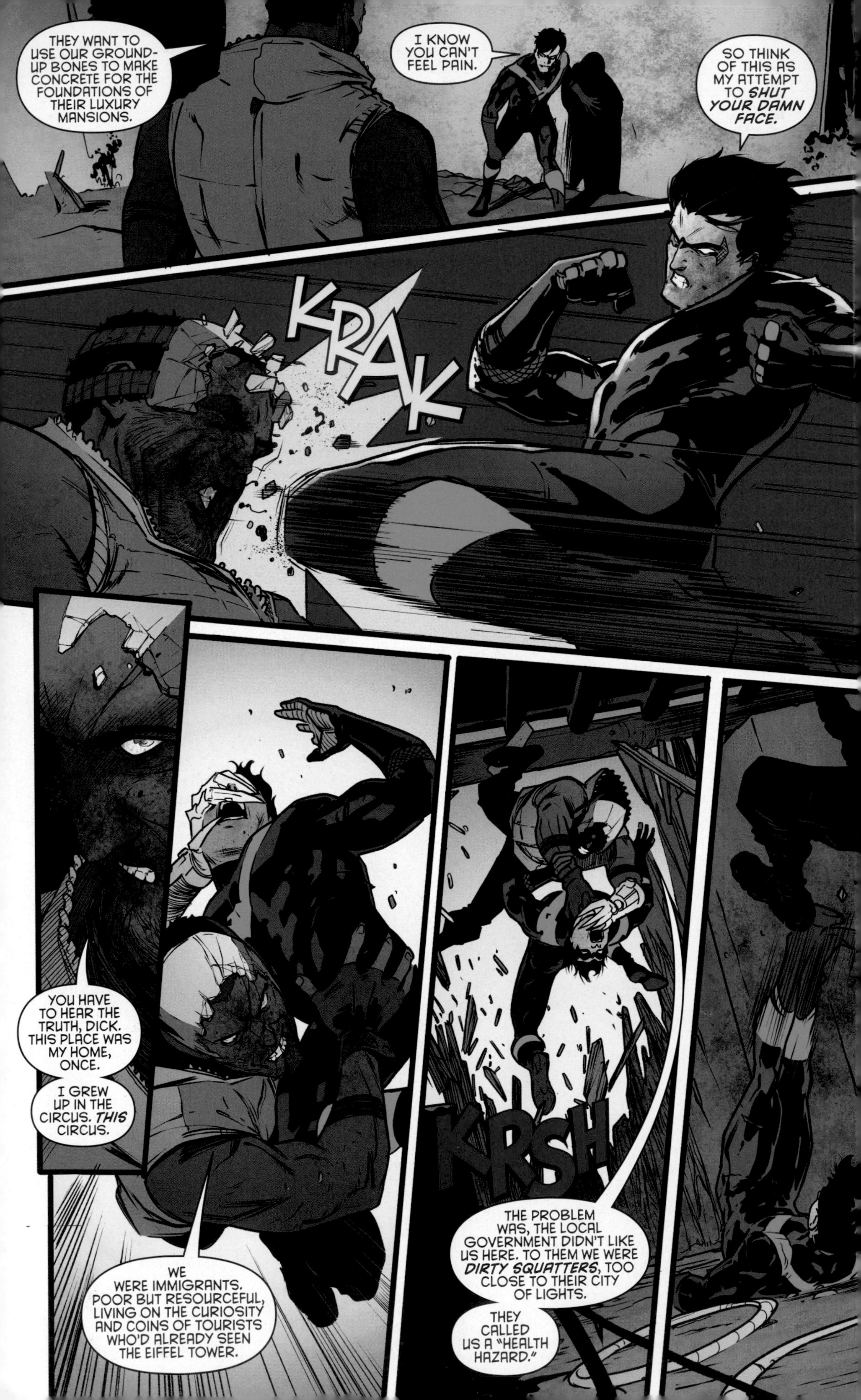
THEY WANT TO USE OUR GROUND-UP BONES TO MAKE CONCRETE FOR THE FOUNDATIONS OF THEIR LUXURY MANSIONS.
I KNOW YOU CAN'T FEEL PAIN.
SO THINK OF THIS AS MY ATTEMPT TO *SHUT YOUR DAMN FACE.*
KRAK
YOU HAVE TO HEAR THE TRUTH, DICK. THIS PLACE WAS MY HOME, ONCE.
I GREW UP IN THE CIRCUS. *THIS* CIRCUS.
WE WERE IMMIGRANTS. POOR BUT RESOURCEFUL, LIVING ON THE CURIOSITY AND COINS OF TOURISTS WHO'D ALREADY SEEN THE EIFFEL TOWER.
KRSH
THE PROBLEM WAS, THE LOCAL GOVERNMENT DIDN'T LIKE US HERE. TO THEM WE WERE *DIRTY SQUATTERS*, TOO CLOSE TO THEIR CITY OF LIGHTS.
THEY CALLED US A "HEALTH HAZARD."

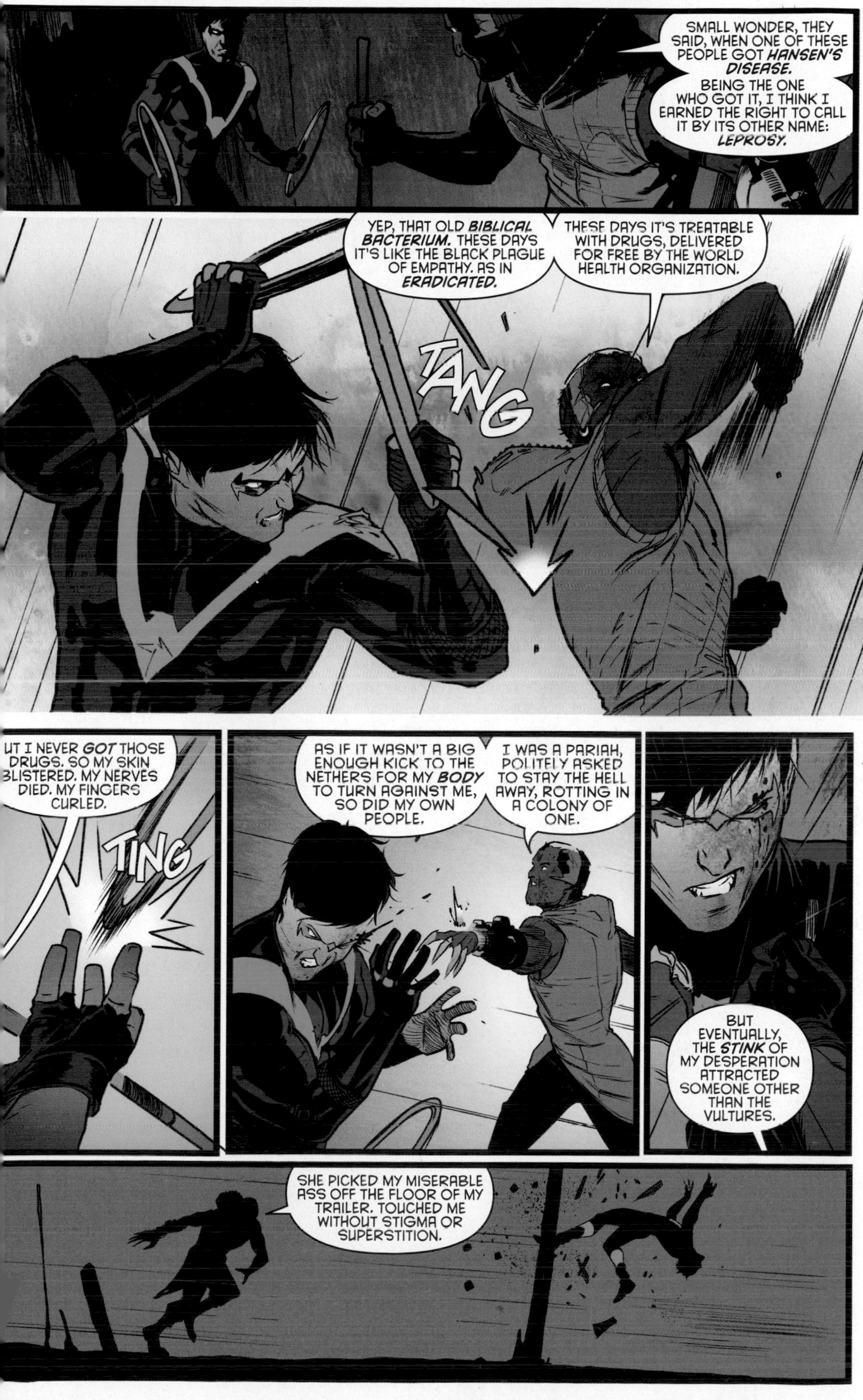
SMALL WONDER, THEY SAID, WHEN ONE OF THESE PEOPLE GOT HANSEN'S DISEASE.
BEING THE ONE WHO GOT IT, I THINK I EARNED THE RIGHT TO CALL IT BY ITS OTHER NAME: LEPROSY.
YEP, THAT OLD BIBLICAL BACTERIUM. THESE DAYS IT'S LIKE THE BLACK PLAGUE OF EMPATHY. AS IN ERADICATED.
THESE DAYS IT'S TREATABLE WITH DRUGS, DELIVERED FOR FREE BY THE WORLD HEALTH ORGANIZATION.
TANG
UT I NEVER GOT THOSE DRUGS. SO MY SKIN BLISTERED. MY NERVES DIED. MY FINGERS CURLED.
TING
AS IF IT WASN'T A BIG ENOUGH KICK TO THE NETHERS FOR MY BODY TO TURN AGAINST ME, SO DID MY OWN PEOPLE.
I WAS A PARIAH, POLITELY ASKED TO STAY THE HELL AWAY, ROTTING IN A COLONY OF ONE.
BUT EVENTUALLY, THE STINK OF MY DESPERATION ATTRACTED SOMEONE OTHER THAN THE VULTURES.
SHE PICKED MY MISERABLE ASS OFF THE FLOOR OF MY TRAILER. TOUCHED ME WITHOUT STIGMA OR SUPERSTITION.

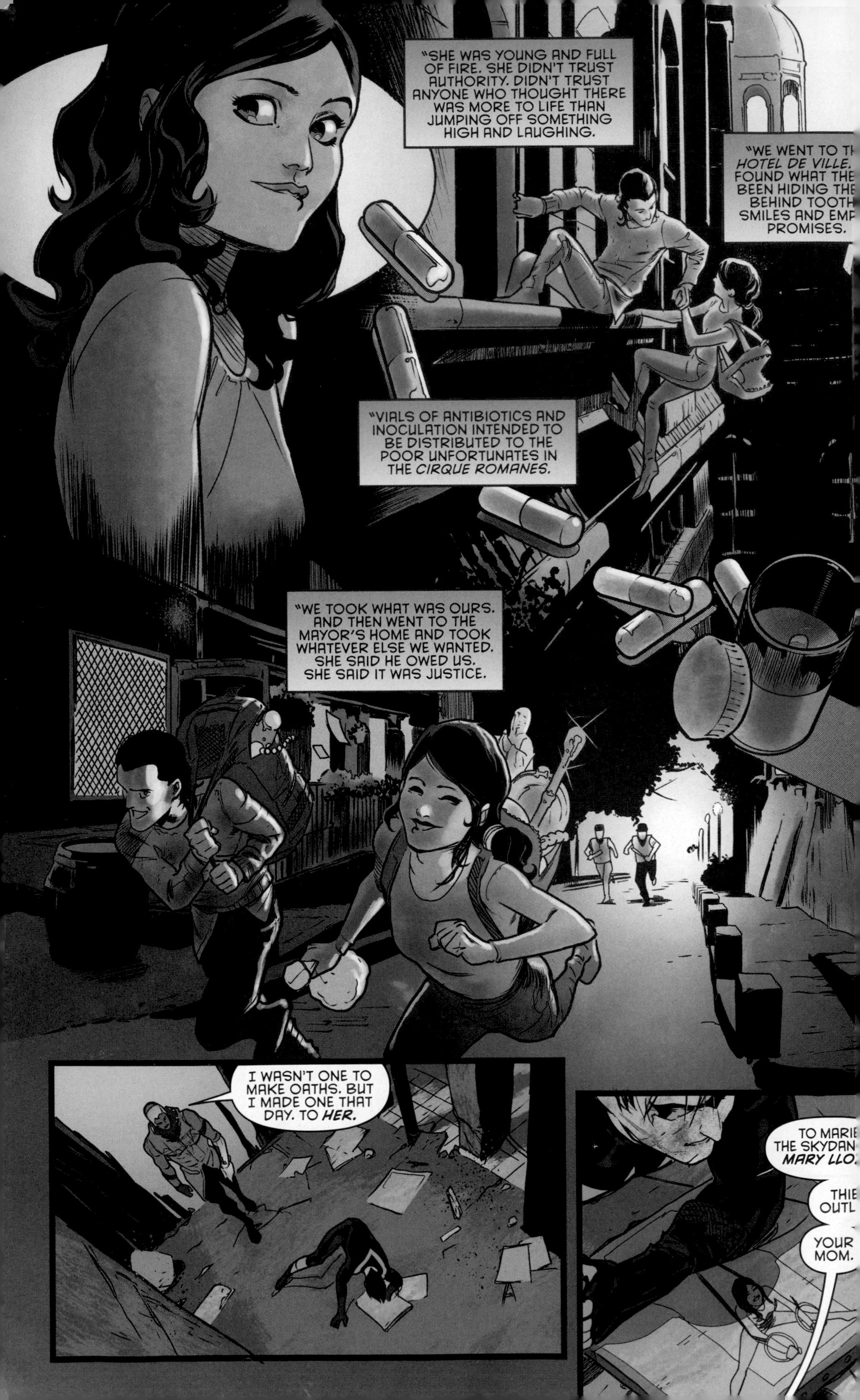
"SHE WAS YOUNG AND FULL OF FIRE. SHE DIDN'T TRUST AUTHORITY. DIDN'T TRUST ANYONE WHO THOUGHT THERE WAS MORE TO LIFE THAN JUMPING OFF SOMETHING HIGH AND LAUGHING.
"WE WENT TO TH
HOTEL DE VILLE.
FOUND WHAT THE
BEEN HIDING THE
BEHIND TOOTH
SMILES AND EMP
PROMISES.
"VIALS OF ANTIBIOTICS AND INOCULATION INTENDED TO BE DISTRIBUTED TO THE POOR UNFORTUNATES IN THE CIRQUE ROMANES.
"WE TOOK WHAT WAS OURS. AND THEN WENT TO THE MAYOR'S HOME AND TOOK WHATEVER ELSE WE WANTED. SHE SAID HE OWED US. SHE SAID IT WAS JUSTICE.
I WASN'T ONE TO MAKE OATHS. BUT I MADE ONE THAT DAY. TO HER.
TO MARIE
THE SKYDAN
MARY LLO
THIE
OUTL
YOUR
MOM.

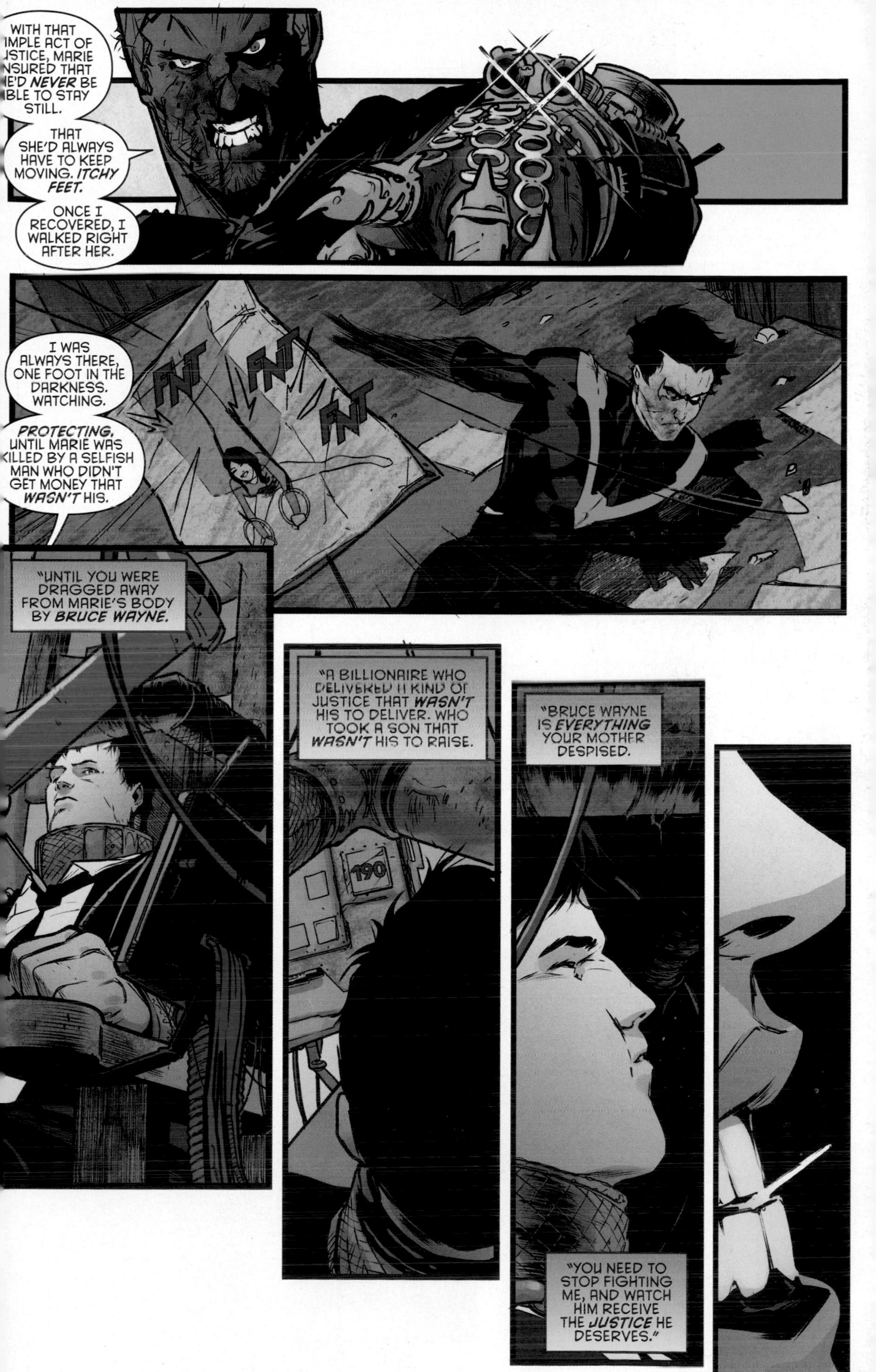

WITH THAT IMPLE ACT OF JSTICE, MARIE NSURED THAT IE'D NEVER BE BLE TO STAY STILL.
THAT SHE'D ALWAYS HAVE TO KEEP MOVING. ITCHY FEET.
ONCE I RECOVERED, I WALKED RIGHT AFTER HER.
I WAS ALWAYS THERE, ONE FOOT IN THE DARKNESS. WATCHING.
PROTECTING. UNTIL MARIE WAS KILLED BY A SELFISH MAN WHO DIDN'T GET MONEY THAT WASN'T HIS.
FNT
FNT
FNT
"UNTIL YOU WERE DRAGGED AWAY FROM MARIE'S BODY BY BRUCE WAYNE.
"A BILLIONAIRE WHO DELIVERED A KIND OF JUSTICE THAT WASN'T HIS TO DELIVER. WHO TOOK A SON THAT WASN'T HIS TO RAISE.
190
"BRUCE WAYNE IS EVERYTHING YOUR MOTHER DESPISED.
"YOU NEED TO STOP FIGHTING ME, AND WATCH HIM RECEIVE THE JUSTICE HE DESERVES."

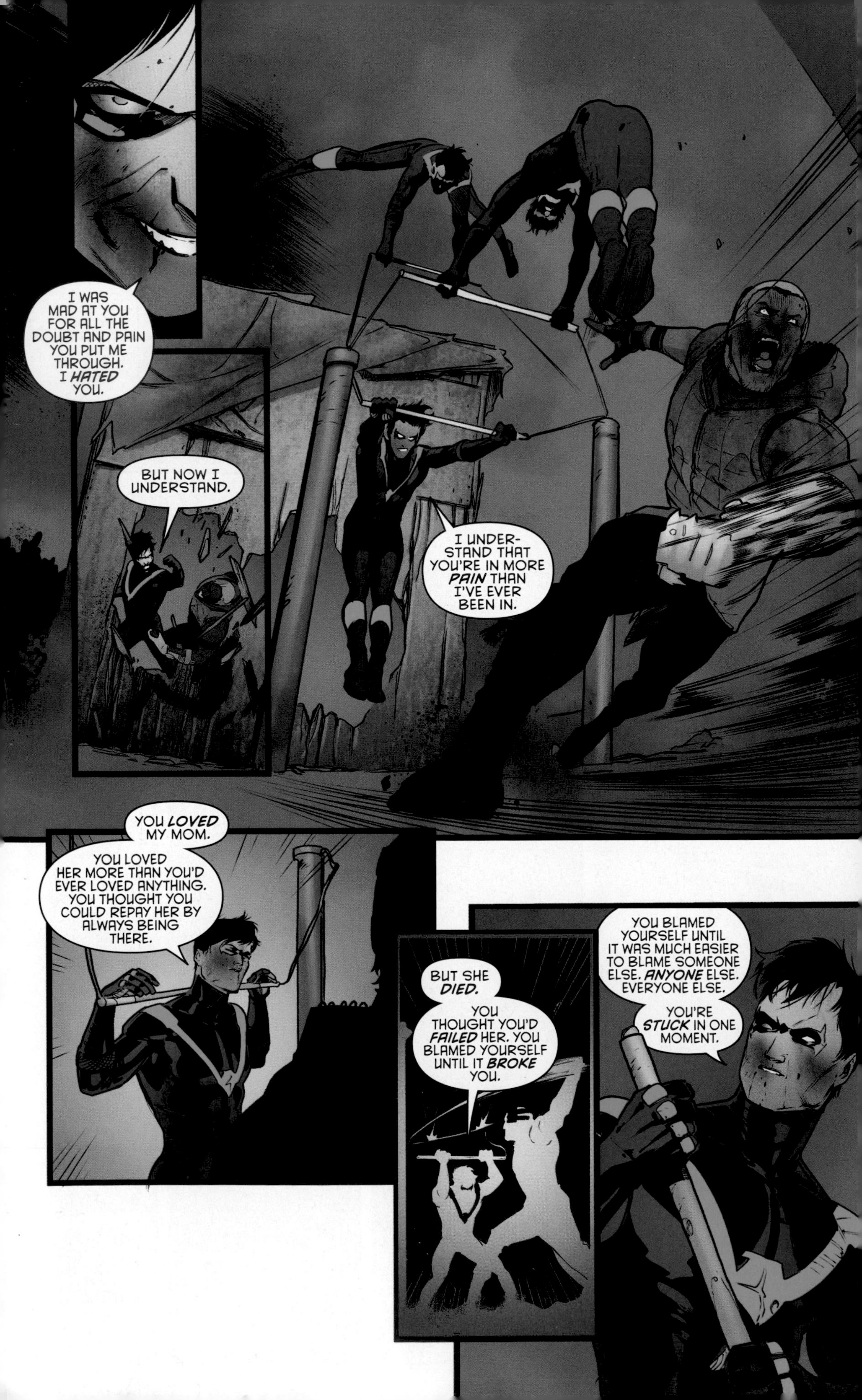
I WAS MAD AT YOU FOR ALL THE DOUBT AND PAIN YOU PUT ME THROUGH. I *HATED* YOU.
BUT NOW I UNDERSTAND.
I UNDER-STAND THAT YOU'RE IN MORE *PAIN* THAN I'VE EVER BEEN IN.
YOU *LOVED* MY MOM.
YOU LOVED HER MORE THAN YOU'D EVER LOVED ANYTHING. YOU THOUGHT YOU COULD REPAY HER BY ALWAYS BEING THERE.
BUT SHE *DIED.*
YOU THOUGHT YOU'D *FAILED* HER. YOU BLAMED YOURSELF UNTIL IT *BROKE* YOU.
YOU BLAMED YOURSELF UNTIL IT WAS MUCH EASIER TO BLAME SOMEONE ELSE. *ANYONE* ELSE. EVERYONE ELSE.
YOU'RE *STUCK* IN ONE MOMENT.

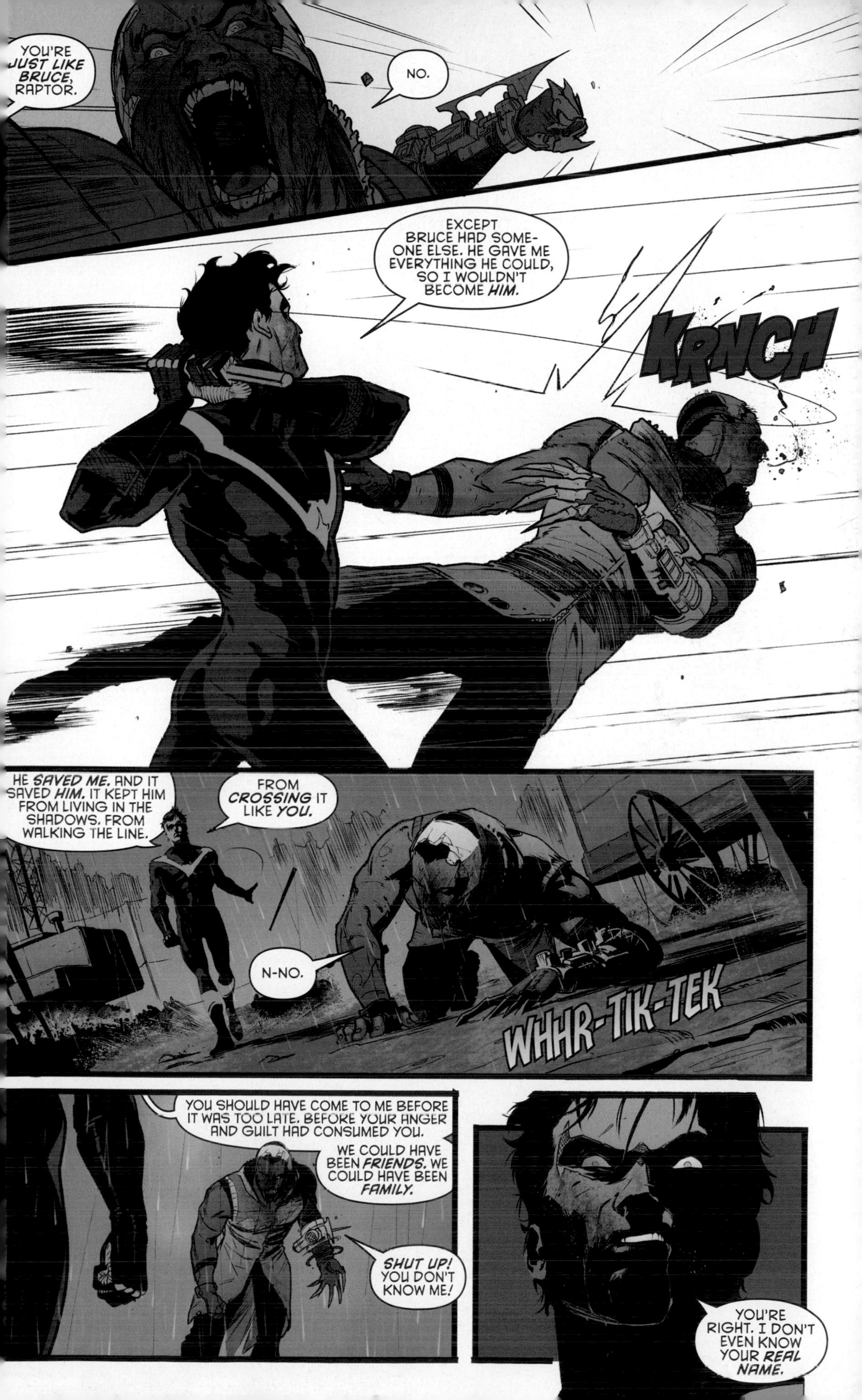
YOU'RE JUST LIKE BRUCE, RAPTOR.
NO.
EXCEPT BRUCE HAD SOMEONE ELSE. HE GAVE ME EVERYTHING HE COULD, SO I WOULDN'T BECOME HIM.
KRNCH
HE SAVED ME. AND IT SAVED HIM. IT KEPT HIM FROM LIVING IN THE SHADOWS. FROM WALKING THE LINE.
FROM CROSSING IT LIKE YOU.
N-NO.
WHHR-TIK-TEK
YOU SHOULD HAVE COME TO ME BEFORE IT WAS TOO LATE. BEFORE YOUR ANGER AND GUILT HAD CONSUMED YOU.
WE COULD HAVE BEEN FRIENDS. WE COULD HAVE BEEN FAMILY.
SHUT UP! YOU DON'T KNOW ME!
YOU'RE RIGHT. I DON'T EVEN KNOW YOUR REAL NAME.

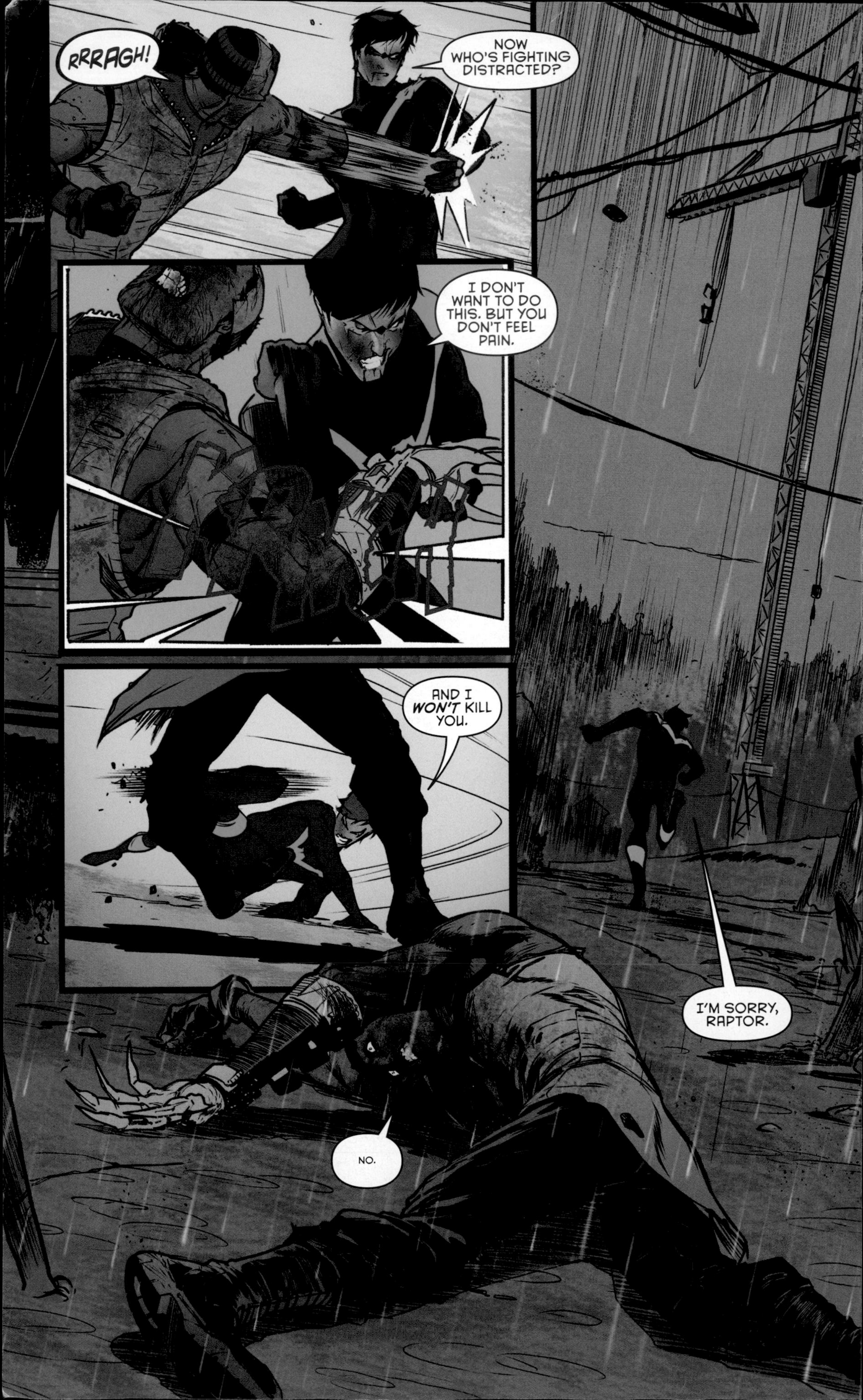
RRRAGH!
NOW WHO'S FIGHTING DISTRACTED?
I DON'T WANT TO DO THIS. BUT YOU DON'T FEEL PAIN.
AND I WON'T KILL YOU.
I'M SORRY, RAPTOR.
NO.

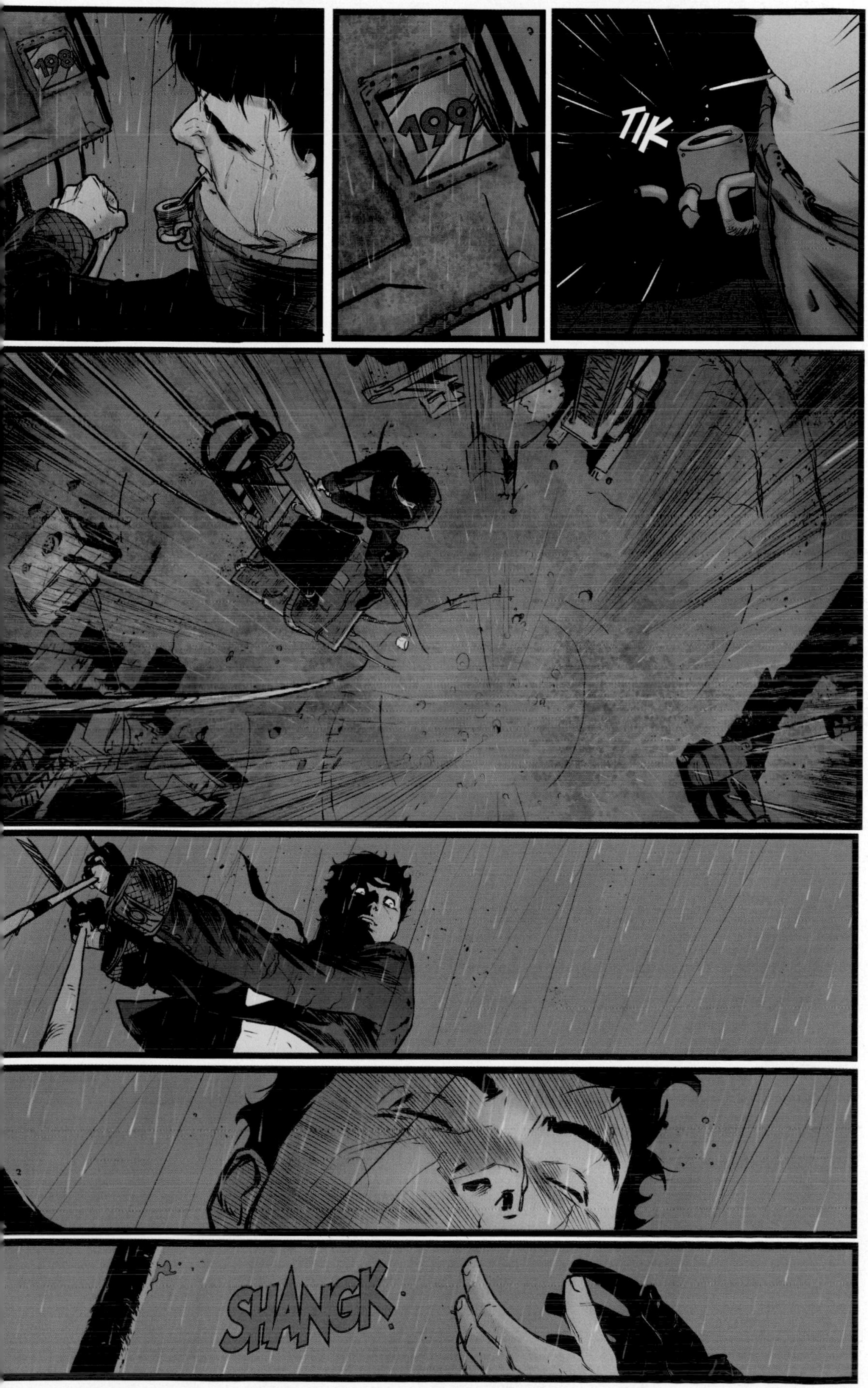
TIK
SHANGK

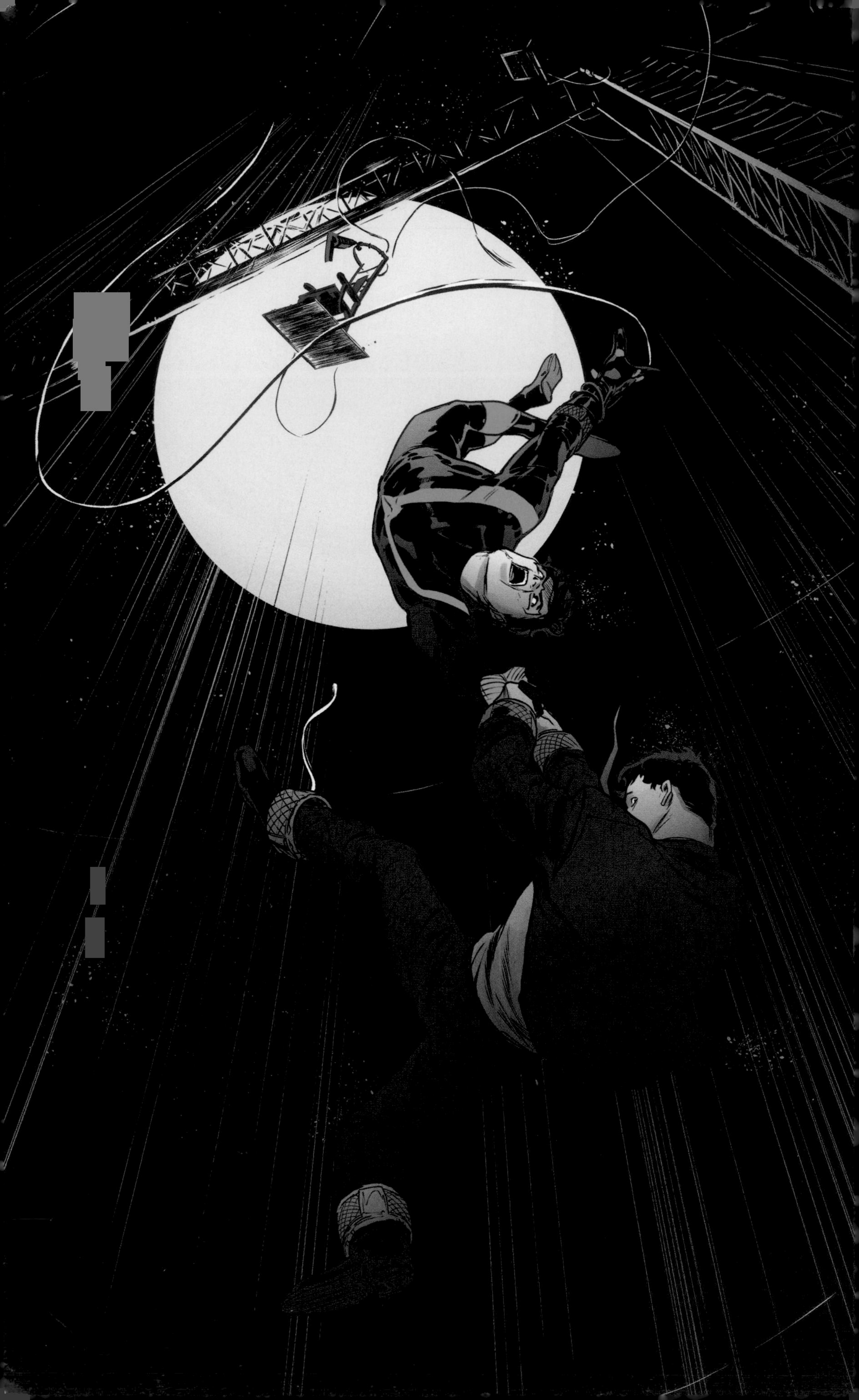

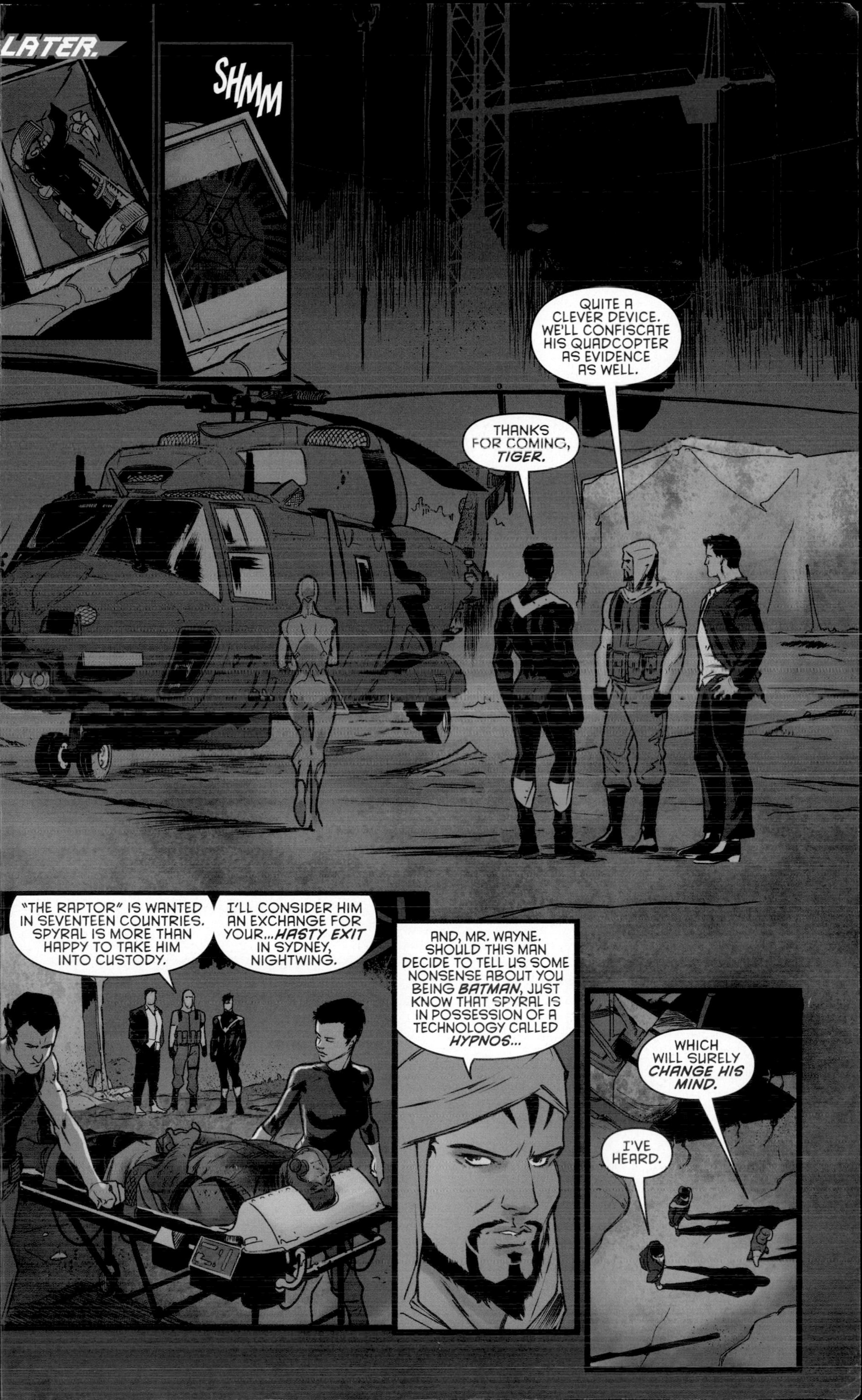
LATER.
SHMM
QUITE A CLEVER DEVICE. WE'LL CONFISCATE HIS QUADCOPTER AS EVIDENCE AS WELL.
THANKS FOR COMING, TIGER.
"THE RAPTOR" IS WANTED IN SEVENTEEN COUNTRIES. SPYRAL IS MORE THAN HAPPY TO TAKE HIM INTO CUSTODY.
I'LL CONSIDER HIM AN EXCHANGE FOR YOUR...HASTY EXIT IN SYDNEY, NIGHTWING.
AND, MR. WAYNE. SHOULD THIS MAN DECIDE TO TELL US SOME NONSENSE ABOUT YOU BEING BATMAN, JUST KNOW THAT SPYRAL IS IN POSSESSION OF A TECHNOLOGY CALLED HYPNOS...
WHICH WILL SURELY CHANGE HIS MIND.
I'VE HEARD.

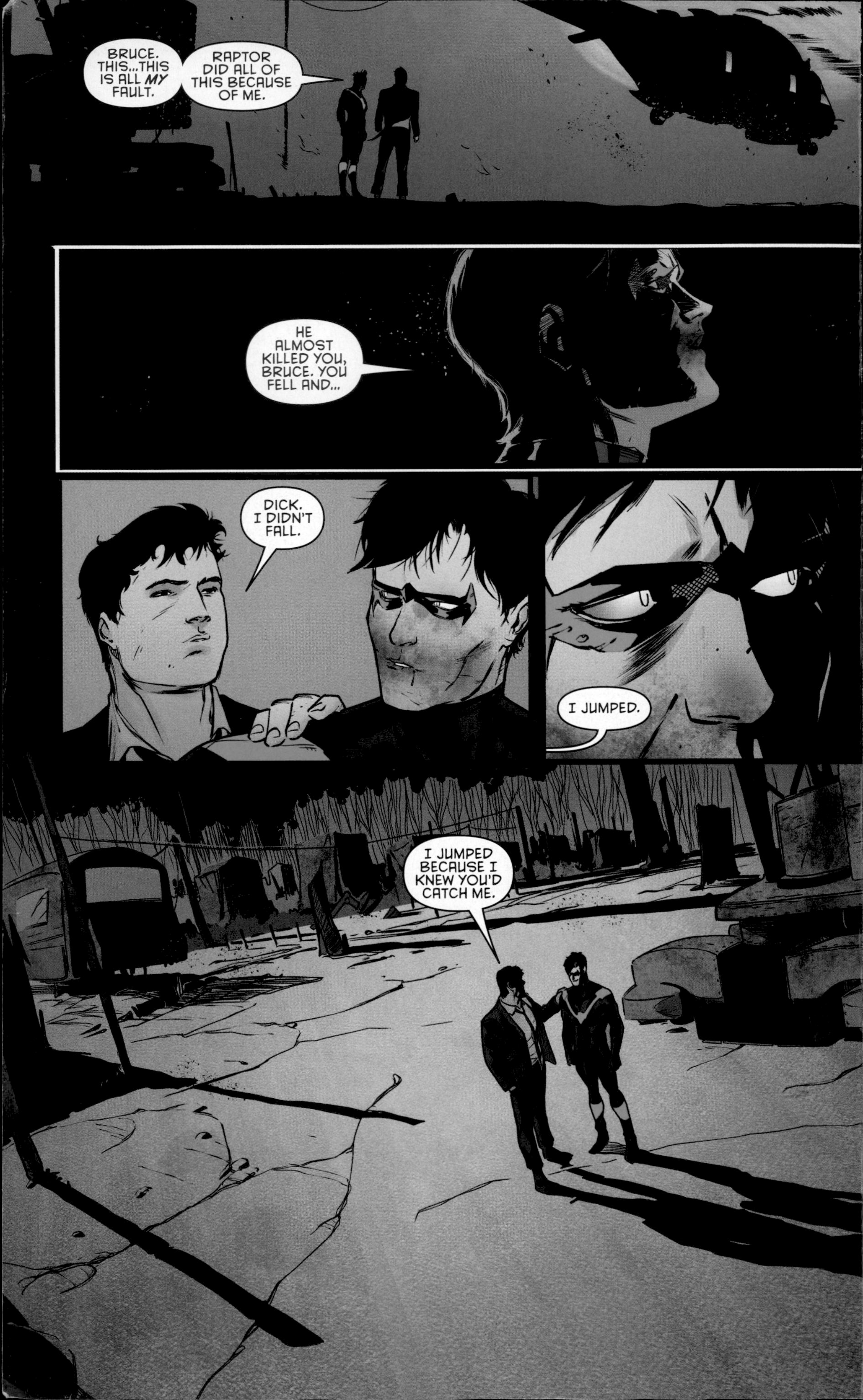
BRUCE. THIS...THIS IS ALL *MY* FAULT.
RAPTOR DID ALL OF THIS BECAUSE OF ME.
HE ALMOST KILLED YOU, BRUCE. YOU FELL AND...
DICK. I DIDN'T FALL.
I JUMPED.
I JUMPED BECAUSE I KNEW YOU'D CATCH ME.

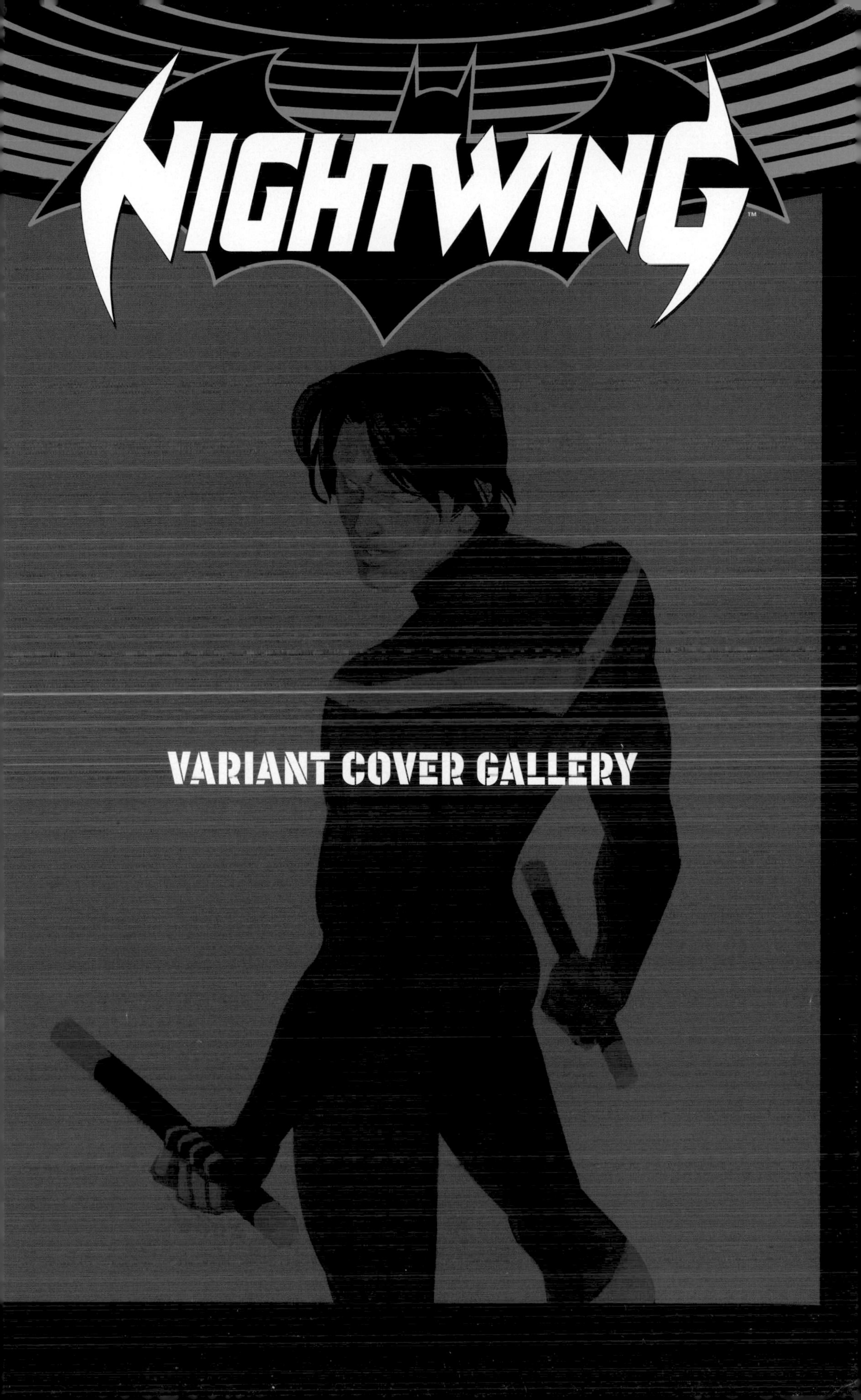
NIGHTWING
VARIANT COVER GALLERY

NIGHTWING: REBIRTH #1 Variant by Babs Tarr

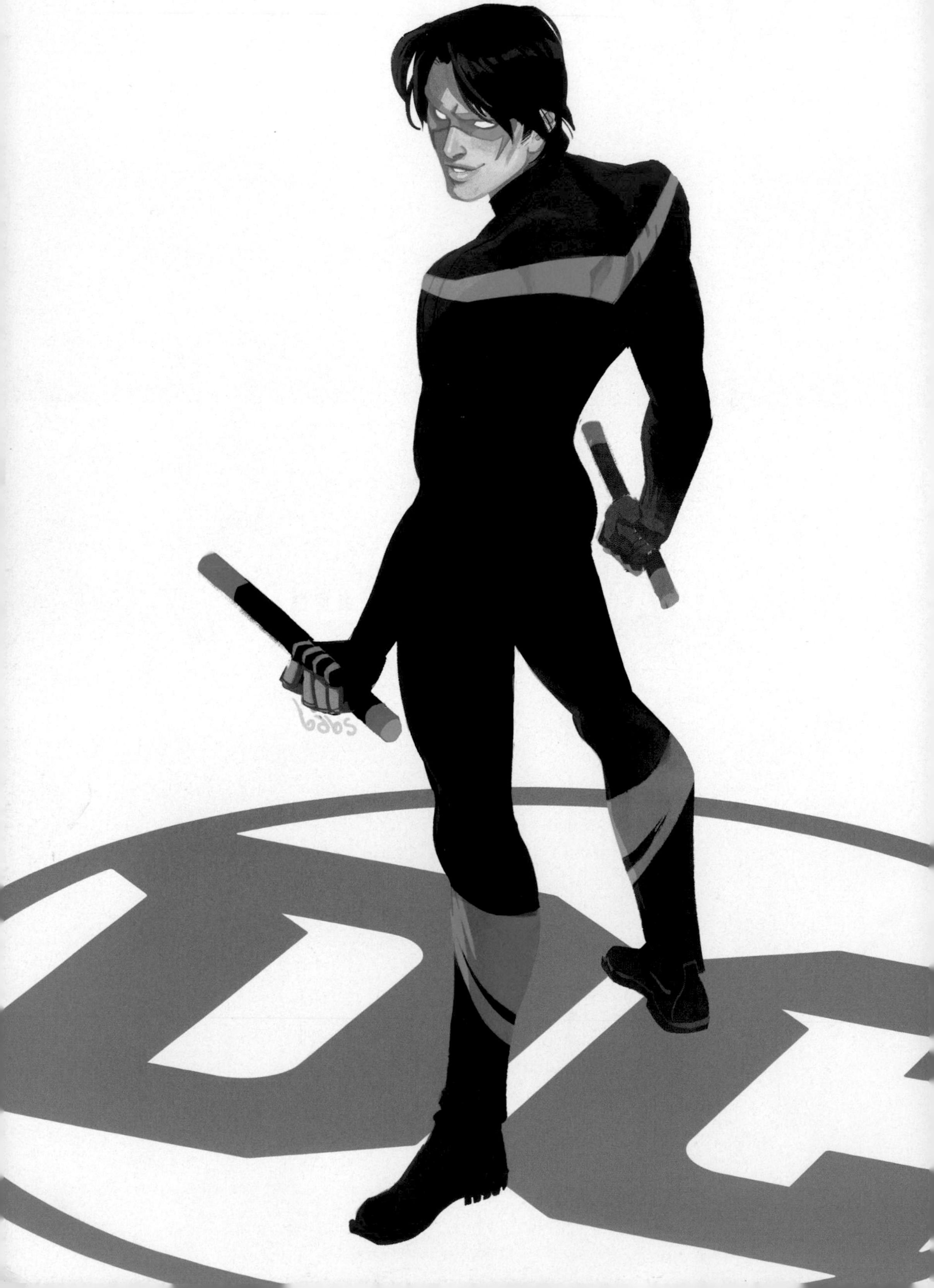
babs

IGHTWING #1 Variant by Ivan Reis, Joe Prado and Brad Walker

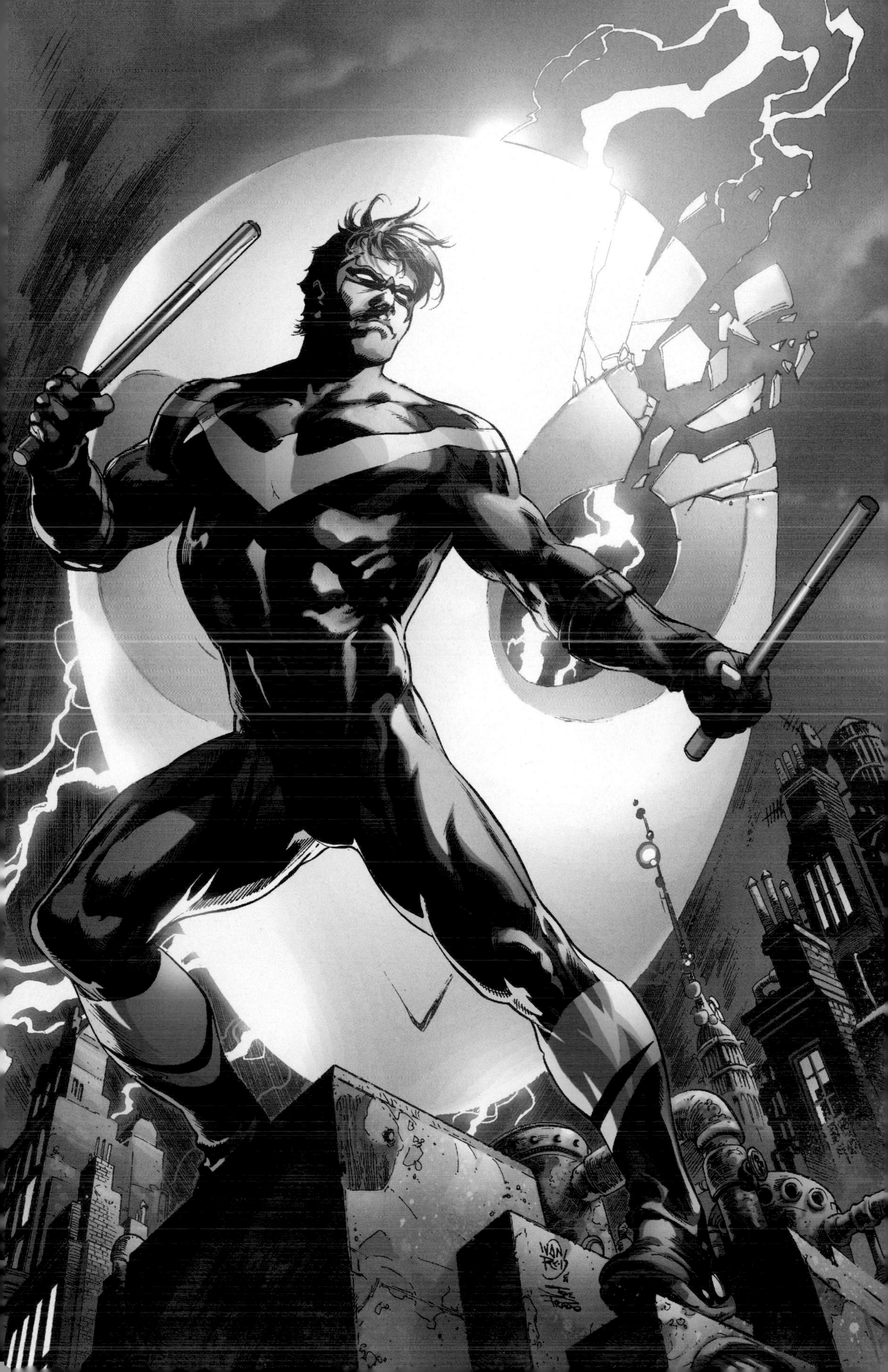

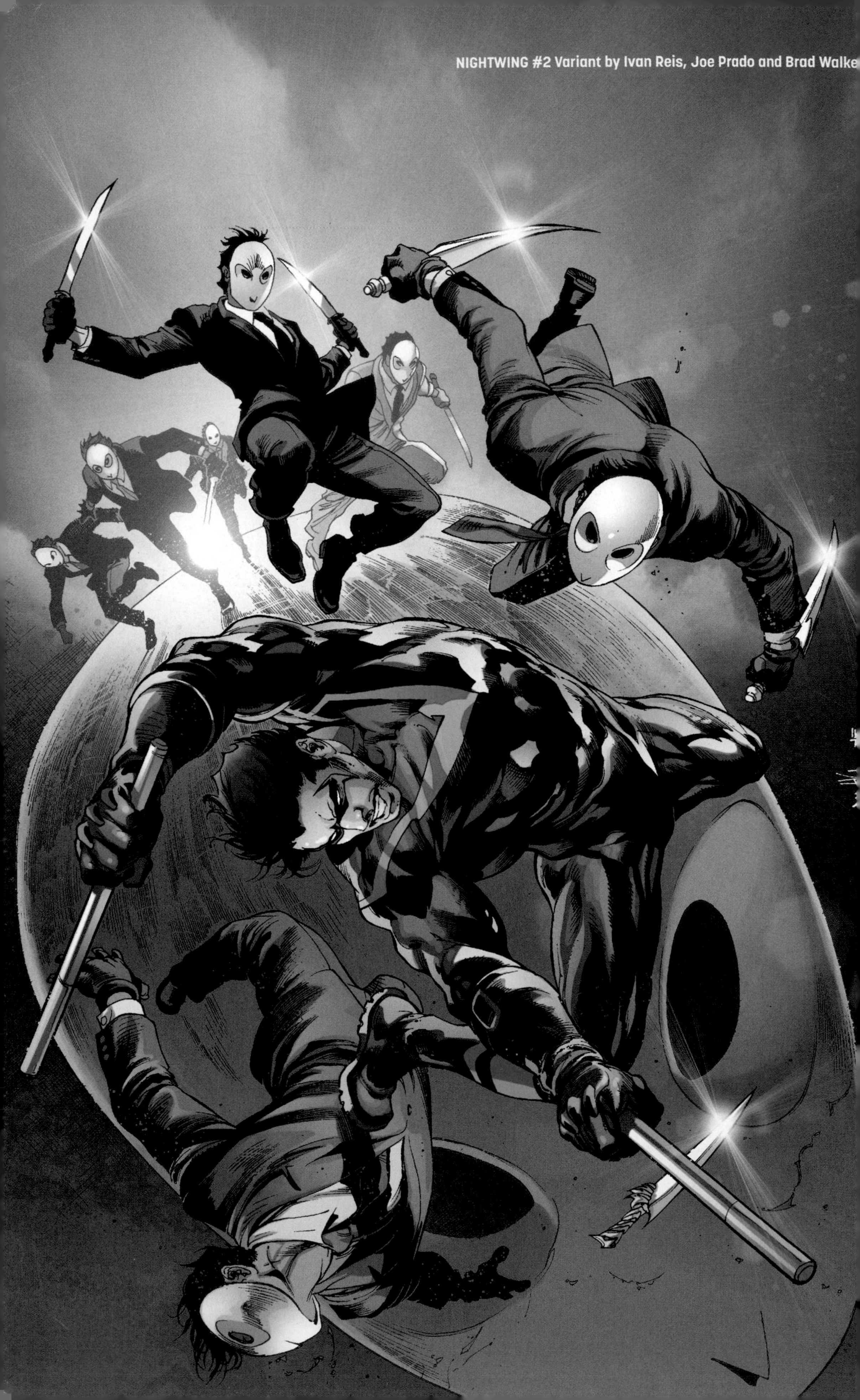

NIGHTWING #2 Variant by Ivan Reis, Joe Prado and Brad Walke

NIGHTWING #3 Variant by Ivan Reis, Joe Prado and Sula Moon

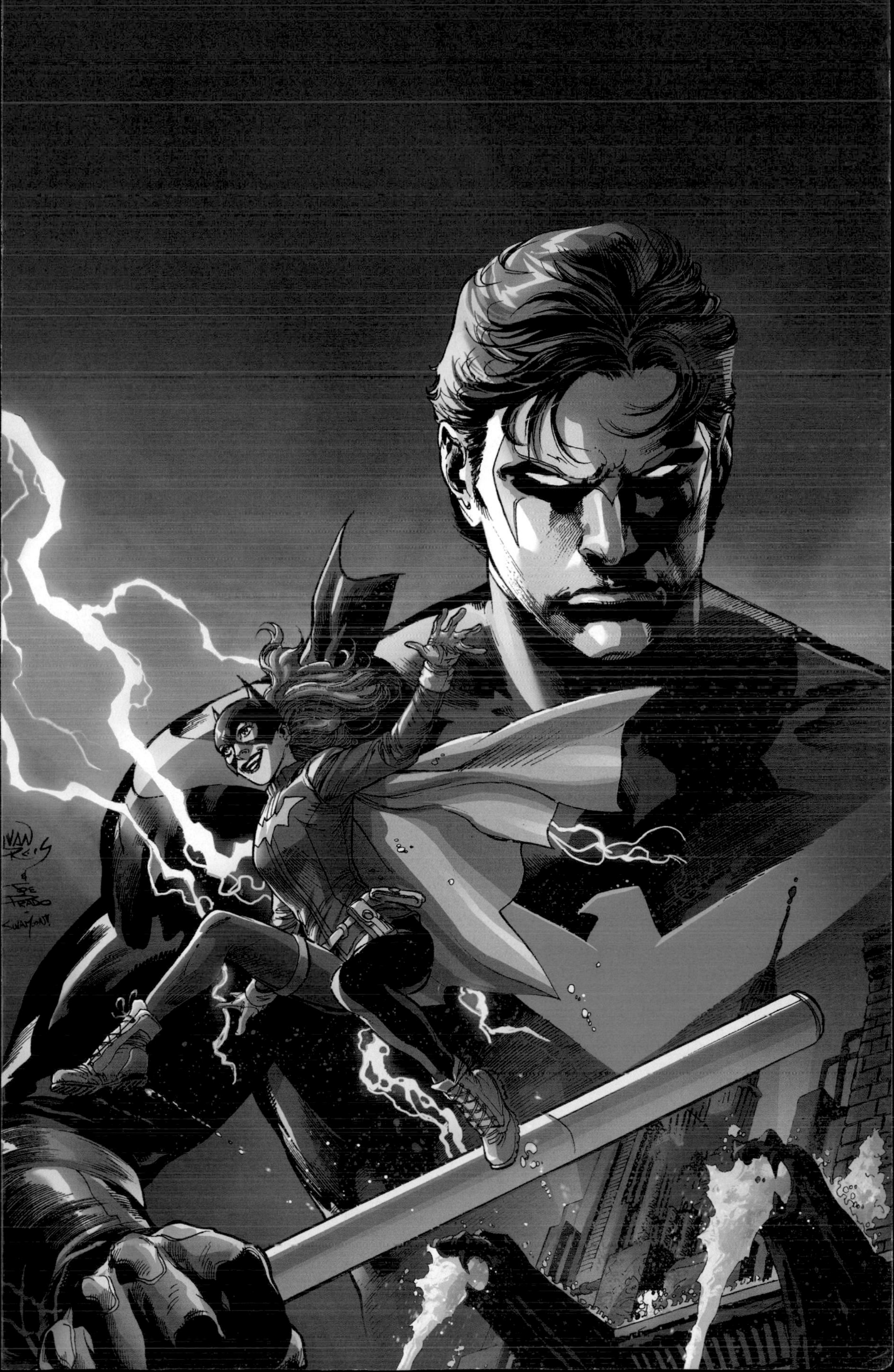

NIGHTWING #4 Varian
by Ivan Reis, Oclair Albert and Sula Moo

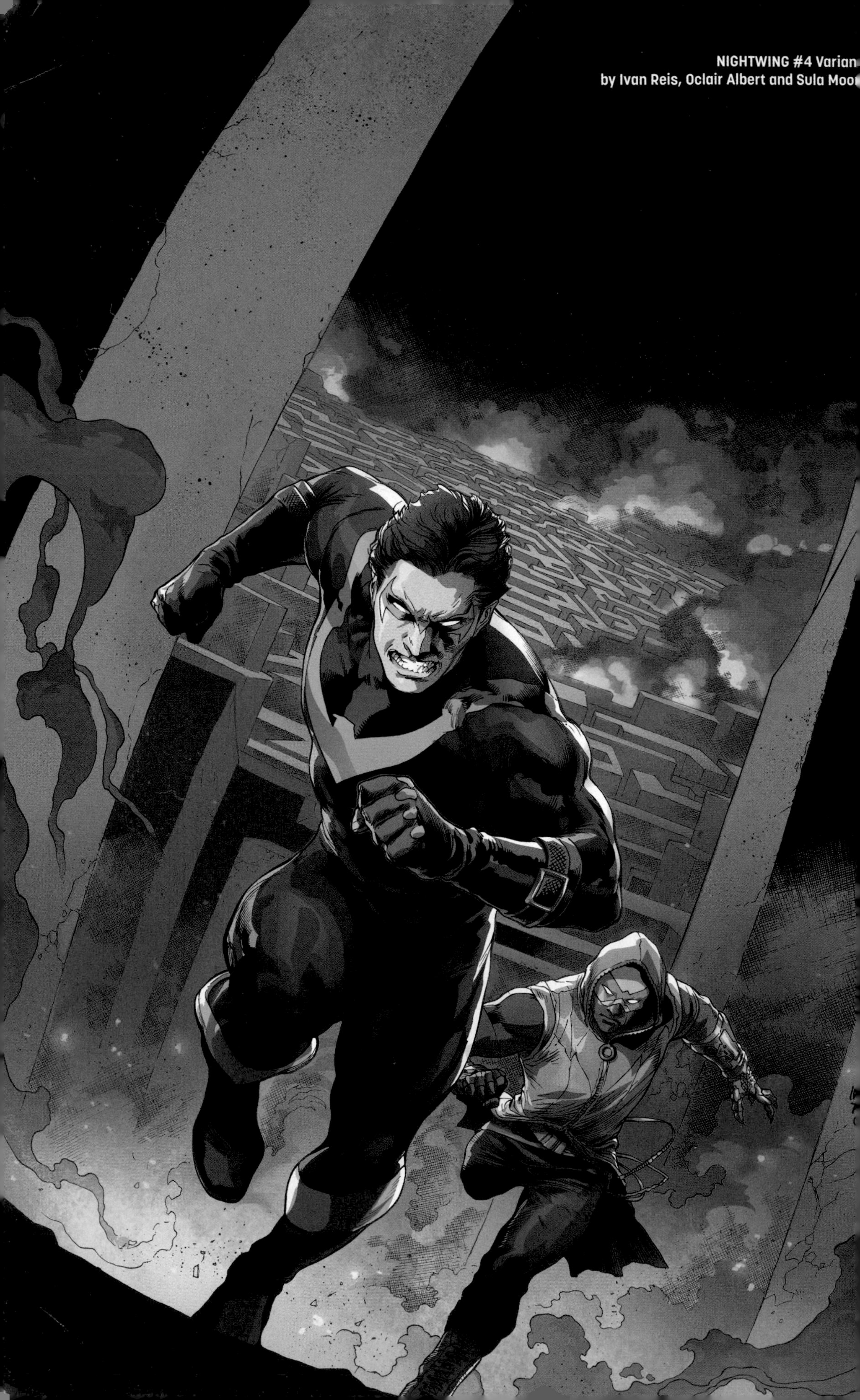

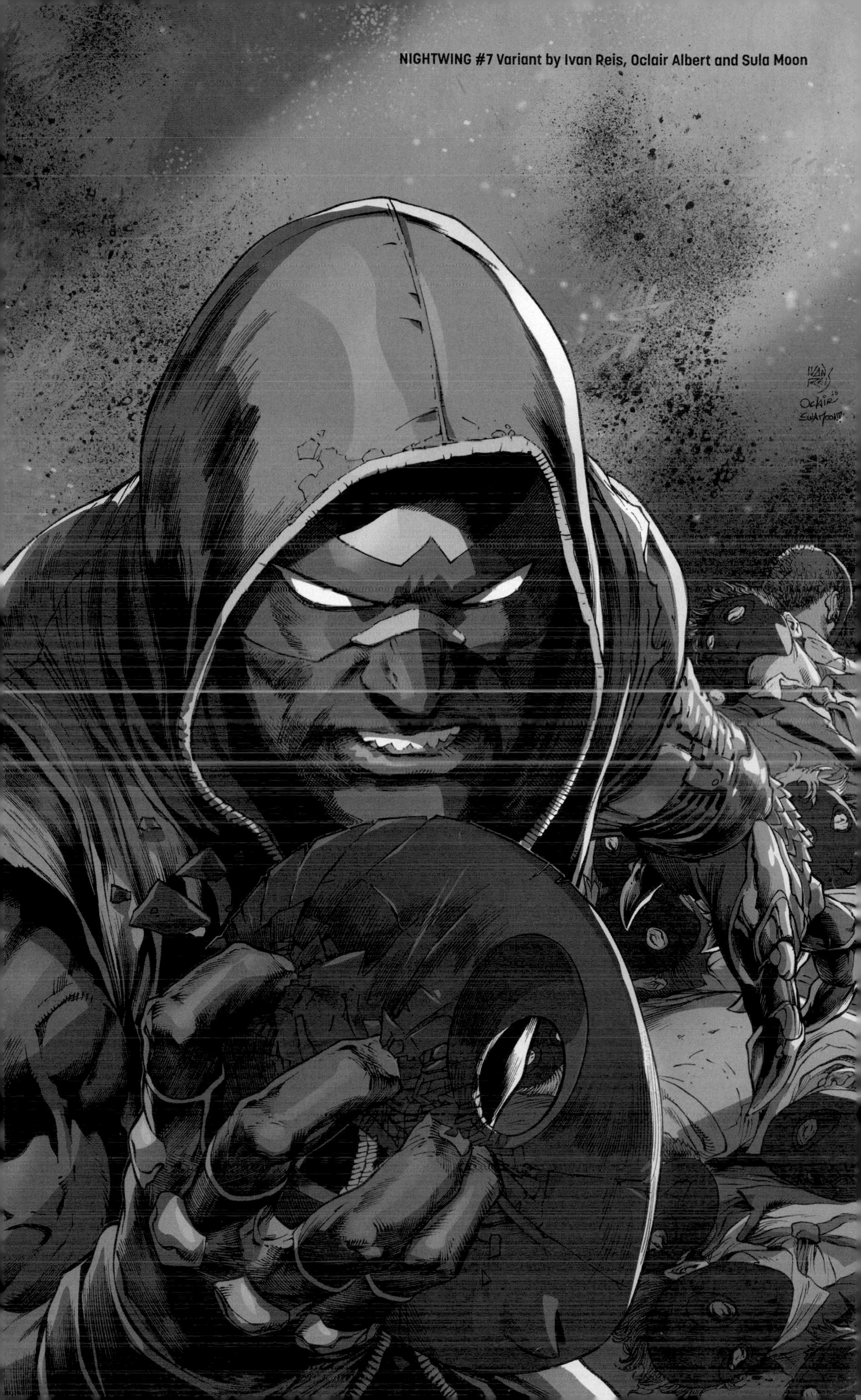

NIGHTWING #7 Variant by Ivan Reis, Oclair Albert and Sula Moon

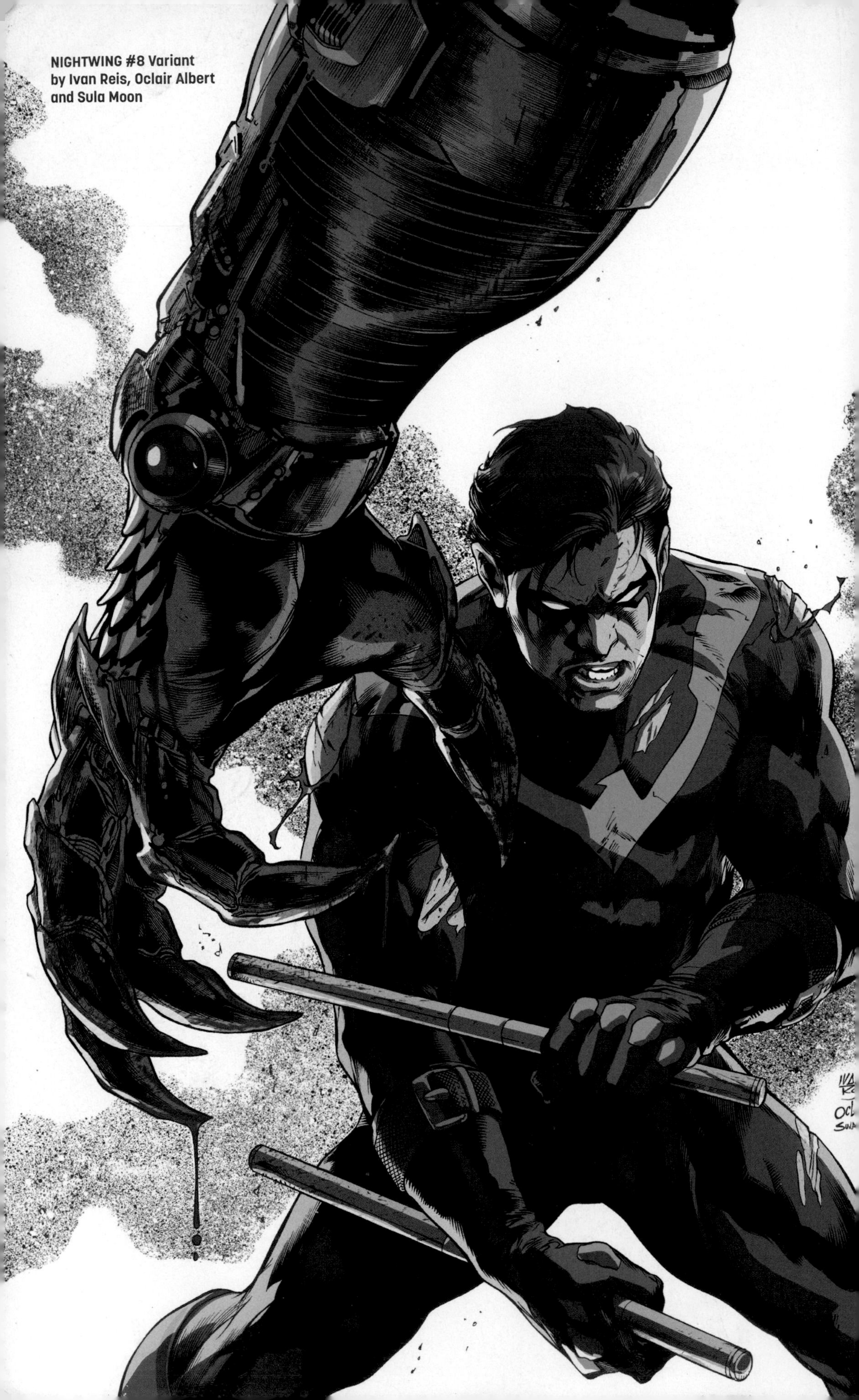

NIGHTWING #8 Variant
by Ivan Reis, Oclair Albert
and Sula Moon

NIGHTWING Sketches by JAVIER FERNÁNDEZ

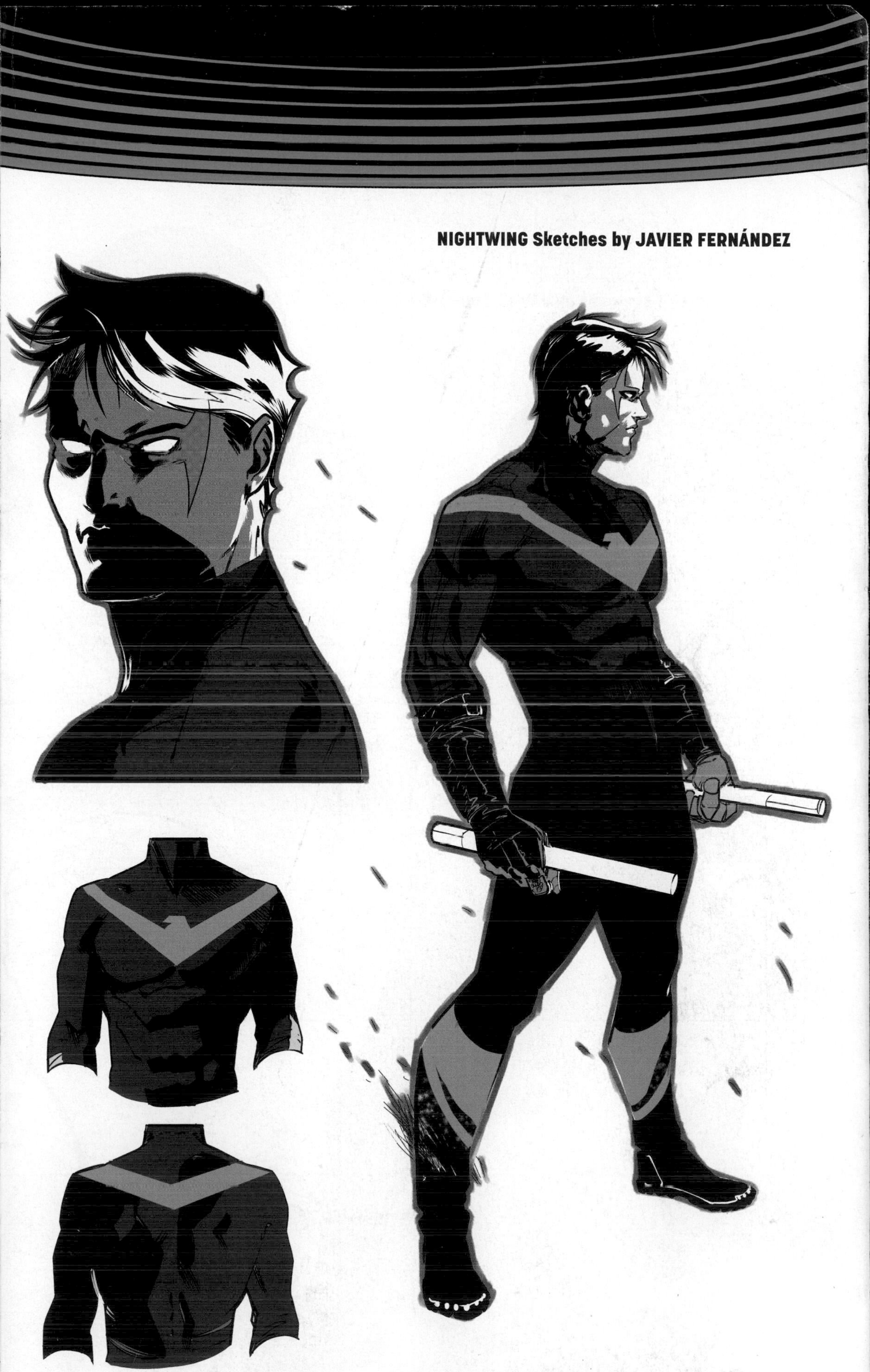

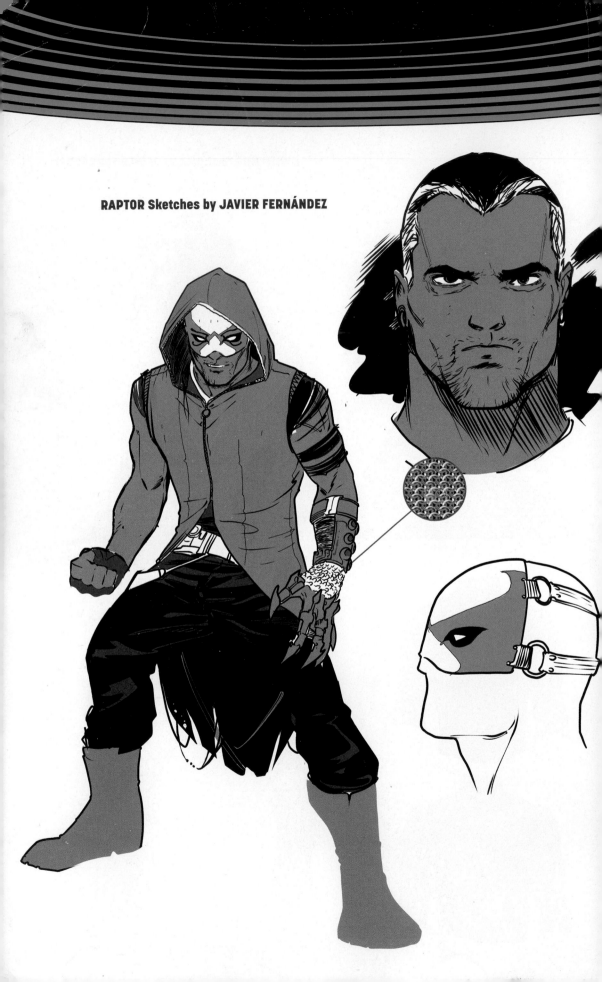

RAPTOR Sketches by JAVIER FERNÁNDEZ

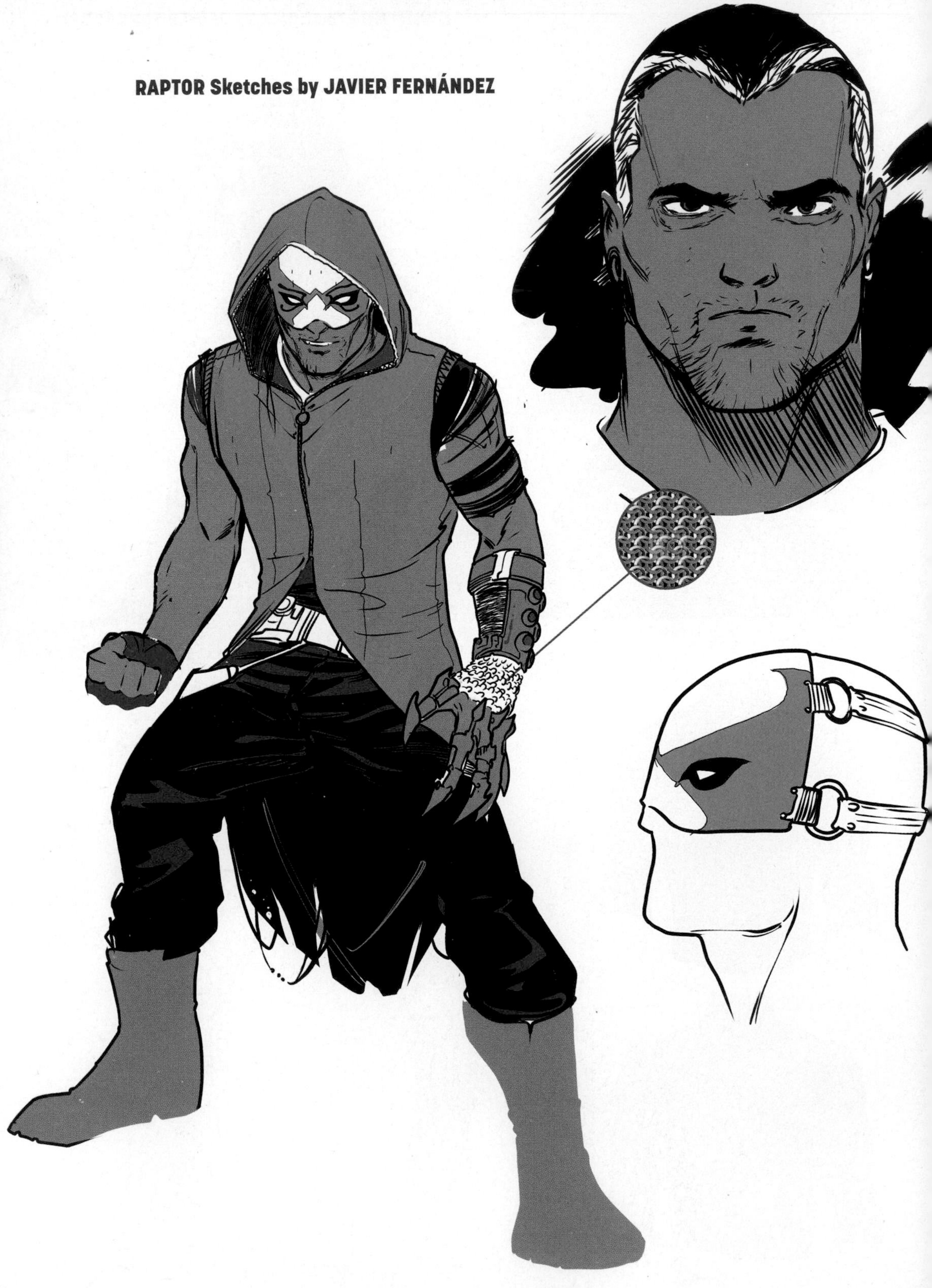